Unlikely Warriors

Unlikely Warriors

General Benjamin H. Grierson
and His Family

By
William H. Leckie and Shirley A. Leckie

UNIVERSITY OF OKLAHOMA PRESS : NORMAN

OTHER BOOKS BY WILLIAM H. LECKIE

Military Conquest of the Southern Plains (Norman, 1963)
The Buffalo Soldiers (Norman, 1967)

Library of Congress Cataloging in Publication Data

Leckie, William H.
    Unlikely warriors.

    Bibliography: p. 349
    Includes index.
    1. Grierson, Benjamin Henry, 1826-1911. 2. United States—History—Civil
War, 1861-1865—Cavalry operations. 3. Indians of North America—Southwest,
New—Wars—1866-1895. 4. Generals—United States—Biography. 5. United
States. Army—Biography. I. Leckie, Shirley A., 1937-   II. Title.
E467.1.G8L43 1984   973.7'3013   84-40275
ISBN 0-8061-1912-8

The paper in this book meets the guidelines for permanence and durability of
the Committee on Production Guidelines for Book Longevity of the Council on
Library Resources, Inc.

To Hazel Enola and Bettie Sue

Contents

Illustrations

Preface

Tʜɪs is the story of an American family whose place in history was secured by the military career of its most illustrious member, General Benjamin Henry Grierson. It chronicles the activities of three generations, all motivated by their pursuit of the American dream of freedom, material success, and occupational mobility. Throughout, the central characters remain the General and his wife, Alice Kirk Grierson.

Benjamin H. Grierson, one of the outstanding leaders of cavalry in the Civil War and a veteran of more than twenty years on the western frontier, has been neglected by historians. Aside from a few articles and an excellent book on his great raid through Mississippi in 1863, he has received far less attention than some of his contemporaries whose contributions were of less importance.

The reasons for this oversight are not difficult to discern. Grierson was a most unlikely cavalry commander. Kicked by a horse at the age of eight and seriously injured, he distrusted all horses for the rest of his life. A talented musician, he embarked on a career as bandleader, composer, and music teacher. After his marriage in 1854, he attempted to increase his income by becoming a merchant. This enterprise failed, and in 1861, Grierson, heavily in debt, was living in his parents' home with his wife and two small sons.

When the Civil War broke out he enlisted as an unpaid aide to the commanding officer of an Illinois infantry regiment. Keen intelligence, hard study, clear judgment, and an abundance of cold courage brought Grierson promotion to major and then colonel of the Sixth Illinois Cavalry. In the summer and fall of 1862, in operations against Confederate units in west Tennessee, he gained the favorable attention of Generals Grant and Sherman.

In the spring of 1863, Grant, needing a diversion from his efforts to invest the great Confederate stronghold at Vicksburg, Mississippi, selected Grierson to lead a large-scale raid into the state. Grierson's sixteen-day, six-hundred-mile dash through the heart of Mississippi and on to the safety of Union lines at Baton Rouge, Louisiana, left a trail of havoc in its wake and was of material assistance to Grant. It made Grierson a national hero and earned him promotion to brigadier general.

His reputation suffered in 1864, while he served under less able commanders, but late in the year, with an independent command, he led another devastating raid into Mississippi. He was promoted to major general and the war's end found him leading a division of cavalry in Alabama.

After giving brief thought to establishing a business, Grierson accepted appointment as colonel of the newly authorized Tenth Cavalry, a regiment to be staffed with white officers and black enlisted men. For the rest of his long term of service, with the exception of two years on recruiting duty, he was stationed on the western frontier.

Three developments compromised Grierson's career in the west. He became the object of ongoing discrimination on the part of General Philip Sheridan, who commanded the Department of the Missouri and later the vast Military Division of the Missouri, and who was for five years, 1883–88, commanding general of the U.S. Army. The obvious favoritism that Sheridan showed younger officers who had served with him during the Civil War—notably George A. Custer and Wesley Merritt—aroused resentment throughout the western army. In Grierson's case, it meant that he was "exiled" to lonely frontier posts where there was little opportunity for distinction, and time and again he was passed over for promotion.

Grierson also paid a price for his views on the Indian problem. It was one thing to fight for preservation of the Union but quite another to make war on the Indian people, which often resulted in heavy casualties among women, children, and old men. Grierson had no desire to take part in such events and argued that negotiation, conciliation, justice, and fair play were more appropriate measures for solutions than guns. He did everything in his power to promote Indian welfare. His position on treatment of the Indians earned few friends and a small army of enemies.

As a commander of black troops, Grierson faced the hostility of many persons, in and out of the army, who despised blacks and regarded them as unfit to wear the uniform. Grierson had both observed and commanded blacks during the Civil War and respected their courage and abilities as soldiers. He managed his troopers with fairness and understanding, insisted on impartial treatment, and seldom hesitated to champion their cause in the military.

That Grierson could fight when necessary was demonstrated in 1880 during the Victorio War, when he outmarched and outfought one of the ablest of all Apache chiefs. But most of his energies were devoted to exploration, construction, and development, solid and essential work that brought little recognition but had lasting results. Fort Sill, Oklahoma, is an example of this kind of effort. Grierson explored the area, recommended the site, and personally supervised most of the construction of the original post.

In the trans-Pecos region, after extensive exploration and mapping of that largely uncharted domain, he pushed to completion an admirable network of roads, telegraph lines, camps, and posts. Within two years, 1878-80, he probably had done more than any other person to bring peace and order to that section of the country.

Despite his achievements, Grierson waited twenty-four years for promotion to brigadier general, and he retired three months later.

In disposition, Grierson was affectionate, kind, humane, humorous, and generous to a fault. He had a temper but rarely lost it and avoided whenever possible a quarrel or petty controversy, often at the sacrifice of his own interests. He was remarkably consistent. The public figure was simply a reflection of the private man.

For Grierson, domestic and family concerns were as important as his participation in national events. The son of a Scotch-Irish immigrant, he remained all his life acutely aware of his responsibilities as son and brother, as well as of those he assumed later as husband and parent. Despite the earlier success achieved by his father, Robert Grierson, merchant and speculator, Benjamin was the only one in the second generation who attained a modicum of financial security. In the absence of the twentieth-century welfare state, the General, having a "paid position for life," found himself in the unenviable position of shoring up the failing fortunes of poorer relatives and in-laws, a task that at times conflicted painfully with his responsibilities to his wife and children. For both Ben and Alice Grierson the close-knit, extended Grierson-Kirk family was a source of strength and support as well as, at times, a heavy burden.

Their marriage was a companionate one in which Alice was accorded the position of moral superior. This advantage gave her substantial authority in terms of family decision-making. Yet, as was true for all the women among the Kirks and Griersons, she had little control over the external events of her life, including even those that affected her intimately. Given her strong religious and moral scruples, she, like many other nineteenth-century Americans, was reluctant to divest sexuality of its procreative function, with the result that she bore more children than either desired or intended. The results for both husband and wife were especially poignant.

Of the four children who survived to adulthood, two suffered from episodes of dementia praecox, or what today would be characterized as manic-depressive psychosis. This circumstance placed a heavy burden on a woman who had assumed her maternal responsibilities with great care and conscientiousness, and it represented a grave disappointment to the man who had once envisioned himself establishing a Grierson dynasty on American soil. Apparently there existed a genetic predisposition to this condition among members of the Kirk family as well as a susceptibility to depression among the Griersons. Nonetheless, the disruptions of family life attendant upon Grierson's military career contributed substantially to the emotional difficulties that plagued two of their children. Few couples have been called upon to face as much adversity as Ben and Alice Grierson. And few have met such challenges with the resiliency and unflinching courage of these two people.

Grierson's military duties often required absences from his family. On these occasions he wrote to Alice almost daily, and she responded just as frequently. They both conducted a wide correspondence with relatives and friends, and at an early age their children became dedicated scribblers. The total number of letters that has survived is astonishing. They present a continuous record of family history for nearly half a century. From these and other pertinent materials we have compiled their story, relating it in the belief that the odyssey of Benjamin Grierson and his family, moving westward across the American continent, is worthy of attention, and that he deserved greater recognition for his contributions than he has received. In an interview with Alice Kirk Grierson, granddaughter and last survivor in the direct line of Ben Grierson's family, she urged, "If you do it, please tell it like it was, plain and unvarnished." We have tried to do just that.

The kindness and consideration of many persons aided our research for this work. We are especially grateful to Sara D. Jackson of the National Historical Publications and Records Commission, Anne Henry of the National Archives, and Mary Williams of the Fort Davis National Historic Site, Fort Davis, Texas. More than generous with the time given us were James Parks and Floreda Harmon of the Millsaps College Library, Jackson, Mississippi; John Morgan of the University of Toledo Library; and Douglas McChristian, superintendent of the Fort Davis National Historic Site. Wayne Daniels and his associates at the Fort Concho Museum, San Angelo, Texas, went beyond the call of duty in providing photographs and other materials.

The courtesy shown us by the staffs of the following libraries is much appreciated: Illinois State Historical, University of Michigan, University of Oklahoma, University of Texas, and the University of Toledo.

President Glen R. Driscoll and Academic Vice President William Free of the University of Toledo provided both encouragement and timely travel funds.

Special thanks go to Jacqueline Wright of Springfield, Illinois, who volunteered to find answers to a number of puzzling questions, and to Don Bufkin, Arizona Historical Society, for the maps. Rebecca Ransom, of Orlando, Florida, typed the manuscript with care, accuracy and unfailing patience.

Asheville, North Carolina   WILLIAM H. LECKIE
                                             SHIRLEY A. LECKIE

Unlikely Warriors

CAST OF CHARACTERS

GRIERSON

Robert
Mary

- Louisa — Steele Semple
  - Mary
  - Thomas Kirk
- Susan — H. B. Fuller
  - H. B., Jr.
  - Ellen Kirk
  - John C. — Marion C. C. Capps
  - Elizabeth
    - Susannah
  - Robert H.
    - Louisa
  - Mary
    - Helen
    - Grace
    - Ettie and Albert
    - Charles
- Benjamin H. — Alice Kirk
  - John (Kirkie)
  - Robert
  - Edith
  - B. H., Jr.
  - George
  - Mary

KIRK

Alice — Benjamin Grierson

John Kirk
Susan Bingham
Ann Bayne

- Thomas
- Mary Fuller
- Mary
- William Fitch
- Ellen
- H. B. Fuller, Jr.
- Henry
- Maria
- John, Jr.
- Rufus

Four others died as small children.

CHAPTER 1

Beginnings

ROBERT GRIERSON, the second son of a farmer and grazier from Meath County, Ireland, was known to be "fond of adventure." Orphaned at seventeen and excluded from the bulk of his father's estate by the laws of primogeniture, he acquired the valuable skills of bookkeeper and navigator. Thus when the captain of a merchant ship offered him the chance in 1810 to visit America in exchange for serving as keeper of the ship's log, the twenty-one-year-old youth eagerly accepted. The voyage included stops in Newfoundland, Boston, New York, and Savannah, Georgia, before returning to Dublin by way of Liverpool.

Back in Ireland the young man, unable to forget the scenes he had witnessed and certain that economic opportunity beckoned across the sea, vowed to make America his future home. In 1815 he married Mary Sheppard, also of Dublin, and three years later, mindful that he was approaching thirty, prevailed upon her to emigrate with him to the United States.

Mary Grierson was not overjoyed at the prospect. The mother of two small daughters—Louisa, age two, and Susan, eleven months—she was already pregnant with her third child. Understandably, she dreaded not only the rigors of an ocean voyage, but also the bearing and raising of children in a strange land. She had spent all of her twenty-seven years in a prosperous Scotch-Irish home, surrounded by a large, loving family. Nonetheless, desiring above all else to please her husband, she yielded to his wishes.

The Griersons booked passage in November, 1818, on a small vessel bound for New York. Once on board their difficulties began, as fierce winter gales prevented the tiny ship from clearing the Irish Channel, forcing it to return to port. After a brief overnight reunion with Mary's family and a second, more tearful farewell, the Griersons again embarked. This time the ship passed through the Channel, but midway across the Atlantic, severe storms left the vessel battered and leaking. Despite frantic efforts by the crew and male passengers, the hold filled with water, compelling Mary, the only woman on board, to move her children and all family belongings on deck and remain there for the rest of the voyage.

Fortunately Robert had brought along his own navigational instruments. His skillful calculations persuaded the captain that the ship, blown off course, now headed towards Bermuda. Their only chance for survival lay in attempting a landing there. By January, as the ship foundered and the crew and passengers prepared for the worst, land was sighted. Even then, if friendly islanders had not sent rescue boats, all on board would have perished. Later, after the Griersons were brought safely to shore, Robert confided to his journal that Mary had borne these dangers "with a fortitude that will ever be remembered by me."

April arrived before the Griersons could obtain passage on a seaworthy vessel. A ten-day voyage brought them to New York City, their original goal. Shortly afterward Mary gave birth to a son, a frail infant who survived only three months despite her unremitting efforts to save him. The grieving parents, attributing his death to the hardships Mary had recently endured, buried him in the cemetery adjacent to the Broadway Street Trinity Church.[1]

Despite the obstacles and delays in reaching New York, it was not their final destination. Robert aspired to become a merchant and, like other Scotch-Irish immigrants before him, had selected Pittsburgh as the most promising site to begin his career. Situated at the far end of the Allegheny Forest, where the Monongahela and the Allegheny flowed into the Ohio River and where two national highways intersected, it was a pivotal point in western and southern trade. In September, 1819, the Griersons set off in a covered wagon and, after a brief stop in Philadelphia, turned west to follow the rough, meandering Washington and Forbes Highway. Their journey led them through a vast expanse of wilderness, containing scenes of "wild, natural grandeur." Nevertheless, it was an exhausted and travel-weary family that arrived at their new home on Tuesday, October 5, after sixteen days on the road.[2]

It had been almost a year since they had left their native Ireland, and after all the distance and hardships, Mary expected to find a large, impressive municipality. Instead, stretched before her beneath a "sulphurous canopy" lay the most unattractive city she had ever seen. As they drove closer she became aware, through the haze of

Robert Grierson. *Courtesy Fort Davis National Historic Site, Fort Davis, Texas.*

black smoke, of the outlines of buildings and streets. Pittsburgh's appearance was so ugly that it precipitated a depression of Mary's spirit that lasted almost a year. Another resident of the town during this period left this description:

> To a stranger, immediately preceding his entrance, the city presents an appearance sufficiently unfavourable to its character, as a place of continuous residence, or even of sojourn. . . . The streets, running at one angle here, and another there; narrow, roughly paved, filthy beyond compare, and filled with hogs, dogs, dray and noisy children, afford a spectacle of any thing but the "sublime and beautiful."

With the exception of the Episcopal Church, all the buildings were "ordinary and common place," and by now, "so begrimed by smoke and soot, that they afforded a most gloomy sight to the visitor from one of the fair cities of the east."[3] Mary saw clearly that while "the fame of its prosperity had drawn them to the infant city," it offered few of the amenities of New York or Philadelphia and far fewer than her beloved Dublin.

The Griersons acquired a building strategically located on the southeast corner of Liberty and Market streets. Part of it was given over to Robert's store and shoemaking establishment, and the rest provided the family with its living quarters.[4] Robert threw himself wholeheartedly into his work, and his business soon flourished. When opportunities arose, he purchased lots in nearby Allegheny Town, shrewd investments that proved profitable. For him there was no doubt. The move to Pittsburgh had been auspicious, and he was now on his way to becoming a man of means.

For Mary it was another matter entirely. Separated from her native land, she pined for her family and the old familiar surroundings she had known. Robert was not insensitive to her feelings, and years later their oldest daughter, Louisa Semple, recalled that her father "saw his wife trying to bear her share of the burden and of the responsibility for two children . . . with her heart too full of cherished memories, drooping visibly, all events and circumstances of the weary days serving to remind her of the past." Despite her husband's efforts to console her, Mary's mind became "unhinged for a time," as sadness gave way to despondency.

Long months passed before two events dispelled Mary's depression. A wise, older neighbor befriended the young mother and taught her the essential lesson for a frontier wife. While Mary could not change her outward circumstances, she could alleviate her personal suffering by accepting her situation more philosophically. Consciously, Mary began changing her attitude, brooding less over Ireland and the past and looking more to the future in America. Soon after, in the summer of 1820, she delivered another child, this time a strapping son whom the Griersons named John. After this event, Mary's old cheerfulness returned, although there were still times when she wept for her native land.[5]

Three more children arrived, a son Robert, who died before his second birthday, a daughter Mary, born in 1824, and on July 8, 1826, a son Benjamin Henry. If the Griersons had dared to hope that the move to America would bring not only prosperity but also a new prominence to the family not possible to achieve in Ireland, this child was destined to fulfill that aspiration.

Ben was not quite three when his father sold his business and town holdings and moved his family seventy miles farther west to Youngstown, Ohio. Pittsburgh had never been attractive to either Robert or Mary, for, in their view, "even prompt access to the very best life it afforded would not have indemnified them for what had been relinquished." They recognized that "with the inhabitants of the place, it was not primarily the business of life to live, but to gain a foothold."[6] Since this description fit them as well, it was only natural that once they had accumulated sufficient wealth, they would look elsewhere for more congenial surroundings. During their nine years of residence there, the number of factories had increased and so had the smoke and soot, making the city an undesirable environment in which to raise the children.

Youngstown, by comparison, seemed at this time almost like a pastoral village. Containing just under fourteen hundred inhabitants, it offered clear skies, relatively attractive streets, and something else as well—a population composed largely of families of Scotch-Irish ancestry and, therefore, compatible with the Griersons.[7] Undoubtedly, Robert had examined the town's prospects earlier and had concluded that they looked promising. Situated midway between Cleveland and Pittsburgh and laid out at the junction of the Mahoning River and Mill Creek, just below Mahoning Falls, Youngstown was surrounded by a region rich in timber, mineral ores, and agricultural products. Since his real estate investments in Pittsburgh had proved profitable, Robert was ready to try his luck elsewhere. Here was a chance to buy land in a smaller town, relatively unknown to speculators, while prices remained low and the opportunity excellent for future profits.

The Grierson family arrived at their new home on Sunday, January 4, 1829. That day snow fell continuously, making it difficult to unpack and carry furniture and belongings from the cart in the street below to the second-story dwelling above Robert's recently acquired store.[8] Ben remembered little of the actual move (and that was just as well, for the necessity of assuring that he did not tumble down the stairs must have greatly impeded progress). Nonetheless, Ben's earliest memories dated back to this place, for it was here that he spent his childhood, skating on the pond behind the public square, hunting rabbits in the fields alongside the Mahoning River, and fishing with his brother John in Mill and Crabb creeks outside of town.

During these early, formative years, Mary, rather than Robert, had the greater influence on Ben's developing personality. His mother transmitted to all her children her enthusiasm for the novels of Sir Walter Scott and the poems of Robert Burns, as well as her appreciation for the plays of Shakespeare. When her voice filled the household with the songs from her native land, however, it was her youngest child who listened most intently. These Scotch and Irish ballads nurtured in Ben an intense, lifelong passion for music. Their lyrics, sometimes humorous, often poignantly sad, so impressed him that in large measure his earliest view of the world was cast in their rhymes.[9]

Mary never forgot the large, extended family left behind in Ireland. As the years passed, however, the memory of these attachments became less a painful reminder of loss and more of an example of the warm, familial ties she sought to create among her own children. With Robert's help she succeeded in instilling a sense of kinship and mutual responsibility that remained evident throughout their lives. By the time the Grierson children reached maturity, their differences of opinion often gave way to bitter and protracted quarrels. Despite this, as a family they functioned at bedrock like an Old World clan. For whatever the nature of their disputes, they never ceased to remember their duties to their parents, to each other, or even to one another's offspring.

Family ties had to be very strong to create such a sense of obligation, for individually the Grierson children were a disparate lot. Louisa, the oldest, was an excellent student whose scholastic achievements not only filled the family with pride but set high standards for the younger ones as well. All her life she remained addicted to "thought and study," leading her brother Ben to conclude that there were "few subjects of interest in regard to which she is not well informed." In stature she resembled her mother, who was small, except that in build, Louisa was thinner. As was common among the Griersons, she had dark hair and deep hazel eyes that at times seemed almost black.[10] She also had the misfortune to be born at least a century too early. Had she lived in the present age, her acute mind could have brought her a life of scholarship or professional activity. No such avenues were open to women in the early nineteenth century. Instead, Louisa's intellectual energies (especially since her marriage to Steele Semple produced no children) were given over to broad, undisciplined forays into various subjects, or more commonly expended upon endless arguments with other members of her family.

Susan, the second-oldest, was the exact opposite of her sister in both temperament and appearance. Like her father she was tall and athletically inclined, and Ben considered her one of the "handsomest" young women in the Mahoning Valley region. She was by nature even-tempered, with no interest in intellectual pursuits, preferring instead the company of horses to books. At an early age she became expert at breaking colts, and over time she developed into an accomplished "equestrienne." At some point in her adolescence she was required to put aside these vigorous activities and confine herself to the more seemly occupations permitted young women at this time. By age twenty-three she was the sedate wife of Harvey B. Fuller of Youngstown and had already borne the first of her eight children.

The youngest of the Grierson daughters was Mary, two years older than Ben and his constant companion. Like Louisa, this tall, thin woman, who bore her father's lantern-shaped face, was gifted intellectually and especially skilled as a writer. Her essays and compositions won the universal acclaim of Youngstown area teachers. Ben remembered that as a child she generally exhibited a "bright, cheerful, sprightly" disposition. There were times, however, when her mood shifted abruptly, and she became "greatly depressed in spirit" for no clearly discernible reason. Unfortunately this painful affliction plagued her until her death at age thirty-six.

Ben's only living brother, John, grew into a tall, massively built man of great physical strength. On one occasion Ben watched him lift half a barrelful of white lead weighing 625 pounds. By profession a bookkeeper, he remained at heart all his life a frustrated entrepreneur, constantly looking for the main chance, whether it be a new business endeavor or an apparently sure-fire investment scheme. If success continually eluded him, it was not for want of trying.

From his earliest years, John, who was "never so miserable as when out of employment," demonstrated a capacity for labor that his younger brother found amazing. This also impressed Robert, who once told his youngest child that he "would rather have one boy like John to work, than a ten acre lot full of boys such as myself." In this assessment Ben concurred, admitting freely that he had no interest in work and not a great deal more in study. Instead he preferred the games and recreations of childhood, availing himself of these at every opportunity. Fortunately he was quick to learn, so that despite his casual attitude towards school, he still performed well. Nonetheless, any objective observer of the Grierson brothers would have identified John as the one more likely to bring honor to the family name.[11]

In reflecting on his childhood Ben remembered not only his mother's warm affection, expressed in loving embraces, songs, and stories, but something else as well—instances of his father's wrath. Robert possessed what family members referred to as "the Grierson temper," and when it exploded, the results could only be described as spectacular. Among Ben's earliest memories was the time his father returned from work one evening and discovered him attempting to recreate his own version of the William Tell legend by shooting an apple off a playmate's head. Robert, armed with a bridle, chased his son with the intention of administering a thrashing. Ben managed to escape, and for days afterward, with his mother's aid, he remained well hidden from his father's sight.[12]

When Ben was eight years old, an injury brought him close to death. One night he overheard Robert and John making plans for a day of log rolling and brush clearing on the family farm outside of town. Even a small boy could sense that this event promised to be lively, and Ben pleaded to be taken along. His mother was opposed, and for good reasons. No task was more strenuous than turning wooded areas into tillable farm land. In order to expedite the work, the able-bodied men of Youngstown formed themselves into competing teams to see which group could clear the largest area of trees and brush and stack the tallest roll of logs. On such occasions whiskey and rum often flowed freely. Under the circumstances, it was difficult for Mary Grierson to see how her young son would be properly supervised.[13]

Ben exerted all his persuasive powers, and at last, against her better judgment, Mary relented and allowed Ben to accompany the other menfolk as they set out for the farm. The morning passed without incident, and then, about noon, John visited a neighbor. As he prepared to saddle a horse to return to the pasture, Ben appeared at his side begging for a ride. At first John refused, but finally, worn down by his brother's cajoling, he hoisted Ben onto the animal. Suddenly the horse bolted. Ben grabbed the animal around its neck and hung on valiantly, actually enjoying the swift pleasure of the ride. Half a mile down the road, however, the horse swerved and threw him to the ground. Ben was bruised but relatively unharmed. But as he struggled to rise in answer to John's frantic call, the horse reared and kicked him, opening a deep gash in the side of his head.

For two weeks Ben lay in a coma, "hovering between life and death." When he regained consciousness and his bandages were removed, his distressed parents discovered that he had no sight in one eye. To their great relief, full vision eventually returned, but Mary, fearful that blindness might still result, confined him to a darkened room for several months. Undoubtedly such forced inactivity at this stage of childhood left its mark on Ben. While his mother and other members of the family filled some of his convalescence with songs and stories, it was a busy household in which there was much to be done. For long periods he was forced to rely solely on himself for entertainment, passing the time as any child does in similar circumstances, recreating his favorite tales in this mind and weaving new ones of his own as well. Such pastimes served not only to heighten his imaginative powers but also to strengthen the sensitive and poetic elements that were already an essential part of his nature.

Eventually he recovered entirely, but he bore the evidence of the accident for the rest of his life in a long facial scar. In maturity he wore a full beard covering as much of the scar as possible. He also emerged from the incident strongly distrustful of horses, hardly the usual characteristic displayed by a future cavalry officer.

Years later Ben noted that some members of the family blamed his brother, maintaining that John's carelessness had caused the accident. Ben's response demonstrated a good deal about his own character. He considered John "entirely innocent of any fault," attributing the misfortune instead to "my reckless desire for a free and unencumbered ride on that horse."[14] This strong tendency to be temperate and fair in his judgment of others was one of Ben's most appealing and consistent traits.

On the whole, Ben's childhood memories were pleasant. His father was strict and, at times, easily angered, but he was not unkind. Aware of his son's love for music, Robert searched for an instrument, finally borrowing a neighbor's flute. It was too large for a child's hands, but this did not deter Ben. After obtaining the music to "Scots wa hae" and "Life Let Us Cherish," he prevailed upon Professor Isaac White, the Youngstown band instructor, to whistle these tunes until he had them memorized. Then Ben returned to his room above his father's store, knelt in the middle of his bed, and practiced until he had mastered these songs. From that time on he described himself as "so infatuated with music that I could think of but little else, being unwilling to give up playing the flute even to eat or sleep."

Professor White provided the eager youngster with a smaller octave flute, and Ben progressed rapidly in his musical studies. Eventually he learned to play all the major instruments including the drum, piano, violin, guitar and clarinet. He became so proficient on the latter instrument that Youngstown citizens raised funds to buy him a "fine cocoa" clarinet. Before long he was playing with the Youngstown Band, and at thirteen, he became by "unanimous vote" its leader. A year later, in 1840, he enjoyed his first taste of political activity when he traveled throughout eastern Ohio, providing the music for the raucous Log Cabin and Hard Cider campaign of "Tippecanoe and Tyler too." After graduation from the Youngstown Academy, Ben assumed a position clerking in Brander's store. In his free time he expanded his musical activities, giving lessons, repairing instruments, and organizing one of the region's earliest minstrel troops. It was about this time that he began courting an attractive young woman.[15]

Alice Kirk was the oldest child of John and Susan Bingham Kirk, prominent residents of Youngstown. Like the Griersons, the Kirks (whose original name had been Kirkpatrick before John shortened it for business reasons) were of Scotch-Irish ancestry and traced their forebears back to the supporters of the Scottish monarch Robert Bruce. Unlike the Griersons, they were not first-generation Americans. John Kirk's grandfather, who arrived in the New World sometime before the American Revolution, had settled originally in New Jersey. Following a common migratory path among Scotch-Irish settlers, he later moved his family to Washington County, Pennsylvania.

About the turn of the century, two of his sons, Thomas and Andrew Kirkpatrick, along with a number of other families from the

John and Susan Kirk with children Alice and Henry. *Courtesy Fort Davis National Historic Site, Fort Davis, Texas.*

same region, relocated in the Mahoning Valley. They established not only Youngstown, but also Warren, Canfield, Ellsworth, Coitsville, Lordstown, and several other small villages in the area. By 1803, Thomas had attained some measure of prosperity. His tax bill for chattel property that year amounted to $1.36, one of the higher amounts levied in Trumbull County. By contrast, Andrew, a blacksmith, owned little worth taxing that year. This fact did not dissuade Andrew from eloping with thirteen-year-old Elizabeth Baldwin, who was the sister of Phoebe, his brother's wife, and the daughter of Caleb Baldwin, one of the town's most prominent citizens. Twelve children were born of this union, of whom John Kirkpatrick was the oldest.[16]

The couple settled in Coitsville, Ohio. Here Andrew Kirkpatrick, with the help of his neighbors, built his bride a log cabin, sixteen feet square, with a clapboard roof to lend it respectability—a typical dwelling in the Mahoning Valley region in the early 1800s. For Elizabeth, a frail young woman who suffered from asthma, and who bore four children in fairly rapid succession, the first years of marriage were especially difficult. In August, 1812, Detroit fell to the British, exposing the entire Northwest Territory to enemy control and the depredations of their Indian allies. Andrew Kirkpatrick, along with fifteen hundred other Ohioans, enlisted in the army under the command of General William Henry Harrison. This left the entire responsibility for maintaining the small family farm squarely on his wife's slender shoulders.

With the onset of winter came the additional problem of keeping the young family from freezing to death. Thomas Kirkpatrick hauled logs to Elizabeth's door, but the task of chopping these into firewood remained to be done. John Kirk remembered that as a small boy of eight he attempted to fill his father's shoes, struggling to wield an ax for his mother, who stood by pale and wheezing in the sub-zero cold. Eventually the work proved too much, and Elizabeth and her children moved in with her brother-in-law and sister to await her husband's return.

Early in the spring, after the victories of Commodore Oliver Perry at Put-in-Bay on Lake Erie and General Harrison at the Battle of Thames brought the Northwest Territory under American control, Andrew Kirkpatrick returned home.[17] Over time, the family's economic situation improved, but these early experiences left their mark on John Kirk. The memory of growing up in a family that was relatively deprived gave him a strong incentive to achieve material success. And the necessity of assuming responsibility at an early age infused a tough resiliency into his developing character.

A man born in a log cabin is a familiar part of an American folk tradition. A self-made man is another, and this is exactly what Kirk considered himself. At twenty he was a school teacher who had managed to save $175 from a small salary. With this capital, he placed an order for $900 worth of merchandise from a family friend and received the entire amount on credit. After selling these goods at a tidy profit, he joined in a partnership with a cousin, Caleb Baldwin Wick, and soon Kirkpatrick and Wick were transacting a large volume of business. Thus established, he successfully petitioned the Ohio Legislature to shorten his name to Kirk, arguing that his customers seldom called him anything else.[18]

In later years, John Kirk attributed his success in merchandising, the "most difficult" enterprise of all, to the virtues of diligent labor, frugality, temperance, and a native shrewdness. The trade secret was simple; buy cheap and sell dear and avoid at all cost the encumbrances of debt and that "monster interest which sucks out the very vitals of the merchant's profits."[19] This was paradoxical for a man who had achieved his start on credit, but he viewed himself as the exception that proved the rule.

If these guidelines provided the answers for doing business, the Bible supplied the rules for conducting one's personal life. That was the simple creed derived from his membership in the Disciples of Christ Congregation, a "New Light" offshoot of Scotch Presbyterianism. When Kirk married Susan Bingham, the daughter of a wealthy farmer, and began establishing their large family, he modeled his role as husband and father on that of the Old Testament patriarch. He set strict rules regarding the behavior of family members, and, despite the long hours he spent conducting business, he devoted much of his free time to his children's upbringing. By this time, the trend among American fathers was to delegate these responsibilities primarily to their wives, but not so for John Kirk. In addition to overseeing his children's moral instruction and education, he took an active role in supervising their diet, selecting their clothing, and prescribing medication when illnesses struck.[20] Even after his children reached maturity, it was John, rather than his wife, Susan, who corresponded most frequently and dispensed advice and counsel, often of the most personal and intimate nature.[21] For example, when Alice had been married for thirteen years and was awaiting the birth of her fifth child at Fort Riley, Kansas, Kirk wrote admonishing her to observe the full period of postpartum celibacy as set forth in the twelfth chapter of Leviticus—sixty days if she bore a female child but only thirty if her offspring was a male.

Children react different to such a powerful father. In the Kirk family, some became increasingly rebellious, pitting themselves against their iron-willed parent. Part of this reaction may have been sparked by a curious contradiction in John Kirk himself. In philosophy and outlook, it would have been difficult to find a more advanced, humanitarian thinker in America before the Civil War. John Kirk was an early supporter of the antislavery movement and during the 1850s, he gave unstintingly of his time and money to assist free blacks threatened by the Fugitive Slave Act. He also was an early champion of suffrage for women, perhaps in part because of his longtime interest in temperance. It should be added that those who knew Kirk socially agreed that no man had a quicker wit or a heartier laugh.[22] And yet there were many occasions in his own home when he could only be described as an unyielding autocrat.

The oldest child often identifies strongly with one or both parents. Alice Kirk emerged from her upbringing heavily influenced by her father, deeply religious and serious in demeanor. An honor student, she shared with Ben Grierson an appreciation for poetry, literature, and above all, music. Years later she recalled that Ben's courtship had consisted largely of love letters and serenades. Often at night he opened his bedroom window and directed his clarinet playing in the direction of Alice's home.[23] The two pledged themselves to one another almost from the beginning, and the courtship appeared to go smoothly until an unfortunate incident led to their separation for a number of years.

One day, while passing the Kirk mansion, Ben spied Alice and her aunt Louisa engaged in conversation on the balcony adjoining Alice's second-story bedroom. He called to them, and, after an exchange of pleasantries, the older woman beckoned the young man to join them. Ben scaled the trellis and the three chatted for some time, apparently unaware of the impropriety of the situation. But when John Kirk learned later that Ben had stood outside his daughter's bedroom, he was furious. After issuing strict orders to Alice never to see Ben again, he took steps to assure her obedience by sending her away to school, placing her first in the Huron Academy in Milan, Ohio, and later transferring her to a school in Hudson, Ohio.[24]

It is unlikely that this single incident was solely responsible for John Kirk's attitude. He objected to young Grierson for a number of reasons. While Ben's family was solidly middle class, he himself had no great prospects. Kirk, moreover, could hardly be expected to welcome his daughter's eventual marriage to a musician and music teacher, and worse yet, an indifferent Christian. The episode on the balcony merely gave Kirk the excuse he had been seeking for some time to terminate the relationship.

The date of Alice's departure from Youngstown—September 5, 1845—remained fixed in Ben's memory all his life. Despite John

Kirk's objections, he found a way to say goodby. He persuaded the neighbor who transported Alice to school to drive so slowly that he could walk alongside her cart and, for several miles, converse with her. After the young couple exchanged farewells, three years passed before they met again.

While Alice was away, Ben continued to establish himself in eastern Ohio as a highly skilled musician. He also had his first taste of military experience. He enlisted in the Ohio Militia, serving as bugler for Captain Samuel Gibson's cavalry regiment. Years later, when he reflected on this early training, he concluded that it had done little to prepare him for actual military service.[25]

When Alice returned home after completing her course of study at Hudson, she and Ben resumed seeing each other. This must have been done surreptitiously at first, since her father still opposed the relationship. At some point, however, he became aware of the situation, and Alice, who was not without influence where her father was concerned, prevailed upon him to relent and invite Ben to call once more at the Kirk home. The letter Kirk sent to this effect was not conciliatory and stated clearly that he intended to enforce a number of conditions. Nonetheless, some progress had been made, and from Kirk's viewpoint, he had made a concession.

As Ben saw it, the conditions attached were insulting. After consulting with Alice, he sent a blunt reply, calling Kirk, among other things, a "pope." Alice was at home when the letter arrived, and she later related to Ben that her father read it, tore it up, and threw it into the fire with no further comment.[26] Even at this point, Alice could have smoothed the matter over in time, but the courtship foundered, not because of Alice's father, but because of strong reservations in Alice's own mind.

By 1848 she was a young woman of twenty. Personal convictions she had long held were now more firmly fixed than ever. Both her religious fervor and her piety had deepened, and, like her father, she had become involved in the temperance movement. She loved Ben, and the attraction between them exerted a strong pull on her emotions. But she now questioned whether he would make a suitable husband, even if in time her father accepted him. It disturbed her that Ben was apathetic towards religion, seldom attended church, and had developed a number of distressing habits. Occasionally he indulged in hard liquor, and he was addicted to tobacco, especially cigars. When they resumed seeing each other, Alice attempted to discuss these differences with Ben, but without a great deal of success.

There was one characteristic Ben exhibited that proved frustrating to Alice. Unlike his brother John or his sister Louisa, he was difficult to involve in disputes. Very likely, as a child he had seen enough of contention, and now as an adult sought to avoid arguments. Only rarely did he exhibit the "Grierson temper" (his blunt note to John Kirk, notwithstanding). And while he did not lack the courage to defend himself, he often went to great lengths to avert a row.

The youngest member of the Grierson family tended not only to smooth over disagreements between himself and others, but to ignore them altogether. Since the differences between them were important to Alice, this trait, which she characterized as "indifference" for want of a better term, had become for her a source of irritation even before the two broke off their understanding of an engagement.[27]

When Alice discovered that Ben passively resisted her efforts to reform him, she became deeply concerned about the future of their relationship. As she explained later in a letter written to her intimate friend, Ben's sister Mary:

> I ought not to have cherished, or have allowed him to cherish such feelings as have been so long increasing and strengthen[ing] and cause so much pain now when crushed. But Mary, blame me for what you will, do not charge me with having wilfully trifled with him in love. I have loved him as I never expect to love another. Yet I always told him I could not marry a man who was not a Christian.[28]

Here Alice was not referring to Christian in the broad sense, but rather, since the Disciples of Christ referred to themselves as the "Christian Association," she was really stating that unless Ben adopted the Disciples' creed and joined the congregation, matrimony remained out of the question.[29]

Despite these personal difficulties and the continuing hostility of John Kirk, both Ben and Alice were reluctant to give up hope of one day being united. For some time, relations between the two remained uneasily balanced between their strong mutual attraction on the one hand and Alice's uncertainty on the other. Then, in 1849, their courtship reached a crisis in which it either had to move forward or end. The entire Grierson family was preparing for another move westward.

The abundance of cheap land, yielding record corn crops in Illinois, a state poised on the verge of a boom, had caught their attention. Along the western edge lay the Mississippi River, funneling agricultural products southward to New Orleans. More recently, the completion in 1848 of the Illinois-Michigan Canal had placed Chicago and its burgeoning commodities market in direct contact with the eastern seaboard. And once the great number of railroad lines already begun or projected had been completed, farmers throughout the state would enjoy access to eastern, and beyond that, European markets.

What this meant was clear to perceptive observers. "In due time these prairies will be attached to the suburbs of New York; the great west will be but a day's ride into the country and its inhabitants will be sending to New York for their flour and garden sauce." When that happened, "adventurers and speculators" would pour in, forcing up land and home prices. For the present, living costs were low (eggs sold for three cents a dozen and prime roast beef brought six cents a pound), work was plentiful, and wages were comparatively high. What better place to explore new business opportunities and, at the same time, speculate in western land.[30]

Specifically, the Griersons were looking at Jacksonville, seat of Morgan County, thirty miles west of the state capital at Springfield, and situated in the midst of fertile, rolling hills. Founded in the 1820s by a group of transplanted New England families, it was attractively laid out, with its broad, tree-lined streets and the inevitable town square in the center. "It looks, I say," wrote one visitor to the city in 1851, "like a model New England village made to order . . . and transported hither by some magic machinery and set down in the midst of the prairie, for picturesque effect or as a wholesale speculation in city lots."[31]

The town's residents could boast of a number of amenities, including Illinois College, founded by the "Yale Band" in 1829 to disseminate learning and civilization on the American frontier. More recently, a female seminary and many reading and discussion groups, as well as musical societies, testified to the population's continuing interest in cultural activities. In addition, there were three asylums, either established or in the planning stages, including an institution for deaf-mutes, one for the blind, and another for the care and treatment of the insane, all avidly sought by city fathers. It was a place, in short, where "the booster's speculative dream of urban success was married to the reformer's zealous plan to uplift and enlighten the West." Also important, the continuing influence of former New Englanders in the town's life gave the Griersons reason to hope that, despite the heavy influx of Southerners from bordering states, some residents would hold political views compatible with their own.[32]

The political climate was a matter of concern. In 1848, Robert Grierson, described as "a strong Democrat" and "an ardent lover of liberty," had bolted his party. Angered over the nomination of Lewis Cass on a platform espousing "popular sovereignty" (allowing settlers moving into territories recently acquired from Mexico to determine for themselves whether they wished to form slave or free states), he had joined the ranks of the Free-Soilers. The newly formed party's platform, calling for a national Homestead Act, federally-funded internal improvements, and reforms of the political patronage system, attracted him. More important was the party's adamant stand against the spread of slavery into the territories. Robert Grierson had not come all the way to the New World and made his way west only to find himself or his descendents competing with slave labor. The territories were for free men.[33]

Years later Ben described his father as having been a "warm friend of Wendell Phillips and Lloyd Garrison." Nonetheless, unlike these militant abolitionists, he did not call for the immediate end to slavery in the United States, nor did he advocate an "unlawful interference" with the "peculiar institution" in the Southern states where it already existed. But increasingly he found himself compelled to speak out against the possible spread of slavery elsewhere, "expressing his sentiments freely and fearlessly on all occasions and often facing large mobs regardless of all threats of violence. . . ." Clearly the matter of community sentiment loomed large as the Griersons contemplated the next move.[34]

Late in 1849, as the time for departure drew near, Ben and Alice met to settle their status once and for all. Ben described the result in his autobiography.

As they talked Ben became aware that, despite her father's objections and her own reservations, Alice was considering accompanying him to Illinois. Realizing that John Kirk's approval was essential to their happiness, he wisely dissuaded her, remarking that "if in time matters so changed as to enable us ever to be united it must be with the free and proffered consent of her father." Since that circumstance was unlikely for the forseeable future, there was no alternative but to part permanently. Their understanding of an engagement ended, leaving each free to form other associations. As a pledge of good faith, they returned to one another all the letters they had exchanged and agreed that in the future there would be no correspondence.[35]

With no hope of marriage in sight, Alice turned to schoolteaching, a common and poorly paid profession for unmarried women in that era.[36] The work was demanding and the conditions trying. Her classes included children of all ages and abilities, and imparting knowledge under these circumstances taxed her ingenuity. Following the accepted instructional practices of the day, she required students to memorize facts in rote fashion and used as textbooks the didactic Eclectic Readers, written by William McGuffey of neighboring Coitsville, Ohio. During the long, almost interminable midwest winters, the poorly lit schoolhouse was dark and difficult to heat, and she wrote Ben's sister Mary, in Jacksonville, of her longing for the "long, bright days."[37]

Alice's friendship with Mary provided both women with strong emotional support. Undoubtedly the similarity of their circumstances strengthened the bond between them. Since neither saw marriage as a distinct possibility, both experienced anxiety regarding their eventual fate. By unburdening themselves in long, intimate, and loving letters, each obtained comfort and release from loneliness.[38]

Despite her dissatisfaction with Ben's character, Alice grieved over their separation. Here the basic Presbyterian cast to her religious faith, with its strong emphasis on predestination, proved a bulwark. "You speak of the way matters stand between Ben and I [*sic*] and tell me to throw away my foolish scruples and now, Mary, whether we are ever united or not, I firmly believe with you, that an overruling Providence will direct all for the best, and if it is right that we will be married, no 'foolish scruples' of mine will prevent it."

Mary, suggesting that the continuing estrangement served no purpose, chided Alice that her conscience was "not so influential in a thousand other matters." True, Alice acknowledged, but she was attempting to live by the Bible, and the basic principle was that "everything dear must be forsaken sooner than violate a positive precept or command." Yet inwardly, she confessed, she often wondered about the wisdom of her actions. "Won't it be a happy time when we get where we all know what is right and always practice what we know?"[39]

Convinced that Alice and Ben belonged together, Mary did her best to play the role of matchmaker, taking it upon herself to act as go-between by passing information on to each of them. She was especially proud of Ben's musical achievements, noting the time when he conducted the Illinois College Orchestra in a series of his own compositions. She also reported on the numerous invitations he received, asking him to audition for the Jenny Lind rehearsals in St. Louis. Finally, Mary was not above dispensing liberal advice to Alice on how she could show interest in Ben in the "right way."[40]

While Mary sought to keep Alice and Ben in contact with one another, the correspondence served another purpose as well. In adulthood, she still suffered from her old nemesis—depression—and her letters contained many references to her emotional difficulties. Alice herself was not immune to wide variations in mood, but she was not as susceptible to despondency as her friend.

Alice was familiar with mental disorders. Among her close relatives, a cousin, John Manning, became so disturbed during his late adolescence that he required confinement. Closer to home, both her brother Henry and her sister Maria were committed to the Columbus, Ohio, asylum. Alice's mother described the onset of sixteen-year-old Maria's difficulties this way:

> There seemed to be a rush of blood to the head, she complained of headache and of her back . . . she suffered very much from fear—she appeared to think that there had been some great crime committed and that she or some one of the family had got to suffer for it . . . she said to me Mother I must go somewhere where I can be taken care of.[41]

Thus Alice was naturally inclined to be sympathetic when Mary Grierson confided, shortly after the move to Jacksonville, that she "felt gloomy . . . sick at heart." Two months later she confessed, "I was rather *low spirited*—but am better again and your words of love and kindness had not little to do with my recovery." Three years later she was still relating to Alice that, although she had experienced "no great outward tangible trouble this summer . . . it has not been a very happy one to me."[42]

Some of the depression experienced by both young women was not because of innate temperament or passing moods, or their concern over future uncertainty. Rather it arose because they were constantly confronting the death of close friends and relatives. Scarcely a letter passed between the two that did not include news of a recent demise. Alice's family was intimately acquainted with death. Of the twelve children borne by Susan Kirk, only eight survived to adolescence, and of these, three would die in their early adulthood. The Grierson family, on the other hand, had been more fortunate, for they had lost only two of their children during childhood.

Pneumonia, tuberculosis, typhus, and typhoid claimed many victims of all ages, while scarlet fever, measles, croup, whooping cough, and diptheria represented grave dangers for children. In the summer, dysentery "of the worst kind," plagued both young and old. "I assure you that you cannot realize," Alice wrote Mary during an epidemic of dysentery in 1853, "how much sickness there is and has been here. The terms dangerously sick, very low, dying and died have become so familiar that they make but little impression on me." A few days later she confided that her whole life now appeared to be given over to attending funerals. "The earth has just closed over the last remains of Lewis Murray," and others who had recently succumbed included four women from Alice's immediate neighborhood.[43]

While the bulk of their correspondence was devoted to sharing confidences, both women, well educated by the standards of their day, maintained a keen interest in the world around them. When the speeches of Louis Kossuth were published, Alice related that her father and brother had traveled to Salem and Columbus to hear the Hungarian revolutionary early in 1852. John Kirk had been so impressed that he remained behind to shake Kossuth's hand. To Mary Grierson, who spent hours in her room reading his speeches aloud, it was very simple; Kossuth was the "greatest man living."[44] And, by the spring of 1852, both women were eagerly awaiting the latest issue of the *National Era* for the next installment of Harriet Beecher Stowe's "Uncle Tom's Cabin."[45]

As an unmarried woman, Alice found her opportunities for socializing limited. She joined a weekly Bible study group, occasionally attended a Methodist Episcopal Church revival, and continued to join her father in temperance activities. She described for Mary one meeting that, fortunately, her father did not attend.

When business matters called him out of town, John Kirk and his friend William Travis (a local leader in educational reforms) persuaded others to appear in their place. An anti-temperance mob stormed the meeting site, a schoolhouse, blew out the single candle, and then pelted the speakers with stones, corn, tomatoes, and eggs "prepared expressly for the benefit of Mr. Travis and Pa."[46]

By the summer of 1852, Alice, finding herself increasingly restless, left home to visit relatives in LaFayette, Indiana. For some time she had felt that change was essential, and she was assured that teaching positions were available in that vicinity. This report proved true, and she soon was mistress of a one-room schoolhouse. Initially she felt exhilarated and passed her leisure hours exploring the area's attractions. She visited the Tippecanoe battleground and on Saturday afternoons sat on the banks of the Wabash and Erie Canal, watching men load barges bound for Toledo, Ohio.

Her new position, however, soon proved both frustrating and unrewarding. Unlike Youngstown (an advanced community for its day), the LaFayette school district was not well financed and relied heavily on subscription fees paid by the students' families. Since there were a number of small, competing schools in the area, salaries were low.

During summer sessions, attendance was even more irregular than during the school year, and Alice found that both her class size and her income varied. As her "light purse" became even lighter, she was hard pressed to pay her board and room. Added to this problem was the strain of living in a one-room house, fifteen by sixteen feet, with three other persons, one of whom was a newborn infant. Before long she was suffering from digestive problems, and her weight plummeted. John Kirk, aware that something was wrong, arrived in LaFayette in September, took one look at his daughter, and immediately packed her bags and escorted her home.[47]

As she recovered her strength over the next few months, Alice found herself at loose ends. She was now a young woman of twenty-four with no prospects for marriage nor any for teaching in the Youngstown schools, at least immediately. More unsettling, her eighteen-year-old sister Mary was already married, and her brother Henry was engaged. Increasingly it looked as if spinsterhood would be her destiny after all.[48]

Thus it was not surprising that when the Springfield Female Academy offered Alice a teaching position, she eagerly accepted. She reached the city well in advance of fall term and took up residence with her second cousin Dr. William Lord and his family. She had no idea that the opportunity to conduct the Springfield Band frequently brought Ben into town as well.

One August afternoon, shortly before school opened, Ben stopped by the Post's Store. On the window was a bulletin announcing the dates the Female Academy would open and listing the instructors. The name Alice Kirk caught his eye, and, dropping everything planned for that afternoon, he prevailed upon the store owner to give him her address. Shortly thereafter, Ben arrived at the Lords' residence.

When Alice received the news that Ben awaited her in the parlor, she braced herself, struggling to collect her thoughts. She decided that the occasion demanded that she act graciously and yet remain aloof. The best way to accomplish this was to address Ben at all times as "Mr. Grierson." But when she actually saw him standing before her after so long a time, she forgot herself entirely, called him "Ben," and clasped his hands warmly. This was all the encouragement Grierson needed, and in his mind the years of estrangement vanished. He was on his way home to Jacksonville and urged her to pack some belongings and accompany him.

All this happened so quickly that Alice stood in the parlor, confused, until her cousin nudged her gently, reassuring her, "you'll be safe in Ben's hands, Alice." Soon after that, the couple boarded the train for Jacksonville, where both received a warm reception from Ben's family. Several days passed before Alice returned to Springfield for the opening of school, but before she left, she and Ben once more were considering marriage.[49]

During the following year, Alice and Ben saw each other at every opportunity, and by the spring of 1854, Alice was busy rehearsing the speech she would make upon informing her parents of her engagement. "Ben & I have decided that we would be happier if we were married than we are now," was the way one version went. "We have seen a great deal of each other during the last year & think we ought to be pretty well acquainted by this time, also we are old enough to have some judgment and look upon life as reality and not all romance."[50]

Ben still remained concerned about Alice's relations with her father and decided that, for his own peace of mind, he needed to obtain John Kirk's unvarnished reaction to their bethrothal. With this in mind he formulated a plan. When Alice returned home after the end of the school year, he would travel first to Cincinnati to visit his brother John and his wife, Elizabeth. Afterward, on his way back to Jacksonville, he would stop at the Kirk home with no forewarning. That way he could determine "whether my presence at your house will be agreeable to your folks or not. Do not," he cautioned Alice, "say anything about my coming—so that folks will have to make up their minds at once whether they are glad to see me or not—without any previous time to consider."[51]

Despite his contrivances to ferret out John Kirk's true feelings, as the time drew near to see Alice again, Ben's overriding emotion was one of joyous anticipation. "Practice *all* you can on the Guitar—so that we can have a *Grand* duet together when I come." After they had completed their version of the "Returned Wanderer," they would enjoy the "*grand* finale from the Opera of the *Grandest Time*

Seated, left to right, John C. Grierson and Benjamin H. Grierson. *Standing, left to right,* Elizabeth Grierson and Alice Kirk Grierson. Date about 1854. *Courtesy Fort Davis National Historic Site, Fort Davis, Texas.*

Imaginable," all of which, he hoped, would be "well rendered."[52]

When Ben arrived unannounced at the Kirk residence, to his immense surprise and relief, he received a cordial welcome from her entire family, including a resigned John Kirk. Alice was now twenty-six, and since she had shown no interest in any other man, it was clear that she would either marry Ben Grierson or no one. More important, Alice was now a mature woman determined to fulfill her own deepest wishes. The notes she had been writing to herself, rehearsing her statement to her parents, demonstrated that she intended to confront them with the situation rather than request their permission. Undoubtedly her father understood this. And while he remained very much the authoritarian parent, he was essentially a kind man who loved his oldest child inordinately and desired nothing so much as her happiness.

On Sunday evening, September 24, 1854, John Kirk, an Elder in the Disciples Church of Canfield, Ohio, officiated at the wedding ceremony, joining together his daughter Alice with Benjamin Henry Grierson. Only one element marred the occasion. Seventeen-year-old Maria Kirk had recently returned to the Columbus asylum. All the other family members were there, and celebrated the event joyously with the happy couple.[53]

Troubling questions remained. How, for example, would Ben adequately support his wife and the children that would inevitably follow. True, he was a talented musician and band leader, but the profession brought little other than accolades. This would hardly suffice, especially since Alice, raised in the Kirk mansion, was accustomed to a high standard of living.

Nonetheless, in the bonds of matrimony that were tied that day, a new family had been established. There was nothing to suggest that anything lay ahead for the couple but the common struggle faced by most newlyweds, which is to keep affection alive while striving to make ends meet.

CHAPTER 2

"Virtually Left Without a Dollar"

IT WAS a common assumption in the nineteenth century that, while women were legally inferior to men, morally they were superior.[1] Thus Alice Grierson was not the only wife who saw it as her duty to improve her husband's character. In her opinion Ben required substantial modification before he could attain salvation in the hereafter. He occasionally drank hard liquor, loved cigars, and at times indulged in billiard playing. Worse yet, he remained indifferent toward religion. This was of grave concern, for it was her duty to establish a Christian home. The importance of this situation was underscored when she found herself pregnant two months after their wedding.

Ben readily concurred; he needed reformation. On their first New Year's eve together, he made a number of sincere resolutions to improve his personal habits, a practice he would follow the rest of his life. But when it came to adopting his wife's religious practices, he resisted. While he had a vaguely defined faith in God, he refused to attend religious services with any kind of regularity. Alice had recognized that this discrepancy in outlook could create problems between them. In the early days of their marriage it appeared that her worst fears were being realized.

They had been married less than four months when Alice was called to Springfield to nurse her sister. Twenty-one-year-old Mary Fitch was seriously ill with an undiagnosed but debilitating disease. Separated for the first of many times in their marriage, Ben and Alice corresponded almost daily. Their long, affectionate letters revealed the high value each placed on marital happiness, their mutual dependence upon one another, and the regret they shared over recent disagreements.

"You don't know how my heart aches when I think you did not want even to come to the Depot with me Monday," wrote Alice after her arrival at her sister's home in January, 1855. "But thank God it was not the feeling you had when I left, and dear Ben, I trust we will never allow it to be so again." After briefly describing Mary Fitch's extreme weakness, her inability to sit up and take nourishment, Alice then returned to her greatest concern—their relationship.

Away from Ben she had time to reflect. "I see so many things in which I have erred, & have been wrong, but I *will try* and do better 'darling,' *do not ever* think I am indifferent *to you.*" While their "differences of feeling & thinking in religious matters" saddened her, she was prepared to accept responsibility for their less than perfect happiness.[2]

When they were apart, Ben eagerly awaited Alice's letters. This one touched him greatly, and his response was characteristically loving. Alice was his "decidedly better half—or rather two thirds," and in no way did he blame her for their problems. These resulted from his deficiencies, and with her patient assistance he would strive to eliminate "at least some of those faults . . . most antagonistic" to peace between them. By nature conciliatory, Ben was never one to hold grudges.

He too had been lonely, but upon her return she would find him more appreciative of her company. Her homecoming would be such a joyous occasion that they would celebrate with a musical duet. With Alice accompanying him on the guitar, he promised her a lively fiddle rendition of "Begone dull care" and "Do it while you're young."[3]

When Mary Fitch failed to recover, the days apart stretched into weeks. Alice could not see her husband unless Ben traveled to Springfield, but there was no money for train fare. A resourceful woman, she found Ben an odd job tuning a piano, thus enabling him to earn the fare between Jacksonville and Springfield.[4] The incident disclosed how limited their financial resources were—so limited, in fact, that throughout the first year of marriage they lived with Ben's parents.

Years later, Ben remembered this period as one of great happiness. Undoubtedly it was, but there were difficulties few couples escape. When it came to describing their residence in his parents' house, Ben viewed the matter differently from Alice, for naturally he was more comfortable there. He painted an almost idyllic picture. "Our own family circle was large and my father and mother's house, which for a time was also ours, became very attractive." His parents were so hospitable that the constant stream of visitors often took complete possession of their Jacksonville home.[5]

All this may have been true. Alice, however, in a letter written years later, recalled that as the months passed her discomfort in her in-laws' home increased. Although she struggled to hide her feelings from others, she was not entirely successful. Ben's sister Louisa Semple recognized the strain Alice was under and attempted to console her at a family gathering. Once they moved out on their own, Louisa assured her, they would be much happier. This simple act of sympathy on Louisa's part left Alice greatly relieved, for at least someone understood her mounting frustration. She was so grateful that for years afterward she tried to overlook much of Louisa's eccentric behavior and was inclined to forgive many, though not all, temper tantrums.[6]

Nor was Alice overjoyed to find herself pregnant so soon after her marriage. She had no illusions about childbearing and understood fully the immense amount of care infants required. At twenty-one she had assisted her mother during the birth of a sister, Susan Ellen, and again a year later had managed the entire household after her youngest brother, Rufus, was born.[7] Although Alice longed for a home of her own, when she delivered Charles Henry, on August 11, 1855, she was relieved to find herself surrounded by in-laws who provided welcome assistance.

The new responsibilities of fatherhood brought matters to a head for Ben. He had enjoyed a creative year writing songs and light comic operas in addition to performing music and conducting bands in the Jacksonville and Springfield area. But this was no way to support a family, and he realized that he had to embark on a more profitable career. After considerable thought, he decided that, since both his father and John Kirk had done well as merchants, he too would enter the mercantile business. An opportunity arose when a former employee from his father's Youngstown farm invited Ben to become his partner.

John Walihan owned a general store in Meredosia, Illinois. Recently his partner, Thomas Holderly, had died, and Walihan found the duties of managing a business alone both physically and financially exhausting. Ben described him as "an honest man," lacking the advantages of education, but enjoying a wide circle of friends, and estimated that Walihan transacted twenty thousand dollars worth of business annually. Given the growing number of settlers and farms in the Meredosia vicinity, it seemed reasonable to assume that the figure would increase to twenty-five thousand before long. Walihan's terms were simple. For slightly less than three thousand dollars and the signing of a partnership agreement binding on both parties for five years, Ben could purchase a half-interest in the country store.[8]

The location appealed to Ben for several reasons. Situated in Morgan County, on the banks of the Illinois River, it seemed a "first rate point for shipping all kinds of country produce." Moreover, it was a proposed terminus along the Northern Cross Railroad. Once completed, this line would link the rapidly growing southern counties of the state with the towns of Quincy to the west, Springfield, the state capitol in the center, and Decatur and Danville to the east. Finally, Meredosia promoters extolled the town as the next "western Athens," although Ben admitted when he visited in October, 1855, that he saw little to indicate the growth of a future center of learning and culture.[9]

The town's chief attraction lay in its westward location, twenty miles from his parents' home in Jacksonville and ten miles from Concord, where Louisa and Steele Semple resided. Alice recognized this clearly, and wrote her father that, while she would not have chosen this place (she preferred western Pennsylvania), she understood the appeal it had for Ben. "'The West' has more charms for him than for me, and, no wonder, all his 'blood kin' are here and aside from that you know yourself that there is a sort of magic in living West."[10]

Ben had little money of his own with which to purchase his share of Walihan's business, but this did not deter him from signing a promisory note due the following March. He knew that the closely knit members of the Grierson family would help in any way possible. John Grierson, having recently obtained a bookkeeping position in Memphis, Tennessee, now enjoyed a reliable income and, after traveling to Meredosia and examining Ben's prospects, he returned home agreeing to send small loans where necessary. Robert Grierson also extended aid. Still, when the entire family contributions were totaled, Ben lacked a thousand dollars. There was no alternative; Ben was now forced to approach John Kirk for a loan.

He assured his father-in-law that the enterprise entailed no risk, because Illinois was enjoying a remarkable boom that brought new settlers into the state every day. Besides, Ben knew the formula for success and could apply it as well as anyone. "I certainly do think that with energy, industry & economy we can not but do very well."

After requesting the use of the money for five years at an interest rate not to exceed 6 percent, Ben added that, if necessary, both his father and his brother would co-sign the note[11]

As it turned out, it was necessary. Not only that, but Kirk stipulated that Ben was to pay the entire 6 percent interest to Alice "to be used as she wishes, and," he warned, "if you fail to pay it over to her promptly and punctually, I shall like the Frenchman call for both principal and interest. . . ." The letter included a draft for five hundred dollars. Ben agreed to these terms, and both Robert and John co-signed the note. This arrangement left Alice with mixed feelings. Ben would cheerfully have given her his last cent, she explained to her father. Nonetheless, she enjoyed having some money entirely of her own.[12]

Notwithstanding his requirements, John Kirk was prepared to be generous. Despite his real estate holdings and his considerable net worth, he had little in the way of liquid assets. Only by collecting on outstanding and, in some cases, questionable debts could he raise the rest of the amount requested. This he promised to do as swiftly as possible, but he also informed Ben and Alice that in his opinion the enterprise was doomed.

Had they asked him, he would have advised them to buy a farm in western Pennsylvania. Merchandising was "one of the most hazardous occupations one can follow," and Ben had now placed himself at the mercy of credit markets and customers. "You will recollect that I told you," he continued, "that the grand secret of merchandising was to buy right and then to guard against being cheated out of your goods." Since Ben had no money of his own, he could not "buy to the best advantage." And, by working with borrowed money, Ben labored under the added burden of interest. Unless luck intervened this "monster interest . . . oftener the cause of merchant's failure probably than all other causes combined" would one day sentence him to "grind in the prison house of bondage."[13]

This pessimistic view filled Alice with foreboding. Her father, she knew, was a shrewd businessman with an almost uncanny ability to judge such matters correctly. Had she known his opinion earlier, she would have "vetoed" the step and could easily have done so, "for Ben told me he would do just as I said about it." Now it was too late, they had embarked on their course, and she would see it through to the end. Whatever the outcome, she was prepared to accept it without complaint as the manifestation of God's will. "If prosperity is the best thing for us, I believe we shall have it, and if, adversity, I hope we shall profit by its severe teachings."[14]

At first Walihan and Grierson prospered, and Ben and Alice began improving the small log cabin that was their home. They whitewashed the walls, carpeted the floor, and decorated the windows with curtains. Initially they made do with a bed, crib, stove, and workstand. Over time, they added a "steamboat" chair, a high, walnut cupboard, three smaller chairs, a workbox, a mirror, and Ben built shelves to display their books and his violin. In the back yard Ben attempted to cultivate a garden. By his own admission he was no farmer, and his efforts yielded meager results.[15]

Both were accustomed to the amenities of life, and, in addition, they shared a common interest in music, literary works, and landscape paintings. As soon as their income permitted, they indulged their tastes, buying books, subscribing to magazines, and acquiring fashionable clothes. Ben was especially insistent that Alice outfit herself becomingly and without regard to cost. Possibly he felt that the way she dressed reflected his success in business. It seems more likely that he realized she longed for and appreciated finery, but hesitated to buy these for herself while they were still in debt. "I shall expect you to make a very respectable appearance," he warned her on one occasion. And on another, he cautioned her not to stint on herself unless she wished to incur his displeasure.[16]

They also shared a deep interest in politics. While Alice could not vote, this did not mean that she remained uninformed on national issues. She had grown up listening to her father—a staunch Whig who later became a Republican—expound passionately on the major topics of the day. She also read widely and was fully capable of holding her own in family discussions, a favored activity among the Griersons.

The elections of 1856 attracted more than the usual interest, for the issues and outcome threatened to cause a dangerous national schism. Since the passage, two years earlier, of the controversial Kansas-Nebraska Act, replacing the Missouri Compromise with the doctrine of Popular Sovereignty, and more recent and disturbing events in Kansas, political dissension had increased. The most significant development had been the breakdown of old party allegiances, worn thin by years of sectional conflict. Anti-Nebraska Democrats, former Whigs and ex-Free-Soilers had come together spontaneously in a variety of places—Ripon, Wisconsin, Jackson,

Michigan, and Washington, D.C., to name only a few. Now there was a new party, the Republican, and in Morgan County, Illinois, Ben Grierson was one of its earliest organizers, a fact that was the source of considerable pride in his autobiography. What he did not tell his readers was that sometime earlier he had been a member of the nativist, anti-Catholic American party, more commonly known as the "Know-Nothings."[17]

There is no record of when he was associated with this group or how much he understood of party principles when he joined. One appealing facet of the American party was its stress on nationalism. At a time when most Americans accepted without question the superiority of their political institutions and their God-given mandate to expand territorially, this fervor expressed itself in many ways. The Young America movement, to which Alice's brother John Kirk, Jr. belonged, was one of these. Particularly strong in the western region, especially among Democrats, it was nourished on a heady brew of exuberance over recent territorial acquisitions from Mexico and a determined belief that the United States should eventually encompass additional lands, including Cuba or Nicaragua. Others were attracted to the American party. Very likely this applied to Ben, and as he confided to Alice with considerable embarrassment years later, once he fully understood the implications of party membership, this son of a Scotch-Irish immigrant quietly withdrew.[18]

The building of the Illinois Republican party occurred at the grass-roots level. Individuals of little or no national stature wrote pamphlets, arranged meetings, made posters, gave speeches, obtained signatures on petitions, and registered voters. Anyone gifted enough to compose songs or write verses was immediately drafted into service. Ben thrived on such activities. After the first Republican National Convention nominated John C. Frémont, the "Pathfinder," for president, on a platform demanding an end to "the twin relics of barbarism—polygamy and slavery," in the territories, Grierson emerged as the town's most enthusiastic party organizer.

The small hamlet of Meredosia was originally settled largely by families who had migrated from Kentucky, Tennessee, and Virginia. For the most part, their sympathies were inclined towards the South and its national proponent, the Democratic party. As Ben described the situation in the summer of 1856, he was for a while "the only man in the town and precinct who openly declared himself a Republican."

One day a group of neighbors, accompanied by the Democratic candidate from the district, stopped their carriage outside Ben's store and, wishing to bring him out, shouted at the top of their lungs, "Thank God we are in a place where there is not a man who dare say he is a Republican or will vote for Frémont." Ben, accepting the bait, bounded out the door and into the street, calling out, "Here is a man who if the Almighty lets him live until the day of election will surely vote for John C. Frémont and who glories in the fact that he is a Republican—Hip, Hip, Hurrah."[19]

If there had been any doubt before, the entire town now knew Ben's politics. He campaigned in and around Meredosia, an activity that brought him into contact with other grass-roots activists working for the new party's advancement. Ben was so industrious that his brother John wrote from Memphis, "I am glad to see you awake to the cause of freedom, but don't be so zealous as to injure yourself in business unless you think you are rich enough." In the same letter, John expressed hope that if Frémont won, Ben would become Meredosia's next postmaster.[20]

Walihan also expressed concern. On the night before the election he visited the Grierson home and warned that threats had been made against Ben's life. The next day Ben, assigned the duty of poll watcher, appeared at his station armed with a pistol and remained on guard throughout the day. No serious incident occurred, though whiskey flowed freely. When the ballots were counted, thirty-two persons, out of four hundred voters in Meredosia, had cast their votes for Frémont and his running mate, William L. Dayton. This was "deemed a remarkable success where the Democratic majority was so great," and Ben's contribution to the party's early struggle earned him the gratitude of Republican organizers and party chiefs. Among these were Richard Yates, the congressman from the Seventh District, and a strong Yates supporter, Abraham Lincoln, the former Whig congressman from Illinois. Two years later when Lincoln arrived in Meredosia for the Lincoln-Douglas debates, he stayed at the Grierson home.[21]

On the surface, the 1856 election results were disappointing for the Republicans. However, party strategists surmised that if they held on to their present gains and won additional support in the North and Northwest, the next election could bring them national victory. In Illinois, though they failed to carry the state for Frémont, their local candidates swept the northern districts, giving the new party a substantial share of state offices. Republicans were now a major force in Illinois politics, a fact that had profound implications for Ben Grierson's future.

On November 1, just days before the election and only fifteen months after Charlie's arrival, Alice gave birth to a second son. Baptized John Kirk Grierson in honor of his grandfather, he was called Kirkie throughout his brief life. The choice of a name demonstrated the strong influence Alice's father continued to play in the Griersons' lives. Undoubtedly both were grateful for the financial help extended. And, since Ben appeared to be prospering (he could now afford to pay a maid $1.50 a week), Kirk's reservations regarding the marriage were beginning to subside.[22]

Kirk, however, continued to compete with Ben in very subtle ways for influence over his daughter. Alice now meant more to him than ever before, for of the six daughters his wife Susan had borne, only two remained—Alice and her eight-year-old sister, Susan Ellen. The others, including Maria and, most recently, Mary Fitch, had died. Kirk wrote to Alice frequently and took an active interest in his grandchildren, offering extensive advice on child bearing. He cautioned Alice against following the "slip and go easy" methods of her mother, and provided her with dietary, bathing, and clothing instructions.

She was advised to begin her day and Kirkie's by drinking a small mixture of brandy and quinine. Until they reached the age of ten, she was encouraged to feed her children mush, milk, molasses, and dark bread and to bathe them often. Once a week was not too frequent. As for clothing, he recommended woolen wraps covering necks, shoulders and arms. Finally to alleviate pain of teething, he instructed her to cut their gums with a small pocket knife.

The health of the entire family could be ensured if she followed Biblical rules. When he discovered that Alice was storing sausages for the winter, he admonished her that pigs were the "vilest and filthiest of all unclean beasts . . . a dish positively interdicted to any & every Christian." By violating the Old Testament, she was also disobeying "Natural Law" and illness would inevitably follow.[23]

Despite his success as a merchant, Kirk had long aspired to live the life of a gentleman farmer. He realized his ambition briefly in 1855, when he moved his family to the "Kirkarian Farm" in western Pennsylvania. Arguing that its location was far healthier than Meredosia, where the Illinois River was a breeding place for fever and ague in the summer and respiratory illness in the winter, he constantly prevailed upon his daughter to bundle up her children and return to her parents' home for extended visits. Alice, left alone with small children during the long hours Ben tended store, was easily persuaded. When she left, she usually stopped along the way at the homes of her numerous relatives, thereby consigning Ben to "Bachelor's Hall" for months at a time.

She made one such lengthy visit in the summer of 1857. By the middle of August, Ben and Alice had been apart for two weeks, and as yet he had heard nothing from her. To comfort himself, Ben untied and reread all the old letters in his possession. It struck him, he wrote Alice, that in some there were "no very warm expressions of love." Others were "sweetly the reverse." What Ben had uncovered was a pattern that would continue throughout the frequent separations of their married life.[24]

Alice never wavered in her love for Ben; that remained constant. She was, however, often preoccupied with the burdens of child care and the constant round of domestic duties that consumed the energies of women in that day. These tasks sapped her physical strength and her emotional vitality as well. There were times when she felt that the burdens she shared with Ben were unfairly distributed, and the resentment that welled up in her tended to be expressed in a series of curt, matter-of-fact responses to the husband that she knew longed to receive affectionate messages. This coolness never lasted long. Alice needed time to struggle with her feelings before putting them into words. Once she shared them in a straightforward manner with Ben, he invariably accepted them in a conciliatory spirit. Shortly afterward her anger would dissipate, and her letters once more would become loving.[25]

By the end of August, with no word from Alice, Ben was despondent. If she failed to return soon, he would be forced to go to her, for he could endure the separation no longer. By now he was "all 'out of sorts' out of a wife & out of children (at home), and" in a message that could hardly have inspired her to return and face the domestic chaos, "my heels are out of my *stockings* & my house is shockingly out of order." Still, she probably smiled when she read his variation of an old refrain they both remembered, "Oh love, I'm all out and alone in the world without you."[26]

Alice returned to Meredosia soon after Ben's lament, and found herself confined almost entirely to the cabin. As a small child, Charlie was susceptible to earaches accompanied by high fevers and convulsions. By March, 1858, Alice wrote her sister-in-law Mary: "I want you to come down as soon, and stay as long as you can, I never was as lonesome as I have been this winter." But Mary by now had responsibilities of her own, for she was serving as a "schoolmarm," teaching the children of black families in Jacksonville. Since the town was a terminus along the Underground Railroad, some of these children were the offspring of fugitive slaves. Mary's task was difficult, for the class was held in a dark, "uncomfortable hole," which suggests that her activity was not public. Given the stringent Fugitive Slave Law then in effect, it was dangerous as well.[27]

Early in that same year, John Kirk had become a sales representative for Jones and Laughlin's American Iron Works, a position that required him to move his family to Chicago. There they rented a nine-room home splendid enough to include brick outbuildings. A shrewd investor, Kirk scouted the city looking for reasonably priced lots for speculation. Thanks to his unerring instinct for a good buy, his earnings were substantial, which was fortunate. By now his two oldest sons—twenty-six-year-old Henry and twenty-four-year-old Thomas required sizable loans. So also did his son-in-law, Ben Grierson.[28]

The balance sheets of Walihan and Grierson no longer showed an encouraging profit. In the aftermath of the Panic of 1857, hard times had descended upon the country, affecting the northern and western states severely. Walihan and Grierson noticed at first that their customers, farmers from the surrounding rural areas, no longer had the cash to purchase goods. Increasingly it was necessary to extend credit if sales were to be transacted at all. Further, their early prosperity had led them to increase their inventory, and by 1858 they had a large stock on hand, all purchased with borrowed money.[29] Although neither understood it at the time, a process had begun whereby both men would lose their business and their homesteads as well. Worse yet, they would emerge from this ordeal deeply in debt for years to come.

Whether or not Ben shared with Alice the full extent of their problems, she was astute enough to suspect that all was not going well. In June she made plans to visit her parents in Chicago, but heavy rains and flash floods hit Meredosia, sending the townspeople scurrying for high ground. She remained with Ben throughout this emergency, and by the time it passed the July and August heat had set in, making it dangerously unhealthy to take small children on trips. As a result, she did not leave Meredosia until October.

Chicago proved no healthier than Meredosia. While there, Kirkie, nearly two years old, became ill with bronchitis. When the disease progressed to pneumonia, Ben received an urgent telegraph instructing him to come immediately. By the time he arrived, Kirkie had died, just three days past his second birthday. Dazed, and grief-stricken, Ben and Alice considered sending his body back to Meredosia, but John Kirk intervened and persuaded them to bury their child in a nearby cemetery alongside the Chicago River.

If Alice had been at all uncertain of their financial circumstances previously, their inability to purchase anything other than a small marker provided a solid clue. Not wishing to lose track of the grave entirely, she and Ben took the additional precaution of planting a small tree close by. Eight months later Alice was still despondent over the loss of their child, and Ben suggested that she investigate the cost of a larger stone. Since their financial situation had deteriorated even further, nothing came of it. Five years later, when Ben's father returned to the cemetery, intending to have Kirkie's remains removed to a Jacksonville cemetery, the tree was gone and sand washed up from the river had covered the small marker. The exact location of Kirkie's grave was lost forever.[30]

Throughout 1859, Walihan and Grierson struggled to remain in business. Ben, by nature an optimist, wrote his brother John in January that he thought the worst had passed and very soon business would improve. John, after congratulating him, warned against "selling more goods than the Suckers can pay for. . . ." But if there was any improvement it was temporary, and by late winter the steady decline continued.[31]

Any lingering doubts Alice may have had about their situation were removed in March when she received her father's response to a report she had sent concerning their business transactions. Her statement of their inventory, assets and debits made no sense to him or to the Philadelphia lawyers he had consulted. "You will have to try your hand again, there is evidently an error, or," there was one other possibility, "they must be doing a much smaller business on a much smaller capital than I supposed."[32]

Affairs continued from bad to worse. Walihan and Grierson took in little cash and what they did obtain were drafts drawn on Illinois banks and subject to discount by Eastern firms. Much of the time Ben and his partner had no recourse; if they wished to move merchandise they were forced to accept corn, wheat, and even ponies as payment. At first these exchanges pleased Ben, for here was a chance to speculate in commodities in a rising market.[33]

When his first such attempts in Chicago made him a handsome profit, Ben concluded that this was the way to recoup some of his business losses. He purchased an additional 214 acres of farmland on credit, hired laborers to plant wheat and corn, and then waited for grain prices to rise in either St. Louis or Chicago. But by the summer of 1859 wheat prices were headed downward, and on the eve of the Civil War reached their lowest point in five years. All Ben accomplished was to increase his total indebtedness.[34]

These were not happy times for the Griersons. Ben worried constantly about their growing financial problems, and Alice continued to grieve over the loss of Kirkie. By June, 1859, she was again visiting her parents, and the correspondence between the two revealed that they had recently quarreled, a fact both regretted. Ben, as usual, missed his wife and was determined that when she returned she would discover a "better & wiser" as well as a "more affectionate and kind" husband. With her patient help, he was certain that the *"dark and sad spots"* of their past life together would become instead "steppingstones to raise us up to something *higher, brighter, happier* and *holier* above. Dearest Alice," he wrote, "will we not extend to each other a helping hand, may we not yet be able to look back on a life not altogether wasted and lost. Hope on hope ever that we may learn to look higher & that God may yet help us & make us happy."

Alice sought to comfort her husband and cautioned him not to surrender to the "blues." Still, three weeks later their recent arguments continued to haunt Ben. "The past cannot be lived over again — the errors that we committed were great & many — they were too harsh & sad & severe to be forgotten." Nonetheless, he was determined that when she returned they would achieve a happier marital state.[35]

Ben counted on his brother to provide financial assistance during difficult periods. By the summer of 1860 it was obvious that John, too, had fallen on hard times. Expecting to turn a quick profit, he had purchased a Memphis lot containing a vacant brick mill and an alley. After paying two thousand dollars down toward the purchase price of ten thousand dollars, he wrote Ben that he could sell it anytime for fifteen thousand dollars. Six weeks later, after quarreling with his employer, Charles Potter, he found himself out of work. Unable to locate a buyer and deeply in debt because of advances he had drawn on his salary (often to send Ben money), John was reduced to desperate straits. There was no alternative but to deed the property over to Potter, at the same time losing the entire down payment. In July, Ben received this message from Memphis: "Our mill speculation has ground itself out at last. . . . It has cost me some time and much trouble & anxiety but perhaps it will be for the better."[36]

John Grierson was beginning to experience a sense of despair. At forty he had not yet found a secure professional niche. Neither he nor his wife, Elizabeth, who suffered from a variety of physical ailments, were fond of Memphis. In addition to his unsettled career, they remained outsiders in the community where they had resided for the past six years. What the future held for them remained an open and troubling question. Like Ben, however, John, from his vantage point in "Egypt," remained avidly interested in national issues and provided his brother with incisive commentary on the growing problems between North and South.

If there was one activity that could divert Ben's attention from business failure it was politics, especially those of the Illinois Republican party. By early summer of 1860, he was hard at work lending his efforts to the national campaign for the presidency that pitted Abraham Lincoln against Stephen A. Douglas, John Bell, and John Breckinridge. He wrote pamphlets and speeches under the pseudonym "Sandburr," distributed leaflets and broadsides, debated opposition spokesmen, and registered voters. It was glorious, for it was 1840 all over again, only better. Now there were the "Wide Awakes," paramilitary Republican campaigners, for whom the talents of Ben Grierson were made to order.

On summer evenings in 1860, as dusk turned to dark in towns all over Illinois, citizens were startled by the sound of martial music. Suddenly, well-drilled formations of men, dressed in black uniforms and covered with enameled capes, appeared on the scene. Marching with precision they carried lamps swinging from thin rails decorated with American flags and bearing the names, Abraham Lincoln and Hannibal Hamlin. Sometimes they were accompanied by "Lincoln Rangers," horseback riders dressed in similar fashion. Invariably these groups erected ramshackle structures that passed for wigwams. There they held their precinct meetings, from which "privates" and "officers" ventured forth to organize and register voters and oversee polls on election day.[37]

They also planned additional activities such as bonfires, fireworks displays, and barbecues. In Meredosia, the task of writing verses for campaign songs, sung to old, well-known tunes, fell to Ben, who relished the assignment. He was especially proud of one entitled "Douglas's Record, or Political Gymnastics," set to the tune of "Rory O'More" and including this refrain: "O! Stephen A Douglas is a wonderful man/ in political gymnastics he leads the van/ Most notable feats he performs with great ease/ On all sides of all questions everybody to please."[38]

John Grierson, acutely aware of Ben's declining fortunes, read of these activities at first with misgivings. Here was his younger brother, totally immersed in a political campaign when there were old debts to settle. "Leave no stone unturned, to collect & pay off," he warned, adding, ". . . get into no fusses and spend no money you can avoid."[39] By midsummer, however, Ben's political enthusiasm proved contagious, and John decided that it was time that he also became involved in Illinois politics. Aside from his own personal commitment to anti-slavery principles, there were practical reasons for returning and lending support. If the Republicans won the November election, and John was certain they would, those who had helped bring this about might be rewarded in the new administration. Such a possibility was worth the effort, and by mid-August John was back in Jacksonville working hard in the local Wide Awake club.[40]

When the election results were in, Republican strategy had paid off. Lincoln had carried all the old states formerly won by Frémont, plus California, Indiana, Pennsylvania, New Jersey and his own home state, Illinois, giving him 180 out of 303 electoral votes, a clear victory in the electoral college. Ben recalled that "no person in the land rejoiced more than myself." There were also other reasons for satisfaction. Ben's good friend and fellow Republican, Richard Yates of Jacksonville, was now the governor-elect of Illinois.

No sooner were the official tabulations completed than John Grierson began pressuring Ben to use whatever influence he had to help John obtain the postmastership of Memphis. His qualifications, he thought, were excellent. A resident and property owner of the city for the past six years, he enjoyed "a favorable acquaintance with a large circle of businessmen. . . ." Most compelling of all, as a loyal Republican, he was "poor and needed the job."[41]

Aside from arranging a meeting with Richard Yates to discuss the matter, Ben gave his brother little help; other matters weighed heavily on him. In the excitement of the campaign he had almost lost sight of his bleak financial situation. Now the unpaid interest on debt was mounting daily, a sure sign that the days of Walihan and Grierson were numbered. Earlier in the summer he had approached his father-in-law for one more loan, but this time no help was forthcoming. "Come to a dead halt, turn all your assets into cash, pay off your debts, & then keep out of debt, adopting the motto 'pay as you go,'" was the response from Kirk, who knew a poor investment when he saw it.[42] Unfortunately, the time had long since passed when advice could rectify the situation.

Despite the precariousness of their fortunes, Ben and Alice looked forward with joy to the birth of their third child. On December 2, Alice delivered a "plump, handsome, live 'Abe Lincoln' Republican boy," an infant who would help fill the void left by Kirkie's death.[43] After considerable debate, they named him Robert Kirk Grierson, thereby honoring both grandfathers.

Whatever elation Ben felt over the election results ended with the onset of the "terrible winter of suspense and anxiety." Less than a month after Lincoln's election, five states in the south—South Carolina, Mississippi, Florida, Alabama, and Georgia—called conventions to debate withdrawal from the Union. On December 17, South Carolina's delegates assembled and three days later adopted an ordinance of secession.

Before Lincoln's election, John Grierson had heard Southerners talk of disunion. Some, he wrote Ben, openly declared that they would never "submit to the rule of the Black Republican President." Given the predominance of pro-Union sentiment in Memphis, John was inclined to discount this, "gas being the principle element in Southern warfare as far as politics are concerned."[44] By Christmas Eve his opinion had changed. Now the telegraph wires in Memphis blazed with reports that South Carolina would occupy the federal forts—Moultrie and Sumter—within the next twenty-four hours. When and if this happened, John predicted, "the first *grand act* in the drama (which may result in heavy tragedy . . .) will have been enacted."[45]

As 1860 gave way to 1861, the movement towards secession gathered strength. By early February, Mississippi, Florida, Alabama, Georgia, Louisiana, and Texas, following South Carolina's lead, had left the Union. Delegates from these states met in Montgomery, Alabama, where they drafted a constitution and elected their officials. With the inauguration of Jefferson Davis as President on February 18, the Confederate States of America had been born. Northerners watched these events unfold with a mixture of disbelief and dismay. It was almost impossible to determine what should be done, for any precipitous action could ignite the spark of secession among the states of the upper South.

"I have made up my mind how the North should act," wrote Robert Grierson in mid-January. "Courage, firmness, no compromise, Act strictly with the Constitution. Free Territory and no interference with slavery in the slave states." This was Lincoln's policy exactly, and as Robert accurately noted: "As long as the Republican party acts and carries out the above it will succeed. If it does not it will fall to pieces."[46]

The secession of Southern states had the effect of hardening not only Republican opinion, but also Northern sentiment. A new standard was being raised that would prove far more effective in rallying the North than the old issue of preventing the extension of slavery into the territories. The Union had to be preserved. Otherwise that government which represented mankind's best hope was doomed. Louisa Semple phrased the issue this way: "The problem which is our destiny, as a nation to solve for all mankind, is simply this. Is man capable of self government." And Robert Grierson spoke for many others when he wrote his son: "Separation is Revolution. So thought Andrew Jackson. I will give to Webster's Motto 'Liberty now & forever.'"[47]

March arrived, and with it Lincoln's inauguration. In his Inaugural Address the new president made it clear that he hoped to avoid confrontation. Nonetheless, he promised to uphold the law and pledged that he would not voluntarily give up the federal forts. John Grierson was convinced that civil war was imminent. Only if the North willingly allowed the seceded states to go peacefully could bloodshed be avoided, an impossibility in his opinion. "Do you suppose the Northern and Northwestern states will quietly submit to the South having full control of the mouth of the Miss? Never I think while grass grows and water runs."[48]

By early April, rumors abounded. Responsible men passed along stories of plots to assassinate Lincoln, while other theorized that Jefferson Davis would soon invade Washington. More concrete, there remained the question of the fate of Fort Sumter off the coast of Charleston. (Fort Moultrie had already been evacuated by federal troops.) Supplies were running low, and on April 6, Lincoln informed Major Robert Anderson, the commander of the fort, that provisions would soon be on the way. What action the Confederacy would take when the ships arrived remained an unanswered question. One fact was certain; if provisioning was allowed, then the federal ships would leave without incident. If not, and the South opened fire, the North was prepared to retaliate. An uneasy nation waited anxiously.

By this time Walihan and Grierson were no longer in business. The store, including the lot and remaining inventory of goods, had

Mary Grierson, sister of Benjamin Grierson. *Courtesy Fort Davis National Historic Site, Fort Davis, Texas.*

been seized to meet the demands of creditors. With heavy debts and no income whatsoever, Ben had no choice. Necessity compelled him to return with his wife and children to his parents' home in Jacksonville, the one Alice had been so eager to leave years earlier.

For Alice it was a very difficult time. Understandably, she was reluctant to give up the privacy and comfort of their Meredosia home. But other considerations made their move even more onerous. No longer could she depend upon Ben's sister Mary to provide comfort and companionship, for Mary had died in February. And more recently, Ben's mother had suffered the first in a series of strokes that eventually took her life.[49] Now she was partially paralyzed, and much of the responsibility for her care would fall on Alice. Ben's father remained at heart a kind man, but the events of the past year had taken their toll. His increasing irritability would hardly abate, given the presence of a noisy five-year-old and a sometimes fretful baby. Worse yet, there was no end in sight to this living arrangement, for Ben and Alice were mired deeply in debt. How deeply would depend upon the proceeds from various auctions and the dispositions of court cases that lay in the future. Despite all this, Alice was determined to bear their hardships without complaint.

A depressed Ben Grierson and his troubled wife, "virtually left without a dollar," took up residence, along with their two children, in the Grierson family home. Ben turned to the only other occupation he knew—that of band leader and music teacher.[50] It would have been difficult in the spring of 1861 to identify a couple less likely to attain prominence or glory in the forseeable future. But the Civil War loomed ahead, a cataclysmic event that would sentence more than six hundred thousand men to death. Among the survivors, a few would find themselves catapulted from obscurity to fame. Ben Grierson, an unlikely warrior, would be one of these.

CHAPTER 3

The Making of a Soldier

OHN GRIERSON's prediction that civil war was imminent came true on Friday, April 12, 1861. At 4:30 in the morning a dull boom was followed by the explosion of a mortar shell high over Fort Sumter in the harbor at Charleston, South Carolina. It signaled the beginning of a bombardment of the beleaguered federal fortress by Confederate shore batteries. Thirty-three hours later Major Anderson capitulated, after firing a fifty-gun salute to his flag.[1]

The fall of Sumter galvanized both North and South into action. On April 15, President Lincoln issued a call for seventy-five thousand militia to serve for ninety days against "combinations too powerful to be suppressed by the ordinary course of judicial proceedings."[2] In quick succession Virginia, North Carolina, Tennessee, and Arkansas seceded and joined the Confederate States of America. John wrote Ben that supporters of both North and South were already drilling in the streets of Memphis. "The secessionists here are firing crackers, rockets and etc. and the principle [sic] part of the programme is drunkeness and speeches from whiskey brains."[3]

Memphis was no exception. In cities and hamlets all over the nation, men rushed to take up arms in what most believed would be a short war. In Jacksonville, Ben spared no effort in aiding with the recruitment and organization of Company "I," Tenth Illinois Infantry.

Despite his contributions, when it came to joining, Ben at first hesitated. A recent stroke had left his mother so weak that death was expected momentarily. Moreover, he flinched at the idea of bearing arms against other Americans. "I am not a volunteer," he wrote John, "it would be hard for me to go and fight my brothers in the South as you are well aware."[4] Nonetheless, as his mother's condition steadily improved, he began viewing the matter differently.

When he finally decided to enlist, however, it was too late. All positions in Company "I" had been filled.

At loose ends for the moment, Ben spent hours poring over books on infantry, cavalry, and artillery tactics. During his only previous military experience as a trumpeter in the Ohio Militia, he had been far more interested in the sound of his bugle than in the drills. He intended to sign up sooner or later, though Alice was hardly enthusiastic over the prospect, considering the state of their finances and her reluctance to be the sole parent of two young boys.[5]

Early in May, Ben was called to Springfield by his friend Governor Yates and given a number of dispatches to deliver to Colonel Benjamin M. Prentiss, Tenth Illinois Infantry, headquartered at Cairo. Prentiss welcomed Grierson warmly, for they had been fellow Republican campaigners in Illinois. Among the dispatches was one appointing Prentiss as brigadier general of Illinois State Troops, and he immediately offered Ben an appointment as aide-de-camp with the rank of lieutenant without pay.[6]

He quickly accepted Prentiss's offer. Unlike many Americans, he felt that this would be a long war, and a position in a command headquarters had distinct advantages over some post at the company level. He was aware, however, that he faced two serious problems. The matter of pay was troublesome, for by now he was supporting his family on borrowed money, and of far greater concern was the likelihood that Alice would disapprove.

Believing his income problem temporary—certainly Prentiss would soon arrange for him to receive a lieutenant's pay—he turned his attention to convincing his wife that his chosen course was right. After outlining his military duties to her, he wrote with a touch of humor that the position gave him a chance to "extinguish" himself. Several days later, in a more serious vein, he disclosed that if he had acted hastily it was out of the conviction that "I must (to be true to myself & country) stand not idly by in this hour of time." He asked forgiveness for the pain inflicted, but he also assured her that "what is is best."

He realized that many of Alice's misgivings arose from her fears regarding the influence military life would have on his character. Recently she had uncovered a hidden cache of liquor stashed away in the Jacksonville residence, along with some wine brought back from his brother's storehouse. Now Alice worried that free from "the restraints of home" he would imbibe heavily. Ben assured her that this was unlikely. Prentiss, his commanding officer, while not a practicing

Christian, was a gentleman and strictly temperate. To further allay her suspicions he then renewed a promise written earlier in pencil, but this time recorded in ink. Never would he "drink as a beverage intoxicating liquors again." As a final gambit he urged her to visit him for a week or two at Cairo and enjoy the excitement "if you desire to see your humble servant. . . ."[7]

Alice's response was immediate and not surprising. She was concerned, of course, about his personal safety and even more apprehensive when she thought of the associations he might form. Morally she felt his situation "fearfully perilous." Most important, she remained unconvinced that he should be in the military. She agreed with her sister-in-law, Elizabeth, that "husbands have no business with situations that separate them from their families. . . ."[8] As to visiting him in Cairo, "young babies and their mothers are more comfortable at home, *if they have a home*," and she did not think in their present circumstances she should spend money for travel. She also advised that she objected to his use of "your humble servant" when writing to her.[9]

More often than not, Ben yielded to Alice's wishes, but the times demanded sacrifice, even his life if necessary. To him the Union was sacred, and he would do all he could to preserve it. Given this difference of opinion between them, he sought to placate Alice with long, loving letters. Writing to her at her parents' home where she had gone to visit for the summer, he acknowledged the difficulty of her situation. "God knows that I would that you had & truly feel you had a home. I regret that it was so uncomfortable for you at Jacksonville, but so it was."[10]

The sorry state of his finances continued to plague him. After borrowing additional funds to apply to the most troublesome debts and provide Alice with living expenses, he and Walihan surrendered their homesteads, hoping that the proceeds raised at auction would satisfy their creditors. His father warned Ben that this action would not release him from future judgments, since the amounts produced would not wipe out the deficit.[11] But Ben, having done all he could for the moment, turned his tangled business affairs over to his father, wishing to give the situations at Cairo and at St. Louis his full attention.

The strategic importance of the town at the junction of the Ohio and Mississippi rivers was apparent to Governor Yates, and he had ordered Prentiss there as soon as a force could be mustered. Cairo was to be held at all costs, for use as a base of operations along both waterways and, when the need arose, to serve as a staging area for campaigns in Missouri and Kentucky.

Prentiss had eight poorly trained and equipped regiments encamped in and around Cairo, six manned by ninety-day volunteers. Given the conditions in their bivouacs, most of them were likely to make all possible speed for home when their enlistments expired, for Cairo that May was little more than a steamy swamp. Many of the men, lacking adequate accommodations, soon fell victim to malaria, dysentery, and a cluster of other illnesses. Still others, unaccustomed either to hard work or the heat, were downed by sunstroke. Rations were poor in quality, short in quantity, and uncertain in delivery. Worse yet, no paymaster had appeared, leaving men unable even to purchase necessities.[12] At this point, affairs took an ominous turn in both Missouri and Kentucky.

Members of the Lincoln administration had hoped that a policy of moderation would maintain peace and order in the border states, and General William S. Harney, a wise and experienced officer commanding federal forces in Missouri, had made strenuous efforts to conciliate contending factions. Activities by near-fanatic Unionists, however, coupled with efforts by secessionists to organize and drill state militia, threatened to plunge the state into civil war.[13]

On May 10, 1861, Captain Nathaniel S. Lyon, a hard-bitten and rash West Pointer commanding the St. Louis "Home Guards" had taken advantage of the temporary absence of General Harney and captured "Camp Jackson," on the western outskirts of the city. After forcing the surrender of a band of secessionists who were using the camp for their drills, Lyon's men then marched their captives through the city streets. A large group of citizens jeered and hissed Lyon and his men. Either on order or otherwise, Lyon's ill-disciplined guards fired into the crowd, killing twenty-eight persons and wounding many more. From that moment on, civil war in Missouri was inevitable.[14]

Governor Claiborne Jackson now moved to arm the state militia on the Confederate side, appointing Sterling Price, former governor and hero of the Mexican War, as its major general. Lyon, meanwhile, was promoted to brigadier general, while Harney, who had sought to arrange a truce, was replaced by John C. Frémont. Despite his unsuccessful campaign for the presidency in 1856, the "Pathfinder" remained a national hero and enjoyed great prestige as a military commander. Both sides began recruiting and organizing on a large scale, and by midsummer a major clash loomed on the horizon.[15]

Prentiss, busily strengthening his defenses at Cairo, viewed developments in Missouri with growing alarm. Equally disturbing were the increasing reports of secessionist activity in neutral Kentucky. Early in June he sent two companies of infantry by steamboat downriver to Elliott's Mill, near Columbus, to disperse a group of rebels rumored to be intimidating loyal Unionists. Aide-de-camp Grierson, armed with a pistol, accompanied them. The little force disembarked at the appointed place, marched a few miles inland, blocked the roads, and charged rebel headquarters. But the "secesh" had fled, and all Ben and his comrades had accomplished was the routing of a herd of hogs, munching contentedly on abandoned supplies.[16]

To keep a wary eye on secessionist activity along the Kentucky shore, Prentiss decided to maintain a river patrol. In mid-June he sent Colonel Richard Oglesby, Tenth Illinois, along with a company of infantry, on the steamer "City of Alton" to the vicinity of Columbus. Grierson went along as an observer. As they drew near the town, a Confederate flag, "a contemptible piece of bunting," according to Ben, was seen waving in the breeze. The steamer was maneuvered close to shore, and Oglesby shouted to a group near the flag to cut it down. When his order was ignored, a small party of volunteers waded ashore and, without opposition, pulled down the nine-by twenty-foot banner. The delighted captors tore their prize into small pieces and handed them out as souvenirs.[17]

Ben's first encounters with his "Southern brothers" had been bloodless and tinged with a bit of comic opera. He informed Alice of his adventures with an almost boyish glee, but he realized that far more serious encounters lay ahead.

Alice, visiting her parents in Chicago, was undergoing a change in her perspective towards the war and the obligations of service to the Union. Shortly after she arrived, the city was plunged into mourning by the death of Senator Douglas. She joined the throng viewing him as he lay in state and paid her respects, for he had supported the Union in its hour of crisis. Her relatives, including her mother and her brother Tom's new bride, Mary Fuller Kirk, were busily occupied, sewing sheets, pillow cases, and cap covers for Union soldiers. The demands of child care consumed so much of Alice's time that she could not join them, but she was able occasionally to enjoy the company of friends and relatives. As she exchanged views with them, she came to the conclusion that the war could go on indefinitely, requiring a great deal of sacrifice from Northern families. Given these circumstances, Ben's decision to enlist for the war's duration was at least worthy of accommodation.[18]

She intended to remain in Chicago as long as possible, though she was not enamored of the place. Her parents' residence was close to the McCormick coal-burning reaper factory, and the surrounding neighborhood was as dirty as any in Pittsburgh. Like her father, she objected to the number of "low Irish" living in the area. Nonetheless, because of her mother-in-law's frail condition and father Robert's increasing irascibility, she was determined not to inflict her two children on the Grierson household any more than necessary. As to visiting Ben at Cairo, she still felt such a trip would be too expensive, for most of the money he had sent her had gone to creditors. Besides, she informed him, ". . . you know we must sacrifice our own wishes for the good of our country."[19]

Despite the tone of coolness evident in her refusal to join Ben, the news of recent casualties from various skirmishes had heightened Alice's concern for his safety. "These little forays and skirmishes I consider as dangerous as greater battles though not to so many." While she was determined to be brave, and maintained a faith "that you will not be killed in this war," she urged her husband to write often and keep her informed of his activities and whereabouts.[20] Under the harsh realities of war, Alice's attitude was beginning to soften, but she still remained distant.

Ben was not a man easily discouraged either by Alice's continued aloofness, his heavy debts, or recent military reverses. Toward the end of June he wrote: "My dear darling, loved one, can you not place in the next letter you write (in one corner at least) some kind or loving words for me . . . nothing more than you truly feel . . . I'm thankful for what you have already sent . . . but like Oliver Twist after food always wanting more."[21]

More was not immediately forthcoming. While Alice agreed that her recent letters had not been very affectionate, the reason was simple; "some of the time I have not felt very amiable or loving." Moreover, Ben was so absorbed in the "novelty" of his new career that her letters were not as important as in the past. If, however, he could manage a trip to Chicago, she would try to make him feel that she was not "altogether indifferent to either you, or any of your affairs or interests."[22]

A week later, her letter was more encouraging, for a small incident had made a dramatic impression on Alice. On July 2, as she had sat with her family on the porch at dusk, a neighbor, anticipating the Fourth of July celebration, startled her by firing a pistol into the street. After regaining her composure, Alice began to reflect that her husband would soon face the "deadly cannon." For the first time, she became aware of a possibility she had not acknowledged earlier. There was no guarantee that Ben would survive the war.[23]

Ben's thoughts paralleled her own. "Different circumstances from former separations surround us at present and we cannot feel so positively certain of seeing each other again. . . ." Still he promised her "a good time coming," if only she would be patient and "forgive and try and forget the past unpleasant occurrences," thinking instead ". . . of the many bright and happy times we have had together and those which await us in the future."[24]

These were brave words, considering that Ben's creditors were hounding his father without mercy. The Meredosia property, auctioned off to the highest bidder, had brought only twenty-three hundred dollars, and two creditors pressed their claims for an additional seventeen hundred dollars. To save his son further trouble, Robert had agreed to liens on his own property, and now Ben was fearful that his father, at an advanced age, faced substantial losses when the notes came due. One way or another, it was essential that Ben raise cash, and his anxiety increased each day that his military pay failed to arrive.[25]

There were other concerns as well. Initially, the federal military effort had gone well in the summer of 1861. Major General George B. McClellan, commanding Ohio volunteers, invaded western Virginia and on June 3 defeated the defending Confederate forces, saving the region for the Union and paving the way for statehood. Northern exultation, however, was short-lived. On July 21, General Irvin McDowell, with a green army of thirty-five thousand men and a slogan "Forward to Richmond," met a raw Confederate force of about equal numbers under General P.G.T. Beauregard at Bull Run, in northern Virginia. After a bloody, day-long battle, the Federals were swept from the field and forced to flee in wild disorder back to the defenses of Washington. Had the Confederates not been as disorganized by victory as the federal troops were by defeat, the nation's capital might have fallen. Deep gloom prevailed throughout the North. "I lay awake for hours thinking of it, the night after the first news" Alice wrote her husband, but in far off Cairo, Ben did not despair. "The result is not as disastrous as first reported. We will pack up our flints and try again."[26]

In Missouri, Lyon's early aggressiveness brought small-scale success, but soon afterward the Union position deteriorated. Frémont proved to be a grandiose planner and an inept administrator. He fired off barrages of letters and telegrams to Lincoln and Secretary of War Edwin M. Stanton, requesting troops, guns, ammunition, and other supplies while presiding over a bevy of foreign advisers in kingly fashion at his headquarters in St. Louis.[27] In a more concrete action, he brought reinforcements personally to a nervous Prentiss at Cairo and gave him command in southeast Missouri, where Confederate irregulars and guerillas were swarming under the loose control of General M. Jeff Thompson. Frémont complicated the situation, however, by assigning a shabby-looking and obscure Brigadier General, Ulysses S. Grant, to immediate command to federal forces in that area. Lyon, meanwhile, continued to operate on his own initiative.[28]

From early summer, Confederate recruitment and organization in the state was improving. In the southwest, Price joined forces with a former Texas Ranger, Brigadier General Ben McCulloch, and formed a motley army some thirteen thousand strong. They posed a threat to Lyon, who was near Springfield with less than half that number. Frémont warned Lyon to retreat, but instead Lyon attacked the Confederates at Wilson's Creek on August 10, where he was badly beaten and lost his life in the process. Little more than a month later, Price forced the surrender of a federal garrison at Lexington, in the northwest corner of the state, took thirty-five hundred prisoners and a large quantity of stores. The federal position in western Missouri looked bleak indeed, and it was little better in the southeast.[29]

Frémont held a long interview with Prentiss while he was in Cairo. He outlined his strategy for campaigning in the western theatre, which began with the elimination of rebel forces in Missouri and then a descent down the Mississippi River. He left the definite impression that Prentiss would be in immediate command of these operations. An excited Grierson attended the interview and found Frémont "very approachable." He also met Jessie Frémont, who had accompanied her husband and who impressed Ben as a "robust good natured, fine-looking woman . . . in possession of considerable good sense."[30]

Prentiss wanted a hard-hitting campaign to drive the Confederates from southeastern Missouri, followed by seizure of Columbus, Kentucky, to forestall probable Confederate occupation of that strategic place. He received orders to take four regiments, proceed to Ironton, terminus of the St. Louis and Iron Mountain Railroad, and assume command of all troops in that area. When Prentiss reached Ironton,

Brigadier General Benjamin M. Prentiss. *Courtesy National Archives.*

he found Grant there, and since it was believed at that time that Prentiss outranked Grant, the latter explained his plans and troop dispositions and took the next train to St. Louis.[31]

As Prentiss marched southeast, scattering guerilla bands in his front, Ben enjoyed his first taste of close-quarter action. With an advance party, he charged and routed a small band of rebels, captured "Dougherty Plantation," and ate his share of the contents of a well-stocked smokehouse. Prentiss was pleased with the outcome of this foray, but lectured Ben for his "recklessness."[32] The column moved on to Jackson, and here Prentiss received a rude shock—the troops here were under Grant's orders.[33]

Within days after Prentiss had succeeded Grant, Frémont discovered a painful error—Grant, in fact, outranked Prentiss—and he wasted no time in removing Prentiss and reappointing Grant as commanding general in southeastern Missouri. Prentiss was outraged, and Ben was unable to calm him. An angry confrontation with Grant followed and, at one point, the two were near fisticuffs, with an embarrassed Grierson doing his best to mediate the dispute. No agreement could be reached in such an atmosphere, and Prentiss left in a huff for St. Louis to lay his case before Frémont.[34]

This mixup was unfortunate, but both army law and practice were clearly on the side of Grant, and Frémont had no choice. Ben's career did not suffer in the long run. Well aware that Prentiss was both wrong and unreasonable, Ben still remained loyal, and his efforts at conciliation were appreciated by Grant. Prentiss did not escape so lightly. He was transferred to Chillicothe, where there was little to do except chase guerillas, and shortly thereafter was ordered to Jefferson City. Poor Ben was tied to a commander whose star was dimming, and he was fast becoming a military gypsy without pay and without opportunity for distinction. His abiding optimism all but deserted him.[35]

In mid-August, Ben had made a quick trip to Springfield to see Governor Yates, who had promised to do all in his power to find him a more promising assignment. So far nothing had materialized. Alice still seemed somewhat distant, his debts were staggering; perhaps home was the best place for him after all. And then, early in September, a letter from Alice sent his spirits soaring. "My dear, darling Ben," she wrote, "wouldn't I like to kiss, hug, love and almost devour you if I could only have you to myself today but I suppose you are safe from any such demonstration at present."[36]

With Alice in a loving and forgiving mood, Ben Grierson's world, with all its frustrations, brightened then and there.

He suffered no lack of imagination, as his answer demonstrated. In his dreams he was with her, she was reading the *Atlantic* and the *Independent* to him, and finally "the Grand Finale—my closing my eyes in sleep with you at my side."[37] A few weeks later Ben, at long last, managed to spend a few days in Jacksonville, where he was reunited with Alice and his young sons. His career also received a boost on October 24, when Governor Yates, true to his word, appointed Ben as major in the Sixth Illinois Cavalry.[38]

Meanwhile, a series of developments occurred that had a profound effect on the course of the war and on Grierson's career as well. Confederate troops seized Columbus, Kentucky, and prevented the move planned by Frémont. Grant, at Cairo, immediately dispatched a force to occupy strategic Paducah, some forty-five miles up the Ohio and at the mouth of the Tennessee River—a waterway meandering into the heart of the Confederacy. Kentucky's neutrality ended and the state became a battleground.[39]

In Missouri, Frémont, trying to cope with widespread guerilla activity and the Price-McCulloch threat in the southwest, issued a proclamation declaring martial law and providing the death penalty for guerillas caught north of a line drawn through the central part of the state. Further, the slaves of persons giving aid and comfort to the rebellion were to be freed. The proclamation stunned President Lincoln, who was following a conciliatory policy in the border states. He realized, as Frémont apparently did not, that many slave owners opposed secession and would willingly fight for the Union. He was also aware that widespread use of the death penalty would provoke Confederate reprisals. Lincoln wanted the manifesto modified at once, but Frémont balked, forcing the President to order him to do so. From that time on, Frémont's days in St. Louis were numbered.[40]

Lincoln's fears were well-founded. Many slave owners, who at least might have remained neutral, cast their lot with the South, while General Jeff Thompson issued a manifesto of his own. For every member of the state or Confederate troops put to death, he would "hang, draw and quarter a minion of said Abraham Lincoln . . . I intend to exceed General Frémont in his excesses."[41]

Frémont's position had also been jeopardized by his frantic and disorganized efforts to raise and equip a large army. Although he was personally honest, many of his advisers were unscrupulous, and contracts issued to suppliers were often subject to serious question. The odor of corruption reached Lincoln and the War Department, and they rightly held Frémont responsible. The latter, well aware of the gathering storm clouds, made last-gasp efforts to save himself. He dispatched his wife to Washington to make a personal appeal to Lincoln for support, while he prepared a full-scale campaign to drive the Confederates from Missouri and then invade Arkansas.[42]

Jessie managed a midnight interview with the President, but her belligerent defense of her husband only served to further alienate Lincoln. Frémont, meanwhile, put thirty thousand men in motion and in late October reached Springfield, seeking a battle with Price and McCulloch, southwest of the city. But here Lincoln's letter of removal reached Frémont, forcing him to turn his command over to Major General David Hunter. Hunter countercommanded Frémont's orders and marched back to St. Louis, where he in turn was replaced by Major General Henry "Old Brains" Halleck, a veteran soldier with a deserved reputation for integrity and administrative efficiency.[43]

These changes marked the beginning of a new direction in the conduct of the war in the West, and, as well, a positive turning point in Grierson's career. At the time, though, Ben felt only a sense of loss. He was not unaware of Frémont's weaknesses, but with his removal, Ben no longer had access to a commander with national power and influence. More important, Ben fully agreed with Frémont that a war on slavery was both morally and militarily correct. It would not only materially shorten the conflict, but it would also hasten the arrival of a more progressive, humanitarian, and harmonious Union. Thus to Ben, Frémont was a brave and honorable man who had been sacrificed to both civilian and military intriguers. "He will always have a warm place in the hearts of lovers of freedom."[44]

Now Ben had seen two friends, first Prentiss and then Frémont, fall from grace. Yet frequent skirmishes with guerillas left him little time to brood or worry. On November 2, he led a sixteen-man detachment on a successful raid out of Jefferson City, routing a band of eighty rebels and returning without any losses. His ability to lead men into action and to adapt swiftly to tactical necessity was growing. He was no longer an amateur. Hours of study, keen observation, and practical experience had prepared him for a more important assignment.[45]

News from home continued to bolster his spirits. Alice, having voiced her anger and resentment in earlier letters, now adopted a more cheerful and conversational tone. She was also greatly relieved that she was not, as she had feared earlier, again pregnant. "Everything is still o.k. in a certain department . . . I am glad to know it." Ben concurred; this was hardly the time for Alice to take on additional burdens. When he learned that his sister Susan, at age forty-four, had borne her eighth child, he answered ". . . if I were called on for advice in their case I would certainly admonish them to 'quit'—'hold up' or 'Stop'—(dat knocking at de door')."[46]

As November waned, Ben prepared to join the Sixth Illinois, but his fierce loyalty to Prentiss compelled him to seek an interview with General Halleck and ask permission to remain for a time at Jefferson City. Halleck gave him a friendly reception and a "good-humored" refusal. Grierson "looked active and wirey [*sic*] enough to make a good cavalry man" and he was ordered to report to Colonel T. M. Cavanaugh, commander of the regiment at Shawneetown, a hamlet on the Illinois shore of the Ohio, some 140 miles upriver from Cairo.[47]

Cavanaugh was absent when Ben arrived, which was not surprising, for the Colonel, a politician rather than a soldier, spent most of his time in Springfield seeking promotion to brigadier. The regiment's condition appalled Grierson. Cavanaugh, with little foresight and less care, had chosen a low-lying field near town for "Camp Yates," and it required only a light rain to turn the place into a quagmire. No arrangements had been made for barracks, and the men were housed in crude huts that afforded scant protection from the elements. Rations were scarce and the water barely fit to drink.[48]

The Colonel's son served as adjutant, though totally ignorant of essential paperwork, and spent his time playing billiards and courting the local belles. Most of the other officers were inexperienced, had quarters away from camp, and rarely appeared for duty. Drills, when held, were a shambles, with untutored officers shouting ludicrous commands to bewildered troopers. Only half the companies had mounts, some of the men were armed with sabers, and a few carried ancient muskets. Nor was this all. The regiment had not been formally mustered into service, and until this task was achieved, no pay was possible. The end result was grumbling, idleness, boredom, and an almost total lack of discipline.[49]

Once more Ben's spirits sank. He had given passing thought before to leaving the service, but now he gave it serious consideration. Having received no pay for seven months, he now confronted "starvation or the poorhouse." Moreover, conditions at Camp Yates seemed unlikely to improve, given Cavanaugh's attitude. Christmas was approaching, and he longed to be with his family. He wrote Alice to set a place at the table for him on Christmas Day and to imagine him there. As matters stood, he felt he would soon be forced to resign.[50]

Even in his gloom, Grierson could not tolerate idleness and disorder. He found quarters in a "rude enclosure," arranged for meals with a poor family nearby, and set out to at least improve conditions in his own battalion. He ordered the officers to move to the camp, where each day Ben instructed them in cavalry tactics. Duty rosters organized the routines tasks, the camp was cleaned thoroughly, and discipline was strictly enforced. Within a few days, morning and afternoon drills brought a marked improvement in performance. Initial resentment at these changes soon gave way to a sense of achievement, and at the first dress parade even Ben was impressed. He addressed the assembled battalion, paid appropriate compliments, and was delighted to hear cheers from both officers and men.[51]

Grierson's normal optimism and good humor returned, as demonstrated by a letter he wrote Alice. He had just learned that his former partner, Walihan, had married a black woman. ". . . if he is satisfied, I'm sure I am and much joy go with them." And, he added: "They can perhaps sing to their boy, if they have one, that old song I used to know and sometimes sing, 'you're all your Papa's hope and all your mama's joy. You're a very merry pretty *curly headed Boy.*'"[52]

Ben needed all the cheerfulness he could muster, for Christmas turned out to be a dreary affair at Camp Yates. Snow, mixed with rain, fell throughout the day, leaving behind an "abundance of mud." The family where he boarded served the usual plain fare for dinner. There were no luxuries or fancy desserts, not even butter graced the table. Later, when he received Alice's description of the Christmas dinner in Jacksonville, his mouth watered. They had enjoyed turkey, mutton, potatoes, turnips, beets, and biscuits for the main meal, and mince, apple, and pumpkin pie and coffee for dessert. By no means had they forgotten him, however, for Alice had set a place for Ben with his photograph alongside.[53]

Despite a grim Christmas, Ben's spirits continued to improve, largely because his battalion was becoming a source of pride. The officers and men were beginning to look and act like soldiers, and morale improved almost daily. The men showed growing respect for their commander, and some of them hinted that he should replace Cavanaugh. Ben felt complimented, but brushed aside all remarks aimed at the regiment's colonel. And Alice made his New Year's Day a happy one, indicating that she would have welcomed his "affection" that day, "but I have faith that this war separation is going to be a benefit to us—this brand of education is certainly not without a purpose and I hope it will develop us for the better."[54]

Ben's fortunes improved even more during the first weeks of January. Nine days into the month the regiment was mustered into service, and ten days later, he received his first pay. Now, at last, he could support his family adequately and begin reducing his debts. To be sure, some problems still persisted. Cavanaugh's absences and neglect left his command largely unhorsed and unarmed, meaning that the regiment was still not ready for battle. Thus Grierson and the Sixth Illinois were destined to be little more than spectators in the early months of 1862 when the pace of war accelerated.[55]

During this time, Ben received the disturbing news that his mother's health had deteriorated further. His application to Grant for a leave was approved, and he hastened to Jacksonville. By the time he had arrived, Mary had recovered enough to allow him to spend most of his time with Alice and the children.

It was scarcely the idyllic reunion of his dreams and letters. His mother's care still consumed much of Alice's energy, and his father, always quick-tempered, was easily irritated by Charlie, a boisterous six-year-old who talked incessantly and paraded through the house resplendent in a blue military uniform his mother had sewn for him. Young Robert, just weaned and suffering from a heavy cold, fretted constantly. But Ben, mindful of oft-repeated promises to be a more considerate father and husband, did his best to assist Alice. And although there was little time for romance, or even peace and quiet, his efforts were both noted and appreciated.[56]

When Ben returned to Camp Yates, he found the officers and men in open revolt against Cavanaugh. They asked him to sign a petition they had drawn up requesting Governor Yates to remove the Colonel. Even though he held Cavanaugh in contempt, Ben refused. The Union cause had already suffered enough from the military in politics and politics in the military. The upheaval did serve, in time, to give the Sixth Illinois a new commander, but meanwhile a series of developments changed the course of the war and thrust the western theater into the limelight.[57]

The first nine months of war had served primarily as a period of preparations. After the initial clashes, leaders on both sides realized that, since a quick victory was impossible, some long-term strategy was essential. For Jefferson Davis and his cabinet the plan was comparatively simple—fight on the defensive and force their antagonists to realize that the South could never be conquered. Union strategy evolved more slowly, but by the fall of 1861, Lincoln and his advisers had decided on three major objectives: a blockade of Confederate ports, the capture of Richmond, and a thrust from Kentucky through Tennessee into the southern heartland.

The first of these aims had been adopted a week after the fall of Fort Sumter. Immediately following Lincoln's proclamation of a blockade, the federal navy had begun strangling Confederate trade and commerce. This tactic proved effective almost at once, forcing the South to rely on swift-sailing blockade runners to escape the Union net.

By the fall of 1861, three blue-clad armies stood poised to strike. After much juggling of field commanders, Lincoln appointed General McClellan as general-in-chief, as well as commander of the Army of the Potomac. A talented organizer, McClellan soon had more than a hundred thousand men armed and equipped for the advance on Richmond. At Louisville, Kentucky, Major General Don Carlos Buell had assembled an army approaching seventy thousand, and Halleck had twenty thousand more, ready to move under Grant at Cairo.[58]

Facing this formidable array was the Army of Northern Virginia under General Joseph Johnston, some sixty thousand strong, charged with defending Richmond. General Albert S. Johnston, commanding the Confederacy's Western Department, had just over fifty thousand men confronting Buell and Halleck—a thin gray line stretching from Columbus, Kentucky, on the west to Cumberland Gap in the east. A coordinated federal attack along the entire front promised to capture Richmond and, at least, drive the outnumbered Confederates from Kentucky and Tennessee.

To President Lincoln's great distress, a Union offensive failed to materialize. McClellan proved overly cautious, insisting he was outnumbered and refusing to move even after personal prodding from the President. Buell, too, had visions of gray hordes attacking at any moment, begged for reinforcements, and remained at Louisville. Halleck, both cautious and methodical, evaluated the situation in Missouri as unstable, and was reluctant to order Grant into western

Kentucky. Moreover, though Halleck knew Buell well, cooperation between them would not be easy.[59]

But above all, Halleck was at heart a shrewd, opportunistic politician. With both the President and the public demanding some action, "Old Brains" decided that his career, as well as the military situation, might be improved if he made a successful strike in Kentucky. He submitted a campaign plan to McClellan, calling for operations up the Cumberland and Tennessee rivers with the objective of taking Nashville, flanking Columbus, and thereby forcing a general Confederate withdrawal southward into northern Mississippi and Alabama.

When McClellan approved, Halleck wasted no time translating plans into action. He ordered Grant to establish a camp for reinforcements at Smithland, Kentucky, near the mouth of the Cumberland, in order to attack Fort Henry on the Tennessee some fifty miles upstream from Paducah. Grant, eager for action, loaded fifteen thousand men on transports at Cairo and, preceded by Rear Admiral Andrew Foote with four ironclad gunboats, reached Fort Henry on February 5. On arrival, Grant found that little remained to be done. Foote's guns had quickly and easily battered the weakly defended Confederate fort into submission. Most of the defenders, however, had escaped overland to Fort Donelson, a dozen miles away on the Cumberland River.[60]

Without waiting for orders from Halleck, Grant marched his infantry to Donelson, while Foote escorted a fleet of transports, loaded with reinforcements, up the Cumberland from Smithland. The assault began on February 13, and three days later, after a fierce Confederate resistance, Brigadier General Simon B. Buckner, commanding at the fort, asked for terms. Grant's reply was "unconditional surrender" to which Buckner reluctantly agreed, making Ulysses S. Grant a national hero. However, one Confederate officer, Lieutenant Colonel Nathan Bedford Forrest, escaped with his cavalry, to become a literal nightmare to Union commanders for the rest of the war.[61]

The fall of Forts Henry and Donelson forced General Johnston to evacuate both Nashville and Columbus. He then fell back to Corinth, in northeastern Mississippi, where he began the task of reorganizing and reinforcing his army for an offensive to recover the lost ground. While there, he gained valuable time. Grant, having dispatched a division to occupy Nashville, prepared to march at once against

General Ulysses S. Grant. *Courtesy National Archives.*

Johnston. But Halleck, upset with his subordinate's rapid movements and sudden fame, charged the hero of Donelson with dereliction of duty and drunkenness and removed him from command.[62]

Grant did not remain in disfavor long. The charges against him were unfounded, and with the strong support of President Lincoln he was promoted to major general and returned to his post. Halleck, having persuaded Lincoln and Secretary Stanton that a unified command was necessary in the West, had been given full control in that theatre. In practice this situation meant that any campaign against Johnston would move at a slow, halting pace.[63]

Union patrols up the Tennessee River had found an ideal campsite on a plateau adjacent to Pittsburg Landing and about twenty-two miles from Corinth. Halleck decided on an unhurried concentration of Buell's and Grant's armies at this place. Once they were in position, he would take the field in person and lead them against a vastly outnumbered Confederate army. By the end of the first week in April, Grant had five of his six divisions, about forty thousand strong, at "Camp Shiloh"—named for Shiloh Church, a small log structure nestled among a grove of trees on the plateau. His remaining division was posted six miles downstream. Buell, with twenty-five thousand men, was still a day's march away.[64]

Aware of Grant's and Buell's movements, Johnston had no intention of simply waiting at Corinth. He had assembled some forty thousand infantry and cavalry, and though many were raw recruits and poorly armed, he set out to strike the Federals at Camp Shiloh before Buell's arrival. At dawn on Sunday, April 6, with his divisions in battle order, he launched a furious assault on the Union lines.[65]

For all that day and most of the next, great masses of men in blue and gray fought with savage ferocity. Only the arrival of Buell and Grant's remaining division during the evening of the sixth saved the Union army from disaster, and only the most stubborn fighting saved the outnumbered Confederates on the second day. Both armies were exhausted by mid-afternoon of April 7, and the battered gray army retired to Corinth, with the Federals content to let them go.[66]

"Bloody Shiloh" sent shock waves both North and South. Casualties on both sides totalled just under twenty-four thousand—more than those of the American Revolution, The War of 1812, and the Mexican War combined. Among the dead was General Johnston, killed on the afternoon of the first day. Despite the unprecedented losses, neither side had gained an inch of ground, though both claimed victory.

Shiloh fell like a hammer blow on Confederate hopes. Not only had Johnston's offensive failed, but Tennessee and Kentucky were lost. The war also had gone badly for Confederate arms in other sectors of the western theatre. In a two-day battle at Pea Ridge in Arkansas, Brigadier General Samuel Curtis had inflicted a decisive defeat on gray forces under Major General Earl Van Dorn. Farther south, New Orleans had fallen to a Union fleet under Admiral David Farragut. Other federal naval forces had taken New Madrid, Missouri, and Island Number Ten, below Cairo on the Mississippi, in addition to destroying the Confederate fleet at Memphis. By early summer the entire Confederate defensive posture in the West stood gravely weakened. Only in the East, where Robert E. Lee's Army of Northern Virginia successfully fought off the federal onslaught, could the South retain serious hopes for ultimate success.[67]

Halleck took over field command after Shiloh and began an extremely cautious advance toward Corinth. As he inched forward, he entrenched, steadily bringing up reinforcements. By mid-May he had more than 120,000 troops in the vicinity of the city, a three to one superiority over Beauregard, Johnston's replacement. On May 29, faced with these overwhelming numbers, the Confederates evacuated Corinth, leaving it to Union occupation. It was an empty victory, however, for Beauregard had saved his army to fight other battles that would prolong the war.[68]

Grierson and the Sixth Illinois played no role in the stirring events of February to May, 1862. The regiment remained at Camp Yates until mid-February, when Brigadier General William T. Sherman, commanding at Paducah, ordered Cavanaugh to send Ben and his battalion to Smithland. The remainder of the regiment continued downstream to Paducah. En route, aboard a transport, a dismayed Grierson discovered many of his troopers drunk and disorderly. When a swift investigation revealed that a bar had been set up on board the ship despite strict orders against the sale of liquor, an irate Ben threatened to throw both the bar and bartender into the river. The men were searched, and their supply of spirits confiscated. Once at Smithland, iron discipline and long two-a-day drills promoted a greater regard for temperance among the men. Sobriety among the officers was assured when Grierson informed a drunken captain that the next bout with demon rum would land him in front of a firing squad.[69]

Ben was eager for action, but his command still lacked arms. He journeyed to Paducah to ask Sherman for weapons, but the latter had none to give. The visit was pleasant, however, and marked the beginning of a lasting friendship between Ben and the fiery, red-headed general. A trip up the Cumberland and an interview with Grant also proved fruitless. Since Forrest had escaped, Grant had no carbines for cavalry in his store of captured weapons. While at Donelson, Grierson examined the works and, considering their formidable structure, found it surprising that the Confederates had surrendered. He concluded that the rebels either lacked courage or the will to fight, an opinion shared by Grant and others at the time, but one that changed swiftly after Shiloh.[70]

Shortly after Ben's return from Donelson, his battalion was transferred to Paducah, where the rest of the regiment was encamped. Once more Ben was forced to report to incompetent "Old Cav." On March 22, orders were received to march to Pittsburg Landing, but the Sixth remained anchored at Paducah for lack of carbines and revolvers. As a result, the first day of Shiloh found a disgusted Grierson sitting on a board of survey, investigating a recent theft of government hams and sugar. His frustration ran high. Visits to Grant and Sherman, letters to Yates and Secretary of War Stanton, and even an order placed with an arms firm in Hamilton, Ohio, had all failed to produce the necessary equipment for his battalion.[71]

Since military action remained out of the question for the present, perhaps time could be spent with his family. However, his letter to Alice begging her to visit him received a discouraging reply. She could not leave Robert with relatives because he cried continually when she was out of sight, and it was beyond her endurance to travel with both children. "It is no wonder women in general have so little energy, they live so shut up in the house, they have no chance to grow hardy." Ben's humor scarcely improved when his brother sought to involve him in a recurrent feud. According to John, their sister Susan's husband, Harvey C. Fuller, was "a dirty dog," a "damned rascal," "naturally a rogue," and "owes every one." Ben was itching for a fight, but he had no desire to become embroiled in family strife.[72]

Even as Ben struggled with his disappointments, his prospects were improving. On April 9, thirty-seven officers of the regiment signed a petition requesting Yates to remove Cavanaugh and appoint Grierson as colonel. Faced with this humiliation, "Old Cav" resigned, along with his son. Four days later, Governor Yates and a large party of friends, en route to inspect Fort Donelson, arrived by steamer at Paducah. Grierson went aboard to pay his respects and "much to my surprise came off a short time after as Colonel of the 6th Illinois Cavalry." He wrote Alice immediately that she could now address him "as—as—yes—as Colonel!"[73]

Within a week Ben was in Cairo, searching through government warehouses, where he found 150 Sharps carbines and obtained the promise of more. By the end of April, a well-drilled regiment was also a well-armed one, performing scouting duty in the vicinity of Paducah. Sherman, having received promotion to major general after distinguishing himself at Shiloh, assured Grierson that important action awaited him in the near future. All this was both gratifying and somewhat disconcerting to a man who, only a year earlier, had been an abject business failure. But whatever the assignments or responsibilities, he was certain he could fulfill them. "The more I have to do, you know," he confided to Alice, "the more I can do—at least you have known it to be some times." Now he was more eager than ever to have his wife with him, and he urged her to visit him, even if it meant inflicting both children on unwilling relatives.[74]

At three o'clock in the morning, May 1, Ben was awakened by the sound of footsteps, followed by shadowy figures entering his tent. Just as he reached for his revolver, he discovered to his great joy that his visitors were Alice and Charlie, who had arrived at Paducah Landing unannounced. With her bags in one hand and Charlie in the other, Alice had first made her way to the hotel. When a disreputable-looking clerk had showed her a "vile smelling" room, she had decided against spending the night there and, instead, obtained directions to the military camp. Leading Charlie by the hand, she had walked along the river bank until eventually she located Ben's tent.[75]

Ben arranged room and board for his family at a private home, but most of their time was spent in his tent, watching the morning and afternoon drills which began at 5:30 A.M. and ended at nightfall. Small wonder that Ben could inform Alice that his regiment was performing "very well." Her questions about the progress of the war gave Ben an opportunity to voice some strong private opinions. Both Halleck and McClellan over-prepared, refused to take risks, and gave the enemy too much time and room to maneuver. The war could only be won by swift, aggressive action and defeat of the enemy's armies. Mere occupation of territory would not suffice.[76]

Alice's visit lasted three weeks before she returned to Jacksonville. During that time, she briefed Ben on family matters. Son Robert had been left with her parents in Chicago, where the opportunity to visit the chicken house and send the hens into cackles of alarm provided compensation for his mother's absence. As for the dissension between John and his brother-in-law, that had eased somewhat. Fuller had recently accepted employment with a Chicago firm, selling one of the newest products available, "wringing machines," for washing clothes, and the prospects seemed encouraging. Meanwhile, both brothers would have to assist Susan and her family, a suggestion to which the ever-generous Ben readily agreed. His pay was now $253 a month, and, while creditors still badgered him, he could afford to send his sister $20 monthly.[77]

Before Alice returned home, she admonished her husband one more time to at least curtail his cigar smoking. She also encouraged him to attend religious services. When Ben protested that Chaplain Jacques's preaching was not very inspiring, Alice's response was that "even poor preaching is better than none at all."[78]

Shortly after his wife and child left, Ben discovered that his desire to see military action would soon be gratified. The fall of Corinth had forced Confederate evacuation of Memphis. On June 6, federal troops under the command of Major General Lew Wallace occupied the city. The Sixth Illinois was ordered to Memphis, and Ben, with five companies of the regiment, embarked on the steamer "Crescent City." They arrived on June 18 and were quartered at the racetrack near the city fairgrounds. The remaining companies of the regiment were ordered to march overland via Union City, Tennessee and scout along the way.[79]

When Ben reported to Wallace, he received instructions to move as soon as possible against bands of Confederate guerillas, concentrated a few miles south of Memphis. On the morning of June 19, Grierson set out with his companies of the Sixth and four of the Eleventh Illinois, some three hundred troopers, each one primed for combat. After an all-night ride, at dawn they reached Hernando, Mississippi, twenty-five miles south of Memphis on the Mississippi and Tennessee Railroad. Here they found a hastily abandoned rebel camp. Grierson, pursuing at a gallop, overtook the fleeing troops in gray twelve miles down the track at Coldwater Station. He attacked with carbines blazing, routed the enemy force, and killed three, wounded seven, and took nine prisoners. Ben tried to capture the rebel leader, General Jeff Thompson, but the latter escaped, though his horse was shot from under him. Grierson would meet the "Bush-whacking, Jay-Hawking, Traitor" in many another firefight.[80]

After destroying fifteen thousand pounds of bacon, some forage, and other supplies, Grierson returned to Memphis, where he reported the Coldwater action to a delighted Wallace. Grant was also there and gave Ben a warm welcome. Grierson noted a coolness between Grant and Wallace and assumed the former was still annoyed at Wallace's tardy arrival on the Shiloh battlefield.[81] Hereafter, Ben was informed, he would report to Grant.

On June 27, Grierson marched his command to Germantown, Tennessee, some fifteen miles southeast of Memphis on the Memphis and Charleston Railroad. Grant's orders were to establish a headquarters there, throw out patrols in all directions, and strike hard at any Confederate forces found in that vicinity. No enemy was found, however, and Grierson's principal task proved to be caring for runaway slaves who came into his lines. Many of these he forwarded to Grant at Memphis, where they were put to work on fortifications.[82]

Although he permitted no searching or looting of private homes beyond the confiscation of food and livestock, Ben encountered problems with the civilian population. Many planters in the area were angry over the Confederate practice of burning cotton to prevent it from falling into federal hands. Ben permitted some bales that had been hidden to pass through his lines for sale, provided the owners seemed favorable to the Union. He also reassured several groups of ladies who visited him that no harm would come to them. They found him, he thought, a "very pleasant gentleman," hardly the ogre in a blue uniform they expected.[83]

Grierson's stay at Germantown was brief. McClellan had waged a costly and indecisive campaign in northern Virginia, and once more Lincoln rotated his commanders. He summoned Halleck to Washington and appointed him general-in-chief. Grant replaced Halleck at Corinth and assigned Sherman to command at Memphis. The latter, concerned over increasing rebel activity south of the city, ordered Grierson's return.[84]

Memphis was far more attractive as a headquarters than Germantown. Confederate withdrawal and Union occupation had, initially, all but paralyzed the city, but vigorous action by Sherman established firm control and encouraged the re-opening of churches, banks, stores, newspapers, and theaters. Many northern commercial houses, sensing quick profits, established branches. Soon the streets were thronged with cotton speculators, traders, army contractors, officers, soldiers, and job seekers, transforming the port into a virtual beehive of activity.

Saloons and theaters carried on a thriving business. For seventy-five cents one could sit in the dress circle and see performances of "The Daughter of the Regiment," "The Innkeeper's Daughter," or the more sensational "Susan Hopely, or the Trials and Vissitudes of a Servant Girl." Through Union patronage Memphis had regained its former bustling prosperity. While this activity was greatly appreciated by the citizens, most of them remained loyal to the South.[85]

Grierson established his headquarters in the depot of the Memphis and Charleston Railroad and for a few days enjoyed the social scene. He loved the theater, though he did not report all his attendances to Alice, who viewed such places with suspicion. He did, however, recount with relish his encounter with a "secesh" lady who accosted him on the street and accused him, as a Yankee, of associating with blacks. Ben felt that he had won the encounter by remaining a gentleman, but he also confided to his wife that Union soldiers "would as soon think of surrounding ourselves with Skunks" as socialize with blacks.[86] Little did he know that one day, as the commander of black troops, he would find himself fighting on their behalf against the racial prejudice he now so casually exhibited.

His "vacation" was brief. Memphis was alive with rumors of an impending Confederate attack, and reports indicated growing rebel activity along the northern Mississippi border. Sherman ordered Grierson out with all his effective force—about two hundred troopers—to break up Confederate organizing efforts. At the end of July he made a hundred-mile sweep through enemy camps, fought three skirmishes, killed two men and took twenty prisoners, with no casualties to his own command. Sherman was impressed and believed the rebels had learned to fear and respect Grierson's cavalry.[87]

There was no pause in the raids. On September 5, Grierson galloped into Hernando, surprised a group of "secesh," and arrested twelve persons. Two days later, while encamped near Olive Branch, the command was attacked by four hundred yelling Confederates. Ben rallied his startled troopers, coolly and skillfully placed them in the line of battle, and counterattacked. Leading the charge on "Old Barber," his favorite mount, and wearing a white linen duster, Ben was an inviting target for rebel marksmen. Two balls pierced his duster, another tore through a pant leg, and a fourth burned two fingers on his left hand. "Old Barber" suffered two bullet wounds, neither one serious. After a two-hour fight the rebels fled, leaving forty dead and thirty as prisoners. Ben's command suffered twenty casualties.[88]

Sherman was so pleased with the results at Olive Branch that he presented Grierson with a silver-plated carbine. He also informed Ben that the rest of his regiment, on scouting duty in Kentucky, had been ordered to Memphis to unite the Sixth Illinois. John Grierson had taken a position in the Memphis Paymaster's Office and wrote Elizabeth of Sherman's regard for Ben. From this and reports in the press, it appeared that his brother was "in a fair way to becoming a lion."[89]

Twenty-four hours after the action at Olive Branch, Grierson was again in the field with 350 troopers, serving as a screen for a regiment of infantry under Brigadier General Morgan L. Smith. At Cockrum's Crossroads, some thirteen miles southwest of Memphis, Grierson, well in advance of the infantry, struck a rebel force about eight hundred strong. An hour of fierce fighting resulted in a rout of the Confederates with a loss of more than a hundred casualties, including forty-one dead. Grierson's loss was one killed and four wounded. He pushed on to Coldwater Station, drove off the defending force, and burned the railroad depot and three cars. Small wonder that Sherman regarded Grierson as the best cavalry leader "I have yet had."[90]

On September 20, there was another surprise in store for Ben. Once again Alice walked "unannounced" into his quarters, this time accompanied by both Charlie and Robert. Sherman called to pay his respects and was amused to find Ben romping with the two boys while Alice sat on the floor mixing ingredients for mince pies. The family enjoyed three weeks together, during which Ben discovered that not all battles were at the front. His father, now seventy-three years old, had gone to Buckingham's store for supplies and while there exchanged words with a Mr. Martin, whom Robert regarded as a "secesh." When Martin threw a paper-weight at Robert, the latter responded with a whistling right to the jaw. Proprietor Buckingham managed to separate the pair, and hostilities ceased. Robert was more concerned about his son's safety than his own. Alarmed by the high casualty rate among officers, Robert suggested that federal officers should wear the same uniform as privates; clothed in this way, they would be less conspicuous targets for Confederate sharpshooters.[91]

Robert's opinions were occasionally a source of amusement to Ben and Alice, but the next words from him were sad ones. On October 8, he telegraphed that his wife, Mary, was dead—the victim of one last, massive stroke. For some time, knowing her death was imminent, Ben had been requesting a leave, but none was forthcoming. His inability to be with her at the end filled him with regret and anguish; "only those who have been placed in a similar position can fully realize my feelings on learning or hearing of her death." Alice returned to Jacksonville immediately to comfort her father-in-law.

Robert was inconsolable, and the decision was reached that he would stay for awhile with his daughter Louisa at Concord, Illinois. John and Ben then agreed to bring both their families to Memphis, where they expected to be headquartered indefinitely. Before long they had located a large home, formerly Grant's headquarters, and in a short time, Alice, Elizabeth, and all the children were comfortably settled.[92]

When Grierson reported to Sherman, he found the general agitated; a major federal offensive would soon begin. After months of effort, Grant had at last persuaded Halleck that a drive down the Mississippi Central Railroad could succeed in flanking the great Confederate fortress at Vicksburg and lead to its fall. Victory there would split the Confederacy and give the Union full control of the Mississippi River, a blow from which the South could never recover. Tactically, Grant proposed to advance with three wings in line, the right under Sherman, the center commanded by Major General J. B. McPherson and the left by Brigadier General C. S. Hamilton. Grierson's cavalry would screen Sherman's march.[93]

By way of preparation, Grierson and his Sixth Illinois struck at guerillas south and east of Memphis in order to secure Grant's rear. A three-day operation resulted in seven "bushwhackers" killed, between twenty and thirty wounded, seventeen taken prisoner, and two dozen horses and mules captured. During these strikes Grierson was impressed with the performance of a young lieutenant in Company "G," Samuel Woodward, and added him to the staff. "Sandy" Woodward would serve Grierson for the remainder of the war and for many years thereafter with unfailing dedication and efficiency.[94]

On November 26, Grierson led his regiment southward in advance of Sherman and, meeting only token opposition, reached Holly Springs on the twenty-eighth. They pushed on to the bankfull Tallahatchie River, swam that stream, and reached Oxford on December 5. Here Grant, urged by Sherman, gave Grierson command of a brigade—the Sixth and Seventh Illinois and the Second

Iowa—with orders "to lead, find and fight" the enemy on Sherman's front.[95]

If Grierson felt he was now in a position to distinguish himself in a major battle, however, he was doomed to bitter disappointment. Colonel John Mizner, Third Michigan Cavalry and West Point 1856, outranked Grierson by seven days and exercised his right to command the brigade. The only satisfaction Ben received was permission to "get out in front" with a single regiment, his Sixth Illinois. On December 6, he reached Panola, southwest of Oxford, crossed the Tallahatchie and broke up two camps of guerillas, capturing their equipment, wagons, and animals.[96]

At this point Grierson received orders from Grant to take important dispatches to General Frederick Steele, commanding in Arkansas and headquartered at Helena. Ben left Panola with seventy-five picked men and headed due west into a region known to be infested with guerillas. The detachment, fearing ambush, jogged cautiously down narrow, tree-lined roads into the tangle of vines, swamps, and canebrakes of the Coldwater. They crossed that stream on the evening of December 12, reached the banks of the Mississippi, and next day arrived at Helena in safety. Carrying Steele's reply, Grierson made the return journey without incident and rejoined his regiment near the Coldwater on December 14. Two days later he reached Oxford and delivered Steele's message to Grant.[97]

Meanwhile, back-door politics and first-rate Confederate planning were combining to halt Grant's advance and force abandonment of the entire project. Illinois politician-soldier, Major General John B. McClernand, a friend of Lincoln's, proposed to the President that Vicksburg be taken by an expedition down the Mississippi River. McClernand would, of course, command the forces involved. The plan was approved without Grant's knowledge, and McClernand established headquarters at Springfield, Illinois, where he began forwarding troops to Memphis, the starting point for the invasion.[98]

Grant heard of the operation from Halleck, who had no faith in either McClernand's ability or integrity. Convinced that he had the general-in-chief's support, Grant moved quickly to forestall McClernand. On December 8, he ordered Sherman to return to Memphis with one division, take command of any troops he found there, and proceed downriver. They could then conduct a coordinated drive on Vicksburg while Halleck took care of any political reverberations in Washington.[99]

But Grant failed to take into account the plans of Lieutenant General John C. Pemberton, commanding at Vicksburg. Pemberton moved thirty thousand men into position along the Yalobusha River in Grant's front and arranged for simultaneous cavalry raids by Nathan Bedford Forrest and Major General Earl Van Dorn on the federal supply routes. And these routes were vulnerable. Grant had established a base at Holly Springs, but the flow of supplies to that point was dependent on the single-line Mobile and Ohio and Mississippi Central railroads. Any serious disruption of traffic along these roads would imperil Grant's entire campaign.

In accord with Pemberton's plans, on December 15 Forrest entered west Tennessee with two thousand men. Grant, having learned of Forrest's movement, warned federal commanders in the area, but the unpredictable Forrest successfully eluded or fought them as chance or necessity dictated. He captured Jackson on December 20 and, like a devastating tornado, pushed north along the Mobile and Ohio, thoroughly destroying sixty miles of track. On his retreat, converging federal columns caught up at Parker's Crossroads on December 31, but Forrest fought his way out of the trap and made good his escape. He had severed Grant's major supply line, left a tangled skein of telegraph lines, inflicted heavy casualties with small losses, and captured large quantities of guns, ammunition, and other supplies. "That devil Forrest," as Sherman labeled him, had dealt Grant's campaign a ruinous blow.[100]

Van Dorn achieved almost as much success. With thirty-five hundred troopers he swept around Grant's left flank and stormed into Holly Springs. A frightened federal colonel, R. C. Murphy, meekly surrendered, and a vast store of supplies fell to the exuberant Confederates. What they could not carry away they destroyed. Grant's wife, Julia, visiting in Holly Springs, received a polite "courtesy call" from the triumphant raiders. Van Dorn then moved off in the direction of Bolivar, Tennessee.[101]

Grant ordered Mizner's brigade in pursuit. Grierson, encamped at Springport, west of Oxford, received orders at 2 A.M. on December 21 to march for Holly Springs, and by 7 P.M. of the same day he reached Waterford, some nine miles out. Here a courier from Grant informed him that Mizner had been relieved and that Grierson was to take command of the brigade. Before noon on December 22, Ben reached Holly Springs, eager to continue the pursuit. The post commander held him there until late afternoon and then, to his astonishment, ordered him to return to Oxford. He had only gone a mile when orders from Grant reached him, directing him to pursue

Van Dorn into Tennessee and either catch and defeat him or rest assured that "West Tennessee is so completely exhausted as to render it impossible to support an army."[102]

Grierson, long delayed and hours behind, moved swiftly to catch up and overtook Van Dorn's rear guard south of Bolivar. The Confederates were now in full retreat, and Grierson pressed them southward, skirmishing with the rear guards. Then at Saulsbury, Mizner arrived and resumed command. The matter of rank and injured feelings had, unfortunately, persuaded Grant to restore the brigade command. Grierson remained in front with the Sixth Illinois, pressing the raiders to Ripley, Mississippi, and beyond. Here Ben urged Mizner to launch a night attack, but the latter refused, and all pursuit ended at Pontotoc on December 28. For the second time in a week Grant relieved Mizner for lack of vigor, and Grierson once more took over the brigade.[103]

Grant, realizing that his central Mississippi campaign was now in disarray, was forced to retire to Memphis. Earlier, Sherman, unaware of Grant's difficulties, had launched an attack up the Yazoo River, a few miles north of Vicksburg, only to meet entrenched Confederates who forced him to retreat. None of these reverses discouraged Grant. As dogged as ever, he decided to assume command of the downriver expedition personally and attack Vicksburg from that quarter. Grierson, meanwhile, positioned himself at La Grange, Tennessee, a few miles east of Memphis on the Memphis and Charleston Railroad.[104]

By this time Alice, having lost all hope of seeing Ben during the Christmas holidays, decided to leave Memphis. With the onset of cold weather, it was impossible to keep the house warm. Moreover, she no longer felt safe, for rumors had reached her that a Mr. Hunt had offered three hundred dollars to anyone who would burn the house down. Besides, Ben's father had returned from Concord and was now living alone in the Jacksonville house. "It is a very different thing," Alice wrote to Ben, "being in Memphis without you, from what it was at the depot. I don't enjoy it as well by considerable."[105]

Elizabeth agreed with Alice, and on December 23, they, along with many other women and children who had been visiting husbands and fathers in Memphis, left on the steamer, "J. D. Perry." After an exhausting four-day journey, they arrived in St. Louis, where they spent a few days visiting relatives, the Sheppard family. One of the Sheppards was studying to become a doctor, and Alice related to Ben that he was "practicing cupping and leeching whenever he gets a call."[106] A few days later, on December 30, father Robert met the train in Jacksonville, giving them an enthusiastic welcome home.

New Year's Day found Ben at La Grange, lonely and weary, trying his best to keep warm before a fire in his tent. His family was far away in Jacksonville, the campaign was a disaster, his mail had been long delayed, and his pay was now two months in arrears. As he dozed before the fire he dreamed of home, of embracing Alice, and of "tumbling cosily into bed." His reverie was interrupted suddenly by the smell of something scorching—He had burned the soles off his boots, and a new pair would cost him his last fifteen dollars. Little did he know that the New Year that had just arrived would bring fame undreamed of, and that in six months he would be a national figure and a brigadier general.[107]

CHAPTER 4

The Raid

By mid-January, 1863, Grant had assembled more than eighty thousand men in four corps, but no more than half of these could be used in the Vicksburg campaign. Occupation duties required thousands, and others were needed for West Tennessee's defense, a task assigned to General C. S. Hamilton, headquartered in Memphis. Grierson's cavalry brigade, consisting of the Sixth and Seventh Illinois and the Second Iowa, was responsible for fending off Confederate raiders along the Memphis and Charleston Railroad. With his rear thus secured, Grant turned his full attention to operations against Vicksburg.

He established headquarters at Milliken's Bend, twenty miles upstream from the city, and spent the next three months in futile efforts to reach the east bank of the river and attack from the north. First he attempted to divert the channel of the Mississippi away from Vicksburg by digging a canal along the west bank, but the current failed to enter it. Next an attempt was made to link a series of streams with canals in order to reach Red River and emerge below Vicksburg, but, after weeks of back-breaking work, this project was abandoned as unfeasible. A third effort to reach the Yazoo River by way of Steele's Bayou just north of the city was easily repulsed by Confederate defenders.[1]

The dogged and determined Grant refused to accept defeat. Instead, he decided to risk a night run with gunboats past the Vicksburg batteries and seek a suitable campsite downstream. On the evening of April 16, Admiral David Porter successfully ran the gauntlet of fire and anchored off the west bank at New Carthage. On April 22, Grant ordered six transports loaded with forage and other supplies to make the run, and five reached the protection of Porter's guns. Grant's remaining task was to march his army, about forty thousand men, through the swamps and knee-deep mud along the low west side of the Mississippi and join the gunboats and transports at New Carthage. If this could be done, he was in position to select a landing site on the eastern bank of the river and attack Vicksburg from the left flank and rear. Meanwhile, he needed diversionary movements to distract Confederate attention from his operations. Sherman was ordered to make a demonstration up the Yazoo, and Hamilton had already received orders in February to have Grierson's cavalry ready for a major raid into Mississippi.[2]

The initial weeks of 1863 found Grierson disheartened. Confederate guerilla activity slowed in the winter, leaving the federal patrols little to do. This was just as well, for the weather, bitter cold, accompanied by frequent snow and rain, had spread illness among the poorly sheltered troopers. Grierson, furthermore, was short on supplies and equipment. Nonetheless, Ben found the inactivity difficult to endure. To add to his foul humor, he was becoming increasingly restive as he awaited promotion to brigadier, a rank warranted by his brigade command. Both Grant and Sherman had written strong recommendations, and when no word of approval reached him, he suspected that opposition had come from General Hamilton. Relations between the two remained correct but barely civil. Grierson regarded his superior as "disgusting . . . disagreeable . . . tyrannical . . . dogmatical and no gentleman."[3] Finally Ben ached to see his family, especially since he had recently learned that both Charlie and Robert had measles. At times, he wrote Alice, the loneliness nearly overwhelmed him, and occasionally he almost gave way to tears, except "that wouldn't be fitting a soldier."[4] Alice's steady stream of correspondence, however, helped to dispel the monotony and ease the pain of separation, and she bolstered his flagging spirits by assuring him he would soon become a general.

Though she wrote tender and, at times, cheerful letters, Alice in private struggled against giving way to depression. Newspaper accounts revealed that the war was going badly for the North; clearly the end was nowhere in sight. In the east, Lincoln had yet to find a general capable of dealing with Robert E. Lee and his lieutenants. General Ambrose Burnside had replaced McClellan, but his solution was a frontal assault on entrenched Confederates at Fredericksburg on December 13, 1862, a disaster that cost the Union twelve thousand casualties and Burnside his command. Whether his successor, General Joseph Hooker, could succeed where others had failed remained an open question.

The more recent battle of Murphreesboro, in eastern Tennessee, had ended without decisive results, despite heavy losses on both sides. For the present, Grant remained mired in the mud and swamp along the west bank of the Mississippi, still unable to find a way to take Vicksburg and open the river to Union forces. Only Lincoln's steadfast support prevented his removal.

As she read all this in newspapers and articles appearing in the *Atlantic,* Alice found it difficult to maintain the serene outward demeanor she felt the situation demanded. But Ben needed her support, and she did her best to provide it, sometimes barely masking the anxiety she felt inside. "I still think you will see stars and wear them too—if no accident befals [*sic*] you, and I don't get so intolerably lonely and low-spirited as to try and induce you to resign your position and come home."

Despite her brave words, she confessed that "I have felt some days since as though I could scarcely endure you being away from home much longer." Her difficulty was compounded now, since she heard from him irregularly. At times she acknowledged she surrendered to tears. Her crying spells never lasted long, for two-year-old Robert would climb into her lap, stroke her face, and set her laughing by telling her "to be a good boy and not cry."[5]

As the winter progressed, Alice struggled valiantly to stave off despondency. The war eventually would claim a fifth of its soldiers as casualties, and the list of wounded and dead now included familiar names from Jacksonville's families. The clergyman from the Meredosia church Alice had attended arrived in the city to visit his son, wounded at Murphreesboro, only to discover that he was too late, his son had already died. While Alice sought to comfort the minister, Ben's father was out among his townspeople soliciting contributions to assist a recently widowed neighbor who now faced the problem of rearing six children alone. His attempts raised enough money to pay for a simple funeral, with some left over to purchase firewood for the rest of the winter. Nonetheless, the family was in dire need, and to assist further, Alice brought the oldest child, a girl of thirteen, home with her as a temporary household helper.[6] As she observed her neighbors coping with tragedy, Alice was reminded that there was no guarantee that her own husband would return alive and unharmed.

Other matters weighed heavily on her mind. She was still depressed over the loss of a younger brother six months earlier. John Kirk, Jr. had been twenty-three when he succumbed to tuberculosis, and the circumstances surrounding his death had been especially painful. An exuberant and headstrong young man, involved in the Young America movement contrary to his father's wishes, he had insisted on coming and going as he pleased in the Kirk household. His father would countenance this from none of his children, and the result had been bitter contention until young John joined the Union Army. Even then, it was only during the last year of his life, as his physical condition deteriorated rapidly, that a reconciliation had taken place.[7] The memory of these events left Alice with a lingering sadness, difficult to dispel.

Less troublesome but irritating, nonetheless, were the increasingly frequent visits of Ben's oldest sister. Since the death of her mother, Louisa felt it her responsibility to look in on her father often, and when she arrived, she generally found much to criticize in Alice's household management. When Alice defended herself, Louisa resorted to slamming doors and shouting invectives, calling her "commander at the post" and accusing her of putting on "martial airs." After these incidents there followed a period of quiet and often sullen hostility, which gave way at last to an uneasy and brief truce as Alice attempted "to bury the hatchet." These recurrent scenes reinforced her deep longing for a home entirely of her own, but she knew that the realization of that hope remained far in the future.[8]

Some activities gave at least momentary relief. When time permitted, Alice joined other Jacksonville women at the Philharmonic Hall two afternoons a week. Here they knitted gloves, scarves, and caps and sewed shirts, sheets, and pillow cases for the Union troops, while at the same time enjoying one another's company and some respite from household chores.

Alice had always looked forward to church services, but never more than during this period. Reverend Walter Russell's stirring sermons reinforced her resolve to bear up bravely. Without any equivocation he believed firmly in the Northern cause, and since last summer had called on his congregation to support the war effort to its very end, meaning not simply restoration of the Union, but the total eradication of slavery. These sentiments echoed Alice's exactly, and she remained convinced that in "the sufferings now endured," she saw the workings of Providence. God was punishing the American people because, like the Pharaoh of the old Testament, "they will not let the slaves go free."[9]

March succeeded February, bringing with it the latest issue of the *Atlantic*. One article appeared to have been written specifically for Alice.

> The great army of letters that march Southward with every morning sun is a powerful engine of war. Fill them with tears and sighs, lament separation and suffering, dwell on your loneliness and fears . . . and you will damp the powder and dull the swords that ought to deal death upon the foe.[10]

The author, Mary Abigail Dodge, writing under the pseudonym Gail Hamilton, exhorted Northern women to face tragedy, including the loss of personal fortunes and the health and lives of their husbands and sons, not only with equanimity but with joy, giving up everything, if called upon, to the holy cause of preserving the Union. "The loss is but for a moment, the gain is for all time." Indeed this fervent abolitionist advised her compatriots who had already endured bereavement: "Count it all joy that you are reckoned worthy to suffer in a grand and righteous cause. Give thanks that you were born in this time, and *because* it is dark, be you the light of the World."

There were other phrases with strong religious overtones as well. If women set themselves on a steadfast path, they would in time have "cleared through the abomination of our desolation, a highway for the Prince of Peace."[11] This article, along with others such as "A Spasm of Sense," which appeared shortly afterward and was attributed to the same author, made a powerful impression on Alice. In her next letter to Ben, she informed him that although she failed to meet the standards of heroism set by Miss Hamilton, she would try harder, for "I have always wanted the war to go on until the destruction of slavery, whatever suffering or calamity it might bring me."[12]

Closer to home, her son Robert had formed a new habit that amused Alice whatever the course of her day. When Ben's letters arrived, she always read them aloud to both children. Lately Robert had taken to snatching them from her hands when she finished and, aware that the curlicues on the bottom of the page were kisses from his father, he would attempt to return them by kissing the page repeatedly. Having heard Ben's opening salutation repeatedly, he now addressed his mother at all times as "my dear Alice."[13]

Alice's letters, filled with the details of everyday life, were of great comfort to Ben during this period. His children, especially his youngest, were changing remarkably with each passing day, something that he regretted not being at home to observe. Instead, here he was encamped at La Grange, Tennessee, in a sea of mud, impatiently awaiting both a change in the weather and the beginning of new military action that conceivably would hasten the end of the war. Then, on February 14, Hamilton, informing him that a long march was in prospect, instructed him to have his brigade prepared to move at any moment. Ben's spirits soared. Six days later orders came from Hamilton to strike at rail and telegraph lines east of Jackson, Mississippi, and, if feasible, make a night raid on that city with the objective of capturing General Joseph E. Johnston, the Confederate commander in Mississippi and Tennessee. But next day, February 21, Hamilton countermanded the order. Grant had been unable to move against the Vicksburg defenses.[14]

Grierson chafed under the restraint, but as the weather moderated Confederate guerilla activity increased, giving his brigade ample work to do. On March 9, after a forced march of thirty-five miles in rain and mud, Ben, with nine hundred troopers of the Sixth and Seventh Illinois, struck the camp of Colonel R. V. Richardson's Tennessee Partisan Rangers near Covington, killed twenty-two, captured seventy, and destroyed the camp. Heavy actions against these partisans later in the month at Belmont and Somerville resulted in severe losses to both sides but served, at least temporarily, to clear west Tennessee of Richardson's forces.[15]

In the lull that followed, Ben was delighted to learn that Grant had replaced Hamilton with Major General Stephen Hurlbut, whom Grierson regarded as a competent soldier and a personal friend. Aware that his brigade might, at any time, be called on for arduous duty in Mississippi, Ben applied to Hurlbut for a brief leave, which was granted. He reached Jacksonville on the evening of April 6, where he found "an oasis of love." Years later he recalled that this visit was "one of the most enjoyable experiences of my life."[16]

His leave lasted only a short time. On April 13 he received a telegram from Hurlbut, "Return Immediately."[17] Grant, prepared to run the Vicksburg batteries, wanted Grierson's cavalry to provide a badly needed diversion. At last Ben had the long-awaited opportunity to distinguish himself. He bade his family a hasty farewell and took the train for St. Louis, leaving behind an anxious wife determined to be brave. It was months later before he received the letter she wrote shortly after his departure. "I felt the clasp of your hand and your last kiss on my lips for a long time after I left you Monday."[18]

Ben reached Memphis by steamer from St. Louis on the morning of April 16 and received his orders from Hurlbut. Although pressed for time, he wrote to Alice before boarding the train for La Grange. "My command is ordered to leave . . . on the expedition I spoke to you about . . . you must not be alarmed should you not hear from me inside a month. . . . My movements are to aid a greater movement which is to take place at a distant point or points. You will understand what I refer to."[19]

Grierson's full brigade was to march south, with the primary objective of cutting the Southern Mississippi Railroad east of Jackson, thereby isolating Vicksburg from the east. En route the expedition was to do as much damage as possible to Confederate installations, stores, supplies, and communications. Speed and deception must be the principal sources of the command's safety, though Grant had ordered several demonstrations to draw attention away from Grierson.[20]

After conferring with General William Sooy Smith, commanding at La Grange, in order to coordinate their operations, Grierson and his adjutant, Samuel Woodward, worked throughout the night completing plans and preparations. Only these two in the brigade knew the full extent of the expedition. John Grierson, recently appointed quartermaster of the Sixth Illinois, assisted in issuing "light rations," making certain that hardtack, coffee, bacon, sugar, and salt were on hand. Each trooper carried a Sharps carbine, a revolver, one hundred rounds of ammunition, and a saber. Six two-pounder guns, each drawn by a pair of horses, formed the battery. Grierson's personal preparation was minimal; he carried a small-scale map of Mississippi and a jew's harp in his blouse. He also possessed an invaluable document supplied by a Mississippi Unionist that showed routes a cavalry column could use as well as locations of plantations, Confederate storehouses, and estimates of local loyalties.[21]

At dawn on April 17, Grierson led the long column, seventeen hundred officers and men, out of La Grange and headed south. If the weather was an omen for the future of the expedition, the prospects were bright, for it was a beautiful spring morning. Private Uriah Fowler, Company "H," Seventh Illinois, believed he was heading for "big things." The men had great respect and confidence in the tall, slender, wiry, Grierson, whom they regarded as "tough as a ten penny nail."[22] The command met no opposition on this first day out and marched at the regular cavalry pace of three miles an hour. After an easy thirty miles, they halted just short of Ripley,

Brigadier General William Sooy Smith. *Courtesy National Archives.*

Mississippi, at the plantation of a Dr. Ellis. Here Ben made what became his standard demand when stopping at a plantation: surrender the keys to the smokehouse and barns and provide food for the men and horses.[23]

While Grierson rested on the evening of April 17, other federal forces were in motion to distract Confederate defenses in northern Mississippi. General Smith, with fifteen hundred men, marched southwest from La Grange, while another column pushed east from Corinth. Still another, thirteen hundred strong, marched south from Memphis, while a cavalry regiment under Colonel Abel Streight left Fort Henry on the Tennessee for a raid into eastern Alabama. All served their purpose, but Streight's efforts met disaster. Relentlessly pursued by Nathan Bedford Forrest, he was forced to fight a continuous rearguard action, and, at the point of exhaustion, surrendered to Forrest on May 3, 1863, at Lawrence, Alabama.[24]

Grierson, underway early on April 18, reached the Tallahatchie at midafternoon. In an effort to confuse the Confederates concerning both his strength and intentions, he crossed the river at three different points. A battalion of the Seventh Illinois under Major John Graham encountered the first opposition when they reached the bridge at New Albany. A few guerillas, pulling up planking on the bridge, opened fire as the bluecoats approached. Graham charged and drove them off with no loss, repaired the bridge, and crossed. The Sixth and Seventh Illinois proceeded along the road to Pontotoc while Colonel Edward Hatch's Second Iowa, after a brief skirmish with home guards, traveled a route some four miles to the east. At nightfall Grierson encamped in a driving rain at Sloan's plantation.

Sloan gave the dripping intruders a cold reception, which turned to rage when the hungry troopers raided his well-stocked smokehouse and devoured his supply of ham and turkeys. When his horses and mules were also rounded up, he launched a tirade at Grierson and, among other things, shouted that these thieves and plunderers might as well cut his throat. Grierson, always one for a good joke, winked at his orderly, a muscular, bearded trooper, and ordered, "Take him out in the field and cut his throat and be done with it."[26] The orderly, with drawn hunting knife, seized Sloan and began pulling him outside, while a terrified Mrs. Sloan begged for her husband's life. One glance at a now much-subdued Sloan convinced Ben that the joke had gone far enough, and the elderly gentleman was released.

At dawn on April 19, Grierson sent one detachment east to contact Hatch and two others north and west to break up reported Confederate concentrations. The main column moved on down the muddy Pontotoc road, and about noon Hatch's regiment and the two detachments caught up. The united command reached the outskirts of Pontotoc after a five-hour march and rode into town at a gallop. They surprised and routed a few armed citizens and a body of state troops. They killed one of the troops and wounded a number of others, as well as capturing all their supplies and equipment. The raiders then moved on through Pontotoc and halted for the night at Daggett's "Weatherall Plantation" on the Houston road, where the troopers once more enjoyed the contents of bountiful smokehouses. They were now seventy miles into enemy territory and had suffered no losses.[27]

During the evening Grierson conducted a rigid inspection of men, animals, and equipment and "culled out" 175 men who were either "sick or inclined to be sick." This "quinine brigade," along with prisoners and unserviceable horses, was placed under the command of Major Hiram Love, Seventh Illinois, and ordered to return to La Grange by way of Pontotoc, marching in columns of fours before daylight in order to create the impression that the whole force had retreated. Ben also gave Love a note for Alice, assuring her that all looked favorable so far, and that he had faith and hope everything would turn out well. Love, with his "invalids" and one of the two pounders, took the back trail at 3 A.M., trotted through Pontotoc before dawn, and reached La Grange without incident.[28]

Two hours after Love's departure, Grierson was again on the move. Bypassing Houston, he took the road to Starkville and spent the night of April 20 at the plantation of Dr. Benjamin Kilgore, a dozen miles south of Houston. A two-hour march the next morning brought the brigade to a fork in the road, one branch of which led southeast toward Columbus. Here Ben detached Hatch and the Second Iowa with a gun from the battery, sending them to strike the Mobile and Ohio Railroad at West Point and destroy the road as far south as possible before returning to La Grange. He also scribbled a final hasty message to Alice and entrusted it to a courier who was instructed to head west, cut telegraph wires along the Mississippi Central Railroad, and seek the safety of Union lines in Tennessee.[29] Grierson then resumed his march for Starkville with a company from Hatch's regiment following for a short distance before back-tracking and creating a maze of muddy hoofprints to

General Edward Hatch. *Courtesy National Archives.*

convince the Confederates that the raiders were either in retreat or heading east for the Mobile and Ohio.[30]

Hatch reached Palo Alto, some ten miles northwest of West Point, where he was struck by a strong force of gray cavalry under Lieutenant Colonel Clark Barteau. Barteau, who had been pursuing Grierson, had concluded from the mass of tracks at the Columbus road that the main body of raiders had turned east. Hatch managed, through the skillful use of lane hedges and fences, to beat off Barteau, but realized he could go no farther south with his available force. He turned north and, avoiding the main roads, marched throughout the night—much of it through swamps—and reached undefended Okolona just before nightfall.

Hatch swept into the town, burned a Confederate barracks, a cotton warehouse, a large quantity of stores, and destroyed a park full of ammunition. After rounding up six hundred horses and mules, he headed for La Grange, fighting off Barteau almost all the way. His losses were ten killed, wounded, and missing, but his efforts had succeeded in drawing off a strong force from Grierson's rear. He had also convinced Confederate leadership that the major objective of the raid was the Mobile and Ohio Railroad.[31]

Grierson, meanwhile, after conferring with the Seventh's lieutenant colonel, William Blackburn, requested the latter to organize a small group of volunteers to pose as Confederate guerillas and ride in advance of the column, seeking information about roads, bridges, streams, towns, and rebel troop movements. Blackburn soon had eight troopers of the Seventh Illinois led by Sergeant Richard Surby. Among the eight was Private Fowler, confident that "big things" awaited him in the days ahead. The men were clothed in gray slouch hats, gray shirts, and butternut jeans taken from houses along the way, and were armed with captured shotguns, rifles, pistols, and sabers. Dubbed the "butternut guerillas," the little band rendered invaluable service for the rest of the expedition.[32]

Grierson pushed on to Starkville and, encountering no resistance from surprised and startled residents, burned government property after rounding up horses and mules. Although it was late afternoon, he urged his command toward Louisville, forty miles to the southwest. He realized that Confederate units throughout the state were by now searching for him. His mission and the safety of his command depended upon the utmost speed and deception. The long column plunged on through "a dismal swamp nearly belly-deep in mud and water."[33] Not until late in the evening did Grierson call a halt and encamp in a torrential downpour.

Before daybreak on April 22, the sixth day of the raid, Ben detached a battalion of the Seventh under Major Graham with orders to destroy a large tannery and shoe factory at nearby Bankston, while the main column pressed on toward Louisville. Graham and his rain-soaked troopers rode hard through a sea of swamp-like terrain, struck like a thunderbolt, effected a complete surprise, and burned the tannery and shoe factory along with a large quantity of shoes, leather, saddles, and bridles consigned to Vicksburg. He captured a startled Confederate quartermaster, who was loading a supply of shoes for the garrison at Port Gibson. Graham caught up as the command approached Louisville.[34]

Grierson, meanwhile, aware that he needed another diversion to deceive the Confederates concerning his major objective, conferred briefly with Colonel Edward Prince of the Seventh Illinois. As a result, Captain Henry Forbes and Company "B" of Prince's regiment were ordered to strike at the Mobile and Ohio Railroad at Macon, about thirty miles to the east. Forbes could rejoin as circumstances permitted, while the main column marched as swiftly as possible for the Southern Mississippi Railroad at Newton.[35]

Citizens of Louisville, alerted to the raiders' approach and fearful of extensive damages to their little town, had "boarded up." The streets were entirely deserted and an oppressive silence greeted the troopers. No Confederate installations or troops were in the place, Grierson allowed no pillaging, and the command passed through without incident. South of Louisville, in growing darkness, the raiders encountered a vast swamp where the water was stirrup deep and studded with sinkholes at swimming level. Several horses drowned, and their riders were fortunate to escape the same fate. Not until midnight did the thoroughly drenched column reach high ground and encamp at Estes plantation, where the owner was forced to supply the usual amenities.[36]

At dawn the command was saddled and on the move. They crossed the bridge over the rain-swollen Pearl River after the butternut guerillas chased away a few timid pickets. Philadelphia offered no more than token resistance, and a few residents were arrested. Among them was the county judge, who informed Grierson that they had resisted only because they feared for their lives and property. Ben then addressed the small crowd and reassured them that he was not there to interfere with private citizens, destroy their property, or insult or molest their families. "We are after the soldiers and the property of the rebel government."[37] Nothing was disturbed in Philadelphia, and the march continued on the road to Decatur by mid-afternoon.

At 10 P.M. Grierson ordered Colonel Blackburn, who had volunteered for the task, to take four companies of the Seventh and advance into Newton. Grierson and the rest of the command would follow within an hour. Blackburn, with the butternut guerillas leading the way, reached Decatur after a five-hour ride. Sergeant Surby, posing as a Confederate soldier, awakened a sleeping householder and learned that no more than a company of infantry garrisoned Newton.

Without further delay, Blackburn resumed his march and by sunrise was within six miles of Newton. He sent Surby and two scouts ahead to gather information, and they soon reached the outskirts of town. Here they learned from a lone citizen that no troops were in Newton, only a military hospital full of convalescents. They were also told that a freight train was due in less than an hour. After digesting this news, Surby rode to the depot to take over the telegraph, but the office was locked and no operator was on duty. Moments later he heard the whistle of a train in the east — the freight was early — and he sent a scout scurrying for Blackburn.

Hurrying forward, Blackburn reached the depot ahead of the train and concealed his men. When the twenty-five-car freight came to a stop on a siding, exultant troopers swarmed from their hiding places and captured it. They scarcely had time to examine the contents when a whistle from down the tracks to the west signaled the approach of another train. This one proved to be a mixed passenger and freight of fourteen cars, and when it slowed at the depot it also was seized, while the passengers attempted to escape at all possible exits including the windows.[38]

When crews and passengers had been secured, both trains were run some distance up the siding, the cars set afire, and the locomotives exploded. Grierson heard the explosion and came at a gallop, fearing that Blackburn was under attack. Relieved and delighted at what he found, he immediately organized the troopers for the work of more serious destruction. Rails were torn up, heated over burning ties, and twisted into grotesque shapes. The depot and a building with five hundred stands of arms were burned. Meanwhile, two detachments were sent east and west along the road to destroy bridges, trestles, rails, and telegraph lines. By early afternoon, with seventy-five prisoners parolled, Grierson, satisfied that he had inflicted major damage, was eager to depart.[39]

After spreading the word that he intended heading east for the Mobile and Ohio Railroad, Grierson set out southeast for Garlandville with his smoke-begrimed command in a gay mood. Their major task had been accomplished. The troopers had found several barrels of whiskey, and many of them were uproariously drunk. As the advance entered Garlandville, a band of armed citizens fired into them, seriously wounding a trooper and killing a horse. Grierson was not making war on old men; he had the group rounded up and disarmed, gave them a stern lecture and ordered their release. Then Ben and his staff, finding themselves famished, searched the houses for food. The enterprising Woodward found a deserted home with lights on and a steaming meal on the table. Grierson and his officers greatly enjoyed the hospitality of an unknown host.[40]

Grierson now faced a decision. Undoubtedly, by this time Pemberton had located him and had ordered troops to converge from all sides. It was essential that he and his troopers reach a safe haven. He could attempt to return to La Grange by way of Alabama or head west, either to Baton Rouge or Grand Gulf on the Mississippi, where he believed Grant was now located. Ben chose the latter course, determined to do as much damage as possible en route.[41]

The long column turned southwest, but despite the need for speed, Ben was forced to ease the pace. Men and animals were exhausted. Reluctantly, he halted at a plantation near Montrose, and bleary-eyed officers and men obtained their first sleep in forty hours. On April 25, the ninth day of the raid, the command marched at a leisurely gait, stopping at convenient plantations for food, rest, and fresh horses and mules. Grierson also sent several small detachments north toward the railroad to create the impression that he intended moving along that line to Jackson.[42]

At dusk the command halted at the plantation of a Dr. Mackadore in the Leaf River valley. Here Grierson dispatched one of the butternut guerillas, Samuel Nelson, to Forest Station on the railroad, with orders to cut telegraph wires there and, if possible, to fire bridges and trestles. Nelson returned before daybreak with alarming news. He had encountered Captain R. C. Love and a strong force of gray cavalry, searching for the raiders. Nelson had convinced the Captain that he had been forced to act as a guide for the blue-coats but had managed to slip away. Love was on a direct route to Grierson's camp, and Nelson obligingly informed the Confederate commander that the Yankees were well to the east, near Garlandville, heading for the Mobile and Ohio Railroad. As soon as possible, Nelson faded into the darkness, hastened back to Mackadore's, and reported to Grierson.

With an enemy force close at hand, Ben was underway at dawn. The command crossed the Leaf River, burned the bridge, and reached Raleigh two hours after sunrise. They met no opposition, but did capture the county sheriff, who had several thousand dollars in Confederate currency in his possession. Grierson wasted little time at Raleigh and urged his troopers westward at a fast pace. All afternoon and into the evening they sloshed on in a driving rain, reached and crossed the Strong River, and were preparing to fire the bridge when they were hailed by an advance party from Captain Forbes's B Company.

Forbes had been unable to cut the Mobile and Ohio and while trying to follow Grierson's elusive trail had run into opposition at Philadelphia and suffered a trooper killed and one wounded. Grierson ordered a detachment to remain at the bridge until Forbes came up and was safely across and then burn the structure.[43]

After a brief halt, Grierson ordered Colonel Prince, with two battalions of the Seventh, to take the advance and push on through the night for the Pearl River, where a single ferry was the only means of crossing. When Prince arrived, the stream was a rain-swollen torrent and the ferry was on the opposite bank. Shouting above the roar of the water, Prince convinced the ferryman that a regiment of Alabama cavalry must cross. The ferry soon took the first load of horses and men to the west bank, and to Prince's vast relief no Confederate guards were there to block his passage. Ferrying both regiments required an anxious eight hours and allowed Captain Forbes to rejoin Grierson, who then marched without delay for Hazelhurst, only fourteen miles away on the New Orleans, Jackson and Great Northern Railroad.[44]

The butternut guerillas were the first to enter the place and managed to file a misleading telegram to Pemberton—the raiders had found the ferry at the Pearl destroyed and, unable to cross, had set off in a northeasterly direction. Prince, in the advance with the Seventh, arrived soon afterward and occupied the town. Hazelhurst provided both some hard work and some excitement for the men in blue. They found a number of freight cars loaded with five hundred artillery shells, other ammunition, and large quantities of stores and commissary supplies.[45]

The cars were set afire and the ammunition exploded, but a strong wind carried sparks to other buildings, and Grierson's troopers joined the citizens in forming bucket brigades to put out the flames. After tearing up several miles of track and allowing his troopers a "banquet" of ham, eggs, biscuits, and bacon in the local hotel, Grierson marched northwest to Gallatin, where a sixty-four-pounder gun, a wagon load of arms and fourteen hundred pounds of powder were captured. After destroying the arms and powder and spiking the gun, the column moved west toward Union Church.[46]

News of the strike at Hazelhurst soon reached an alarmed Pemberton at Vicksburg. He had expected an attack on the Southern Mississippi Railroad at or near Jackson and had ordered a strong force of infantry to move by rail and bring the raiders to bay. Now they were virtually in his backyard, and he telegraphed General John Bowen at Grand Gulf to send Colonel Wirt Adams's cavalry — Bowen's only significant mounted troops — to pursue the audacious Yankees. Grierson's next move, Pemberton informed Bowen, "is only a matter of conjecture."[47] Pemberton tried to calm a concerned Jefferson Davis by telegraphing, "all the cavalry I can raise is close on their rear."[48]

And on April 28, near Union Church at midafternoon, Grierson met a scouting detachment of Adams's cavalry. After a sharp skirmish, the graycoats were driven off and the raiders encamped in the village. At this point Grierson all but gave up hope of reaching Grand Gulf. Confederate forces were close on his heels, his command was in danger of being overwhelmed, and sober judgment argued that he should head for Baton Rouge.[49]

Next morning, to confuse his pursuers, he ordered Colonel Reuben Loomis and the Sixth Illinios to make a strong demonstration westward toward Fayette, and then marched swiftly southeast through a thick pine forest for Brookhaven, on the New Orleans, Jackson and Great Northern Railroad — the Confederates would certainly not expect him to turn back east. Upon reaching the outskirts of town, Grierson ordered a charge by both regiments and "There was much running and yelling but it soon quieted down into almost a welcome."[50] Over two hundred prisoners were taken, including sick soldiers, their nurses, and other attendants at the local hospital. According to Confederate surgeon R. B. Maury: "I have to state that the conduct of the enemy towards the hospital and its officers was entirely proper. Nothing was injured or disturbed in the slightest particular."[51]

As prisoners were parolled, creating a great deal of paper work for Adjutant Woodward, detachments tore up the railroad in the vicinity of Brookhaven and burned trestles and a bridge. The depot and several freight cars were fired, along with the buildings in a deserted training camp. But as sparks threatened to ignite homes and other buildings, the troopers, as they had at Hazelhurst, became fire-fighters and prevented further destruction.[52]

Grierson left Brookhaven early in the evening but halted after eight miles to give his weary command some rest. It proved well that he did so, for there would be little rest for the next three days. Colonel Adams, deceived temporarily by Grierson's feint toward Fayette, was now hot on the trail, and Colonel R. V. Richardson, Ben's old antagonist in Tennessee, was pushing hard for Brookhaven. Other gray units were closing in from the west.

On April 30, the fourteenth day of the raid, Grierson resumed his march along the railroad, destroying track, trestles, and bridges as he passed. At Bogue Chitto Station he burned the depot and a number of freight cars. He could not have known, as the smoke swirled from the depot, that Grant had made an unopposed landing that very morning at Bruinsburg, on the east bank of the Mississippi, and was pushing inland to high, dry ground. Much of the credit was due Grierson and his brigade, who had demanded so much of Pemberton's attention and drawn away so many of his troops.[53]

The work at Bogue Chitto required little time, and Ben decided to proceed down the railroad to Summit. Here the raiders received a surprisingly warm welcome; Union sentiment was not lacking in the small town. One lady's sympathies for the North were so strong that she informed Grierson that if the North won the war and he ran for President, her husband would either vote for him or face her divorce petition. Search parties found little in the way of military stores, but they did uncover forty barrels of Louisiana rum under the sidewalks. To the dismay of his thirsty troopers, Grierson had the "vile stuff" poured on the ground.

Further questioning of the citizens revealed, mistakenly it later developed, that a strong Confederate force awaited the bluecoats at Osyka, eighteen miles to the south.[54] With enemy forces to his front, in his rear, and closing in from the west, Grierson decided to abandon the railroad and further destruction, and make an all-out run for Baton Rouge. Accordingly, after an inspection of men and animals, he marched in the late afternoon toward Osyka to deceive onlookers, and then veered southwest along the road to Liberty.

The column halted that evening at the plantation of Dr. Spurlark. Grierson, as usual, turned the smokehouse and barns over to his troopers, but he was determined that he and his officers would also dine well, and he placed a guard over a chicken coop. He noticed a short time later that the chickens had all disappeared except one, and that a trooper was about to steal the lone remaining hen. As he related the incident later:

> [I] drew my saber and went for that private like a flash of lightening. I jumped clean over the hen cage around the pig-sty, through the stable, behind the smokehouse, between the horses and under the horses, dodging the trees and shrubbery. . . . smashing the trellis and vociferating in language more forcible than polite, I pursued that soldier and squawking hen . . . until finally the soldier went scrambling and tumbling over a high rail fence dropping the fowl on my side under the stroke of the saber.[55]

Grierson had his chicken at last, and the much abused fowl provided a tasty morsel for the staff.

On Friday, May 1, the command left Spurlark's in the early morning and marched southwest for the Wall's Bridge crossing of the Tickfaw. Near noon, Sergeant Surby and his butternut scouts reached the bridge, but encountered pickets from a force of Tennessee cavalry that had crossed Grierson's front en route to Osyka and halted for a noon bivouac. Firing on the picket line alerted the Tennesseans to Grierson's approach and they prepared an ambush on the east bank in the trees and undergrowth that bordered the Tickfaw.

Lieutenant Colonel Blackburn, riding forward alone to investigate the gunfire, ordered the scouts to follow him, and rashly charged the bridge. A hail of bullets cut him down and seriously wounded Surby. A platoon from the advance galloped to the rescue and crossed the bridge, but were met by a curtain of fire that brought down seven horses and wounded three troopers. Five others were captured, and only four managed to escape unscathed back across the bridge.

The heavy firing brought Grierson to the front, where he calmly and skillfully organized an assault. After the two pounders laid down a barrage, three attack columns struck the front and both flanks of the Confederates. The Tennesseans, badly outnumbered, retreated precipitously. Grierson sent Loomis and the Sixth in pursuit and halted to assess his losses.[56]

Blackburn, hit in three places, appeared mortally wounded. Four others, including Sergeant Surby, were wounded, and five men had been captured. Colonel Prince was highly agitated and wanted to encamp, but Blackburn urged Grierson to move on, arguing that the command was in grave danger and must be saved. Grierson was fond of Blackburn, respected his courage, and agreed on the need to move on, but he felt the colonel's rashness had caused unnecessary casualties: "Unfortunately Lieutenant Colonel Blackburn, calling on the scouts to follow him, dashed forward to the bridge without waiting for the column to come within supporting distance."[57]

Grierson made swift arrangements at a nearby plantation for the care of his wounded and, when the Sixth returned from pursuit, pressed on toward Greensburg, Louisiana. He scattered a small force of graycoats encountered on the way and entered the town without opposition.[58]

After a brief halt, Grierson raced into the night for the only bridge—Williams'—over the Amite River, fourteen miles away. The butternut guerillas, leading the way, succeeded in surprising and capturing the small bridge guard. With this obstacle removed, the command clattered across the two-hundred-yard span at midnight. And none too soon, for they were just two hours ahead of Wirt Adams's cavalry, under forced march in their rear. There were still other streams to cross before they reached Baton Rouge, thirty long miles away. With their safety still not assured, Ben pushed on through the early morning hours, allowing no stops for rest.[59]

Near dawn they reached Sandy Creek, where the scouts sighted an enemy camp just beyond the ridge. A charge by forward units of the Sixth swept through the tents and captured about forty convalescent soldiers, left behind when the effectives of their regiment had marched to the defense of Osyka. After ordering the camp of about one hundred and fifty tents destroyed, Grierson resumed his march.[60]

The strain of fifteen days of almost constant campaigning was beginning to exact its toll; riders and their animals were near exhaustion. Some troopers, with the aid of their comrades, tied their feet under the saddles to stay astride. Others fell asleep as they rode, swaying to the motions of their mounts. A final barrier remained— the Comite River crossing.

As the column approached, Grierson halted while the scouts went forward to investigate. A small Confederate camp on the east bank barred the way. Ben summoned his troopers to a final effort, and a thundering charge routed the unsuspecting graycoats. Once across, Grierson slowed the pace, and when he reached a convenient plantation, ordered a halt. On this warm Saturday morning of May 2, officers and men sprawled in any available space to get some badly needed sleep. They had marched seventy-six miles in twenty-eight hours and fought four engagements, all without food or rest.[61] A frustrated Wirt Adams telegraphed Pemberton:

> During the last twenty-four hours of their march in this state, they traveled at a sweeping gallop, the numerous stolen horses previously collected furnishing them fresh relays. I found it impossible to my great mortification and regret to overhaul them.[62]

Colonel R. V. Richardson expressed similar sentiments:

> He [Grierson] has made a most successful raid through the length of the State of Mississippi and part of Louisiana, one which will exhilerate for a short time the fainting spirits of the Northern war party. We had forces enough to have captured and destroyed him but his movements were so rapid and uncertain of aim that we could not concentrate our scattered forces.[63]

With his command enjoying the first sound sleep in many days, Grierson, a man of extraordinary stamina, spied a piano in the parlor of the plantation house and, with Woodward and the family in attendance, sat down to play. He was still playing when, at noontime, an excited orderly interrupted to report that enemy cavalry was approaching from the west. Grierson knew better. He mounted his horse and rode forward to meet the oncoming force. When he came in sight of them, he dismounted and walked to meet them, waving his handkerchief. Soon he shook hands with an astonished Captain J. Franklin Godfrey, who had marched with a patrol from Baton Rouge to investigate reports of enemy cavalry in the vicinity.

Ben was provided with an escort into the city, where he met General C. C. Augur, commanding there, who insisted on a parade. Grierson tried to dissuade the general. His troopers were bone tired, their clothing in tatters, and their animals in poor condition. Augur remained firm, however, and the Sixth and Seventh Illinois, a thousand strong, in torn, dust-covered, and sweat-stained uniforms, reached Baton Rouge in midafternoon and began their parade. They were followed by a throng of blacks who had flocked in from outlying plantations to enjoy a newfound freedom. The long procession wound through the streets lined with cheering citizens and ended in the early evening at pleasant Magnolia Grove, where the troopers encamped for a long and well-earned rest.[64]

By any standard the raid had been an overwhelming success. Grierson had marched six hundred miles in less than sixteen days, through the heart of enemy country. His command had killed and wounded over one hundred, captured and parolled five times that number, and had seized a thousand horses and mules. Sixty miles of rail and telegraph lines had been destroyed, along with three thousand stands of arms and an immense amount of commissary supplies and stores. Most important, thousands of Confederate troops (Grierson estimated the number at thirty-eight thousand), had been drawn away from the defense of Vicksburg, thereby simplifying Grant's task. All this had been accomplished at a cost of only three killed, seven wounded, five left sick, and nine missing.[65]

Small wonder that hard-bitten General Sherman, not given to superlatives, described the raid as "the most brilliant expedition of the war."[66] Grant, aware of Grierson's talents, was also impressed: "It was Grierson who first set the example of what might be done in the interior of the enemy's country without any base from which to draw supplies."[67] When Hurlbut, Grierson's superior in Memphis, learned of the results of the raid, he telegraphed Army headquarters in Washington, "I desire especially to call attention of the General-in-Chief to this gallant exploit of Colonel Grierson, one, I think unequalled in the war."[68]

As the plaudits poured in, Ben and his officers were wined, dined, and elaborately entertained, but in all the furor he did not forget Alice. At the earliest opportunity, he dashed off a note. "I, like Byron, have had to wake up in the morning and find myself famous."[69] And famous he was. News of the raid spread rapidly throughout the North and thrilled a public longing for a triumph of Union arms, rather than defeat and stalemate. Grierson's picture appeared on the front cover of *Harper's Weekly* and *Leslie's Illustrated,* and John Grierson wrote his father that the *New York Herald* and the *Memphis Bulletin* were filled with stories of Ben's "great raid through Mississippi."[70]

At the first opportunity, Ben and several of his officers visited New Orleans, where he received a warm welcome from Major General N. P. Banks, commanding the Department of the Gulf. Banks's attention was riveted on the Confederate stronghold at Port Hudson, some twenty miles upriver from Baton Rouge, which thus far had repulsed all efforts to take it. He needed cavalry and felt there was none better than Grierson's. Ben was flattered, but expressed his desire to join Grant in the Vicksburg campaign as soon as possible.

Grierson spent four days in the city, enjoying a continuous ovation, and, among other gifts, received a magnificent bay horse. He managed to obtain his back pay, which was four months in arrears and, ever conscious of his family, mailed presents to "My dear Alice," Charlie, and Robert, along with a draft for five hundred dollars.

On May 9, the day he left New Orleans for Baton Rouge, Ben wrote Alice a long letter describing his reception and experiences and indicating that he expected to join Grant within a few days. The following day Banks received a telegram from Grant urging the release of Grierson's cavalry, but Banks had other ideas. He intended keeping these hard-riding troopers in his own Department.

While Ben and his officers enjoyed a week of relaxation and entertainment, their men were given the "freedom of the city" in Baton Rouge. Bathed, rested, and in clean uniforms, the soldiers took full advantage of the opportunity. At the insistence of proprietors, they had the best the city could offer in food, refreshment, and entertainment at no cost. Some of the more exhuberant spirits invaded the Provost Marshal's office and captured it. Another group took complete charge of a saloon, to the consternation of the bartender. Many simply roamed the streets in good-natured inebriation, savoring the sights. No ill-feeling resulted, for such recreation seemed a reasonable reward for a job well done.[73]

Their "vacation" ended on May 12. Despite his busy schedule, Grierson had succeeded in getting his gun carriages repaired and his animals reshod, all in preparation for joining Grant. But orders from Banks sent the Sixth and Seventh to the Port Hudson front. Here they skirmished with a familiar opponent, units of Wirt Adams's cavalry. Grierson made a hurried trip to New Orleans with General Augur for a conference with Banks and met with a cordial reception but no indication of when he would release the Illinois regiments.[74]

Upon his return to Baton Rouge, Ben was still hopeful of serving under Grant but was also determined to give his best while in the Department of the Gulf. On May 20, with eleven hundred troopers he "tore up" the railroad between Clinton and Port Hudson and felt certain that thirty days of fighting would free the Mississippi "of the tread of traitors' feet." "This great artery of the West," he wrote Alice, "will be of more value to us by far than Richmond or Charleston."[75] A few days later Banks ended speculation on Grierson's immediate future by appointing him to command the First Cavalry Brigade, Fourth Division, Department of the Gulf, consisting of the Sixth and Seventh Illinois Cavalry, the Second Massachusetts Cavalry, the First Louisiana Cavalry, and the Fourth Wisconsin Mounted Infantry. The brigade's primary task was to screen the advance of Banks's infantry in their efforts to surround Port Hudson.

An assault on the fortress was repulsed by hard-fighting Confederates on May 27. Although Ben lost forty horses during the struggle, he escaped with minor casualties. He also gained a new respect for the valor of black troops as they charged the gray entrenchments. In a letter to Alice the next day, he remarked, "the negro regiments fought bravely yesterday . . . there can be no question about the good fighting qualities of negroes hereafter—that question was settled beyond a doubt yesterday."[75]

For the balance of May and into June, Grierson and his brigade obtained little rest. On June 3, near Clinton, after fighting a savage, four-hour engagement with a determined force of Confederates, he was forced to retire when his ammunition ran out. Three days later he resumed the attack, drove the stubborn defenders off, and entered the town, a major source of supplies for beleaguered Port Hudson. He destroyed the depot, a locomotive, machine shops, two factories producing wool and cartridges, and a large quantity of ammunition. All this was a severe blow to Major General Franklin Gardner, charged with the defense of Port Hudson, but Grierson also paid a price for his victory. He sustained losses of eight killed, twenty-eight wounded, and fifteen missing. In directing the attack, Ben took three balls through his coat, but miraculously he escaped injury.[77]

Despite the setback at Clinton, Gardner's troops continued to hold out. Twice in mid-June, Banks tried to storm the works, and twice he was repulsed. Grierson believed part of Banks's problem was in the composition of his infantry. "Eastern troops do not fight like Western troops and Banks has very few Western troops in his Department."[78]

With Banks stalled before Port Hudson, Grierson's cavalry was assigned the more routine task of defending the Federal rear and cutting Gardner's communications. This created a frustrating situation for the aggressive Grierson, for given the prolonged siege that now seemed inevitable, he lost all hope of joining Grant. Upriver the Vicksburg campaign had also bogged down. After crossing at Bruinsburg, Grant had pushed rapidly eastward, forcing Johnston to evacuate Jackson and capturing the city on May 14. Swiftly he turned west, met Pemberton's forces at Champion's Hill and drove them into the Vicksburg fortifications. Efforts to assault these formidable defenses failed, and Grant settled in for a siege. For the moment,

the Federal campaign to open the Mississippi and split the Confederacy had ground to a halt.

Ben had other reasons to fret as well. On leaving La Grange, the
brigade had left even minimal comfort and convenience behind. Few
carried more than a toothbrush. In the field before Port Hudson,
Ben and Adjutant Woodward discharged the essential administrative duties under the most trying conditions. Their headquarters
consisted of a sheet of canvas thrown over tree limbs, while ammunition boxes provided chairs, desks, and served as beds when covered
with a blanket. Food was scarce and frequently non-existent. Banks
had never been noted for an efficient commissary. Grierson's basic
good humor sustained him, however, and on June 14 he received
welcomed news—his "star" had finally arrived. On June 3, President
Lincoln had appointed him Brigadier General of Volunteers for "gallant and distinguished service."[79]

Pleased as he was with the promotion, Ben's morale needed additional reinforcement. He could stand the heat, flies, mosquitoes, and
irregular meals; he could laugh when he and Woodward were occasionally soaked by a downpour that cascaded into their "canvas
castle," and he was not concerned about injury on the battlefield.
He was, however, troubled over lack of word from Alice, since he
had not heard from her in weeks. Faithful as she had always been
to write, he was fearful something was wrong at home.

Alice, too, was deeply disturbed. During the course of the raid
she had understood his long silence, although that did not make it
easy for her, since she expected at any moment to receive a telegram announcing his death or capture. When she finally heard of his
safe arrival in Baton Rouge, she had shed tears of joy and relief.
Now she realized from his letters, which she received regularly, that
hers were not reaching him. Nonetheless, after reading of his ex-
ploits in the newspapers she wrote that the *New York Herald* reported
that he was modest and unassuming, "which I'm glad to know is true,
nor do I think your present notoriety will make you otherwise."[80]

This was the longest separation they had ever endured. If the
transfer to Grant's command materialized, it seemed likely to continue indefinitely unless Ben was assigned to Tennessee. Meanwhile,
certain that he would receive her letters eventually, Alice continued
to write almost daily, describing in great detail even the most routine
incidents. Since she also maintained a large correspondence with
relatives and friends, she kept her husband informed of their affairs
as well. For her own part, her religious faith provided a strong source

of personal strength. She prayed to God each night to keep Ben from physical harm, but as her father had reminded her upon the death of her brother John, "The Lord giveth, the Lord taketh away." Thus she also beseeched the Almighty to at least open her husband's eyes "to the beauty of a Christian life." Then if the war claimed him, at least he would attain salvation in the hereafter.[81]

The siege of Vicksburg, seemingly interminable, came to an abrupt end. Pemberton, cut off from all hope of relief and finding his army and the citizens of Vicksburg on the verge of starvation, decided that further resistance would result only in additional and unnecessary suffering. On July 4 he surrendered to Grant. Port Hudson, the last Confederate stronghold on the Mississippi, had held out for months against Union troops led by the incompetent Banks. The valiant Gardner's position, however, was now desperate, for Grierson's cavalry in May and June had severed his communications and lines of supply. When news of Pemberton's capitulation reached him, Gardner realized his own situation was hopeless, and on July 8, surrendered to Banks.[82]

Gardner asked to meet Grierson, the instigator of so much trouble in the area surrounding Port Hudson. After asking many questions, including some about the Mississippi raid, Gardner observed: "The trouble was, my men ambushed you where you did not go; they waited for you till morning while you passed in the night."[83]

With Port Hudson in federal hands, Grant renewed his efforts to pry Grierson loose from Banks. On July 10 he telegraphed, "I am very much in want of cavalry and Grierson to command them."[84] Sherman, laying waste far and wide between Vicksburg and Jackson, also wanted Grierson's services. On July 13, he inquired of Grant: "Cannot Grierson be brought up here. In a month he could make the State of Mississippi forever useless to the rebels."[85] With Grant and Sherman both applying pressure, Banks at last yielded, though reluctantly. On July 18 he issued orders transferring Grierson and his cavalry to Grant's command.[86]

Grierson left Port Hudson on the steamer *Imperial* with twenty-two Confederate officers, prisoners of war, in his charge. Grant gave him a warm welcome at Vicksburg and a guided tour of the fortifications. After discussing options with Grant, Grierson expressed a desire to return to Tennessee. His wish was granted, and he was ordered to report to Hurlbut at Memphis. As he rode through rows of cotton bales and other cargo to reboard the *Imperial*, Ben was kicked on the right knee by the horse given to him in New Orleans, and suffered a painful injury. Only the high cavalry boots prevented more serious damage.[87]

When he reached Memphis, a delighted Hurlbut appointed him chief of cavalry for the Sixteenth Army Corps, a three-brigade command of some eighty-six hundred officers and men. Grierson's principal task was to prevent enemy disruption of supplies and communications in west Tennessee. Pleased with his new responsibilities, Grierson, with the aid of Adjutant Woodward, set about at once to establish his headquarters, though hampered by constant pain in his knee. He was unable to mount a horse, and even riding in a carriage caused much discomfort.[88]

Once settled into his official duties, Ben made haste to lease quarters and make arrangements to bring his family to Memphis. It had been almost four months since he had last seen Alice and the children, and now the opportunity was at hand to have them with him indefinitely.

CHAPTER 5

Frustration, Defeat and Final Victory

I N THE summer of 1863, the fate of the Confederacy was decided, though few persons either North or South realized it at the time. The fall of Vicksburg and Port Hudson gave control of the Mississippi to the Union and severed Texas, Arkansas, and Louisiana from their sister states. Robert E. Lee, after soundly defeating "Fighting Joe" Hooker at Chancellorsville in May, invaded Pennsylvania with the finest organization of fighting men the South could muster. During the first three days of July, he met and fought the Army of the Potomac under Major General George G. Meade at Gettysburg. When fierce Confederate assaults on strong Union positions failed to dislodge the Federals, Lee was forced to lead his battered army back to Virginia on July 4, the same day that the Vicksburg fortress surrenderd to Grant.

The twin losses at Vicksburg and Gettysburg were death blows to the Southern cause. Thereafter it was only a matter of time until the Confederacy would be forced to yield. Myopic Union strategy and Southern valor, however, conspired to prolong the war, and the bitter struggle continued for almost two more years. Union strength was frittered away on unnecessary efforts such as Banks's campaign to conquer Texas and Halleck's piecemeal breakup of Grant's army to garrison conquered territory. Not until Grant became general-in-chief in March, 1864, did the North adopt the single-minded strategy essential to ending the war—the destruction of the armies of Lee and Johnston.

At the height of his career in the latter part of 1863, Ben Grierson would fall victim to the nearly constant shuffling of troops and commanders and find his new and hard-earned star tarnished by agonizing defeat in campaigns over which he would have little or no control. In the summer of 1863, however, he assigned the brigades under his command to strategic points along the Memphis

and Charleston Railroad to fend off enemy raiders seeking to enter
west Tennessee. Once these troops were in position, Grierson, always eager to see his family, applied for a leave. a request that
was reluctantly denied by Hurlbut. Rumors abounded that Bedford
Forrest was planning a raid, and if this proved true, Hurlbut wanted
Grierson to direct field operations against the wily Confederate.[1]

Ben, in extreme discomfort from his injured knee, wrote Alice
to join him in Memphis, and grew impatient when she failed to
appear. Alice, meanwhile, assuming that Ben would certainly receive a leave, had gone to visit her parents in Chicago pending
his arrival. Ben became increasingly restive each day that she failed
to appear. When he discovered her whereabouts, for once his temper
flared, as he dashed off a letter that left no doubt as to his feelings.

> If this letter should find you at Jacksonville, Chicago or in the State of
> Michigan or some other pleasant state—and you should prefer remaining
> there to coming to see me here at Memphis—I hope you will do so—as
> I would always regret that any wish of mine should deprive you of any
> pleasure.[2]

Stunned by her husband's anger, Alice made immediate preparations to leave for Memphis, when tragedy, no stranger to the Grierson family, intervened. Dysentery "of the worst form" struck the
youngest children of Ben's sister Susan. On August 8, Ettie Fuller,
age two, died; and six days later, three-year-old Albert also succumbed. These were bitter losses for the Fullers. The older child
had delighted both parents and relatives alike with a remarkable
ability to sing and whistle patriotic songs, while Ettie had charmed
her mother, by constantly admonishing her to "mind her baby,"
who was also "mother's bird." As Louisa Semple confided to Ben,
"these sounds ring in the memory and make the outer silence terrible."[3]

As the close-knit Grierson family rallied to Susan's support, Alice
at last left to join her husband. She, along with Charlie and Robert,
made it as far as Cairo where they boarded a packet for Memphis.
After several false starts and numerous delays, they arrived at their
destination where they were greeted by an almost frantic Ben. For
weeks he had hobbled down to the landing each day, where he sat
for hours, anxiously awaiting their arrival and praying that each
steamboat brought his family.

Now that the waiting was over, any strain between Ben and Alice
evaporated "for it was well understood by both," Ben recorded

later, "that no lack of affection between us had caused the delay, and that all which had been done seemed best at the time." Shortly thereafter, the division surgeon, finding that his knee was not mending properly, ordered him to take a twenty-day leave to hasten the recuperation.[4]

When Ben and his family arrived in Jacksonville, he was greeted with a hero's welcome, complete with bands playing "Home Again" and "Welcome to General Grierson" set to the tune of "Scots wa hae." In addition there were speeches, a parade, and a formal reception. Among the many gifts presented was a "rich and elegant service of solid silver." Later Ben, resplendent in a new uniform, received resounding applause from an overflow crowd when he addressed them with patriotic fervor, while deprecating his own achievements. No longer did his Jacksonville neighbors perceive him simply as their local music teacher. Instead, he had assumed a new stature in their eyes—that of military hero. One citizen summarized the change this way: "Twelve years ago a man came among us and commenced teaching a brass band. . . . I knew him to be open, simple-hearted, earnest and I take credit to myself today for seeing then and saying so, that there was far more in him than bugle-blowing."[5]

In mid-October, Alice and the children returned with Ben to Memphis, where they took up residence in a comfortable suburban home. During the day, Ben's energies were given over entirely to drilling and inspecting his command in preparation for a spring offensive. But when evening arrived, he yielded to his wife's admonitions to set aside time for activities with his children.

Alice worried constantly that neither she nor Ben was providing Charlie and Robert with the quality of care desirable in a Christian home. Her failure, she felt, was due to a lack of stamina; her other domestic duties were so pressing that she had too little energy to give her children all the attention and teaching they required. As for Ben, his military duties separated him from his family so often that when they were together it was important to Alice that Ben compensate as much as possible for past absences. When he was cooperative, then she was inclined to make her own concessions. Aware of his love for the theater, she softened her attitude to the extent of attending a number of "not very well performed comedies."[6]

A frequent visitor to the Griersons' home was General Sherman, newly appointed as commanding general of the Department and Army of Tennessee, Grant's old command. In October, the latter had been named commanding general of the Military Division of the Mississippi, which included the Armies of Ohio, the Cumberland, and Tennessee. Grant established headquarters at Chattanooga, where Union forces under Major General William S. Rosecrans, were under virtual siege by a Confederate army under Major General Braxton Bragg.

After bringing up reinforcements, including Sherman and his units from the Army of Tennessee, Grant attacked the strong Confederate positions. After two days of savage fighting, resulting in heavy casualties on both sides, Bragg retreated on November 25. Grant's victory at Chattanooga opened the way for the Union invasion of Atlanta, only a hundred miles away, a major objective.

Since a secure line of supply was essential to the success of the federal campaign, Grant was concerned about strikes by gray raiders in his rear, most notably by the redoubtable Bedford Forrest. His concern was not unfounded. Forrest and his superior, Major General Stephen D. Lee, commander of all cavalry in Mississippi, were planning widespread raids into Tennessee to round up cattle and horses, secure recruits, and disrupt Union communications and supply lines.[7]

Early in December, Forrest, with a few hundred men, crossed the Memphis and Charleston Railroad at Saulsbury, some sixty miles east of Memphis, and headed for Jackson, which he planned to use as a center for his activities. To distract attention from Forrest, Lee conducted demonstrations between Corinth and Memphis. Hurlbut ordered Grierson to move on Forrest from the west, while other columns converged from the north and south. Grant sent his chief of cavalry, Brigadier General William Sooy Smith, with five regiments from middle Tennessee to close from the east.[8]

Interception of so elusive a foe as Forrest was difficult under the best conditions. Now Union efforts were hampered by cold, driving rain that turned to sleet and snow. Lee's detachments pinned down many of Grierson's troopers, and Forrest, as was his custom, threw out many small parties in all directions to raid, harass, and screen the movement of the main body. Grierson, still handicapped by his injured knee and forced to conduct most of the operations of his cavalry from a desk in Memphis, fretted over the conflicting reports of enemy strength and movement that came from the field.[9]

For more than three weeks, in an ocean of mud and water, small columns in blue and gray maneuvered and clashed in a confusing swirl of engagements at Saulsbury, Estenaula, Collierville, LaFayette

Station, and Moscow. At the latter place, the gallant Colonel Hatch, a close friend of Grierson, was badly, though not mortally wounded. Smith's two battalions, slowed by the weather and a tardy start, played no role in the fighting, for they did not arrive in the vicinity of Memphis until January 8.[10]

Forrest, after gathering up several hundred recruits and a large herd of cattle and horses, managed to weave his way through the swarm of bluecoats and reached safety behind the Coldwater on December 27. Chagrined, Grierson must, nonetheless, have been reminded of his own success in eluding Confederate pursuers earlier in the year.[11]

With Forrest at least temporarily out of west Tennessee, Sherman planned to lead a strong force of infantry across Mississippi from Vicksburg to Meridian. A swift-moving cavalry column was to strike the Mobile and Ohio Railroad in northern Mississippi and move down that road to join him at Meridian. From that point, the combined command would move on east to Selma, Alabama, and destroy the large arsenals and foundries there. Grierson expected to lead the cavalry forces, but Smith outranked him and desired the command for himself. Sherman preferred Grierson, for he believed Smith indecisive, but he was unwilling to offend Grant's chief of cavalry.[12]

Grierson, believing that two brigadiers were unnecessary for the expedition, felt he would be only a "supernumerary." Sherman, however, pointed out that Smith, unfamiliar with the country to be traversed, would need advice. Sherman also assured Ben that when Meridian was reached, he would send Smith back to Grant and give Grierson command of the cavalry column. Grierson argued no further, but inwardly he still felt slighted, for he considered himself better qualified than Smith to lead a fast-striking, independent command. Events of the next few weeks proved him right.[13]

Before departing for Vicksburg, Sherman ordered Smith to start for Meridian by February 1. He also warned him to be prepared to deal with Forrest, who undoubtedly would attack with "vehemence" at some point along the way. It was essential that Smith not only repel that attack, but make every effort to destroy Forrest's entire force. Smith, after expressing a keen desire to close with Forrest, promised Sherman that he would attain the desired outcome.[14]

Sherman reached Vicksburg on February 1 and two days later launched twenty-thousand men eastward for a swift march to Meridian. Brushing aside weak and sporadic attacks by Wirt Adams's cavalry, he reached and burned Jackson on February 7 and a week later entered Meridian, which had been evacuated by Confederate defenders. There was no sign of Smith, and Sherman spent the next five days laying waste to the city and the railroads in the vicinity. "Meridian," he wrote, "with its depots, storehouses, arsenals, hospitals, offices, hotels, and cantonments, no longer exists."[15] But, on February 20, when Smith still had not appeared, Sherman abandoned the idea of an advance on Selma and instead, began his return to Vicksburg.

Smith, meanwhile, had begun concentrating his three brigades of cavalry at Collierville, near Memphis, shortly after receiving his orders from Sherman and soon had his Second and Third Brigades on hand. The First Brigade, under Colonel George E. Waring, Jr., marching from Union City, Tennessee, was delayed by washed out bridges and flooded streams. Nonetheless, Smith decided to wait, a mistake, as it turned out, for Waring did not arrive until February 8, and by that time his animals were entirely worn out. Smith delayed another three days in order to give Waring's command some rest. Thus it was not until February 11, a day after he was supposed to have reached Meridian, that he and his force of seventy-five hundred men were finally underway.[16]

Grierson and his staff, by Smith's order, rode with the Second Brigade, Hatch's command, though because of the latter's wound it was now led by Lieutenant Colonel William P. Hepburn. This placed Grierson on the right flank of the march and out of immediate contact with Smith. Progress was slow, for the roads were in poor condition caused by heavy rains. Smith's insistence on carrying out widespread destruction along the way, coupled with encouraging slaves to desert from plantations and join the column, slowed their movements even further.[17]

As the command slogged southeast toward West Point on the railroad, Smith became increasingly nervous and wary. On the evening of February 17, seven days late for his junction with Sherman, he called a conference of his officers. Given the scouting reports of a Confederate concentration at West Point, he now harbored serious reservations about proceeding farther. Grierson urged Smith to continue and received approval to cut loose with the Second Brigade and make a dash for Meridian. Before Ben could get underway, however, Smith changed his mind and ordered Grierson to remain with the rest of the command.[18]

On February 20, the advance reached West Point, where it encountered its first resistance. After a sharp skirmish, the graycoats withdrew and Smith occupied the town, but all his initial eagerness had vanished. Believing that Forrest had set a trap for him along the streams and swamps south of West Point, he was convinced that defeat awaited him. Ben believed Smith "absolutely sick and unable to properly command in such an emergency." Close to midnight, Smith called another conference, and despite Grierson's advice to push on southward along the railroad, announced his decision to return to Memphis.[19]

Next morning, on February 21, Smith began his retreat, encumbered by some three thousand blacks who had joined his lines. If he believed he could return unmolested, he was badly mistaken. Forrest, outnumbered nearly two to one, had been prepared to attack south of West Point. Once convinced that Smith was actually in retreat, he moved to assail the federals on both flanks and in the rear.

Grierson and the Second Brigade, acting as rear guard, managed to fight off the attacks and stall pursuit about four miles north of West Point. As night fell, Forrest halted to rest his command, but Smith continued northward until 2 A.M. before feeding and resting. He was underway again at daybreak, with his Tennessee brigade protecting the rear and Grierson leading the advance.[20]

Forrest caught up near Okolona and attacked. One of the Tennessee units broke under the pressure, abandoned five field guns, and fled precipitously, throwing the entire rear guard into confusion. What had been an orderly retreat became a five-mile headlong flight that ended only when Grierson took charge and, with battalions from the First and Second brigades formed in line of battle, let the runaways pass through and took Forrest's charge. A furious, hour-long action followed, with heavy losses on both sides. Among those who died was Forrest's brother Jeffry, who had been killed leading an attack.

After the attack was beaten off, Smith resumed his retreat and Forrest gave up the pursuit. Smith did not pause to rest, but pushed on headlong for Memphis, which he reached on February 26. His return had required only half the time of his outward march. According to Colonel Waring, the retreat to Memphis was "a weary, disheartened, almost panic-stricken flight."[21] In addition to more than three hundred casualties, Smith had also lost more than two thousand animals.

A disgusted Grierson retrieved his command from a thoroughly chastened Smith, who, in turn, was censured by an outraged Sherman. To the end of his days Grierson believed he could have gone on with the Second Brigade and joined Sherman at Meridian. He also felt that had Smith chosen to fight at any point, he could have defeated Forrest.[22]

With Ben in the field, Alice and the children had gone to visit her parents, who were spending a few weeks at the "Kirkarian Farm" in Pennsylvania. She kept well informed on military operations, for her father, an avid reader of newspapers, subscribed to the *Pittsburgh Gazette* and the *Chicago Tribune,* among others. While Smith's fiasco was upsetting, Alice was relieved that Ben had escaped unscathed from the campaign. As usual, however, it was not simply his physical safety that concerned her. While her husband had been in the military now for almost three years, this fact had not dispelled her fear that the immoral influences of army life would corrupt his character.[23]

He assured her that he was not involved in the drinking that was so widespread, but Alice desired more. "I can't help wishing that you would give your influence more strongly against the use of all sorts of liquors." There were other steps he was to take as well. As long as they were apart, she enjoined him to avoid the theater as an unhealthy environment.[24]

At this point Ben made it clear that he had received enough advice for the present. Gently but firmly he again informed Alice that there was one subject on which she could set her mind at ease. Not only was he not drinking now, but he had no intention of doing so in the future. But when it came to attending plays, that was a different matter entirely. "I go to the theatre occasionally and presume I will continue to do so while I remain and do not think it is wrong." Ben hastened to add that recently he had done some thinking about his character, and he had come to a novel conclusion. On balance, he was a pretty good fellow after all.[25] Considering that Ben was depressed over what he regarded as Smith's disgraceful behavior, as well as the rundown condition of his command, he had suffered his wife's lectures in good humor.

Toward the end of March, Forrest again struck in west Tennessee and Kentucky and caught Grierson's cavalry in woeful condition. Military policy provided furloughs for veterans whose enlistments were expiring—probably wise in encouraging re-enlistments—but Grierson's ranks were sorely depleted. His old regiments, the Sixth and Seventh Illinois and the Second Iowa, all filled with veterans, were reduced to mere skeletons of their former strength. In the entire District of West Tennessee, Grierson could count only twenty-two hundred men, many of whom were raw recruits, and even these were poorly armed and mounted.[26]

Forrest, throwing out small detachments in all directions, pushed into Tennessee on March 14. At Jackson, he sent one regiment northwest to Union City, where a timid Union commander surrendered without a fight. Forrest, with the main body, marched north to Paducah, drove the garrison there into a fortified work on the outskirts, and sacked the city.

After consolidating most of his far-flung units, Forrest moved against Fort Pillow, on the Mississippi some forty miles above Memphis. Here, on April 12, he assaulted the fort and, after savage, close-quarter fighting, forced the garrison to surrender. Of 557 federal defenders, 221 were killed. Of 226 black soldiers in the garrison, 168 were either killed or wounded, and Forrest was accused, perhaps unjustly, of condoning a massacre. From Fort Pillow, Forrest returned loaded with booty to the comparative safety of northern Mississippi.[27]

Forrest's successful raid left both Grierson and his superior, Hurlbut, mortified, but there was little they could do. Many of Hurlbut's troops had been transferred to Sherman's army for the invasion of Georgia, leaving the District of West Tennessee painfully short of manpower. Grierson, under orders to intercept and attack Forrest "at all hazards," was hard pressed, with the cavalry available, even to fend off small bands of raiders in the vicinity of Memphis. Alice, well aware from his letters of the condition of his cavalry, hoped Ben would not have to fight Forrest with the "odds and ends of your cavalry."[28]

If Alice was sympathetic and understanding concerning her husband's problems, General Sherman was far less charitable. Upset by what he regarded as a lack of initiative and aggressiveness on the part of both Hurlbut and Grierson, he replaced the former with Major General C. C. Washburn. Then he ordered Brigadier General Samuel D. Sturgis, Commander of the Cavalry in the Department of Ohio, to Memphis with instructions to take command of "all cavalry at or near Memphis" and conduct a campaign of complete destruction against Forrest. Sherman had no intention of allowing his lines of supply and communications to become vulnerable to Forrest's raids.[29]

Washburn and Sturgis soon discovered that Hurlbut and Grierson

General William T. Sherman. *Courtesy National Archives.*

had not exaggerated conditions in their district. Grierson could now mount less than two thousand troopers, and of these, three hundred had mounts that would not last "over a three day march." Ben requested a leave to return to Illinois to "reorganize, equip, arm and mount the regiments of my old division." When his appeal was denied, he wrote despairingly to Alice that the forthcoming Sturgis campaign would have no better outcome than Smith's.[30] Unfortunately, Ben's prophecy proved correct.

Brigadier General Samuel D. Sturgis. *Courtesy National Archives.*

Both Washburn and Sturgis appealed for reinforcements, and these were forthcoming. By late May, Sturgis had assembled near Memphis three brigades of infantry totalling five thousand men and two of cavalry under Grierson numbering thirty-three hundred. In addition, and much to Ben's dismay, Sturgis had five batteries of artillery with twenty-two guns, 250 wagons loaded with supplies and ammunition, as well as a number of ambulances and other conveyances.[31] Ben felt that if success were to be achieved, it could only be done by strong and mobile cavalry columns living off the country and unencumbered by a slow-moving train of wagons.

On June 1 the long column left Memphis and pushed southeastward into Mississippi, heading for the Mobile and Ohio Railroad. On the second day out, heavy rain began to fall, turning the roads into rivers of mud and slowing the march to a crawl. Averaging scarcely ten miles a day, the advance did not reach Ripley until June 8. Here Sturgis, who had shown little enthusiasm for the expedition from the beginning, asked Grierson and the infantry commander, Colonel William McMillen, if discretion did not require a return to Memphis. Grierson, who had no confidence in Sturgis, agreed, but McMillen argued forcefully that the march should continue, and Sturgis reluctantly decided to go on.[32]

Rain was still falling next day, as the thoroughly soaked command plodded along toward Guntown, some thirty-five miles southeast, where Sturgis planned to strike the railroad. From his saddle, Ben penned a note to Alice, complaining that in nine days of marching only ninety miles had been covered and "the cavalry could have travelled . . . three times that distance."[33] Sturgis halted for the night at Stubb's Farm, fourteen miles east of Guntown, and officers and men welcomed a letup in the rain. A hot June sun would quickly dry out the roads and make the march far less arduous. They were unaware that less than ten miles to their front, Bedford Forrest was preparing to contest their advance. Grierson, however, had forebodings. Concerned about the slow pace which must certainly have allowed Forrest to ascertain the federal strength and concentrate his own forces, Grierson cautioned Sturgis that he was convinced:

> from what I had learned then and the day previous, that the enemy was in large force and not far off and learning that the mules of the train were exhausted and in bad condition, after their great exertions in pulling the heavily loaded wagons through the deep mud, in which they were frequently mired thus far, I advised the General to remain where he was, as the position was a good one, and that in my judgment the

enemy would attack us there if no further advance was made, and our chances of victory would be greatly strengthened if the Infantry and Artillery could be quietly put in position for battle while the Cavalry, unencumbered continues to operate in such a manner as to fully develop the enemy's strength and draw his presence to a general engagement.[34]

Grierson and his two brigades were underway for Guntown at 5:30 A.M. Sturgis, however, unaccountably made a fatal error by allowing the infantry a leisurely breakfast, and his lead brigade did not take to the road until seven o'clock. Thus a muddy gap of five miles separated the cavalry and infantry. After a three-hour march, Grierson reached and crossed a causeway, nearly a mile in length, that spanned the muddy flood plain of rain-swollen Tishomingo Creek. A narrow bridge provided the only means of crossing the stream, and it was almost ten o'clock when the command ascended a slight incline to a small plateau where the road was crossed at right angles by another that led southwest to Pontotoc.

Here, at a small plantation known as "Brice's Crossroads," Grierson halted in order to send patrols along the various roads to probe for any enemy defenders that might be between him and the railroad. The patrol on the east road that led to the little town of Baldwyn, some six miles away, had scarcely covered a mile when gray skirmishers emerged from heavy brush and timber to the front and opened fire. Grierson called in his patrols and established a line of battle on the east slope of the plateau.[35]

After beating off three attacks by increasing numbers of yelling graycoats, Grierson hastened a courier to Sturgis apprising him of the situation and indicating that the cavalry, in a strong position, could hold if the infantry was brought up promptly. Sturgis ordered McMillen to move as rapidly as possible and then galloped to Brice's to take command of the forces then engaged.

Forrest, meanwhile, had begun the action with less than a thousand of his forty-eight hundred men, but all were converging on the battlefield and were thrown into action as they arrived. Never one to fight on the defensive, Forrest ordered charge after charge on the Union positions, but these were repulsed as Sturgis fed his arriving infantry into line, though many of them were exhausted from the heat and speed of their march. Grierson's cavalry, their ammunition nearly depleted after three hours of fighting, pulled out of line to replenish their supply.

Close to five o'clock, after Sturgis had committed his last brigade, Forrest summoned his troops to a final effort and launched coordinated and slashing attacks on the federal front, rear, and both flanks. The bluecoats recoiled and then broke, despite the pistol-in-hand efforts of Sturgis, Grierson, and other officers to hold them in line. According to Sturgis, "The road became crowded and jammed with troops, wagons and artillery sinking into the deep mud, became inextricable, and added to the confusion that now prevailed. No power could control the panic-stricken mass."[36]

The demoralized Federals threw away their guns and packs, abandoned their wagons and ambulances, and fled across the narrow bridge or plunged into the bank-full Tishomingo, while vengeful Confederates, pressing close on their heels, exacted a fearful toll. When the distraught Sturgis reached the far side of the causeway, he was met by Colonel Edward Bouton, commanding a brigade of black infantry. Bouton had rallied his troops and begged Sturgis to supply his men with ammunition and let them fight. Sturgis's only answer was to instruct Bouton to save himself and his men. Grierson was prepared to make a stand at Stubb's Plantation, but, he, too, discovered that Sturgis would think of nothing but escape.

Not until after nightfall did Forrest call a brief halt to the pursuit to rest his weary troops, but by early morning his graycoats were again on the trail of the fleeing Federals. Only when he had driven them beyond Ripley did he turn back to collect the spoils of his greatest victory. He had captured fourteen pieces of artillery, the entire train of 250 wagons, a large supply of ammunition and more than 1,600 prisoners. In addition he had inflicted 617 casualties, bringing Sturgis's total loss to 2,240. Forrest's losses totalled 492 killed and wounded.[37]

Though Forrest gave up the pursuit north of Ripley, Sturgis and his beaten army continued their flight until they boarded trains at Collierville for Memphis on June 13. Their march to Brice's Crossroads had required ten days; their retreat took only three.

A Board of Inquiry was convened to investigate Sturgis's conduct during the expedition amidst charges that he drank heavily on the march and was intoxicated during the battle. Grierson, as well as other officers called to testify, did not support the charge of drunkenness, but Ben's testimony clearly impugned Sturgis's military abilities. Sturgis was cleared of the charges, but saw no further service during the remainder of the war.[38]

On Grierson's part, he had once more shared in an ignominious defeat under a commander in whom he had no confidence. He believed Sturgis lacked aggressiveness and that the large train had stripped the command of essential speed and mobility, thus permitting Forrest not only to accurately assess federal strength but also to concentrate his scattered forces in time to meet the blue advance. Finally, he blamed Sturgis's delay in bringing up the infantry as a key factor in the defeat.[39] Louisa Semple offered her own explanation for the disaster. If Sturgis was not drunk then, "some other evil spirit must have possessed him. I think nothing can redeem him in the eyes of the country."[40]

Stung by the twin failures of Smith and Sturgis and concerned about his lines of supply, Sherman ordered Washburn to send out a force to take care of Forrest regardless of the cost. Washburn, keenly aware of Sherman's concern and his temper, ordered Brigadier General Andrew J. Smith, freshly arrived from Louisiana with two veteran divisions of infantry, to take command of a third expedition into northeastern Mississippi. In addition to Smith's divisions, Washburn added Grierson's division of cavalry and a brigade of black troops under Colonel Bouton for a total of 14,200 officers and men and twenty pieces of artillery.[41]

On July 5, Smith left La Grange, marched to Ripley, and after partially destroying it moved on to New Albany, leaving a wide swath of destruction in his wake. He met the first serious resistance on July 11 at Pontotoc, but a charge by Grierson's cavalry dispersed the enemy. From Pontotoc, with detachments from Forrest's cavalry snapping at his flanks and rear, Smith turned due east and headed for Tupelo on the Mobile and Ohio Railroad. On the evening of July 13, he encamped at Harrisburg about one mile from the railroad.[42]

Forrest, aware from the beginning of Smith's strength and intentions, had concentrated some six thousand men at Okolona to contest Smith's advance. He was, however, cautioned by his superior, Major General Stephen D. Lee, to avoid a battle until reinforcements arrived. Lee in person brought up two thousand men and a trap was set for Smith at Okolona. Smith's eastward march to Tupelo caused a change in plans, and, with Lee in command, the Confederates moved to Harrisburg and made dispositions to attack at dawn. Forrest was reluctant to make the assault, for Smith had entrenched his encampment and was in a strong position, but Lee overruled him. Forrest found himself, though he would not have made the comparison, in a position similar to that of Grierson under

Sooy Smith and Sturgis—less than eager for an encounter under the circumstances.[43]

Early on the morning of July 14, Grierson led his division east to Tupelo, took the city and immediately began destroying the Mobile and Ohio for miles north and south. Smith, his infantry posted in combat readiness on a knoll, was ready to receive an attack if and when it came. The wait was not a long one. Shortly after six o'clock the assault began with "Forrest's characteristic impetuosity," but the entrenched Federals mowed down the attackers. Four wild charges failed to dislodge the bluecoats and left Confederate dead and wounded piled in heaps before the Union lines, some within thirty yards of Union positions. Near noon the attacks ceased, and quiet descended on the blood-soaked field. The afternoon was spent in caring for the wounded and burying the dead.[44]

Late in the afternoon, when the renewed Confederate attack was easily beaten off, Smith decided that his mission had been accomplished. Grierson had torn up ten miles of railroad, and Forrest had suffered a severe defeat. Now, with federal supplies and ammunition running low, a return to Memphis seemed in order. On the morning of July 15, Smith began retracing his steps, fending off with ease graycoat attempts to disrupt his march.[45]

On reaching Memphis, Smith felt he had done well. He had lost 650 killed, wounded, and missing, while Forrest admitted to 153 killed, 794 wounded and 49 missing, though his losses could have been higher. But if Smith was satisfied, Sherman was far from pleased. Forrest remained a threat that must be destroyed, and Smith was ordered to undertake another expedition for that purpose.[46]

Meanwhile, Alice and the children had arrived in Memphis for a visit, but they saw little of Ben. Under orders to take the field once more with Smith, he was required to spend long hours getting his command in readiness, and Alice found time on her hands. She was reluctant to leave the house for fear Ben might manage a few hours of freedom. She also felt that it was unsafe to tour the city, even with other army wives. "I did think some of going out with Mrs. Kendrick but Lieutenants Redfern & Pike thought I had better not go . . . as a train had so lately been fired into." Despite the drawbacks, however, she was determined to remain in Memphis, at least until Ben returned from the expedition.[47]

Smith concentrated eighteen thousand effectives, including Grierson's cavalry, at Grand Junction east of Memphis. Early in August he marched into Mississippi, but this time, in an effort to pull

Forrest westward away from Sherman's rear, Smith moved down the Mississippi Central Railroad. By August 8, he had taken Holly Springs and forced a crossing of the Tallahatchie at the expense of a portion of Forrest's army. The next day, after sharp skirmishing, Grierson entered Oxford, and thus far all had gone well.

Forrest had awaited developments at Okolona, but finally satisfied that Smith intended to move through central Mississippi, he left with the rest of his command for Oxford, and Grierson was forced to retire and rejoin Smith near the Tallahatchie. Heavy August rains stalled both the blue and the gray and gave a badly outnumbered Forrest time to devise a means of frustrating Smith's advance. Late on August 18, Forrest, with two thousand picked men, skirted Smith's right flank and headed for Memphis.[48]

At 4 a.m. on Sunday morning, August 21, Forrest dashed into the city virtually unopposed. Pandemonium broke out as gray raiders raced through the streets and took up positions at strategic points. General Washburn managed to escape capture only by fleeing in his nightshirt. John Grierson, awakened by the rattle of gunfire, recorded that, "the Rebs passed through the city with impunity."

For a few hours the raiders enjoyed the "freedom of the city," but Forrest, aware that he must retire before reinforcements arrived, sounded the recall and by nine o'clock was racing southward. He had accomplished his objective, however, for alarmed federal officials demanded protection. Smith was obliged to call off his invasion and instead throw a ring of defense around the city.

While Sooy Smith and Samuel Sturgis had suffered defeat at the hands of Forrest, and the second Smith had achieved only limited success, the three had occupied Forrest to the extent of keeping him away from Sherman's communications and lines of supply. Ben Grierson, chafing under slow-moving and timid commanders, had carried out his responsibilities as best he could, fearing all the while that he would become a scapegoat. At the same time, he longed for an opportunity once more to lead an independent command. That chance would come, but not before he spent another four months in frustrated obedience to orders from higher headquarters. A private in the ranks of Grierson's cavalry, in a letter to his family, expressed feelings that were very similar to Ben's:

Surrounding circumstances are so dismal as to unnerve the soul for such an undertaking as letter writing. We fit [*sic*] all day yesterday with a cavalry loss of about 50 k.w. & m. but although the rebs *of course* lost a much larger number we don't feel very jolly—because the battle was useless. I am bored in the superratty manner.[50]

But Grierson had little time to worry about his career. His command, the Cavalry Corps of the District of West Tennessee, consisting of two divisions under Hatch and Colonel E. F. Winslow, Fourth Iowa, had returned from the expedition in poor condition. He had virtually no ammunition and his troopers were ragged and badly in need of clothing. Since there was no forage for the animals, they were fed green corn. Always concerned about the welfare of his men and determined to have his divisions in a state of instant readiness, Grierson spared neither himself nor his staff in providing equipment for his command.[51]

Sherman's drive into Georgia, even with Forrest occupied elsewhere, proceeded slowly because of the defensive genius of Joseph Johnston. He fought a series of delaying actions with Sherman in May and June, as he retired toward Atlanta and prepared extensive entrenchments to defend the city. The Davis administration, however, dissatisfied with Johnston's tactics, did Sherman an enormous favor by replacing him with General John B. Hood. Hood incautiously left Johnston's carefully prepared works and assailed Sherman at Peachtree Creek, only to lose the battle. Atlanta came under siege, and Hood was forced to evacuate the city on September 1. Sherman occupied it the following day.

Though he had not destroyed Hood's army, Sherman, after several weeks of preparation, launched his "march to the sea." To counter this move, Hood, deciding that he would operate in Sherman's rear, drove his army into Tennessee. This turn of events cast a long shadow over Ben Grierson's plans and dashed for the present his hopes of again achieving distinction.

In October, with his division in good condition once more, Grierson wrote Sherman complaining about his service under Sooy Smith and Sturgis, and asked for an opportunity to take the field "untrammeled." He received an encouraging reply, which Sherman signed "your sincere friend." But a need for reinforcements in Tennessee and in Missouri all but destroyed Grierson's command.

On October 14, Ben received orders from General O. O. Howard, commanding the Army of Tennessee, to forward Hatch's division to the vicinity of Rome, Georgia, and to "keep your own division in best possible condition ready for a movement through Mississippi, Alabama, and Georgia to join cavalry corps there."[52] Howard explained that Hatch's move had been ordered in part to counter raids by Forrest and General Joseph Wheeler into Tennessee.

The order was a blow to Grierson. Previously, under instructions from Washburn, he had dispatched most of Winslow's division to Missouri and Arkansas, where last-gasp operations by Sterling Price had aroused concern. Now Howard was taking a full division, leaving Grierson with fewer than two thousand men. Ben, of course, obeyed orders, but he could not resist a bitter reply to Howard:

> I have worked hard for the past six months to place my command in condition for the field and, in spite of several unsuccessful expeditions made by General Sturgis and others who were sent here to command my troops, I had at length succeeded in organizing, mounting, and arming my entire force and at the time my command was scattered, I had the finest and most effective cavalry command in the West.[53]

Grierson understood the need for additional troops in Tennessee to counter Hood. His objection was simply that he wanted to command a corps that he regarded as his own and not have it assigned piecemeal to others.

Disheartened and feeling unappreciated, he applied for a leave of absence, which Washburn approved, and took his family to Chicago for a visit with Alice's parents. The trip was not entirely social, for Ben, a dedicated officer, spent a part of his time securing two thousand remounts for Winslow's cavalry. He was unaware that orders had been received in Memphis transferring both him and his division to General George Thomas at Nashville.

When Ben returned to Memphis in mid-November, he found himself in difficulty with Thomas and Sherman's new chief of cavalry, Major General James H. Wilson. Wilson, angry at what he regarded as a deliberate disobedience of orders, questioned the legitimacy of Grierson's leave and demanded to know why Grierson was not in Nashville with his division. Ben, not easily intimidated, responded to Wilson in clear and measured words. The leave had been approved by his superior, General Washburn, and he had remounted Winslow's cavalry while away. Further, how could he possibly bring his division to Nashville when it was scattered from Missouri to Tennessee. The few troopers in the vicinity of Memphis were held there on specific orders from General Washburn.[54]

As Grierson and Wilson engaged in this exchange, Hood attacked a portion of Thomas's army at Franklin and suffered a bloody repulse. Two weeks later, On December 15 and 16, Thomas took the offensive and routed Hood at the Battle of Nashville. As the battered Confederates retreated they depended for supplies and equipment on the Mobile and Ohio Railroad, long a target for Union raiders, and at last Grierson was given the opportunity for which he had both prayed and begged.

Under orders from Major General N. J. T. Dana, Washburn's replacement at Memphis, Grierson readied his division for a strike at the Mobile and Ohio. His command numbered thirty-five hundred men organized in three brigades under colonels Joseph Karge, E. D. Osband, and Winslow. In addition, fifty blacks were formed into a "Pioneer Corps" to repair roads and bridges. Pack mules carried rations and other essential supplies—no ponderous slow-moving wagons for Ben Grierson—this command would move swiftly and live off the country.

On December 21, in "wretched weather," Grierson got underway "without a wheel to cumber their difficult and dangerous mission."[55] Despite heavy rain and knee-deep mud, the long column swept southeastward over terrain thoroughly familiar to Grierson. After passing through Ripley, strong detachments were sent to Booneville and Guntown on the Mobile and Ohio to tear up track while the main body converged on Tupelo. When his detachments came in, Grierson marched swiftly south, leaving a destroyed railroad in his rear.

On Christmas Eve, in a cold, driving rain, Grierson launched a surprise attack on Forrest's huge dismounted camp at Verona. Disorganized gray defenders were driven off and the camp taken with ease. The exultant raiders began the work of devastation immediately. They burned two trains of sixteen cars each, loaded with supplies for Hood, and destroyed two hundred wagons that Forrest had taken from Sturgis, as well as eight warehouses, and four thousand new English carbines. They then exploded a vast supply of shells, creating a fireworks display that continued into Christmas Day.

With the work of destruction completed, Grierson resumed his march south along the railroad toward Egypt Station. He knew from wires tapped at Okolona that the Confederates intended holding that place "at all costs."[56] On the morning of December 28, Grierson reached Egypt and launched his attack. He met instant and stiff resistance and a savage firefight developed. As the fighting raged, two trains with reinforcements appeared in the south, and Grierson threw two regiments into the path of the oncoming trains and drove them off.

For two hours the Confederates held out, but a final blue assault carried the station. Five hundred graycoats surrendered, while others fled into the trees and brush along the tracks. After setting a torch to the station and a fourteen-car train, Grierson turned west and headed for the Mississippi Central Railroad. He passed through Houston, crossed the route of his previous raid, and sent detachments far and wide while the main column struck the railroad at Winona. A shoe factory was burned at Bankston, and Grenada was heavily damaged. Continuing west, Grierson drove off a brigade of Wirt Adams's cavalry at Franklin and reached Vicksburg on January 5.

In summarizing his sixteen-day, 450-mile raid through eastern and central Mississippi, Grierson listed as destroyed 100 miles of railroad track, 20,000 feet of bridges, 20 miles of telegraph lines, four locomotives and tenders, 95 railroad cars, 300 army wagons, 32 warehouses, 5,000 stands of new arms, and 500 bales of cotton. He took 600 prisoners, 800 head of stock and brought in 1,000 blacks. All this was accomplished at a cost of 27 officers and men killed, 93 wounded and seven missing.[57]

More important, Grierson had effectively cut off Hood from desperately needed supplies and delivered a savage blow to confederate sources in Mississippi. Ben Grierson "untrammeled" was a fearsome antagonist, and General Dana believed the raid "second to none in the war."[58] Certainly Grierson was vindicated in his belief that swift movement, surprise, and the concentration of fire-power at the point of attack were keys to success. He had also proved that Grant and Sherman had erred in assigning Grierson's cavalry to the likes of Sooy Smith and Samuel Sturgis.

When Ben returned to Memphis, he telegraphed the Adjutant General in Washington, asking to be given parts of his command, notably the Sixth and Seventh Illinois and the Second Iowa. With these troops, "I would be willing to undertake the destruction of every railroad and arsenal and depot of supplies in possession of the enemy."[59] The answer, however, was an order sending Grierson and his division to Louisville, Kentucky, a transfer that would disrupt the harmony of the Grierson household for several months.

Alice wanted to accompany her husband, but Ben very quickly vetoed the idea. Uncertain as to how long he would be stationed in Louisville, he felt that it was not feasible to take his wife and children with him. Alice, interpreting this as a personal affront, withdrew into herself and spent a great deal of time brooding and weeping. And Ben, who hated confrontations, especially among family members, tried the approach of ignoring the issue, hoping that, in time, Alice would become reconciled to his decision and the dissension would pass.

This was the wrong strategy to use with Alice. The problem did not go away; instead it festered. At such times Alice tended to conjure up all the real and imagined marital injuries she had ever sustained. Her ability to recall in minute detail events that had happened years earlier was impressive. By the time she had packed her belongings to take the children back to Jacksonville, she was angry at Ben over a long list of what she considered delinquencies.[60] But her husband, preoccupied with military matters, either failed to notice or chose not to acknowledge her coolness. Inside she smoldered.

While she longed to be with her husband after their many separations, Alice had other reasons that accounted for her reluctance to return to Jacksonville and resume sharing her father-in-law's home. The death of his wife had not improved the older man's disposition. Robert, now given to periods of despondency, often barricaded himself in his room and insisted on taking his meals alone. When he did join Alice and the boys, other problems were created, for plainly he favored his namesake. Young Robert, "one of the most charming little mortals," was a bright, inquisitive child, who, even at age four, possessed an appealing personality. "Such a childlike child, and yet so brimming with thought" was the way his Aunt Louisa described him.[61]

Nine-year-old Charlie, by contrast, tried everyone's forebearance. Always in motion, he was constantly bumping into furniture and frequently falling down and injuring himself. A few months earlier he had chipped his two front teeth while playing at the "Kirkarian Farm." His incessant activity was accompanied by almost equally incessant chatter, with the result that Charlie often incurred his grandfather's wrath. Alice considered much of grandfather Robert's anger unjustified and, in true maternal fashion, defended her son.[62]

Alice had another problem; once again she was expecting a child. With the exception of Robert, each succeeding pregnancy was more difficult to accept. She consoled herself that this time the infant might be a girl, but the thought of facing childbirth in August, followed by almost a year of nursing afterward, left her irritable and prone to tears.[63] Under these circumstances, she felt that Ben should have been more considerate of her feelings.

Her return to Jacksonville proved a miserable experience. At Decatur, the full waiting room compelled some women, including

Alice, to sit on the floor, where it was impossible to escape the puddles of tobacco spit. The train arrived six hours late and was so crowded that Alice was forced to hold Robert on her lap throughout the entire trip. At Jacksonville, no one met her at the station, for, after waiting for hours, grandfather Robert had gone to spend the night at his daughter Susan's home. Alice, loaded with baggage and coaxing two tired children behind her, trudged wearily home, only to find the house dark and cold.[64] Small wonder that she vented her feelings to Ben in a long letter, tracing "the clouded atmosphere" to his "thoughtless inconsideration of my feelings & wishes, or the aversion to the bother of finding out what they are."[65]

She delineated a long catalog of grievances stretching all the way back to the time Ben had failed to pay Kirkie sufficient attention before his death. More recently, Ben's complaint that moving his family to Louisville would be expensive was absurd, given the amounts he had wasted on cigars, liquors, and billiards. But uppermost in Alice's mind was the concern she felt over the kind of home she and Ben were providing for their children. Sons especially required the influence of a father, but even when they were together, in her view, Ben still failed to allot a sufficient amount of his "leisure time to the *care & teaching* of our boys." There was no point in looking to Ben's father to rectify this situation, for Robert was "acting just as he pleased, without regard to his family or friends." Clearly Alice was sorely wounded, and it would be many weeks before she would allow Ben the privilege of a forgiving and loving letter.[66]

Fortunately for Ben's spirits, he did not receive Alice's letter for nearly a month. His stay in Louisville was brief, for he received orders on February 8 to report personally to General Grant in Washington. When he arrived, Grant congratulated him on the success of his recent raid and then informed a happy Grierson that he would be promoted to Brevet Major General. Grant then took Ben to see President Lincoln, where Ben enjoyed "a delightful interview of nearly an hour." After that there followed a visit with Secretary of War Stanton and other notables, all of whom were generous with their compliments. "In short," Ben related to his wife, with innocence and enthusiasm, "I've had a big time."[67]

Ben's visit to Washington ended all too quickly. On February 12 he received orders to report immediately to Major General E. S. Canby at New Orleans, where he was to take command of the cavalry of the Military Division of West Mississippi. Canby was under instructions from Grant to organize an expedition against Mobile, Alabama. Canby had asked for Major General William W. Averell to lead the cavalry, but Grant had demurred—he had no confidence in Averell and sent Grierson instead, explaining to Canby that Grierson had been a successful commander of cavalry: "He [Grierson] set the example in making long raids. What is wanted is a commander who will not be afraid to cut loose from his supplies and make the best use of the resources of the country. I do not think I could have sent a better man."[68]

Canby greeted Grierson warmly and explained clearly his plans and needs for the attack on Mobile. Rear Admiral David Farragut, in early August 1864, had defeated the Confederate fleet defending Mobile Bay and sealed off the port. Now operations must be conducted against the city of Mobile, and after that, a plunge into the heart of Alabama was planned. Grierson's responsibility was to ready some twelve thousand cavalry to take the field.

Grierson, with the resourceful Woodward as his adjutant, set about at once to carry out his new duties, conscious that the South could not hold out much longer. Grant was driving Lee into the defenses of Richmond, and Johnston, who had replaced Hood, could only retreat before Sherman's advance into the Carolinas. Mobile could not withstand the 45,000-man battering ram that Canby was assembling, and there was little left in Alabama to oppose a federal sweep. In this situation Ben could be forgiven for making some plans for the future.

After paying off some of his huge pile of debts, he had managed to save some money. Now he wrote his brother John urging him to put aside some cash so that they could combine their resources and go into business after the war. He mentioned no specific endeavor and would not have tried another mercantile establishment, if for no other reason than that Alice would have vetoed it.

Always ready to assist a member of the family, Ben did loan money, against John's advice, to his brother-in-law, Harvey Fuller. John regarded Fuller as a "jackass and crook as well as a secesh."[69] But Fuller's fortunes were at a low ebb, and Grierson, remembering his own recent misfortunes, extended a helping hand even though the possibility of repayment was slight. At heart, there was no way that Ben would have turned his back on his sister Susan and her children.

Shaken when he finally received Alice's long and accusatory letter, Ben responded immediately, begging her forgiveness and promising once more, as he had done so often in the past, that "you shall not have so much cause for complaint against me in the future." He enjoyed little immediate success in softening her attitude. Late in February, after describing her full round of social activities, she added, "so you see I am not staying at home weeping for your absence," and signed the letters, "yours truly, Alice K. Grierson."[70]

She did, however, write regularly, keeping Ben well informed of affairs in Jacksonville and Springfield, as well as the activities of his children. Charlie was progressing rapidly in his musical studies, a great relief to Alice, since earlier he had encountered difficulty in learning to read. Robert, on the other hand, was precocious. He not only constantly asked questions, but often challenged the answers he received. When Alice instructed him to pray for his father each night, his response was to inquire "how praying to God could keep the rebels from shooting him." Most recently he had decided that he was a soldier, entitled to the rank of major. Each day he awaited his commission, and to satisfy his grandson, grandfather Robert had written out an official-looking document, signed it "Abraham Lincoln" and mailed it. When young Robert received his "appointment," he accepted it as genuine, especially after his mother sewed him a uniform complete with a major's insignia.[71]

As February faded and March arrived with a hint of spring, Ben's long distance love-making began to pay dividends. Alice, pleased with a new plaid dress, wrote, "I presume you would fall in love with me again if you could see how nicely it looks on me."[72] A few days later, she capitulated altogether and, in a lengthy letter, called him "dear darling," asked for a kiss, and added "I want to love you a great deal more than that." She also requested a long letter, "a real loving one—right from your heart—one all for myself. I mean that will be too precious for other eyes than mine, do you think me selfish?"[73] When Ben received this message of forgiveness and conciliation, he was only too happy to comply.[74]

Now that his relations with Alice were once again warm and affectionate, Grierson dispatched his duties at New Orleans with renewed vigor, though they were largely routine. Canby moved his headquarters to Fort Gaines, Alabama, to personally conduct the investment of Mobile, leaving Ben behind to forward regiments of cavalry as they were outfitted. As Ben went about the city making necessary arrangements for forage and supplies, he observed with distaste the conduct of some of his fellow officers. They had taken over private homes, busily stripping them of fine furnishings, which they then replaced with cheaper items. After witnessing the exchange of a thousand-dollar piano for a fifty-dollar one, Ben confided to Alice, "How much short do such men fall of being thieves."[75]

While Ben was thus engaged, Grant pierced the defenses of Richmond, and, after President Davis and other Confederate leaders fled, Union troops entered the city on April 3. Wild rejoicing swept the North, and in Jacksonville a spontaneous celebration erupted in the town square. The crowd that gathered brought out fireworks, shot off guns, and sent teams of boys and men racing into the various neighborhoods with bells, horns, tin pans, and whatever other noisemakers could be found to alert the population to the glorious news. That afternoon there was a band concert, followed by a parade, and in the evening, in a setting illuminated by Chinese lanterns, politicians brought the day of festivities to an end with their inevitable speeches. Alice, who did not feel like "merry-making" with Ben so far away, remained at home throughout the jubilee.[76] Six days later General Lee surrendered to Grant at Appomattox, and the end of the war was clearly in sight. Ben believed "A grand jollification" could occur by the Fourth of July.[77]

Grierson, having completed his work at New Orleans, left for Fort Gaines on April 11. While he was en route, Mobile fell to Canby's troops, and Ben had the pleasure of a relaxed inspection of the city with General Canby as his guide. He then set to work organizing his cavalry into three brigades for the invasion of Alabama.

In the midst of these activities came the news of Lincoln's assassination at Ford's Theater on the night of April 14. Grierson felt a deep sense of personal loss as well as fear for the country's future. He had known Lincoln for more than a decade, had campaigned ardently for him, and only two months ago had visited with the President at the White House. Now Lincoln's murder, "a savage thrust at the heart of the Nation," left the country again in great peril. But there was no time to nurse either private grief or anxiety. Instead, all his energy and wit were required to prevent his troopers from going on a rampage and destroying everything in sight, an event that unquestionably would "have resulted in the death of many comparatively innocent people."[78]

Jacksonville, along with the rest of the Union, was thrown into mourning. Businesses closed, while citizens draped their establishments and private homes in black. At the Grierson residence grandfather Robert, Alice, Charlie, and Robert bordered the house in black crape and lowered the flag to half-mast. Two weeks later, when Lincoln's body arrived in Springfield, special trains were scheduled to carry the crowds from Morgan County to the state capitol, where they paid their final respects. Alice had no confidence in Lincoln's successor, Andrew Johnson, wishing instead that either Senator Charles Sumner or Chief Justice Salmon P. Chase had assumed the presidency.[79]

Ben agreed, but he had little time to worry about the ascendancy of Andrew Johnson. On April 16 he received orders to march for Columbus, Georgia, tearing up rails and communications east of the city. He was then to turn west and join A. J. Smith's corps, converging on Montgomery, Alabama, original home of the Confederacy. Ben did not believe in wanton destruction, and before setting out he issued orders that no private home was to be entered without special permission and "straggling and pillaging are positively prohibited and will be punished with utmost severity."[80]

Keeping a wary eye on Smith's right flank and rear, Grierson pushed eastward until he reached Eufala, Alabama, near the Georgia line. Here he learned that Johnston had surrendered to Sherman at Durham Station, North Carolina, on April 26.[81] With the war's end now clearly in sight, Grierson turned west to join Smith at Montgomery and dashed off a note to Alice that "we are well, gay and festive. . . ."[82]

En route to Montgomery, Grierson threw out detachments in hopes of intercepting Jefferson Davis, who, with a small party, was fleeing for sanctuary in Texas or Mexico. Davis's course, however, was through Georgia, where he was captured near Irwinville by cavalry from General Wilson's command, early on the morning of May 10.[83]

When he reached Montgomery on May 7, Grierson learned that Lieutenant General Richard Taylor had surrendered the rest of Confederate forces east of the Mississippi to General Canby. Among these was the cavalry of Ben's old antagonist, Bedford Forrest. Only in Texas, where General Kirby Smith still held out, was there any organized Confederate resistance, and Ben believed that Smith would soon surrender.

Relieved for the moment from active campaigning—though there was a small chance that he might have to go to Texas—Ben's attention again turned to the future. After four long years he was tired of war and military service. He might get a commission in the regular army, though there was not yet any policy toward volunteer officers, but he preferred to go into business. A partnership with John was appealing and another, involving raising cotton with Woodward either in Arkansas or Mississippi, also seemed promising. Meanwhile, he would keep his options open.[84]

On May 11, Grierson was ordered to Mississippi to garrison the towns of Columbus, Macon, and Okolona. His duties included taking charge of government stores, receiving and collecting arms, and paroling Confederate soldiers. Ben carried out his orders promptly, but received no instructions concerning how to deal with the blacks who thronged to his camps. With no policy to guide him, he issued rations and clothing, but could do little more.[85]

Grierson's stay in Columbus ended when he was orderd on May 26 to report to General Canby at New Orleans, where Kirby Smith had just surrendered. With the war now finally over, Ben was in high spirits and wrote Alice: "I feel kindly toward all mankind and some women and one in particular . . . comprenez vous?"[86] He should have qualified "all mankind," for he distrusted the planter class, whom he saw as bitter in defeat and determined to do all in their power to preserve at least the vestiges of slavery, that "barbarous institution."[87]

When Ben reached New Orleans he was assigned to command the cavalry in the Department of the Gulf. He expected a major post with the cavalry in Texas, but Major General Philip Sheridan, commanding the military division that included the Department of the Gulf, had other ideas—he preferred either Brevet Major General Wesley Merritt or George A. Custer, who had served with him in the east. Ben's military future thus became uncertain, as once more he lost command of a cavalry he had organized. He felt he would soon be mustered out and at the time saw this as "no great calamity."[88]

In mid-June, Grierson was sent to Memphis to organize five regiments of cavalry for Sheridan's new division. While there he managed a quick trip to Jacksonville for his first visit with his family in five months and found Alice in better spirits than when they had last parted. She was busily engaged in sewing infant's clothing while awaiting the arrival of their fourth child and was certain that this time the infant would be a girl. Ben, having lost weight in the southern heat, was down to 145 pounds, but teased his wife that she had gained what he had lost. He returned to Memphis with the expectation that he would soon be out of the service.

After completing his duties in Memphis, he returned to New Orleans and reported to Canby. The latter had received no orders concerning Grierson, and Ben found himself at loose ends. All he could do was bide his time and wait, either to be mustered out or

Alice Kirk Grierson about 1865. *Courtesy Fort Davis National Historic Site, Fort Davis, Texas.*

to receive a new assignment. Fortunately for his morale, Alice wrote daily in a light-hearted manner.

She regaled him with Jacksonville's celebration of the "Glorious Fourth." A huge crowd had assembled at the fairgrounds, where some soldiers had "ranted," a professor had tried, without success, to read poetry to the multitude, and a party of Indians had attempted

General Benjamin Grierson at the close of the Civil War. *Courtesy Fort Davis National Historic Site, Fort Davis, Texas.*

to dance and perform with a buffalo. The press of the crowd had been so great that all their efforts had failed. Some citizens did manage to fire cannons, and there was a fine display of fireworks. Ben's father had capped the festivities for the family by shooting his pistols from the front yard.[89]

Besides recounting events in Jacksonville, Alice also reviewed her reading material. She had recently finished two books, *Substance and Shadow* and *Conjugal Love*. She assured Ben that on the latter subject he need not fear that she would become a fanatic. As for the other, here was a work that presented a less conventional view of religious matters, one which might well "commend itself to your understanding & heart," and she added, as she had done so many times before, "it has always troubled me darling, that we seem to have so little belief in common on such subjects."[90] Alice had still not given up hope that one day she would convert her husband.

After waiting a month without receiving any orders, Ben discussed his situation with Sheridan. He was directed to proceed to Jacksonville and apply from there to the Adjutant General in Washington for a leave. No sooner had he reached this understanding with Sheridan than he learned that he would be ordered to report for duty to Major General C. R. Woods, commanding the Department of Alabama. Clearly he was destined for a minor post, and Ben was determined to appeal to either Sherman or Grant for a more favorable assignment. He felt Sheridan had shunted him aside, and for the rest of his life Ben never forgave him for the slight.[91]

His orders failed to arrive, however, and he left for Jacksonville, where he hoped to be with Alice when she gave birth. He was not disappointed, and, on August 27, Alice delivered a nine-pound daughter. After three sons, Edith Clare Grierson was warmly welcomed. Ben barely had time to greet "Edie" before his long delayed orders—they were dated July 28—overtook him, instructing him to leave at once for Alabama.

He stopped off in St. Louis to visit Sherman, who gave him a note to General Woods. His old friend also wrote a recommendation to the Adjutant General for Grierson's appointment to colonel in the regular army. When Ben reached Mobile he had no difficulty, particularly in view of Sherman's dispatch, in explaining his delay to Woods. While there he roomed at the "Battle-House," where, he informed Alice, "they can come as near starving a person at $4.00 per day as any hotel I ever stopped at."[92]

Assigned to command the District of Northern Alabama, head-

General Philip H. Sheridan. *Courtesy National Archives.*

quartered at Huntsville, he came into close contact with what he found alarming—the results of presidential reconstruction. Andrew Johnson's lenient policies toward the formerly seceded states were having the effect of bringing into power the old Confederate officials, determined, in Ben's view, to rule as they had before the war. He became more firmly convinced than ever that this group adamantly opposed the extension of basic civil rights and suffrage to the newly freed blacks.[93] Ben now agreed completely with the opinions voiced by John and Louisa.

From the quartermaster's depot in Memphis, John relayed his pessimism. "The secesh are putting on extra airs in the city and Loyalty to the Govt is the exception. I hear the roar of cannon in the future—it is merely a matter of time as to when the 2nd Rebellion will begin."[94] In Jacksonville, Louisa echoed the sentiments of many Northerners.

> Glad there are some men, who will never give their consent that the redeemed national life shall be dishonored by a breech of faith towards the freedmen. The world shall see, I trust, that we are not only able to sustain ourselves but to hold over the blacks the mighty shield of just and humane protection.[95]

By November, Louisa looked forward with relish to the confrontation certain to take place between President Johnson and members of the Congress due to convene shortly. She was confident that "until they prove themselves worthy of admission," the newly elected Southern congressmen would not be seated. Men such as Charles Sumner would "stand fast," while their old friend, Richard Yates, now Senator from Illinois, "will not flinch and . . . everything will be done for the protection of the freedman."[96]

This was not all that Louisa expected. With slavery eradicated, the "redeemed" nation now stood poised on the verge of "astounding events" when "everything will be made new." Among the most encouraging signs was the growing recognition, both at home and abroad, that "something was essentially wrong in the condition of women." Now that the suffrage was being extended to black men, surely it was only a matter of time before women secured the vote. As Louisa saw it, "if women would demand the right in the United States, they would obtain it in a very few years."[97]

Ben, whose spirits had often been sustained during the war by his sister's idealistic letters, agreed with her on all these issues. Nonetheless, aware that he would be in Huntsville for several months longer, his immediate concerns were more prosaic. He wanted his wife and family to join him as soon as Alice could travel. White troops were being mustered out, and soon he would command only half a dozen regiments of blacks. Thus he instructed Alice to "bring your detachment."[98]

As soon as she received Ben's letter, Alice began preparing for the journey, but the recent stress of childbirth had left her depressed and physically exhausted. She also had the delicate task of persuading her father-in-law not to accompany her. When her departure was delayed by fatigue and ailments, she wrote Ben, "I feel as if a good cry would do me good—very silly am I not? Well I am the best wife you have."[99] Ben, his patience at an end, replied that if he did not see her soon, "I should not wonder if I should set fire to this town and run off by the light."[100]

Grierson did not have to "run off by the light." Alice and the children arrived in mid-October, and the family settled into a comfortable private home. Their letters to relatives and friends about conditions in Alabama brought a wave of response. John Kirk was curious to know, "Are the freedmen industrious? Or, are they indolent & lazy?"[101] Ben's response to that question, posed by others as well, was that he "found the negroes much more willing to work and less disposed to depend upon the aid of the government than I had supposed they would be. I had been surprised to see them go to work so freely and so cheerfully."[102]

Others opportuned Ben to assist them in finding "some golden opportunity down in Dixie." To most such entreaties Grierson turned a deaf ear, but he did aid John in securing an appointment in the quartermaster's office in Mobile. He also recommended his brother for the rank of captain in the regular army.[103]

Given Sherman's encouragement, Ben's interest in continuing his military career revived. The idea appealed to Alice as well. The Grierson-Walihan venture had ended in disaster with many debts still unpaid, and Ben knew nothing about raising cotton. When Woodward, who had been mustered out, wrote about a partnership in the cattle business in Mississippi, Grierson showed little interest.

The Griersons' stay in Huntsville ended on January 15, 1866, when Ben received his mustering out orders. The family lost no time in returning to Jacksonville, where Ben wrote a friend, "I am now free from orders—am a high private citizen and outrank all generals."[104] After nearly five years of service, however, the pull of a military life was strong, and he would not remain a "high private citizen" for very long.

Grierson had scarcely reached Jacksonville when he received an invitation to testify in Washington before the Joint Committee on Reconstruction. Congress, at loggerheads with President Johnson on Reconstruction policies, had created the committee in December, 1865, to develop recommendations for new legislation. At the time Grierson was approached, the committee was seeking information from persons familiar with conditions in the South.

Ben appeared before the committee on March 2 and found many members in accord with his views. He was sympathetic towards the needs of freedmen and felt that many poor whites would be loyal to the Union. But he was suspicious of the majority of Southerners, especially those who had served in the Confederate army. As for the former slave-owning class, he had no trust in them whatsoever. "They do not appear to think that they have done anything wrong. Their only regret seems to be that they had not the means to carry out their designs." Unless they were rendered powerless to control affairs in the South, a second rebellion was not only possible, but probable as well. Indeed, Ben was convinced that a secret "organization" had been created and was functioning throughout the South "for the renewal of the rebellion." Under no circumstances did he believe that either the army or the Freedmen's Bureau should be withdrawn.[105]

After completing his testimony, Ben spent several days visiting friends in Congress and army acquaintances. He secured a petition to President Johnson, signed by the entire Illinois delegation, recommending him for the rank of colonel and Brevet Brigadier General in the regular army. Both Grant and Sherman wrote similar recommendations. He was also offered the position of Deputy Port Collector at New Orleans, a well-paying position in a city he had found attractive.[106]

When he wrote Alice about these matters, she unhesitantly replied that she thought it best that he enter the army but: "Ex Brevet etc. . . . proceed to build your beloved wife Alice K.G.—etc. a house . . . to be modelled in its main features like the house in which said Alice is at this present time, more comfortably ensconced waiting with extreme serenity the arrival of her Lord and Governor.[107]

Above all else, Alice wanted a home of her own, in or out of the army. That was totally in character, but the humorous tone she adopted was not for a very unusual reason. Alice, suffering from a severe sore throat, had just consumed five bottles of ale and was definitely feeling better by the time she composed this letter, a fact that amused Ben greatly, considering all the temperance lectures he had endured. She hastened to add, however, that the ale had been consumed for medicinal purpose only, an entirely proper use of alcohol.[108]

After he succeeded in having his mustering out orders temporarily revoked, Ben received promotion to a full Major General of Volunteers obtaining fifteen hundred dollars in back pay as a result. Given this small bonanza, he decided to remain in Washington for a few days longer and, since Alice was visiting in Chicago, take a brief eastern tour.[109]

At a reception for Grant, he met President Johnson and his family, and shortly afterward was required to assist his old friend Richard Yates, who became uproariously drunk. It required the better part of a day and night, along with physical force, to sober up the good senator. Ben then journeyed to Philadelphia, where he visited the U.S. Mint and obtained some new coins for Charlie and Robert.[110]

After trips to New York and Boston, Ben returned to Washington, where, on April 30, he was formally mustered out of the service. He was certain now of a regular army appointment and gave no further thought to going into private business. Satisfied with the results of his travels, he returned to Alice and his children in Jacksonville, content to await the passage of a new army bill.

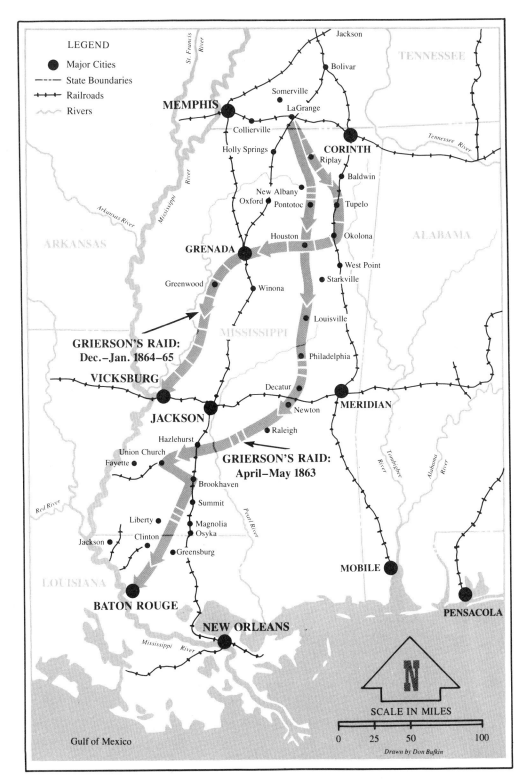

LEGEND

- ● Major Cities
- ----- State Boundaries
- ✛✛✛ Railroads
- ∿ Rivers

TENNESSEE

St. Francis River

Jackson

Bolivar

Somerville

LaGrange

MEMPHIS

Collierville

Holly Springs

CORINTH

Riplay

Baldwin

Tennessee River

New Albany

Oxford · Pontotoc

Tupelo

Arkansas River

Mississippi River

ARKANSAS

Houston

Okolona

ALABAMA

GRENADA

West Point

Greenwood

Winona

Starkville

GRIERSON'S RAID:
Dec.–Jan. 1864–65

MISSISSIPPI

Louisville

Philadelphia

VICKSBURG

Decatur

JACKSON

Newton

MERIDIAN

Raleigh

Hazlehurst

Union Church

Fayette

GRIERSON'S RAID:
April–May 1863

Brookhaven

Summit

Red River

Liberty

Magnolia

Osyka

Pearl River

Jackson

Clinton

Greensburg

Tombigbee River

Alabama River

LOUISIANA

MOBILE

BATON ROUGE

NEW ORLEANS

Mississippi River

PENSACOLA

N

SCALE IN MILES

0   25   50   100

Drawn by Don Bufkin

Gulf of Mexico

Grierson's area of operations in the Civil War.

CHAPTER 6

"Come—To My Medicine Bluff Mountain Home"

THE SPRING OF 1866 ended the separation between Ben Grierson and his family. Now he could assist Alice in directing some of the energy of Charlie and Robert into constructive activities, and he joined others in spoiling Edie. Above all else, however, he wished to give Alice the home she wanted and deserved after so long a time. He also wanted to please and care for his father, and he decided to reconcile these objectives by expanding and renovating the family home at 852 East State Street.

When the work was completed, eight thousand dollars had been spent, and John Grierson thought the house "fine enough for Andy Johnson."[1] But, while Alice now had a large, comfortable home, it was still not entirely her own, since she was compelled to share it with grandfather Robert. In his desire to please everyone and avoid controversy, Ben had refused to acknowledge that the relationship between his wife and father had evolved into an armed truce. Neither was comfortable in the other's presence, and no house in the world would have been large enough to quarter these two permanently. By trying to satisfy everyone, Ben, unfortunately, had pleased no one. Furthermore, both he and Alice failed to realize that the demands of a military career would deny them a permanent home for many years to come. Thus, after all the expense and trouble, they were destined to spend little time in the "mansion" on State Street.

Now that his future seemed secure, Ben began looking for ways to earn a quick return. For some time Jacksonville civic leaders had been searching for inexpensive sources of power in order to lure machine shops to their city, as Decatur and Bloomington had done. When coal was discovered in several local shafts in 1866, a number of citizens, including Ben's brother-in-law H. B. Fuller, began entertaining hopes that here was an easy route to prosperity. Promotional literature was enticing. "Immense sources of wealth are now lying dormant in the valuable layers of coal beneath our surface soil, requiring only the hand of capital to develop."[2]

Ben sought his brother's advice and was urged to be cautious. John's opinion of Fuller's business ability was "not very exalted." Nevertheless, both he and Ben did buy stock in Fuller's venture, only to observe that luckless individual preside over a business that faltered from the start and soon failed. Both the equipment and outfitting proved expensive, while the coal extracted was too inferior in quality to be of any industrial value. It was a blow, not only to the investors but to Jacksonville's civic leaders as well. Gone were their hopes for expanding the town's economic base through manufacturing.[3] Soon afterward, in 1867, the site for the state university was awarded to Urbana, another sore disappointment to the community that had produced Illinois College and Jonathan Turner, the great proponent of education for the "industrial masses." As for the Grierson brothers, it was not the first nor the last time that they lost money in shaky business enterprises.

If Grierson had any lingering doubts about his future, they ended in the late summer of 1866 with the enactment by Congress of a new army bill. The superb Union Army had been demobilized rapidly at the end of the war, and within a year the authorized strength had been cut to fewer than fifty-five thousand men, with the actual strength even less. On July 28, Congress approved legislation for the organization of six regiments of black troops—four of infantry and two of cavalry. Grant recommended Grierson to command one of the cavalry regiments—the Tenth—and when this was approved Ben accepted immediately. He had had ample opportunity to observe and assess the soldierly qualities of black troops during the war, and he had no reluctance at serving with them, a feeling not shared by many of his fellow officers.[4]

John Grierson was delighted to learn of Ben's appointment through the *New York Tribune* and wrote, "I presume it is a fixed fact and you have a paying position for life, or during good behavior, but suppose you should be ordered away out upon the Western Frontier among Howling wolves and Savage Indians, where civilization is entirely in the prospective—that might not be pleasant—however this may not occur and on the contrary you may be assigned to pleasant locality." John's concern was real enough. For most of his long career Ben would be "among Howling Wolves and Savage Indians."[5]

On September 10, Grierson was ordered to report to Major General Winfield S. Hancock, commanding the Department of the Missouri, with headquarters in St. Louis. After a pleasant visit with Hancock and General Sherman, who was also stationed in the city, Grierson proceeded to Fort Leavenworth, Kansas, where he was to organize his regiment. He set to work at once to secure officers, preferably ones who had served with black troops. He also contacted his old associate Sam Woodward and urged him to return to the service as adjutant in the new regiment.[6]

At first Woodward hesitated. His brother had recently died from cholera, leaving him solely responsible for his aging parents, and, in addition, he was attempting to raise eight hundred acres of cotton. With all these obligations he feared that the slender army pay would be inadequate. The inducement of serving with his old commander, however, was too great, and Woodward soon changed his mind. For the next twenty years he served on Grierson's staff as the latter's most trusted friend and confidante.[7]

Grierson had scarcely reached Fort Leavenworth when he was ordered to report to Washington for a special examination before a board of officers appointed by the Secretary of War. While this was required of all officers serving with the new black regiments, Ben, who lacked no physical courage in combat, faced his inquisitors with trepidation. Once the results were in, indicating that he had passed without difficulty, he confessed to Alice his great relief. His anxiety had brought on the stomach disorders he was susceptible to under stress, but, he assured her, "I hope to be well again soon."[8]

Before he left Washington, General and Mrs. Grant entertained Ben, taking him to a concert and providing a night's lodging. The next morning—a beautiful fall day—the General, driving a span of swift horses, treated him to a carriage ride. Ben had enjoyed another "big time."[9]

He returned to Fort Leavenworth late in October, determined to have his family with him before Christmas. It would be none too soon, for all was not well at the "new" home in Jacksonville. Once again Alice and Ben's father were feuding. This time the source of contention was not Charlie, but young Robert, who after calling his grandfather "a little snip," had been held up by his heels and soundly spanked. Alice was incensed. Not only had the punishment been inflicted "before one of the carpenters," but she had expressly forbidden father Robert "to strike a child of mine." As she informed her husband, she desired no "assistance, in your absence, from any person whoever [*sic*] in training my children."[10]

Major Samuel Woodward. *Courtesy Illinois State Historical Library, Springfield, Illinois.*

Ben located a fine cottage only three miles from the post, with large grounds and beautiful trees. After obtaining a cow, so the family could have their own milk and butter, he wrote Alice that it was Indian summer "in all its varied glory," and their new home awaited her and the children. There was one problem, however, and that was the "millions of grasshoppers—they actually darken the sun." As Ben observed:

> . . . they were grasshoppers impolite and unceremonious enough to hop up, get up or in some way make their merry way up under the hoops and skirts of the ladies who are bold enough to promenade among them. From motions I have myself seen made by ladies walking the streets I am of the opinion that they were being tickled almost to death by grasshoppers—in some instances wiggling was most excruciating—even enough to drive a man with a heart of stone promptly to the rescue . . . should the grasshoppers remain here very long, I have no doubt some Yankee will invent some new pattern for the relief of the ladies in way of *solid drawers*.[11]

Alice and the children arrived in mid-November, and all were pleased with their quarters, though Alice suspected correctly that this was hardly a "fair test" of army life. She was certain they would soon be "roughing it."[12] Charlie provided swift evidence that his mother just might be right when he brought home an oppossum that Alice swiftly banished to the back yard.

Ben spent long hours at his office, devoting much of his time to recruitment, a slow and time-consuming task. Many officers refused to serve with black troops, and Grierson's insistence on a high standard for enlisted men brought in recruits at a snail's pace. To officers on recruiting duty he constantly urged care in their selections, ". . . the very best you can. . . . look well to their physical and military appearance. Recruit men sufficiently educated to fill position of Non-Commissioned officers, Clerks and Mechanics in the regiment."[13]

The end result was a mere trickle of men to the depot at Fort Leavenworth, and not all of them were "superior." Of fifteen men who arrived in November, one deserted after a few days, another was arrested by civil authorities in Leavenworth City and thrown in the "calaboose," and a number of others turned out to be sickly and unfit for duty of any kind. An irate Grierson lectured Captain H. T. Davis, recruiting at Memphis, on effective means of enlisting men and then warned: "You will have to foot the bill for your rejects in the future."[14] After that, the quality of recruits improved, but by the end of January, 1867, Grierson could report that only seven officers and eighty enlisted men had joined the regiment.[15]

He also encountered difficulty in procuring suitable mounts. Despite frequent trips to St. Louis to inspect horses, he usually returned disappointed. On one such occasion he inspected fifty animals in a single day and rejected all of them, determined that, "The Government will not be swindled in any horse I receive."[16] It was the beginning of years of effort, often frustrated, to properly mount his command.

While in St. Louis, Ben usually called on his friend General Sherman, commander of the vast Military Division of the Missouri. Invariably Sherman received him cordially and attempted to be helpful. He wrote General Hancock that Grierson was "energetic, dedicated, skillful, takes good care of his men," a recommendation that was certainly an asset to Ben's career.[17] Sherman helped in other ways as well, often providing tickets for an opera, ball, or the theater, knowing that his guest thoroughly enjoyed such entertainment. When Ben did attend one of these affairs, he was always careful to reassure Alice that his behavior was above reproach. On the eve of one ball, he wrote her that he would "use my eyes more than my heels."[18]

Grierson's problems with mounts, recruitment and organization were compounded by the commanding officer at Fort Leavenworth, Brevet Major General William Hoffman. Hoffman despised blacks and was contemptuous of officers who served with them. He went out of his way to make their stay at his post disagreeable by bombarding them with complaints over alleged tardiness at meals, untidy quarters, and improper training methods. When spring brought a sharp rise in enlistments and accelerated the organization of companies, Hoffman's campaign of discrimination increased.[19]

During inspections, Grierson's company commanders were instructed to keep their troopers ten to fifteen yards from white troops, and were not permitted to take part in parades—the blacks were ordered to remain at parade rest! Grierson confronted Hoffman in angry protest, received no satisfaction, and ordered Captain George Armes with Company F to parade anyway. Hoffman's answer was to prefer charges, among them that Grierson had "behaved with contempt and disrespect toward his said commanding officer."[20]

Grierson, nevertheless, fearful for the future of his regiment at the hands of "Old Fogies" like Hoffman, was determined to organize his companies at "double-quick" and get them out of Fort Leavenworth. Company A had been equipped, mounted, and sent west in

February, and it had required two months more before Company B followed. Company C, however, was mounted and equipped and departed the post within two days after the arrival of sufficient recruits from the depot. Hoffman was "highly incensed" that a hospital attendant had been put in C to fill out the ranks, but Grierson paid no attention to the protest.[21]

Grierson also ordered Captain J. W. Walsh, on recruiting duty at Little Rock, Arkansas, to organize Company D at Fort Gibson, Indian Territory, with the men he had on hand. And Ben received approval from the Adjutant General to assign only eighty-four men to each company rather than the normal ninety-nine. In part this was because of haste and in part because of the need to hold slots for better qualified personnel.[22]

In the midst of this frantic activity, Ben received word that his father was gravely ill. Hancock immediately approved a leave, and Ben hastened to Jacksonville, where doctors told him that Robert could not survive. Ben and Louisa scarcely left the old man's side—he was seventy-nine—until he passed away on May 16. Robert, while a stern and often ill-tempered man, had been at heart a kind, loving, and always generous father. In his last hours he expressed his love for his sons, leaving Ben forever thankful that he had reached Robert's side before his death.[23]

While in Jacksonville, Grierson was kept minutely informed of affairs at Fort Leavenworth by Alice and the regimental adjutant, Lieutenant Henry Alvord. Alice, four months pregnant with their fifth child, was in good health and relatively high spirits, considering that this pregnancy, like most of the others, was neither planned nor welcomed. Taking upon herself the responsibility for keeping in close contact with Grierson's staff, she relayed to her husband in frequent letters all the noteworthy news on the post. She also kept a watchful eye on the morale of enlisted men and reported that new recruits from Philadelphia were vastly disappointed on arrival "as they all expected to be non-coms."[24]

When Grierson returned to Fort Leavenworth early in June, he resumed his "war" with Hoffman by issuing orders that the word "colored" was not to be used in any reports, the command "is simply the Tenth Regiment of Cavalry U.S. Army."[25] And, he bent every effort to complete organization of the remaining companies. E, F, G, and H were outfitted in June and July and marched west. Then, on July 30, Grierson received welcome orders to transfer his headquarters to Fort Riley, Kansas. He wasted no time in complying, and on August 7 he telegraphed the Adjutant General that the move had been completed.[26] Ben's sister Louisa thoroughly approved of the transfer; influenced by the romantic notions of the age, she thought that "there must be an indescribable charm in getting a little nearer the unvarnished face of nature."[27]

"Unvarnished" may have been the proper word to describe conditions facing Grierson and the Tenth. The regiment had been ordered west in response to a sore need for cavalry on the Central and Southern plains. With the outbreak of the Civil War and the withdrawal of federal garrisons, Kiowas and Comanches raided the Texas frontier with impunity, and made life miserable for the Civilized Tribes in Indian Territory. In 1864–65, white pressure on the Cheyennes in Colorado led to all-out war that set the Central Plains afire. Temporary peace was achieved with these tribes by the Treaty of the Little Arkansas in October, 1865. Unfortunately, lands assigned them under the treaty were in Texas and Kansas, and both states refused to tolerate reservations within their borders.

When it became clear that the terms of the treaty would not be carried out, the Kiowas and Comanches renewed hostilities against their Texan foes and a menacing restlessness swept the Cheyenne camps. In an effort to prevent a Cheyenne outbreak, General Hancock took the field in April, 1867, to "overawe" the potentially hostile tribesmen. Hancock knew little of Indians and less of the nature of Indian warfare, and his floundering attempt provoked a full-scale war. By the summer of 1867 the plains frontier was ablaze from the Río Grande to the Platte.[28]

On orders from department headquarters, Grierson sent three companies, D, E, and L, to Indian Territory. Five others were thrown into action along the line of the Kansas-Pacific Railroad in central Kansas, where hostile Indians were teeming. At Fort Riley, Grierson continued organizing and equipping the remaining four companies at a rapid pace. He also made an important and lasting change in his staff. "Sam" Woodward finally arrived and was appointed regimental adjutant, replacing Alvord who was assigned to command Company M. Ben and Alice had expected to greet a Mrs. Woodward, but the romance had soured, and Sam telegraphed, "*me and mine* will consist of myself and *trunk* and nothing more."[29] While the handsome Woodward had no difficulty in attracting women, he always managed to evade the joys of matrimony.

Grierson's troopers at stations and posts along the Kansas-Pacific, guarded railroad workers, stages and trains and fought off hostile war parties. Their initial combat action came on August 2, when Captain George Armes and Company F engaged seventy-five to eighty Cheyenne warriors on the Saline River. After a six-hour fight the Indians broke off the action. Armes suffered a hip wound and Sergeant William Christy was killed—the first combat death in the Tenth Cavalry. For the rest of the summer and into the fall, the Tenth's black troopers proved their courage and worth—no surprise to Ben Grierson—and earned the respect of their Indian antagonists. The Cheyennes called them "buffalo soldiers," a title the troopers accepted and wore proudly.[30]

Grierson's busy schedule at Fort Riley was interrupted in mid-September when he was ordered to Fort Leavenworth for court-martial duty. Brevet Major General George A. Custer had commanded the Seventh Cavalry during Hancock's ill-starred campaign. After a series of long and frustrating marches during which he was forced to cope with mass desertions, Custer left his command without proper authorization to join his wife at Fort Riley. He was placed under arrest, and General Grant ordered a general court-martial to try Custer at Fort Leavenworth.[31]

The trial could not have come at a more inconvenient time for Grierson. Alice was due to deliver any day, and Ben was trying to solve a number of troublesome problems in the regiment. While the quality of recruits had improved, there were still too many misfits arriving at Fort Riley. Grierson once more had to reprove Captain Davis for one enlistee who arrived with badly ulcerated legs and another who was not only illiterate but lacked a skill of any kind. All in all, they were receiving some "very ignorant specimens of humanity."[32]

There were also problems with many of the officers. Some were tardy in reporting for duty, while others managed to obtain lengthy leaves from higher headquarters, leaving many of the companies temporarily understaffed. A few officers were inclined to mistreat their men and quickly established reputations as being graduates from the "knock down and drag out" school. Lieutenant Charles Nordstrom of Company L was prominent among these. He had five men "tied up" for "going through a Dutch woman's watermelon wagon."

Numerous complaints also reached Grierson that Captain John B. Vanderviele, commanding Company B, was both harsh and brutal with his troopers. Indeed, two men had left the company and appealed directly to Grierson. By nature and disposition Grierson was kind and tolerant toward the enlisted men and insisted on humane treatment. When an officer failed to respond, Grierson did his best to rid the regiment of the offender.[33]

The Tenth was also afflicted, though no more so than any other regiment, with petty rivalries and jealousies among the officers. Drastic reductions in personnel following the Civil War found most officers who remained in the service at much lower rank than they had previously enjoyed. Often they were forced to serve under officers whom they had formerly outranked. In addition, promotion was slow and pay inadequate. Under such circumstances small grievances became large ones, feuds were common, and sheer hatred not unusual.

Grierson and his staff were not immune. Lieutenant Colonel John W. Davidson of the Tenth, had been a Brevet Major General at the close of the Civil War, and his commission predated Grierson's. Woodward was convinced that Davidson schemed to have Grierson placed on extended detached service in order that the lieutenant colonel could command the regiment. If true, Davidson never succeeded in his strategy, nor was his relationship with Grierson ever close.[34]

Despite his problems at Fort Riley, Grierson had no choice but to journey to Fort Leavenworth, where court convened on September 15. Long days of hearing testimony followed, but on September 28 a number of witnesses failed to appear. Grierson took advantage of the opportunity to move that the court adjourn for a few days. His motion carried, and he hastened to Riley to be with Alice. She still had not delivered on October 2, when he was ordered to return to court. Nine more days were required to find Custer guilty on all counts. He was sentenced to suspension from rank and command for one year and forfeiture of pay for the same period.[35]

Meanwhile, Benjamin Henry Grierson, Jr. had arrived at Fort Riley, and Woodward notified Ben that the name was the unanimous choice of the garrison and that the child would be called, "Harry," subject "of course to the approval of the *War Department.*" Alice was a bit disappointed at first that the new arrival was a boy, but she informed Ben that she "soon got over that." As for Ben, he was elated, "If the name of Grierson be not *perpetuated* it will be no fault of mine."[36] Louisa Semple echoed his sentiments. "It will always be possible to initiate a war whoop where there is a Grierson in the field and by prognostications there will soon be at least a score of them. They promise to become an institution on American soil."[37] Alice, by this time, hoped that her childbearing could come to an end, but Ben gloried in the thought that the Griersons were on the way to becoming an American dynasty.

Upon his return to Fort Riley, Grierson found that peace, of a kind, had returned to the Central and Southern plains. In July, Congress had created the Indian Peace Commission with instructions to make contact with the warring tribes, arrange for a cessation of hostilities, and hold councils designed to prevent further outbreaks. Weeks were required to get word to the various tribes, and it was mid-October before the Southern Cheyennes and Arapahoes, Kiowas, Comanches, and Kiowa-Apaches assembled for a council at Medicine Lodge, Kansas.

Here, after much oratory and discussion, treaties were agreed upon. The Kiowas, Comanches, and Apaches were given a reservation of about three million acres between the Washita and Red rivers in Indian Territory and, immediately to the north, the Cheyennes and Arapahoes were alloted more than four million acres. Other treaty provisions included guarantees of food and clothing, as well as the right to hunt buffalo south of the Arkansas River. Resident agents would live among them to provide assistance in adjusting to a new way of life. The Indians, in return, agreed to keep peace and stay away from the great roads across the plains.[38]

Grierson welcomed the news of Medicine Lodge. Sensitive to the grievances and needs of the Indians, he deplored the bloodshed that all too often had marked the course of white-Indian relations. Now he and his growing family could enjoy the comforts and social activities at Fort Riley, and more time could be given to the details of regimental organization. When Alice's six weeks of convalescence had ended, she and Ben once more attended dinners, hops, and concerts, and were often guests at games of whist.

Alice, disposed at times to wide variations in mood, gave no evidence of this at Riley. For the first time in her married life there were ample funds and servants. Besides, she was now called upon to play the agreeable role of the colonel's lady. She made a large circle of friends among the women of the garrison, which helped her to keep well abreast of tales and rumors. Alice was no gossip, but she remained ever alert to information concerning the Tenth. With Ben she shared a fierce pride in the regiment and enjoyed discussing with him the personal lives and problems of officers and men. Thus, for example, they were both relieved to learn that Lieutenant T. C. Lebo of C Company, had broken off his engagement to Miss Scott of New York

City. Miss Scott, "an accomplished flirt," would have been a threat to the peace and good order among the officer corps.[39]

Unfortunately, family problems soon clouded the pleasant days at Fort Riley. John Grierson was in serious trouble in Mobile, where he had continued to serve as a captain in the quartermaster corps. For sometime, John had given thought to seeking a commission in the regular army but had changed his mind and was merely serving out his time as head of the depot in Mobile. Ill health had plagued both John and his wife, Elizabeth—she had been near death from cholera in the fall, and he had contracted yellow fever. In both instances he had been forced to take leaves of absence, leaving him unable to attend to business with his usual close attention. Suddenly, in November, he was charged with irregularities in the conduct of the depot, and a Court of Inquiry was convened to conduct an investigation.[40]

Confronted with a long list of charges, John was forced to retain a lawyer. Among the more serious were the allegations that he had permitted the use of government employees and materials for the building of homes for two men named Fuller and Spence; that he had allowed Fuller to exchange poor mules for good ones owned by the government and that he had awarded contracts to a "Mobile Trade Company" at abnormally high rates. Until these matters were satisfactorily resolved, John would receive no pay or allowances.[41]

Fearful of a court-martial and hard pressed for funds, John appealed to Ben and Louisa for assistance. They did not hesitate—one of their own was in trouble—and responded at once with money and verbal support. John believed his difficulties stemmed from "some rascals on duty with me as clerks, and Superintendent." The witnesses called before the court had not implicated him and could have done so only by lying.[42] Since John was rigidly honest, his troubles clearly arose from misplaced trust in his associates. His experience with Reconstruction in Alabama convinced him that "all a man needs is a few thousand dollars in ready cash—be a consummate scoundrel and liar—a coward and thief and have a little political influence and he can get anything he asks for at Washington."[43] While the charges against him were eventually dropped, he was not permitted to leave Mobile and return to Jacksonville until the summer of 1868.

Trouble of another kind developed in Indian Territory and soon brought an end to the Grierson's halcyon days at Fort Riley. When Congress failed to implement the Medicine Lodge treaties promptly, the Kiowas and Comanches resumed their raids against the Texas frontier and continued to strike the herds of the Choctaws and Chickasaws. Conditions were such that in November, 1867, Grierson ordered Captain Alvord and Company M to Fort Gibson to join Company L, while D and E remained at Fort Arbuckle.[44]

Both Gibson and Arbuckle, however, were too far east to allow the buffalo soldiers to intercept raiding parties or to exercise any real control over the belligerent Indians. A new post farther west was necessary. In March, General Sheridan, who had replaced Hancock as commanding general of the Department of the Missouri, ordered Grierson to move his headquarters to Fort Gibson. As soon as possible, Grierson was to organize a strong column, march west, and after exploring the country, recommend a site for the new post.[45]

While Grierson prepared to change stations to assume command of the District of Indian Territory, he also agreed to take Alice and the children to Fort Gibson. Charlie and Robert were eager for adventure in Indian country, little Edie was a good traveler, and infant Harry, bundled against the spring chill, presented no real problem. Louisa added her words of approval. "It is better to advance among the Indians in a solid body than for the head to go distinct by itself."[46]

On May 1, the little party, consisting of Grierson and his family, Adjutant Woodward, Chaplain W. T. Grimes, and nineteen troopers, set out. They arrived at Fort Gibson four days later in a heavy downpour, only to find the commanding officer's quarters unfinished. Alice had exchanged comfortable and commodious lodgings at Fort Riley for a pair of tents. Nevertheless, the family remained in good spirits and enjoyed the "camping out."[47]

Grierson spent a busy three weeks concentrating his companies and supplies at Fort Arbuckle in preparation for his march west. He also hurried construction on his quarters and assured Alice that she would soon have a roof over her head. He left Gibson on June 1, and after conferring en route with Creek and Seminole leaders, arrived at Fort Arbuckle on June 8. Three days later, in a driving rain, he left for the west with an interpreter, two Caddo Indian scouts, and companies D, E, L, and M of his regiment. One company of the Sixth Infantry guarded the train.[48]

For three days the rain continued, soaking the column and turning the trail into a river of mud and water. To get the train through, long stretches had to be corduroyed, with the troopers pushing and tugging to move the heavy wagons mired in the muck. Finally the skies cleared, the command "dried out" and the pace accelerated. They soon reached a pleasant valley at the edge of the Wichita Mountains; here Grierson encamped.

After a week of scouting along Cache and Medicine Bluff creeks, followed by an ascent of Mount Scott, Grierson was convinced that the site was superior to any other in the region. Water in the creeks was clear and pure, and fine springs bubbled nearby. There was also ample wood, excellent stone, and the "grazing surpasses anything I ever saw." From a strategic point of view the location satisfied all necesssary requirements.

Wild game abounded, and Woodward estimated that one herd of buffalo numbered more than ten thousand head. After feasting on buffalo steaks and wild turkey, the command moved on west to Otter Creek, where Grierson held council with a band of Comanches—his first experience with these wide-ranging Indians of the plains—and managed to secure the release of six captives. Satisfied with the results of his expedition, Grierson reversed his march and headed for Fort Arbuckle. His one regret was his failure to capture a buffalo calf for Charlie and Robert.[49]

During Ben's absence, Alice and the children had finally moved into permanent quarters. Unlike those at Fort Riley, these were small and cramped. Furthermore, few amenities were available, for here the post sutler carried only a small supply of goods. The variety of food was limited, and the scarcity of produce, eggs, and meat other than army beef supplemented by wild game, made the dietary fare monotonous. Nonetheless, there were some compensations.

Charlie and Robert, enjoying the run of the entire post, found ample outlet for their energies. Edie struggled to the "dood girl" so pleasing to her father, and Harry, cutting teeth, only whimpered occasionally. While Alice found that her social activities were now limited to visits with Chaplain Grimes and Mrs. Alvord, she "enjoyed the quiet." At Riley she had found it difficult at times to reconcile the demands of small children with the social obligations of a colonel's wife. Here there was welcome respite from many of these duties.[50]

The period of "quiet" ended early in July. A violent storm struck the post and blew rain into the recently completed home. Fresh plaster fell from the walls, damaging Alice's favorite red rug, along with a chair and a number of books. And Alice clashed with Mrs. Alvord, who insisted on the arrest of three enlisted men for "disrespect and impertinence" in not hitching a horse to her buggy promptly. Alice intervened and secured the release of Sergeant Brown, but Privates Innes and Woods remained in the guardhouse. She wrote Ben, however, that "I have not allowed it to disturb my serenity."[51] When Ben returned, Innes and Woods were quickly released, and "quiet" returned to Fort Gibson, though Alice and Mrs. Alvord were never again on close terms.

Both Ben and Alice were deeply concerned about an education for their children. While there were occasional tutors at the frontier posts, as the children grew older and required more advanced schooling, other arrangements were necessary. This meant that there were two choices. Mothers could leave husbands and other family members behind and return east while their children pursued secondary school studies; or the children could depart alone, going off to live with relatives or enrolling in a boarding school. Either way it meant that, at some stage, separation from older children was an inescapable fact of family life on frontier army posts.[52]

As fall approached, the Griersons decided that Alice should return to Jacksonville and place Charlie and Robert in school. Ben applied for a leave to accompany her, since he wished to attend to some business matters and was determined to vote for Grant in the November presidential election. Early in September, when the leave was approved, they left for Illinois. Thus Grierson was far away when a major Indian outbreak struck the Southern Plains.[53]

Congress delayed ratification of the Medicine Lodge treaties for nine long months. In the interim many of the Indians went to the assigned reservations but found no agents there and drifted away. Early in the summer they moved north to the Arkansas River, where they expected to receive the promised annuities. When none were forthcoming, they grew sullen, suspicious, and wary, and many, plied with whiskey by bootleggers, talked of war.

Late in July, Congress finally approved the treaties, but it was August before funds were available to implement the agreements, and by then, it was too late. Cheyenne war parties, with a sprinkling of Arapahoes, were swarming in the valleys of the Saline and Solomon rivers in northwestern Kansas. More than a dozen settlers were killed, a number of women were raped—one by more than thirty warriors—and a few women and children were carried away as captives.[54]

General Sherman received approval from both the War and Interior departments to drive the Indians into their reservations, killing those who resisted. It was understood, however, that those innocent of any hostilities would be separated from the guilty and escorted to their reservation, where they would be out of harm's way. As interpreted by Sherman, this meant unrelenting war against the Cheyennes and Arapahoes, while the Kiowas and Comanches were presumed innocent.[55]

To carry out this plan of operation, Sherman created a Southern Military District and appointed Brevet Major General William B. Hazen to head it. Hazen's immediate task was to hold council with the Kiowas and Comanches, arrange for food and other supplies, and then escort these tribes to Fort Cobb to Indian Territory. Meanwhile, General Sheridan would organize sufficient forces to thoroughly thrash the Cheyennes and Arapahoes.[56]

Sheridan and Hazen held council with the Kiowas and Comanches on September 19–20, and the Indians agreed, reluctantly, to go to Fort Cobb. Hazen then set about securing the necessary rations. This task required about ten days, and the Indians, uneasy about traveling with troops, left to continue the trip on their own. Hazen delayed his own departure until he was reasonably certain of the direction the tribes had taken. Realizing his charges would reach their destination well before he did, Hazen forwarded instruction to Fort Arbuckle to send an officer to Fort Cobb to receive and ration the Indians as they arrived. This task fell to Captain Alvord of Grierson's Tenth.[57]

When Alvord reached Fort Cobb in mid-October, he was astonished to find several hundred Indians already there. In addition to incoming Comanches and Kiowas, there were bands of friendly Wichitas, Caddoes, Wacos, Anadarkoes, Keechies and Tawakonies— all hungry and waiting to be given rations. Alvord immediately issued supplies from his meagre stores, and hastened a courier to Fort Arbuckle for troops. Company L of the Tenth and a company of the Sixth Infantry were soon on hand, and Alvord hoped he could keep the Indians in the vicinity until Hazen appeared.[58]

To Alvord's vast relief, Hazen finally arrived on November 7 and replenished the almost depleted supplies. Faced by this time with feeding and controlling about a thousand Indians, Hazen ordered two additional companies of the Tenth from Arbuckle to reinforce the troops already at Fort Cobb. And he began a continuing round of talks with chiefs and headmen of the assembled tribes. In this way he learned that large bands of Cheyennes and Arapahoes were encamped above the Kiowas and Comanches on the Washita River. This important information he forwarded to General Sheridan.[59]

While Alvord, and then Hazen, struggled with the problem of feeding the "friendlies," Sheridan completed plans for the conquest of the Cheyennes and Arapahoes. He had not attempted a serious summer–fall offensive, for the swift-moving warriors were all too difficult to pursue and bring to bay. He waited for winter, when the war ponies were weak on a diet of bark, and the warriors sought the warmth of their tipi fires. Then he would strike them in their villages.

Four strong columns were in motion by mid-November, though Sheridan's principal reliance was on a "main column" under Custer, restored to duty by specific request from Sheridan. The other three columns were to serve principally to drive any roving hostiles into Custer's path.[60]

At dawn on November 27, in piercing cold and deep snow, Custer surprised and destroyed a large Cheyenne camp at a bend in the Washita in the western reaches of Indian Territory. According to Custer, Cheyenne losses were heavy — more than one hundred men, women, and children, among them Chief Black Kettle, long an advocate of peace. Custer's own losses were severe including twenty-two killed and fifteen wounded. Late in the afternoon, when hundreds of warriors appeared from other camps downriver, Custer withdrew and returned to newly established Camp Supply.[61]

After a brief rest, Sheridan, with Custer and his command, made a sweep down the Washita, driving the Kiowas and Comanches toward Fort Cobb. Sheridan wished to attack these tribes, but information from Hazen indicating that they had remained peaceful caused him to desist. He did, however, arrest two Kiowa chiefs, Satanta and Lone Wolf, and brought them in irons to Fort Cobb.[62]

On hand to welcome Sheridan was Ben Grierson, though their relationship at best was coolly correct. Grierson had just returned from a pleasant sojourn in Jacksonville, Chicago, and St. Louis. Having cast an enthusiastic vote for Grant, he was elated over the latter's victory in the presidential election; in Grierson's view the nation was in excellent hands. He had enjoyed a visit with General and Mrs. Sherman in St. Louis, Alice was comfortably settled in Jacksonville, and Louisa was tutoring Robert. Charlie was enrolled in school in Chicago under the watchful eye of his grandfather Kirk. The only clouds on the family horizon were John Grierson's inability to find suitable employment and the final demise of the Jacksonville coal company at a substantial loss to both Ben and John. Despite this financial jolt, Ben returned to Indian Territory in a good frame of mind; Alice and the children would join him in January.[63]

More than four thousand Indians were encamped in the vicinity of Fort Cobb, and many of them milled around the little post under the watchful eyes of hundreds of troops. The Kiowas had been tardy in arriving, and only a threat by Sheridan to hang both Satanta and Lone Wolf had brought them in. And it was only concern over the fate of these chiefs that kept them from bolting. Grierson described the scene as "lively as well as warlike."[64]

A cold drizzle ushered in Christmas Day, and Grierson, apart from his family, welcomed Sheridan's invitation to dinner. "I am hungry all the time and like *Lo* the poor Indian, I am always ready to eat."[65] With Hazen, Custer, and Sheridan's staff, he enjoyed a bounteous feast of buffalo, venison, and wild turkey. Eggnog was also served, but Ben reported to Alice that he did not care for the drink. Nor was he overly fond of Custer, whom he believed "exaggerated as usual" in reporting Indian casualties in the Washita battle. Grierson wrote his father-in-law, John Kirk, that after discounting women and children, there were more soldiers than Indians killed.[66]

Much of the table discussion centered on the whereabouts of the Cheyennes and Arapahoes, and Sheridan assigned to Custer and the Seventh Cavalry the task of driving these people onto their reservation. All were agreed that Fort Cobb was unsuitable for a permanent military post and Indian agency. Sheridan questioned Grierson at length about the site the latter had visited the previous summer and decided to send a small party there for another survey. If the opinion was favorable and there was sufficient grass for the animals, then troops and Indians would move there immediately.[67]

Grierson, Hazen, Woodward, a number of other officers, and Company D of the Tenth, left Fort Cobb on December 27 and reached Medicine Bluffs the following day. Grierson's previous impressions were confirmed quickly, and there was ample grass for the livestock. A mishap did occur that served to confirm Grierson's chariness of horses. While riding along the steep banks of Cache Creek, his mount stumbled, and he was thrown headlong down the slope. His companions feared he had been badly injured, but he scrambled up and remounted with appropriate profanity.[68]

A cold norther swept their camp that night, and the return next day was made in howling wind and sleet. The weather failed to dampen their enthusiasm for Medicine Bluffs, however, and Sheridan was pleased with the report. He ordered Fort Cobb abandoned, and the move made to the new site as soon as the weather permitted.

If Ben's Christmas holidays were given over to business, his family, by contrast, enjoyed a traditional celebration in Jacksonville. Even though the Griersons were once more in debt, Ben had telegraphed Alice two hundred dollars with instructions to "buy whatever you wish," and she had loaded the "very pretty tree" with gifts for the children.[69] Alice was so anxious for Christmas to arrive that she had given Edie her new doll two weeks early. Nonetheless, her Christmas spirit was dampened; here was one more holiday season away from her husband. "The main thing," she wrote him, "is that it is unnatural and wrong for families to be so separated. I never see John and Elizabeth together, but what I see the bad effects of their being apart all these years. Louisa notices it too." And there was one other matter that depressed Alice as well. She found it hard to believe but once again she was "in the family way."[70]

Torrential rains ushered in the New Year at Fort Cobb, delaying the move to Medicine Bluffs. The Washita overflowed and literally washed Grierson out of his bed. Along with bitter cold, the continuing downpour turned the camps into miserable quagmires, and there was general rejoicing when, on January 6, the rain stopped and Sheridan ordered the troops to march for Medicine Bluffs. Two days later, Sheridan supervised staking out "Camp Wichita" and gave Grierson and the Tenth responsibility for both building and manning the new post. For the moment, officers and men threw up shelters with any material available—tentage, logs, and brush. Once all the troops had arrived, Hazen moved the Indians into nearby camps and housed his stores in a large tent.[71]

Supplies from Fort Gibson to Camp Wichita via Fort Arbuckle, were slow in arriving, and both men and animals suffered from lack of food and grain. Grierson's immediate task was to improve the road between Arbuckle and Camp Wichita. He personally supervised the work of Captain George Robinson and Company E in bridging Beaver Creek and restoring the badly rutted and eroded road. Soon supplies were flowing between the two posts without difficulty. Grierson was never happier than when he directed work of construction.[72]

Work also continued apace on more substantial, though temporary, wooden structures at Camp Wichita. These were to be replaced as soon as possible by permanent buildings constructed of limestone quarried from a hill near the post. Sheridan, satisfied that all was going well, ordered Grierson to move his headquarters from Fort Gibson to Camp Wichita and concentrate six companies of his regiment there. This done, Grierson was to assist Hazen in controlling and rationing the Indians. Sheridan also held a long council with the Kiowas and Comanches and, after receiving their assurance of good behavior, he released Satanta and Lone Wolf. On February 23 he left for St. Louis to assume his new duties as commanding general of the Military Division of the Missouri.[73]

While a few Cheyennes and Arapahoes surrendered before Sheridan's departure, the bulk remained out. An effort by Custer early in February to bring them in produced no results, and, on orders from Sheridan, Custer left Camp Wichita on March 2, for a second attempt. After nearly two weeks of searching, he found a large camp on the Sweetwater River at the eastern edge of the Texas Panhandle. Learning that the Indians held two white women captive, Custer did not attack, but instead negotiated the women's freedom. Convinced that the Indians, who were destitute, would go to their reservation, Custer ended his campaign and moved in to Camp Supply.[74]

While Grierson and Hazen strove to feed and supply the bands of Indians in their charge—and many Cheyennes and Arapahoes came in to Camp Wichita where they were fed and transferred to Camp Supply—a band of another kind arrived at Fort Gibson. Alice had intended leaving Jacksonville for Indian Territory early in the new year, but when Robert and Edie contracted chills and fever, her departure was delayed. Once the children had recovered, and with Louisa Semple accompanying her, Alice and her family took passage on the packet "Luminary," from St. Louis to Memphis. There they boarded the "Ozark" for Little Rock, and after ascending the Arkansas on the "Fort Smith," they arrived at Gibson on February 24. For Louisa and the children, the two-week trip was a welcomed adventure, with Edie describing everything as "Hunky Dory." Ben, chained to his duties at Camp Wichita, was unable to meet them and sent Woodward instead. They arrived in a cold drizzle, but Chaplain Grimes had their quarters warm and comfortably furnished.[75] Although five months pregnant, Alice had withstood the rigors of her journey well.

She had hardly settled into her quarters before she took up the cause of a pair of enlisted men. It was well known among troopers of the Tenth that the colonel's wife had a sympathetic ear when one of them got into trouble, and Sergeant Moss and Private Lewis sought her assistance. Moss, who had killed trooper Maybee, insisted it was in self defense. Alice wrote Ben asking for a swift court-martial "so Moss can get out of that wretched guardhouse."[76]

Lewis, Captain Alvord's orderly, had a sore leg that "needs attention" and further, wanted to rejoin his company at Camp Wichita. Lewis was in the guardhouse for "drunkenness and fast riding," and it was Alice's recommendation that he be released and ordered to Camp Wichita.[77]

Alice's attention was soon diverted from the mishaps of enlisted troopers. Her maid, Maria, was charged with setting fire to a small cabin near the stables, and Woodward applied for a guard to arrest her and then escort her to the Arkansas River. Here she would be released, with the understanding that she never return to Indian Territory. When Alice stated that the evidence was not conclusive enough, Maria remained in her service.[78]

On March 18, Fort Gibson bustled with activity. Six companies of the Sixth Infantry arrived to garrison the post, bringing with them "an immense amount of traps, ladies, children, dogs, and servants."[79] Their commander, Colonel R. P. Jones, attempted to exercise his prerogative by taking over Grierson's quarters. It was not uncommon for the wives of army officers to find themselves forced to vacate their quarters when the family of a higher ranking officer made an appearance. As the colonel's wife, Alice had not been subjected to attempts to oust her before, and she was determined that Colonel Jones, the first to try, would not succeed. She stood her ground, refusing to move, asserting that she was there by special permission of Lieutenant General Sheridan. Under those circumstances, she would remain until her husband came for her. Meanwhile, she would do her best to entertain the officers and ladies of the Sixth.[80]

Ben was well aware of Alice's uncomfortable position at Fort Gibson, but for the moment there was little he could do. Bands of Indians continued to drift into Camp Wichita, requiring him to be on hand to receive them, along with Hazen and the recently appointed agent, A. G. Boone. Once she arrived, however, he assured her, she would find Camp Wichita delightful. There was "much more life and stir" at the post than anywhere else in the Indian country. He wrote lyrically of the place, "the music of the rushing—dashing—foaming and sparkling mountain streams" and added, "will you come love will you come—to My Medicine Bluff

Mountain Home."[81] Fifteen years of marriage had failed to dull Ben's ardor for his Alice.

It was late April before affairs at Camp Wichita were such that Ben could leave for a few days and journey to Gibson for his family. He rode horseback, covering the 250 miles between the two posts in six days, "good time even for a cavalryman."[82] Within a day the ambulance and wagons were loaded and the move to Camp Wichita got underway. Ten days of camping out in pleasant weather brought them into the post, and Alice set up housekeeping in a tent. Once again, she was "roughing it" on a wild frontier.

With his family provided for, Grierson turned his attention to the construction of permanent buildings, personally supervising much of the work. He also spent many hours in council with chiefs and headmen of the various tribes and, as he became familiar with their views and the condition of their people, he found himself increasingly doubtful that a military solution was appropriate for the Indian problem. Moreover, it was far costlier than the newspaper stories reported. Once more he wrote John Kirk that if Indian women and children were excluded, more soldiers than Indians had been slain. Moreover, in the recent Cheyenne war, every Indian killed had cost the government over $200,000.[83]

Grierson enjoyed meeting and talking with Indian leaders and often invited them to dinner. On one such occasion, he entertained the redoubtable Satanta and Horseback, and they expressed great satisfaction with the food, commenting, "Heap, heap, wano."[84] From these men and other Indians he learned that their rations were insufficient to last between issues and that their people often went hungry for several days. Some of the chiefs told him they must either go to the plains or starve, and Grierson felt that to keep them on the reservation under such conditions was "a gross injustice."[85] Frequently he gave visiting Indians an order on the post bakery for bread, and more than fifty years later old Indians were still asking for "that good army bread."[86]

Grierson came to believe that the proper solution to the Indian problem was simple. Supply them with plenty of substantial food, furnish them promptly with annuities of good quality, and faithfully keep all promises made them. "Without strait [*sic*] forward manliness, generosity and integrity the case is hopeless."[87]

Since these views were not shared by Colonel Hazen, their relationship became one of mutual distrust. Sheridan, prior to his departure in February, had instructed Grierson to hang any Indians guilty of murder in Texas and to arrest those who committed depredations there. If this proved impossible, Grierson was to consult with Hazen on taking hostages to insure good behavior. Hazen was in thorough agreement with Sheridan, but Grierson had no interest in killing Indians and was not going to operate "on the principle of the Irishman at the Fair—which was whenever he saw a head to hit it."[88] Moreover, he suspected that Hazen sought to supersede him as commanding officer of the District of Indian Territory. If this happened, Grierson would resign from the army "even if I go to the poor house in the end."[89]

Federal Indian policy, meanwhile, was undergoing a major reform, one which Grierson favored and fully supported. With the close of the war on the Southern Plains, restoration of civil control over the Indians was imminent, but there was little sympathy either in or out of government for this course, because of the previous record of corruption and inefficiency on the part of the Indian Bureau. Demands for reform echoed across the land, and the recently inaugurated Ulysses S. Grant reacted swiftly. Under his leadership and encouragement, a series of measures, collectively called "Grant's Peace Policy," soon took form. To achieve dedication and integrity in the Indian service, he called upon the religious denominations of the country to nominate persons to supervise the agencies. The most enthusiastic response came from the Society of Friends, and earnest Quakers were soon staffing the Central and Southern superintendencies, which included most of the Plains Tribes.

The new emphasis on peace required a refinement of the military's role in Indian affairs, and this led to extensive discussion between the War and Interior Departments. Agreement was reached that from now on, Indians on the reservations would be under the exclusive control of their agent who could, if the need arose, call on the military for assistance. The Indians remaining off the reservations were subject to army jurisdiction and would normally be regarded as hostile.[90]

To implement the new policy, Congress created a Board of Indian Commissioners, appointed by the President to serve without pay and supervise the disbursement of Indian appropriations. The commissioners, all philanthropists, were free to visit and inspect the agencies at will, and in addition, the treaty system, which regarded Indians as "domestic dependent nations" was discontinued.

Henceforth, all Indians were to be concentrated on reservations, Christianized, educated, and taught to practice agriculture.[91]

In June, 1869, Grierson welcomed a Quaker agent, Lawrie Tatum of Iowa, to Camp Wichita, while Hazen, to Ben's profound relief, returned to duty with the Sixth Infantry. A man of great industry and enthusiasm, Tatum made swift arrangements for construction of a schoolhouse, dwellings for agency employees, a sawmill, and shingling machine, and ordered land plowed for the cultivation of corn, squash, and melons. This done, he brought in his wife, Mary Ann, and a staff of employees sufficient to run the agency. A warm friendship soon developed between Ben and Alice and the friendly and pious Tatums, one that was strengthened by the faith both couples shared in the new peace policy.[92]

As permanent construction grew, Camp Wichita was renamed Fort Sill in honor of Brigadier General Joshua W. Sill, a West Point classmate of Sheridan's, killed at the Battle of Stone River, Tennessee. Grierson did not like the change and would have preferred Fort Elliott, after Major Joel Elliott, who died in the Battle of the Washita. Nonetheless, he was characteristically philosophical, "it matters not as a rose will smell as sweet by any other name."[93]

The construction also included a picket house for the Griersons. With her sixth child due shortly, Alice was greatly relieved to move from the tent and set up housekeeping in small, but comfortable quarters. Moreover, Charlie was already on his way to Fort Sill for the summer. Having finished his year of schooling he wanted nothing so much as to see his family again, and over his grandfather's opposition, he was determined to make the long trip alone. John Grierson, who had recently formed a business partnership in Chicago, took care of Charlie's travel arrangements, though he too felt it "a considerable trip for a boy of his age."[94] The fourteen-year-old youth reached Fort Sill without incident, to the great delight of his younger brother Robert, who now had a hunting and riding companion. And on August 9, the united Grierson family welcomed Theodore McGregor "George" Grierson, who weighed ten and a half pounds on arrival. Ben wrote John that all had gone well, adding joyously, "It seems the name of Grierson is to be perpetuated."[95] Here was another son to add to the dynasty.

Affairs at his post, however, prevented Ben from spending much time with George or his other children. Six companies of his regiment were now at Sill, but he was dissatisfied with their state of readiness. They were not scoring well on the firing range, their mounts were in poor condition, and discipline was only fair. The remaining six companies were concentrated at Camp Supply under Davidson, to support Quaker agent Brinton Darlington in dealing with the Cheyennes and Arapahoes.

Frequent drill and target practice soon improved both discipline and marksmanship, and Grierson took steps to eliminate another lurking problem—the presence of bootleggers who plied their illicit trade among both troopers and Indians. Determined to stop the traffic, Ben made an example of two teamsters who arrived outside the post with several kegs of whiskey—"foolish water" to the Indians. Grierson had the kegs seized and broken up and the teamsters arrested and escorted to Van Buren, Arkansas, for trial.[96]

The most serious problem was the behavior of the Kiowas and Comanches. They conducted themselves reasonably well on the reservation, but their war parties continued to strike the Texas frontier. When Tatum reproved them for these raids, one chief told the agent that if Washington didn't wish his young men to raid in Texas, then Washington must move Texas far away, where his young men couldn't find it. Such attitudes troubled both Grierson and Tatum, but they clung to the belief that generosity and fair dealing were more appropriate instruments of policy than military force.[97]

In response to mounting criticism from Texas officials, citizens, and newspapers, Grierson did establish patrols along Red River to turn back raiding parties. No success accompanied these efforts, for the Indians, with an intimate knowledge of the country, easily eluded the patrols. Grierson then requested the aid of Colonel James Oakes, Sixth Cavalry, commanding at Fort Richardson, but Oakes, with every available man in the field, had been unable to turn back a single raiding party.[98]

Given this state of affairs, Grierson decided on a tour of the reservation and a visit to at least some of the Indian camps. With a small force, sixty men drawn from four companies of the Tenth, he set out west and then southwest to the North Fork of Red River. After some exploration of this area, he turned northeast and found a large camp of Comanches on the Washita, near the mouth of Rainy Mountain Creek. Grierson and his troopers received a friendly welcome and they encountered no "bad talk," but it was also clear that a number of Kiowa and Comanche bands were off the reservation and this did not bode well for the peace policy.[99]

Before Ben left on his "tour," he bade goodby to Louisa and

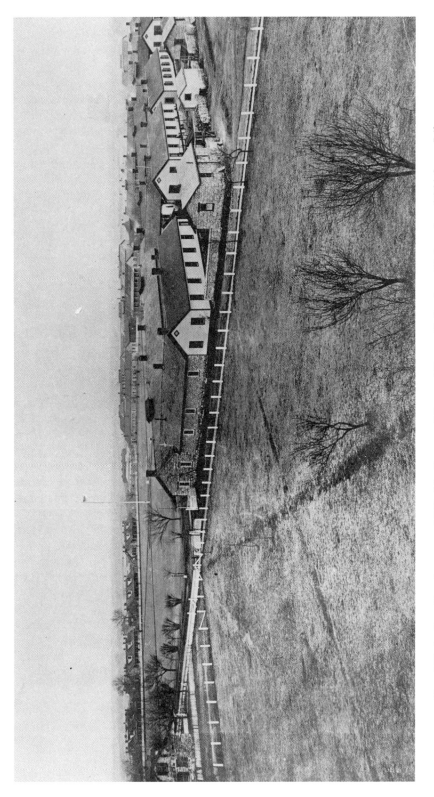

Fort Sill, Indian Territory, ca. 1890–95. *Courtesy Western History Collections, University of Oklahoma Library.*

Charlie. They were returning to Illinois so that Charlie could resume his studies. A detachment of buffalo soldiers escorted them to
the railhead in Kansas, giving Louisa the long-awaited opportunity
to "roam the prairies." Along the way the troopers provided feasts
of wild game from herds of buffalo, deer, and antelope, and Louisa
and Charlie entrained for Jacksonville via Kansas City with appe-
tites fully satiated.[100]

A depressed John Grierson met them at the station. His real estate
and loan business in Chicago had closed its doors after only nine
months of operation. John's partner, James Boyden, using large sums
of the firm's funds for private purposes, had plunged the business
into bankruptcy. According to John, Boyden was a "church-going
and loud-praying member in good standing of the Congregational
Church—the meanest men I know are church members in good
standing—too cowardly to be Highwaymen, but a thousand times
meaner in every respect. Hereafter all I wish to know of a man
is, is he a member of any church—that will damn him in my es-
timation."[101]

John's sentiments may well have evoked a silent nod of approval
from Ben, whose own indifference to formal religious activity so
distressed Alice. She, however, most emphatically disagreed that
Church membership produced rascals, though she held her brother-
in-law in high regard. Nonetheless, Alice had largely despaired of
ever converting her husband, and her letters no longer contained any
references to the subject.

During Ben's absence, Alice spent what little leisure time she had
available in reading. Always an avid devourer of books, she was
delighted when four hundred volumes arrived from Fort Arbuckle
to augment the slender holdings at Fort Sill. She formed a reading
and discussion club among the officer's wives and held bi-monthly
meetings in her quarters. That fall, her list of works included John
L. Motley's *Rise of the Dutch Republic,* an influential work that
attributed the ascendency of Holland to Protestantism. She was also
absorbed in Horatio Storer's *Why Not? A Book for Every Woman.*
This last dealt with abortion, which the author viewed not only as
a sin but also as one of the major causes of insanity among women.[102]

Even with servants, Alice's leisure was limited at best. Four young
children demanded her full attention; two were infants, while Edie
and Robert required tutoring. Moreover, she still bore the major
responsibility for sewing almost all the family's clothing and linens

and oversaw the production of household soap, medicine, ointments, and other items not available from the post sutler.[103]

Finally, as the wife of the commanding officer, she was expected to provide lodging and hospitality for prominent visitors. In October, 1869, while Ben was in the field, she entertained William E. Dodge, one of the Indian Commissioners, and his wife, Melissa. With Georgie only two months old, it was difficult to accommodate guests, but Alice found the Dodges both compatible and understanding. The two women became fast friends, and for years afterward carried on a warm correspondence. Mrs. Dodge showed her appreciation by sending Alice many gifts for both herself and the children. Others who enjoyed the Griersons' hospitality, however, often expressed little gratitude, accepting it simply as their due.[104]

At the end of October, Ben returned reasonably satisfied with what he had seen and heard. True, too many Indians were "off limits," but cold weather had arrived, and most of them were sure to come in. If they were issued ample supplies of food and given understanding and guidance, he believed they would take "the white man's road." Accompanied by Alice, he hastened to visit the Tatums and offer words of encouragement.[105]

Grierson had other reasons for optimism. He maintained close communications with several of the Indian commissioners and knew the recent visit from the Dodges had gone well. He was certain that the support of these wealthy and influential people would insure honesty and efficiency in the Indian service. Further, they could give him some protection from removal for his too Quaker-like opinions regarding Indian policy.[106]

The last few weeks of 1869 seemed to confirm Grierson's beliefs. The raids all but ceased, most of the Kiowa and Comanche bands encamped on the reservation, and an air of peace prevailed. The garrison at Fort Sill relaxed and prepared for the holiday season. Ben found time, on occasion, to direct the regimental band—a labor of love—and evening concerts under the stars brought out the garrison en masse. Dinner parties and "hops" were frequent, though Alice left the "hopping" to Ben, who thoroughly enjoyed these affairs.

For Ben and Alice, this Christmas was far different from the previous one, when she had been in Jacksonville and he in cold, wet, and dreary Fort Cobb. With the exception of Charlie, who was sorely missed, the family was together, and once again the children were smothered in presents. Well in advance of the holidays, Alice had made long lists, ordering gifts from Chicago and New York. In the afternoon the Griersons held open house for the officers and ladies of the Tenth and offered a table loaded with sandwiches, cakes, cookies, pies and nuts, along with coffee, tea, and punch.[107] As they celebrated the season of peace and joy, they failed to hear the distant rumble of trouble in the Indian camps.

CHAPTER 7

Peace Policies Falter

T HE FAITH and hope that Ben Grierson and Lawrie Tatum shared in the peace policy received a rude jolt early in 1870. On the afternoon of January 11, about forty miles south of Camp Supply, Satanta and a large force of warriors stampeded a trail herd of Texas cattle. The trail boss and his crew of cowboys were surrounded and robbed of all their supplies and money. Chief Kicking Bird of the Kiowas, an advocate of peace, reached the scene in time to prevent bloodshed, but the cattle were never recovered.[1]

When word of the affair reached Camp Supply, Major M. H. Kidd, with four companies of the Tenth, set out to drive the Kiowas back on their reservation. They went first, however, to Kicking Bird's camp, where the chief convinced Kidd that the Kiowas would behave in the future. Thus assured, Kidd returned to Camp Supply. A serious confrontation had been avoided, but Satanta's raid sent a shiver of uneasiness through the garrison at Fort Sill and at Tatum's agency.[2]

Apprehension eased as weeks passed with no further reports of raids or depredations. Alice wrote Charlie that white horse thieves and whiskey peddlers were a greater threat to peace than the Indians. Ben, free of restraint in dealing with the former troublemakers, managed to make their occupations precarious through a policy of vigorous pursuit and swift punishment.

After many interceptions and arrests, a signal success was achieved early in May. A report reached Fort Sill that a gang of thieves had stolen 139 mules from a government train at Bluff Creek, Indian Territory. Grierson immediately ordered Lieutenant William Harmon, who had already earned some fame as a thief catcher, to take a detachment and pursue the robbers. Harmon overtook his quarry in Montague County, Texas, and after a chase of eighteen miles, cornered them in a wooded ravine. In the exchange of fire that followed, he killed one and captured the remaining seven. He

171

recovered 127 mules, three horses, and two wagons, and escorted his prisoners to Fort Smith, Arkansas, for trial.[3]

Meanwhile, the lull in Indian activity allowed Grierson to turn his attention to post construction and family matters. The erection of permanent structures proceeded rapidly and generally according to plan. When it came to the family, however, all was not well, either in the Grierson household or in those of their relatives.

Months after Georgie's delivery, Alice had failed to regain her full strength. To make matters worse, the infant was not thriving. Alice experienced great difficulty and pain in nursing him; nonetheless, she persisted, fearing that if she gave up, he would not survive. Becoming "greatly debilitated," she sought assistance from the post physician, but there was little he could recommend, other than to prescribe for her "the constant stimulant of Sherry wine." So, by immersing herself in a slight but constant alcoholic haze, Alice endured the spring and summer of 1870 until Georgie was strong enough for weaning.[4]

Ben observed this situation with growing concern. At one point he considered sending his wife to visit her parents in Chicago. Ordinarily, Alice would have gone with delight, especially since long months had passed since she had seen Charlie. Moreover, recent letters from her sister Susan Ellen, now a twenty-one-year-old schoolteacher (who was always called simply Ellen), had heightened her anxieties regarding her oldest son. "I think Charlie needs a father and mother to watch over him every minute—more than he needs an education . . . a book education I mean," was the way one disturbing letter began.

> When he is told to do a thing, and if the mood is upon him he does it—if not, he don't—and if Pa happens to be good natured it is just about the same one way or the other—if not—feeling all serene—Charlie is scolded unreasonably sometimes I think—children cannot discriminate and understand that the undue punishment one time will balance the lack of it another time—really it does not.

Ellen then noted that Charlie's disposition, not generally cheerful to begin with, was often subject to abrupt changes, especially when he competed with others. "Charlie plays well, but if sometimes he is reckless and loses, he is tormented and he talks back—Very often he says very nasty things but," she added, "I don't think he is half to blame."[5]

Despite her longing to visit Chicago, Alice remained at Fort Sill, not daring to subject Georgie to travel and unable to leave him behind while she was still nursing him. Nevertheless, her frame of mind did not improve when she learned in late July that Ellen had left home, driven away by the arbitrary rules John Kirk had abruptly imposed on the entire family. The emotional scenes described in John Kirk's letters, in which he sought to restrict the reading of "fool" novels and enforce a 9 P.M. curfew, reminded Alice of earlier confrontations with her deceased brother, John Kirk, Jr.[6] Alice loved and respected her father, but she understood that, on occasion, he could be autocratic, despite his strong humanitarian impulses. Obviously too, such a highly charged emotional atmosphere was bound to affect her son negatively. Still, there was little Alice could do. Life on a frontier army post offered few educational opportunities for a bright fifteen-year-old boy, and this was especially true when the boy's parents held strong hopes that one day he would follow in his father's footsteps. Indeed the Griersons wanted something more for Charlie—an advantage Ben never had, to the detriment of his own military career. Ben and Alice had their hearts set on sending their oldest son to West Point.

Throughout that difficult summer, Ben, casting about for other ways to improve Alice's situation, seized upon the idea of inviting Louisa Semple to live with them. At first Alice hesitated, but after giving the matter further thought, finally consented, acknowledging that despite Louisa's erratic temperament, she could assist with the children. The idea delighted Ben's sister, who immediately responded "I have no home but with you." She prepared to leave at once, but a "summer sickness" delayed her arrival.[7]

The year 1870 had brought its discouragements to John Grierson as well, and once more, with his fortunes at a low ebb, he sought Ben's assistance. After the failure of his real estate business the only employment he had found was a $150-a-month bookkeeping position with the Memphis and Arkansas River Packet Company. At a time in which many families survived on an annual income averaging between $500 and $1,000, this was not a meager salary. But John, still harboring great ambitions, was unable to view the matter in that light. It was the exact sum he had received fifteen years earlier in Memphis, and at his age (he was now fifty) it seemed a great setback.

Whatever his circumstances, John was not inclined to blame himself. Rather, in his view, something had happened in American life, making it more difficult for his generation to repeat the successes achieved earlier by his father. Where Robert Grierson had managed

Cadet Charles ("Charlie") Grierson. *Courtesy Fort Davis National Historic Site, Fort Davis, Texas.*

to amass a small, comfortable fortune through shrewd business dealings and judicious speculations, John's efforts had produced only loss and frustration. Nor could it be said that his brother's investments had yielded much better results. "The fact is Benj, a poor man has no right to live now-a-days . . . business is becoming monopolized. Monopoly is the order of the day and the big fish (rich men) swallow all the lesser ones." There was a good deal to be said for the accuracy of John's perceptions, but he was allowing himself to become not only disillusioned but increasingly bitter. "The greater the scoundrel (if only successful) the more you are respected. An honest man has no right to live. Damn all poor men, I hate them, and of course hate myself."[8]

As usual, John was not the only relative requiring help. Ben's

Robert Grierson, age seventeen. *Courtesy Fort Davis National Historic Site, Fort Davis, Texas.*

brother-in-law Harvey B. Fuller had given up trying to sell wringer washing machines to his neighbors and instead was trying to convince them to buy sewing machines, but with no greater success. Laboring under a crushing load of debt, largely the result of the coal-mining failure, and facing a long list of suits, he, too, turned to the Colonel in desperation. Surely his brother-in-law, who enjoyed the benefits of a secure income, could advance enough funds to prevent creditors from seizing his home and throwing his family into the street.[9]

But Ben's own finances were shaky. He had also lost heavily in Fuller's mining venture, and while he had recently made a healthy profit in Jacksonville real estate, the possibility of future gain had lured him into reinvesting the entire amount. John Kirk had recently inherited large tracts of Kansas land from his brother-in-law, William Morley, and having an instinctive sense of when to let something go, had found a willing buyer in his son-in-law. When the balance owed— a note for one thousand dollars—came due at the first of the year, Ben was unable to make his payment. As usual, and in good humor, John Kirk simply renewed the note, but not without first noting that the 10 percent interest was still due Alice "punctually for pin money."[10] Somehow, despite his own problems, Ben raised enough funds to aid both John and Fuller. Griersons might disagree with Griersons on business, politics, religion, childbearing practices, and any number of other issues, but they never failed to lend a helping hand when one of the clan was in need.

Whatever demands family matters and post construction made on Ben, the actions of the Kiowas and Comanches increasingly diverted his attention. As the weather moderated and the war ponies grew strong on the greening prairie grass, the old restlessness stirred the Indian camps. By early May, war parties swarmed along the Fort Dodge–Camp Supply road, stealing stock and attacking unwary trains. They showed no reluctance to skirmish with detachments of buffalo soldiers who sought to protect traffic on the road, and both sides suffered a few casualties.[11]

Fort Sill and Tatum's agency also became inviting targets. The Comanches led off with a raid on Tatum's beef corral and captured twenty horses and mules. On the night of June 12, White Horse, a noted Kiowa raider, with a few warriors, ran off seventy-three mules from the post quartermaster's corral. Captain J. W. Walsh and Lieutenant Harmon, with two companies of the Tenth, pursued them, following the trail for a hundred miles before losing it in a maze of fresh buffalo tracks.

A few nights later, Kiowa warriors, led by Big Tree, killed and scalped a member of a wood-cutting crew near Fort Sill and then rode into the agency grounds. They fired into the camp of some employees of the quartermaster and severely wounded a man. A few minutes later, they shot and killed a Mexican herder near the beef corral. After rounding up a few horses, they dashed among the buildings, shrieking and yelling at the top of their lungs while firing their weapons. A group of white horse thieves lurking in the vicinity took advantage of the tumult and rode to the rear of Grierson's house, where they fired into it. No harm was done, but the family lost a night's sleep.[12]

Tatum called his staff together shortly after this incident and admitted there was some danger in working at the agency. He then told them to use their own judgment in deciding whether to remain or return to their homes. To his great disappointment, all except the two school teachers, Josiah and Lizzie Butler, left immediately.[13]

If Tatum regarded conditions at his agency as "dangerous," they were far more so on the north Texas frontier. Within a month Kiowa and Comanche raiders killed fifteen persons in Jack County and ran off hundreds of head of stock. White Horse, with a handful of warriors, crossed the Red River into Texas, surprised and killed Gottlieb Koozier, and took Mrs. Koozier and her five children as captives. The Indians did not always escape unscathed, and one prominent casualty of this raiding season was the eldest son of Kiowa chief, Satank. Tatum regarded the latter as the "worst Indian on the reservation."[14]

So widespread were these raids that a harrassed Colonel Oakes at Fort Richardson charged that Tatum or Grierson or both were issuing repeating rifles to the Indians. Texas newspapers, taking up the charges, heaped abuse on the pair. Oakes's accusations were untrue, and in a less tense atmosphere he would have known better.

Outraged, Grierson fired back his reply. After outlining the restrictions under which he operated, he pointed out that he had kept patrols along Red River all summer, notifying authorities in Texas whenever he learned of the departure of a war party, so that interceptions could be made. Beyond this, there was little he could do. He then went on to list stolen stock that had been recovered from both Indians and white thieves and suggested that, since the legislature of Texas took measures to protect their borders from raiding Indians, it should also take steps to suppress the bands of white thieves who stole impartially from Indians, citizens, and the government alike.[15]

Grierson's position received strong support from his superior, General John Pope, commanding the Department of the Missouri. Pope set forth clearly the limitations imposed on Grierson and his regiment.

> Indian reservations and the Indians upon them are wholly under the jurisdiction of the agents in charge who are alone responsible for the conduct of the Indians, and for the protection of the rights of persons and property both of the Indians and of white men on Indian reservations. The military forces on or near such Indian reservations are placed there solely to assist the Indian agents to preserve good order on the Reservation.
>
> Under no circumstances except specific orders from Department Headquarters or higher authority will any commander of troops assume jurisdiction or exercise control over reservation Indians or their agents, nor originate nor execute any act of their own volition in regard to affairs on such reservations.[16]

Privately, while Grierson admitted to being "anxious and perplexed" over Indian behavior, he still supported the peace policy. Among family and friends, however, his position evoked disagreement. John Grierson, no lover of Indians, warned his brother to be "careful not to allow any of your Red-faced friends to comb your head with their tomahawks," adding, "Put no confidence in the Red-Skinned Skunks." Adjutant Woodward, while conceding that possibly some progress had been made, thought that "if two or three Kiowa chiefs were killed off it would have a good effect."[17] But in far-off Jacksonville, Louisa Semple gave her brother unqualified support. "I am not at all surprised at the conduct of the Indians," she wrote in July, 1870, while waiting to recover from dysentery before joining the Griersons. "That a savage is a savage and not a civilized man, takes away all wonder at anything they do, especially as they have generations of unredressed wrongs treasured in their memories, and that civilized 'fire water' will find its way among them through the kindness of their mortal enemies. . . . the Indians have had such a splendid exhibition of 'the white man's path' that it is strange that they are not worse than they are, if there be an imaginable worse."[18]

Such sentiments afforded some comfort, but Grierson realized, as did Tatum, that additional measures must be taken to restrain Indian raiding. After a lengthy discussion, Grierson recommended, and Tatum agreed, to withhold rations until both captives and stolen mules were returned, and assurances of future good behavior extracted. In mid-July, when Kiowa and Comanche runners came to the agency with word that their people wished to be friendly and draw rations, Tatum informed them of his conditions.

On August 7, the main body of Kiowas arrived with thirty-seven mules, the Kooziers, and a young captive named Martin Kilgore. The chiefs wanted to bargain and asked Tatum for a council, to which he agreed and invited Grierson to attend. The agent opened proceedings with a stern lecture on the many misdeeds of spring and summer.

Raids into Texas must stop. Texas was a part of the United States and, as such, helped supply the Indians with rations and annuities. The only Texans who injured them were those who came on the reservation and sold them "foolish water." They were also instructed to cease molesting the people at the agency who were their friends and sought only to help them. Finally, Tatum refused to issue rations until they had given up their captives and returned the stolen mules. Grierson spoke in a similar vein, warning them that unless the raiding stopped, troops would be sent against them.[19]

Lone Wolf and Satanta spoke for the Kiowas. They made no apologies for the Texas raids, indeed they boasted about them. They pointed to White Horse, identifying him as the one who had stolen the mules and taken the Kooziers. And for those weak and miserable tribes who had accepted the white man's road they had nothing but contempt. If Tatum and Grierson were angry, so be it. In the midst of this show of defiance, several warriors twanged bows and readied arrows. Others repeatedly loaded and unloaded their rifles. One warrior drew a knife and, standing in front of Tatum, sharpened it on a whetstone. A dangerous tension filled the room.

Grierson rose quietly, approached Satanta, and took his hand. He urged the voluble chieftain to be calm—there was much business to be done. Lone Wolf strode to Tatum's side, thrust his hand under the agent's vest and over his heart to see if he could "feel any scare." He found it beating normally. This exhibition of cold courage impressed the excited Indians, who now ceased their hostile gestures and promised to behave around the post and agency. The council ended without further incident.[20]

A few days later the Kiowas returned the mules and Tatum made them a "gift" of one hundred dollars for each of the Kooziers. Shortly thereafter he secured the release of the Kilgore boy. This accomplished, he issued rations but refused demands for guns and ammunition.[21]

The summer raids had shaken Tatum's faith in the peace policy, and he asked Grierson to send a military guard to the agency on issue days. He also wrote the Executive Committee of Friends in Philadelphia that he did not believe the raids would cease until the perpetrators were punished. Unless the Indians were willing to surrender the guilty, which was unlikely, force must be used to apprehend and punish them. The committee gave Tatum cold comfort. Force was out of the question, and he was to report facts and cease making suggestions. Grierson recognized the possibility of an Indian war and prepared his regiment accordingly, but he remained firm in his belief that the peace policy would eventually succeed.[22]

After the August council, the Indians kept their word, causing no further trouble at Fort Sill or around the agency. Sporadic raids, however, continued to plague the Texas frontier. White Horse and Satank were the principal offenders, along with the implacable Kwahadi (also called Quohada) Comanches, who had never set foot on the reservation.[23]

In the comparative quiet of the fall and winter of 1870, Grierson pushed his construction program, attended to some pressing regimental matters, and found time to relax with Alice and the children. By the year's end, at "practically no cost to the government," as Grierson proudly reported, the quartermaster's storehouses, commissary, post headquarters, a stone corral, and two other small structures had been completed. Most of the barracks and officer's quarters, however, were still under construction, and one more year of inadequate housing faced the garrison. Unfortunately, the weather was unusually cold, and the enlisted men suffered in below freezing temperatures. Captain Byrne, C Company, asked Grierson for stovepipe to provide some warmth for his unfinished barracks, and the Colonel, always responsive to the needs of his men, sent the stovepipe from his own quarters.[24]

In 1870, Congressional economizers forced a reduction of military personnel. Grierson received orders in July to submit a list of officers to Department headquarters whom he regarded as unfit to properly carry out their duties, unless their inadequacies stemmed from injury or disease incurred in line of duty. From such lists, forwarded by commanders throughout the army, "benzine boards," sitting in Washington, determined the fate of those named. Grierson

Lone Wolf, Kiowa chief. *Courtesy Western History Collections, University of Oklahoma Library.*

Satanta, Kiowa chief. *Courtesy Western History Collections, University of Oklahoma Library.*

was not vindictive (many in higher headquarters regarded him as too tolerant), but he did take the opportunity to attempt to rid the Tenth of some men he considered undesirable. Prominent casualties among those in this category were Major Kidd, for his gambling habits, and Captain Byrne, whose actions while in temporary command at Fort Arbuckle, had alienated Grierson.[25]

The regiment also needed replacements for three company commanders who suffered court-martial. Captains George Armes, G. W. Graham, and Charles Cox were dismissed from the service on lengthy lists of charges, and in each case for "conduct unbecoming an officer and gentleman." It is doubtful that Grierson mourned the loss of Cox and Armes, but Graham had compiled an excellent combat record and was held in high esteem by other officers of the Tenth Cavalry.[26]

Grierson had one other problem, a most sensitive one. As permanent quarters for the officers were completed, assignments, according to rank, fell to the commanding officer. Inevitably, old jealousies, petty grievances, charges of favoritism, along with fears of the benzine board, merged to create a wave of prickly unhappiness among officers of the Tenth. When Captain William Beck, who had served with Grierson since 1862, had made uncomplimentary remarks about the Colonel commanding, Ben felt constrained to ask Beck for an explanation. Beck denied the allegations in writing, but resigned as regimental quartermaster in the same letter. Woodward, certain that an "anti-Grierson clique" existed in the regiment, advised Ben to take necessary steps to "break it up." Louisa Semple also offered her views on the subject. In her opinion, the officers at Fort Sill—with the exception of her brother—were a "bunch of drinking, swearing, gambling, domineering men," many of whom were also "shiftless."[27]

Despite the actions of benzine boards and court-martials and a wave of malaria and typhoid that swept the post in the fall, the tempo of activity at Fort Sill continued apace. And both officers and men, even with the heavy demands on their time, managed to find avenues for recreation and entertainment.

The officers formed the Fort Sill Jockey Club and prepared a one-mile racetrack. At the first race, held on October 1, Captain Walsh's "Leather Lungs" won the main event and considerably enhanced the financial fortunes of his owner. The troopers, burdened with work details, stepped up drills, and target practice, still managed to organize a number of "shows." During one performance a "sword-swallower" fascinated Alice and Edie. Alice thought the act a hoax, but it was so well done that she could not be sure.[28]

If Alice was uncertain that a soldier had actually swallowed a twenty-inch blade, she was sure of one thing—to her utter dismay, she was again pregnant. And her "condition," along with John Grierson's gloomy reports from Memphis, cast a shadow over an otherwise festive Christmas. John believed Reconstruction in Tennessee a total failure. "I think the Government could justly hang about one half the population of this city. The people are getting worse instead of more loyal. Rebellion No. 2 is now an embryo." And, given the strength of opposition to both the Fourteenth and Fifteenth Amendments, John strongly suspected that Tennessee Democrats were getting "furtive aid" from Northern conservatives. As for Andrew Johnson, still a power in the state, in John's view, he was "so mean the Devil wouldn't have him for an associate." There was no use in looking for help from Republican leaders, however, for Grant, afraid of losing votes for the Party, had turned into an indecisive do-nothing for whom John Grierson would not vote in 1872.[29]

Alice's cold resignation to the birth of another child and John's forecast of another civil war combined to dampen Ben Grierson's usual good humor and optimism. But it was the Kiowas and Comanches who plunged him into a state bordering on despair, one that stretched to the limits his faith in the peace policy.

The normal winter "raiding holiday" failed to occur in 1870–71. Late in December, war parties crossed the Red and killed three men, a woman, and her child in Parker and Montague counties. In January, Big Bow led twenty-five Kiowa warriors into Young County and attacked four black men who were hauling supplies from Weatherford to their homes near Fort Griffin. The men, after killing their horses for a barricade, fought desperately for their lives, but all were slain and scalped. One of these, Brit Johnson, was already a legend on the Texas frontier for his successful efforts in recovering captives from the Comanches. Before the month was out, nine more persons had been killed and scalped in the northern counties of Texas.[30]

When the raids continued into February and March, Tatum called on Grierson for patrols along Red River. Soon two companies of the Tenth were working the north bank, but Indian bands easily eluded them. Tatum feared the summer of 1871 would be a bloody one, but Grierson disagreed and blamed most of the trouble on the tardy arrival of annuities and the appearance of railroad survey crews on the reservation.

The annuities arrived in April, but they had no effect on the scale of Indian hostilities. Alarmed, Grierson, with an additional company of the Tenth, toured his outposts along the river, seeking a more effective disposition of his troopers. But his entire regiment could scarcely have turned back the red tide.[31]

Meanwhile, outraged Texans were bombarding Washington with letters and petitions relating details of Indian depredations in the state and demanding that something be done to stop them. In a formal resolution the state legislature reviewed the previous five years of Indian raids and depredations. Several hundred citizens had been murdered and millions of dollars worth of property had been destroyed, activities which had "not only retarded the settlement of the frontier counties of the state, but have almost depopulated several counties thereof."[32]

General Sherman was not convinced that conditions were as bad as described, but finding himself deluged with protests, he decided on a personal fact-finding tour and invited Inspector General Randolph B. Marcy to accompany him. They arrived in San Antonio on April 28, and a few days later, with a picked escort of seventeen buffalo soldiers from the Tenth Cavalry, set out to visit the outer line of Texas posts.

Stops at Forts McKavett, Concho, and Griffin produced ample rumors of raids, atrocities, and property losses, but they saw no Indians nor any solid evidence to support claims of widespread Indian activity. On the evening of May 17, they encamped among the ruins of abandoned Fort Belknap, a day's journey from Fort Richardson, the last stop along the ring of Texas posts. Sherman felt the flood of reports he had received had been exaggerated, but Inspector Marcy disagreed. He had traveled through this same country before the Civil War, and there were fewer settlers along the route now than there had been during his former visit. In his view, unless the Indians were punished and disarmed, the border settlers of Texas would be annihilated.[33]

Next morning, they took the road for Fort Richardson and, early in the afternoon, trotted across a broad prairie, the site of frequent Indian attacks. Seeing no Indians, they were blissfully unaware that from the brow of a nearby hill a powerful Kiowa war party watched their eastward progress. Only strong restraint from their chiefs prevented a swarm of eager warriors from attacking what appeared to be easy prey. The chiefs preferred to wait for a richer prize. By the thinnest of margins, the Commanding General of the Army escaped with his scalp.[34]

When Sherman reached Richardson, he was welcomed by Colonel

Ranald S. Mackenzie, Fourth Cavalry, who had replaced the ineffective Oakes. After some rest and refreshment, Sherman received a delegation of citizens who voiced the now familiar complaints about Indian raids, including accusations that Grierson and Tatum were arming the warriors. Sherman knew that such charges against his old friend Grierson were ridiculous, but, not knowing Tatum, promised to investigate when he reached Fort Sill.

In the early morning of May 19, Sherman's view of conditions on the Texas frontier changed abruptly. A wounded teamster, Thomas Brazeale, staggered into Fort Richardson with a tale of horror. At midafternoon on May 18, on the same road over which Sherman had passed, an overwhelming force of warriors had struck a ten-wagon train loaded with corn en route to Fort Griffin. Five of his fellow teamsters had been killed in the first rush, and Brazeale, with six others, fled on foot for some nearby timber. In the mad dash for safety two more of his companions had been killed, and he was uncertain of the fate of the remaining four.

After interviewing Brazeale, Sherman ordered Mackenzie to take every available man at Richardson and pursue the hostiles. He also authorized Mackenzie, if necessary, to enter the reservation, attack the Indians there, and recover the stolen property. He was then to move on to Fort Sill, where Grierson would provide all necessary cooperation. Mackenzie was underway by noon, and late in the evening, in a driving rainstorm, reached the scene of the attack. Seven mutilated bodies were found, including that of the wagon master, Samuel Elliot. Contents of the wagons were scattered over a wide area, and five dead mules were found, while forty-one others were missing.[35]

Mackenzie pushed on in rain and mud in an effort to overtake the raiders, while an "enlightened" Sherman set out for Fort Sill. He arrived on May 23 to the martial strains of the Tenth Cavalry band and a mass turn-out of the garrison. Sherman was pleased to see Grierson, but he was in no mood for the planned round of receptions, reviews, and inspections until he had attended to the business of Indian raids into Texas. He wanted to see Tatum immediately.

Ben escorted his hot-tempered friend to the agency, where he introduced him to the agent. Sherman related the details of the wagon-train affair to an increasingly distressed Tatum and then asked if the latter knew of any of his charges who might be raiding in Texas. Tatum, who impressed Sherman as a "good and honest man" was not sure, but thought he could find out. When the Indians came in for rations in a few days, he would question them. Tatum added, in words that could not have been lost on Grierson, that some of his Indians were out of control. The strong arm of the government was needed.[36]

While he waited for a report from Tatum, Sherman inspected Fort Sill and pronounced it one of the best he had ever seen. He also received the officers "in sashes and belts, but not epaulettes," along with their wives, at Grierson's quarters. Young Robert Grierson had a "splendid" time, showering Sherman and Marcy with questions and later recording that General Marcy told "very funny stories."[37]

When the Kiowas came in for their rations on Saturday, May 27, Tatum called the chiefs into his office for a conference. After preliminary greetings and hand-shaking, the agent related what he had been told about the wagon-train attack and asked if they knew who had done it. Satanta rose, and in a lengthy speech, accused Tatum of robbing the Indians and denying them many things rightfully theirs, including guns and ammunition. For these reasons, Satanta thundered, he had led a war party into Texas. Chiefs Satank, Eagle Heart, Big Tree, Big Bow, and Fat Bear had accompanied him. They had attacked the train, killed seven men, and taken about forty-seven mules. Three of his warriors had been killed, but he was prepared to call matters even. Satanta concluded by saying, "If any other Indian comes here and claims the honor of leading the party, he will be lying to you, for I did it myself."[38]

Tatum instructed his clerks to proceed with issuing the rations, then went to his office, and penned the following note to Grierson:

COL. GRIERSON
Post Comd.

Satanta, in the presence of Satank, Eagle Heart, Big Tree, and Woman's Heart, in a defiant manner, has informed me that he led a party of about 100 Indians into Texas, and killed 7 men and captured a train of mules. He further states that Chiefs Satank, Eagle Heart, Big Tree and Big Bow were associated with him in the raid. Please arrest all of them.

LAWRIE TATUM
Ind. Agent[39]

After sending one of his employees with the note, Tatum went in person to post headquarters and conferred with Grierson and Sherman. Sherman had only one question—did the agent want Satanta arrested on the spot. Tatum replied that he "not only desired it, but requested that it be done." A decision was then reached to hold a council on the front porch of Grierson's quarters, at which time the arrests would be made. Tatum left immediately for his agency to round up the chiefs, and Grierson alerted his company commanders to station their troopers to seal off possible avenues of escape.

Satanta arrived just as these arrangements were completed. He understood that a big Washington officer was there, and he "wished to measure him up." When Sherman questioned the chief closely, Satanta readily admitted his part in the raid. Just as readily, he changed his story as Sherman mentioned arrest and trial in Texas. He then rose to go to his pony, but Grierson's orderly drew his revolver and forced the chief to sit down.

At this point a number of other Kiowas, including Satank, arrived for the council. Sherman informed them that the guilty chiefs were under arrest and would be sent to Texas. Satanta shouted that he would rather be shot on the spot and clutched at a pistol under his blanket, but at that instant the shuttered windows of Grierson's parlor flew open, revealing a squad of buffalo soldiers with carbines leveled. Satanta's desire to die on the spot ceased immediately. Grierson gave a pre-arranged signal, and four companies of the Tenth moved out of the stables and trotted into position. For the Kiowas at Grierson's porch there was no escape.

Kicking Bird was one of them, and he begged Sherman to release Satanta and Satank in view of his own attempts to guide his people along the road to peace. He would see to it that the stolen mules were returned. Sherman acknowledged the chief's efforts, but remained firm in his intention to punish those guilty of murder. As this exchange ended, a belligerent Lone Wolf arrived carrying two carbines, a bow, and a quiver full of arrows. Striding toward the porch he gave a carbine to one unarmed warrior, the bow and quiver to another, and, with the remaining carbine at full cock, faced the porch and glared at Sherman. The mounted troopers brought their weapons to bear on the assembled Indians, and a savage hand-to-hand fight seemed imminent.

Grierson's courage and quick thinking provided a bloodless solution. He launched his slender, wiry body at Lone Wolf, grasped the carbine, and wrestled the chief to the ground. At the same time, he shouted to interpreter Horace Jones to tell the Indians that violence would not save their chiefs. Satanta and a number of others contributed their bit by shouting, "No, No, No," and the crisis passed. After Kicking Bird promised to return the mules, Satanta and Satank were taken to a cell and manacled hand and foot. The other Indians were permitted to leave.[40]

Orders had also been issued for the arrest of Big Tree and Eagle Heart, but they had not appeared at the council. Woodward, with Lieutenant Pratt and D Company, received the order to apprehend the two, who were reported to be at the trader's store. When Woodward reached the store, he entered with a few men, while Pratt and the remaining troopers stood guard outside. Big Tree, behind a counter helping himself to some desirable goods, spied Woodward and, with no wasted motion, dashed to the rear and plunged through a window, carrying away both glass and sash. Pratt and his men pursued, surrounded the burly chieftain, and forced him to surrender. Shortly thereafter, Big Tree was keeping company with Satanta and Satank. Eagle Heart, who had left the store just before Woodward's arrival, witnessed Big Tree's capture and made his escape.[41]

With three chronic troublemakers safely in the guardhouse, Sherman prepared to leave for Fort Gibson. He left instructions for Mackenzie to take the chiefs to Jacksboro, Texas, for trial and advised Grierson to occasionally send a "well organized" patrol to the Indian camps. He was pleased with Tatum and satisfied that the agent would issue nothing to the "Kioways" until the stolen mules were returned. Marcy's preparations were less businesslike. He borrowed Grierson's "hair-trigger" rifle and double-barreled shotgun to do some hunting en route.[42]

When Mackenzie came in to Fort Sill after two weeks of futile, mud-splattered pursuit, he was surprised to find the principle objects of his search in confinement. Three days of rest restored his energy and good humor, and on June 8 he was ready to take the chiefs to Texas. Two wagons were driven to the guardhouse, and the prisoners, completely shackled in irons, were brought out. A subdued Satanta and Big Tree gave no trouble and were lifted into one wagon with two troopers to guard them. Satank was another matter. He swore at his captors, refused to move, and had to be shoved into the other wagon. A corporal and two privates, assigned as guards climbed in beside him. Interpreter Horace Jones, standing nearby warned: "You had better watch that old Indian, he means trouble."[43]

As the column got under way along the Fort Richardson road, Satank began his death song, while under his blanket he struggled to free his hands from the manacles. Less than a mile down the road he succeeded, tearing his flesh badly in the process. His chant ended and, grasping a knife that he had somehow managed to conceal, he lunged at the corporal and stabbed him in the leg. All three guards tumbled pell mell from the wagon leaving their carbines behind. The old Kiowa seized one of these and worked at the lever to chamber a cartridge. Troopers riding behind the wagon opened fire, and several slugs struck Satank, sending him sprawling, but he rose and again tried to fire the carbine. Another volley mortally wounded him, and his body was thrown by the roadside.[44]

In July, Satanta and Big Tree, indicted for murder, stood trial in Jacksboro, where they were convicted and sentenced to hang. However, the proceedings had attracted national attention, and strong pressure from eastern humanitarians, including many prominent Quakers, led Texas governor Edmund J. Davis to commute the sentences to life imprisonment. Davis's action was unpopular in Texas and in military circles, where commutation was regarded as simply a first step in the release of the chiefs. Sherman was a severe critic, for he had earlier warned that if Satanta and Big Tree were freed, "no life from Kansas to the Río Grande will be safe, and no soldier will ever again take a live prisoner."[45]

The events of May and early June had provided the garrison at Fort Sill with more than the normal amount of excitement and activity, and many of the residents may have looked forward to a quiet and routine summer. If so, they were greatly disappointed. Most of the Kiowas remained in their camps, but there were disturbing reports that some of the more belligerent ones were trying to stir up the Cheyennes. Kicking Bird had not returned the mules, and Comanche raiders were active in Texas. Mackenzie wrote Grierson and proposed a joint campaign to whip the Comanches, seize Eagle Heart, Big Bow, and White Horse, and retrieve the mules. Grierson agreed and so did Tatum, for both had reached the conclusion that the Kwahadis had to be whipped and driven on the reservation before there could be any real hope of peace. Immediately Grierson began concentrating nine companies of his regiment at Fort Sill. Several weeks were required to prepare the troopers and gather the necessary supplies for extended field operations, and in the interim both joy and sorrow came to the post.[46]

On June 23, Alice gave birth to a daughter, her seventh child. Ben wrote John that "the young children are especially delighted" at the arrival of Mary Louisa Grierson and, "our family is equal in number, if not in rank, with the Generals of the Army." Louisa, having returned to Jacksonville briefly, was complimented that the infant bore both her name and that of Ben's deceased sister. As for Alice, while she had not wanted another child, she was greatly relieved that this time the baby was a girl, a fact which helped to reconcile her to the event. Only a heated battle between Kate, the cook, and Taylor, the male servant, over policies in the kitchen, marred the occasion.[47]

Shortly afterward, the garrison celebrated the "Glorious Fourth" with a good deal of spirit and appropriate ceremony. A six-company review, with sabers flashing, filled the morning, and at noon "a cannon was fired thirty-seven times." In the afternoon a children's party, complete with punch, ice cream, nuts, and candy, competed for attention with a baseball game between H and B Companies. In the evening Grierson played host to an officer's ball held in his flag-draped office. Alice, still convalescing, did not attend.[48]

On the heels of an enjoyable Fourth came somber news. Near Santa Fe, New Mexico, while escorting a party of railroad surveyors, Lieutenant Robert Price, C Company, had shot and killed two members of his detachment, Privates York Johnson and Charles Smith. Price, a graduate of West Point, with the regiment only a year, was being held by civil authorities. These actions shocked members of the Tenth and were deplored by Grierson, whose firm, but kind and often close relationship with the enlisted men was emulated by most of the officers. Price was soon released and returned to Fort Sill, but shortly thereafter, he resigned from the army.[49]

Grierson completed preparations for his campaign on August 8 and arranged to rendezvous with Mackenzie on Otter Creek, a two-day march southwest of Sill. At the last moment he made two additions to his six-company command. He yielded to Robert's pleadings to be taken along and, to Alice's great relief, chose Private Taylor to accompany him as cook. Peace would reign in the Grierson kitchen at least for the duration of field operations.[50]

The long column got underway on the morning of the ninth and encamped on Otter Creek the following day. For Robert, the second day's march of twenty-four miles was a tiring one. He rode his pony "all the time" and found that "my belly ached all the time." Captain Vandewiele of B Company prepared some "Jamaica Ginger" for the youngster, but Robert decided that he preferred to endure his stomachache "rather than drink the stuff." Whatever his pain, he obviously recovered quickly, for that evening he caught a fish "almost as big as he is" from Otter Creek.[51]

When Mackenzie arrived, he and Grierson spent that evening making plans by the light of "prairie fires glowing all around." By August 15, the commands were on the move in steaming temperatures, with Mackenzie following the Salt Fork and Grierson the North Fork of Red River. The oppressive heat and broken country turned the march into a near nightmare of sweat and dehydration that left both men and animals exhausted. Despite these conditions, Grierson pushed doggedly on to the Staked Plains but encountered no Indians. He did, however, find evidence of a lively trade in guns, ammunition, and whiskey between the red men and stealthy "comancheros" from New Mexico.

On August 24, Grierson turned eastward, where he was overtaken by a courier from Tatum with a report that Kicking Bird had brought in the mules. Grierson gave up the hunt and returned to the camp on Otter Creek. After leaving four companies behind to patrol Red River, he then came into Fort Sill. Shortly thereafter, Mackenzie returned to Fort Richardson, having failed to see a single Indian.[52]

If Ben expected to find tranquility when he and Robert returned home, he was disappointed; awaiting him was a most unhappy household. For several days Alice's best efforts to break Mary Louisa's high fever had been of no avail. Plagued by searing heat, swarms of flies, and sleepless nights, her nerves had become frayed, and recently she had quarreled bitterly with Louisa. In a fit of rage, she had slammed and locked a door in her sister-in-law's face, and now the two were not speaking and communication between them was carried on through written notes. This was hardly the welcome Ben had hoped for after an exhausting march, but he did his best to calm the flaring tempers. It was impossible to mollify Alice, however, for her baby's condition was steadily declining. On September 16, Mary Louisa, less than three months old, died in her mother's arms.[53]

Ben tried valiantly to comfort his wife, urging her to "bear up darling, she was with us for some purpose." This time, however, Alice was inconsolable, informing her husband that she failed to see the workings of Providence in recent events. Rather, she was convinced that if she had not borne the responsibility as the post commander's wife for entertaining an almost constant stream of company, she could have given her child better care and Mary Louisa might have survived. Still she struggled to overcome her bitterness, attempting to find within herself "a great deal more philosophy and religion," so that she could take "life as it came without any fretting. . . ." Unfortunately, as she acknowledged later in a letter to Ben, she was "neither saint, nor angel."[54] She was simply an anguished woman. But even while Alice dealt as best she could with her turbulent feelings at Fort Sill, a series of events was having a profound impact on all members of the Kirk family.

At the Kirk household at 53 Warren Avenue in Chicago, a number of changes had transpired. The mental condition of Alice's mother, Susan Bingham Kirk, impaired for some time, had deteriorated rapidly in the space of a few months. What John Kirk referred to as "softening of the brain" proceeded so far that at times the sixty-three-year-old woman had no knowledge of where she was, the year she was living in, or who was in attendance. For the first time in their marriage, John Kirk was compelled to take a leave of absence from employment, for given his wife's state, it was impossible to continue traveling as a salesman for the Jones and Laughlin American Iron Works.

Other matters troubled John Kirk as well. While his relations with Ellen had improved considerably after her marriage a year earlier to Ben's nephew, Harvey B. Fuller, Jr., John Kirk was now deeply concerned about the way his son, Tom Kirk, managed his financial affairs. Tom's hardware business appeared to be flourishing, but he had incurred large debts (he owed enormous sums to his father), which he made little attempt to repay. Nevertheless, Tom devoted no time to worrying about such matters, consigning that responsibility to his father, until a series of occurrences entirely altered the course of his future and adversely affected other members of the family as well.[55]

The fall of 1871 had been an especially warm, dry season for the residents of the "Windy City." Since the last heavy downpour on July 3, little rain had fallen, and in the open fields outside town (once covered with tall trees, but now stripped of timber by the settlers of the past thirty years), rural residents constantly battled prairie fires. Within the city, lawns were parched and the water supply in cisterns and wells was running dangerously low. By the end of September, the combination of warm weather and drought had stripped trees and shrubs of most of their leaves. Predictably enough, in a place where most construction was of wood, the under-staffed fire department found itself battling a large number of blazes, most notably the spectacular conflagration on 16th Street near State. There on September 30, the Burlington warehouse was entirely destroyed—a loss that totalled over $600,000, at that time one of the largest in the city's history.

In the week that followed there were forty other fires, none as serious. Then, on Saturday night, October 7, shortly before midnight, a planing mill located on Canal Street erupted in flames that spread quickly over a four-square-block area and destroyed $750,000 worth of property before finally being extinguished after sixteen hours of unremitting and arduous labor. The city's two hundred firefighters, responsible for protecting a population exceeding 330,000 inhabitants, were left utterly exhausted, while a third of their hose was ruined and several of their engines were disabled.[56]

Thus the city was ill prepared when a fire broke out the next night on the west side of town. When the initial alarm was sounded, the directions received were so confused (fatigue and blundering playing their roles), that the four fire companies closest to the blaze were not alerted. By the time engines arrived, the fire, fanned by a strong southwest wind, had exploded into an inferno, enveloping surrounding buildings. By midnight, three hours after it started, it had crossed a branch of the Chicago River, almost half a mile away, and was headed in a northeasterly direction.[57] Before a gentle rain helped bring it under control after twenty-seven hours, the fire, "the largest that ever occurred in the world," burned an area of over two thousand acres. This covered, as Charles Grierson wrote his mother, "all the South side from Harrison (from the West side) to the river & lake and the North side from the River and the north branch to the lake and above Lincoln Park."[58] Included was almost the entire business section, all public buildings, virtually all retail and commercial establishments, transportation centers, the waterworks and other utility companies, all brokerage offices, over thirty churches, many schools, and two-thirds of the city's stores. Not even "fireproof" structures, such as the court house and the Tribune building, were spared. The human and social costs were even greater. Three hundred persons perished, and ninety thousand were left homeless.[59] On the morning of October 11, a dejected Tom Kirk stood on the charred earth , the site of his former store, surveying the ruins and wondering what percentage of his losses would be covered by insurance.[60]

When news of these events reached Alice, she immediately began preparing to visit her family in Chicago. Ben, saddened by recent events and increasingly anxious over the fate of the peace policy, was not in good spirits himself. Nonetheless, as much as he regretted losing his wife's company, he recognized that it would be therapeutic for her to leave the post for a time and began making the necessary travel arrangements. Toward the end of October, Alice embraced her husband one last time and, along with Edie and Harry, set out by stage for Sedalia, where she would board a train for Chicago. Louisa had agreed to remain at Fort Sill to care for Robert and Georgie, while acting as hostess for Ben during Alice's absence. Ben's sagging spirits were buoyed up by his expectation that Alice would return home before Christmas.[61]

Travel between Fort Sill and Sedalia was not easy under the best of circumstances. The stage on which Alice and the children traveled day and night provided a notoriously uncomfortable ride over poorly maintained roads. During the first night out, an early cold wave plunged temperatures far below freezing. After dressing the children in every article of clothing she had brought, Alice huddled with Edie and Harry under a large buffalo robe until the morning sunlight dispelled the chill.

At Tishomingo, during an eight-hour wait, Alice managed to locate the unexpected, "a room with a floor, a bed, and a fireplace," and here for a few hours, they all rested comfortably. That was the extent of their blessings, however, for supper that evening was almost inedible and lacked such basic staples as bread, butter, or sugar. Fortunately, when they resumed their trip, the weather had moderated. But during the long stops at Boggy Depot and Gibson Station, Edie, who by now had lost all enthusiasm for this adventure and was already missing her father, spent her waking hours either crying or complaining. At last they reached Sedalia, where a worn-out Alice and two tired children sank gratefully into the plush, comfortable seats of a palace dining car for the ride into Chicago.[62]

When they arrived at the station, the weary travelers received a warm welcome from Charlie and John Kirk, eager to share with Alice the latest news. While they were thankful that all members of the family had escaped the fire, there was no doubt that Tom's business had sustained heavy damages. As John Kirk drove home, Alice was struck by the miles of leveled buildings and acres upon acres of debris. Her father assured her, however, that the "undaunted" Chicago businessmen had already begun the massive task of rebuilding. He was less optimistic about his wife's condition. While Susan had regained some physical strength, her contact with reality remained tenuous at best. Still, even with this preparation, it was a painful blow to Alice when her mother scarcely recognized her. Susan Bingham Kirk was lost in her own private world.[63]

Despite her mother's illness, Alice, free from the responsibility of post life, found her parents' home a welcome haven. She passed her days visiting with friends and relatives and found ample opportunity to indulge in one of her favorite pastimes, visiting the various and constantly expanding Chicago department stores, many of which had reopened at new locations since the fire. During these outings she often had to fend off peddlers attempting to sell "relics" of the recent disaster.

In the evening she frequently attended lectures with her father, Charlie, and her twenty-year-old brother Rufus. Among the more memorable were presentations given by Mark Twain, Frederick Douglass, and Thomas Beecher. For the first time in many months she began sleeping soundly throughout the night, a gratifying relief after her recent bouts with insomnia.[64]

At Fort Sill, Louisa found herself stretched to the limits of her endurance. As she tried to cope with the myriad and often conflicting duties of domestic affairs and post life, she developed a growing appreciation for the way Alice had met the demands placed upon her as mother and hostess. One problem stemmed from the difficulties of dealing with Kate and Taylor, who engaged in several "thunderous encounters," leading Louisa to fear that something "disastrous or fatal" would soon occur. Matters were not helped when two-year-old Georgie, having acquired some of their language, ran around the quarters shouting unprintable expletives in front of company. But when Louisa turned to Ben for assistance, he provided little help. Instead of being alarmed as she expected, he found the situation amusing and took great pleasure in describing Georgie's new vocabulary in his letters to Alice.[65]

The dedicated brawling of two servants was not the only behavior Louisa found upsetting. The assignment of permanent quarters according to rank continued at Fort Sill, with the accompanying dislocations, dissatisfaction, and feuding among the officers and their ladies. A steady parade of persons came to the Grierson home to lodge complaints, take meals, or spend a night or two or even more. Louisa felt she was running a hotel. The house was "invaded every day by men, women, and children," who often departed without so much as a thanks. "The idea of the family of the Post Commander being made the servants of a whole regiment of shiftless

Louisa Semple. *Courtesy Fort Davis National Historic Site, Fort Davis, Texas.*

things is simply disgusting."[66] Generally, Ben was easygoing and tolerant of such matters. Since he was genuinely fond of Kate and Taylor, he rarely intervened in their quarrels. As for extending hospitality, having been raised in the home of Robert and Mary Grierson, he placed a high value on generosity and felt it incumbent upon him as post commander to maintain at all times an open door.[67]

There were, at any rate, a number of concerns that loomed so large in his mind that the ongoing uproar in his household seemed inconsequential by comparison. Tatum's Indians still refused to behave, and there were rumors of a major outbreak. If this occurred the Tenth Cavalry was ill prepared for extensive field operations. The August campaign had broken down many of the horses, and Grierson could mount only half his command. The two hundred fresh mounts he had applied for had not arrived, leaving him hard pressed even to maintain his Red River patrols.[68]

Luckily the rumors proved untrue, and most of the Kiowas remained in their camps, but a few revenge-bent relatives of Satank and Satanta made their presence felt. They ambushed one of Grierson's patrols and killed bugler Larkin Foster of Company B. The loss of a buffalo soldier so incensed Grierson that his impulse was to take every available man and strike the Kiowas. But Tatum, feeling there was insufficient evidence to link the Kiowas to the murder, refused to give his approval. Shortly thereafter, the same parties struck again, killing and scalping two of Tatum's herders, Patrick O'Neal and John Johnson. When pinpointing the perpetrators proved impossible, Tatum again was unwilling to punish the entire tribe for the acts of a few.[69]

The Comanches, unworried about imprisoned chiefs, made life both miserable and uncertain for settlers south of the Red River. Mackenzie reported from Fort Richardson that the northern and western counties of Texas were experiencing more outrages committed "by these Indians" than "I have ever known them, here or at any other point."[70] In October, Mackenzie launched a campaign against the Kwahadis, but bad weather stalled his efforts and these Indians escaped unscathed. As usual, when cold weather set in, the raids declined, and frustrated officers and their troopers, both north and south of the Red, enjoyed a brief respite.[71]

The garrison at Fort Sill took full advantage of the "winter vacation." Horse racing, interrupted by Indian activity in the summer and fall, was resumed in November, and Robert Grierson reported to his mother that the result was a fiasco. The main event, a race between the steeds owned by Captain Little and Lieutenant Spencer, struck a snag when Little's horse "ran away with its rider," and Spencer's "threw the man off." According to Robert, "that settled the race."[72]

Picnicking, when weather permitted, was another favorite pastime, and one such party of five officers' wives, their children, guest Robert Grierson, and a proper escort, paid a visit to a patrol camp on Cache Creek. After a delightful afternoon of feasting, the party prepared to return to Fort Sill, and Lieutenant Orleman attempted to assist one of the ladies, Mrs. Meyers, into the wagon, but "he was drunk and he turned her heels up and her head down."[73] The only damage done was to Mrs. Meyers's composure.

As the Christmas holidays approached, Ben began urging Alice to make her travel arrangements to return to Fort Sill as soon as possible. Her reply caught him entirely by surprise.

> Nerves that have been for eleven years at least, getting in the state mine are, at present, and that have arrived at such a pitch of sensitiveness, as mine have been in, for the last eighteen months, will need large and long continuous doses of rest, and quiet to soothe them into a desirable state of composure.[74]

In short, Alice would not be back at the post earlier than spring and possibly not until summer.

She tried hard to soften this news, arguing that she was needed in Chicago. Her mother was ill, and Ellen had just borne a daughter, thus it was her responsibility to assist in managing the Fullers' household during her sister's recuperation. Nonetheless, there was a sharpness in her comments when she assured Ben that these tasks would be a pleasure and not a burden, unlike the situation at Fort Sill. Then Alice outlined for her husband, in this and subsequent letters, those aspects of frontier life that disturbed her most. Clearly Alice had decided to remain in Chicago longer, despite Ben's objections, but it was also apparent that she intended using this separation and her husband's discomfort and loneliness as a means of effecting some desired changes in her daily circumstances.

Chief among her complaints was the number of post visitors. Like Ben, she was "social by nature, and believe[d] hospitality to be a sacred duty. . . ." She now declared herself, however, "unwilling to make a martyr of myself for any individual or any garrison." Several weeks later she admitted, to Ben's consternation, that one couple, the Carltons, had stayed so long that at last she had bluntly asked them to leave.[75]

This was by no means her only problem. In spite of repeated pledges that additional help would be obtained, Alice was still compelled to serve as the family's seamstress, an additional demand that "was greater on me, than you can estimate." Finally, it appeared that in the daily relations between husband and wife, communication was sometimes circumvented. Otherwise it would be hard to explain why Alice raised the following issue by letter rather than discussing it earlier in person. "I mean no unkindness to you, nor do I say it reproachfully," she began, "but simply say what I honestly believe true, that your disagreeable habit of jingling your cup, when you wish it refilled at the table, has hurt me more than all I have done, since I left Ft. Sill put together." She concluded one letter by noting that if Ben were as lonely for her as he maintained, he could obtain a leave and visit with the family in Chicago.[76]

Such a trip was impossible for Ben to make at this time. His administrative duties at the post weighed heavily, often keeping him at his desk until ten in the evening. His concerns regarding the fate of the peace policy were so great that recently his rest had been disturbed, causing him to awaken every morning at three, unable to return to sleep. There were some nights, increasingly frequent now that Alice was away, when he tossed and turned until dawn.[77]

As for Alice's list of complaints, he begged her to return quickly, promising that she could "rest perfectly assured that I will do everything in my power to make you the happiest woman in the world and will make arrangements to relieve you from all work possible and have you do in every respect only what you wish to." Two days later he again implored her "to make me more than happy do come home." Never before, in all their absences, had he been "so lonely and miserable . . . when separated from you." At one point he even declared that at long last, after so many futile attempts, he had sworn off cigars and could now give her proper kisses.[78]

Obviously Alice had won some concessions, but these alone were not sufficient to bring her back to Fort Sill immediately. There was another matter that preyed on her mind. She was now forty-three and approaching menopause. If she was careful, then perhaps she could avoid another pregnancy altogether. Her most recent conceptions had occurred shortly after she stopped nursing. Now that Mary Louisa had died, Alice wished to remain in Chicago as long as possible to forestall the same eventuality.

A week before Christmas she gave some indication of this when she sent Ben a package containing copies of Theodore Tilton's recently published *Account of Mrs. Woodhull,* one for him and the other for Louisa. "I want you to read it, to please me, it will not take you more than an hour," was the accompanying message. This biography of the radical feminist and proponent of free love, Victoria Woodhull, had struck a responsive chord in Alice. Among the doctrines espoused by the controversial figure, was the dictum that love, not marriage, should form the basis of sexual relations. While Alice was not prepared to accept the idea of sex outside marriage, she was receptive to Woodhull's subsequent reasoning that within the state of matrimony, wives had the right to say "no" to marital relations, and that in all cases motherhood should be voluntary.[79]

Two days later, a long and intimate letter to Ben revealed that the couple's attempt to control fertility by relying on a common method of the time had been not only ineffective, as seven children demonstrated, but, also given Alice's religious scruples, morally objectionable. As she explained to Ben, "*We are* the temples of the living God, and those temples must never again be desecrated by an incomplete act (union)." She then continued in a vein that reflected the impact the proponents of voluntary motherhood were having on her thinking:

> I think it is desirable that the parents of every unborn human being, should from the first hour of knowledge, that by their own voluntary act, such being exists, accept the existence with at least quiet joy and thankfulness.

Unfortunately, in her own history of childbearing, this had not been the case.

> Charlie's existence, I accepted, as a matter of course, without either joy or sorrow, Kirkie's with regret for so soon succeeding him. Robert came nearer being welcomed with joy than any other. Edie was gladly welcomed as soon as I knew her sex, but I was exceedingly thankful she did not come until the close of the war. Harry succeeded her too soon . . . and it was so hard for me, to learn to harmonize public life with nursery duties, and other family cares, that I feel as if I had scarcely natural affection for Harry, and told you before he was a year old that I would rather die than have another child.[80]

Two more children had followed, but Alice maintained that she had been "neither tempted to commit suicide, nor the fearfully frequent national crime of abortion." (Her mention of both indicates that these thoughts at least crossed her mind.) Nonetheless, her existence at this point became almost intolerable and "life had ever since, been nearer a burden to me, than at all desirable." With the birth and death of Mary Louisa, Alice felt that she had almost lost her mind, a fear which haunted her still, considering her mother's state.

Yet, while she had originally thought of staying in Chicago at least until summer, Ben's loneliness had touched her, and she was prepared to compromise and return home in March. What she asked of him in return was his assurance that never again would she become pregnant.[81]

It was some time before Ben received this letter at Fort Sill, and, in the meantime, he continued to press Alice to return quickly. He described himself as a *"poor cuss in exile out in the Wilderness* left in the meantime lonely and miserable without his wife and children." He revealed too that, in his mind at least, he and John Kirk competed for Alice's affection, for he reminded her that however much her father loved her, his love could not compare with Ben's.[82]

Alice's books arrived, along with a collection of speeches by the feminist Elizabeth Cady Stanton, also a proponent of "voluntary motherhood," and a reprint of an address by William Lloyd Garrison on women's suffrage, "one of the best" Alice had ever seen. As he promised, Ben read them and wrote his wife that when it came to the subject of women's rights, there were no differences between them. He considered the topic "too sublime to be written down in *hasty* chapter." He was much more interested in discussing with her the other issues between them, for his emotional state was now one of great sadness. It hurt him, he acknowledged, that Alice could look upon their separation "with much more complacency than I could possibly summon to my command or manifest under like or the same circumstances. And now," he added, "perhaps I have said something I should not have said. I will think and believe so long as possible that you do love me—even if I never see you again."

His mental attitude had deteriorated, allowing self pity and loneliness to surface. "I do not know of any great reason why any one should love, or even care for me. There never was anything very inviting or captivating about me—even in my young and best days." Now, at forty-five, he had grown "old and gray," and his attractiveness was entirely gone. "Besides," he added, "I have no right to have any friends as I am *a poor miserable Cuss* and have no peach or class."[83]

Shortly thereafter, his letters revealed a different mood. He had turned to his old companion, music, to relieve his sadness, playing all the songs he remembered in the minor keys. "I *have* had my cry *on the violin* and feel as much relieved after it as any woman can after a veritable cry out of the eyes." He also shared with Alice a recent dream. She had been attending a woman's rights convention and had been so absorbed in the proceedings that she failed to notice him. Poking fun at himself, he acknowledged, "I would prefer to see you even in my dreams where you would have sufficient leisure to pay a little more attention to me." Once more Ben's natural optimism and good humor were struggling to the fore.[84]

This separation, difficult as it was, gave Ben and Alice the chance to air their differences. Alice admitted that she would be much happier living in a city such as Chicago or even Jacksonville, rather than at a lonely frontier outpost such as Fort Sill. Ben disagreed with her on the virtues of city life. Chicago was too crowded for his tastes, and Jacksonville seemed less like home with each passing year. "My only home is the United States and the territories especially." In his opinion, modern cities had been "spoiled," for the woods, hills, and other natural surroundings had all been destroyed.[85]

Finally, Alice confided to Ben that, from her perspective, what motivated him was ambition, an ambition so great that at times he placed his military duties ahead of his family's needs and interests. This remark cut Ben deeply, for he took strong exception. He had enlisted in the Civil War, not for glory, but because of "the deep interest I felt in the cause." His advancement had been due to "my natural pluck and devotion to my country & family & last and not the least reason of my success—by any means—ever your assistance during the struggle." All he sought now, "the height of my great ambition is to be worthy of & to be able to retain at all times your love."[86]

Early in January, Ben received a letter from Alice that dispelled the shadows over their relationship. She had placed one of his recent letters on the Christmas tree as her most prized gift and then went on to assure him that never in their seventeen years of marriage had she regretted her choice; she was not a dissatisfied wife. As he had done so often in the past, Ben wasted no time in replying. Once more he asked forgiveness for any harsh or unkind words he had uttered, and he admitted that at times they misunderstood one another. He concluded by pleading that in the future she should make it a special point to confide in him, without hesitation, her "earnest hopes and fears," as well as "the joys & sorrows of your heart." Ben recognized that better communication might have served to ease many of the recent tensions between them.[87]

When Alice arrived, earlier than expected, at the end of February, she received a joyous welcome from her husband. For awhile all in their quarters was serene. Then, a few weeks later, a violent quarrel erupted in the kitchen, and Kate felled Taylor with a flat-iron. Fortunately he was not seriously injured. Not to be outdone, Georgie lost his temper at the table, mouthed a few choice bits of profanity and was sent to bed by his indignant mother, while Ben tried hard to stifle his laughter.[88]

In the midst of efforts to restore some semblance of order and propriety to her quarters, Alice received word that her mother had died. The news was not unexpected, and Alice's reply to Charlie in Chicago showed little emotion. Nonetheless, for a time she limited her social activities, confining her visits to seeing Mary Ann Tatum. The two had become intimate friends, for Alice found much in common with the warm, kind, and God-fearing Quakeress. To her surprise she learned that the Tatums were disillusioned with the peace policy. Though Indian raids had, as usual, declined with the onset of winter, and Grierson's patrols along Red River reported no significant activity, Lawrie Tatum felt certain that when spring arrived, red marauders would again strike the Texas frontier. The Indians might remain in their camps if several chronic troublemakers were arrested and imprisoned, but Tatum's superiors would not countenance such a course.[89]

Comanche and Kiowa raiders soon confirmed Tatum's view. From Fort Richardson, Colonel Mackenzie informed department head-quarters that war parties were active all along the line from his post to Fort Stockton in far west Texas, a distance of more than four hundred miles. Grierson's thin line of troopers along the Red rarely intercepted the elusive Indians. Once again, it was the Kiowas who inflicted the greatest losses. On April 20, White Horse and Big Bow, with a strong force of warriors, attacked an unescorted government train at Howard's Well on the San Antonio–El Paso road. The swarm of braves overwhelmed the train's defenders and seventeen civilians were killed. Emboldened by their success, the Indians remained in the vicinity long enough to fight off pursuit by two companies of the Ninth Cavalry.[90]

Raids by reservation Indians were not the only concern facing Grierson and his regiment in the spring of 1872. Construction of the Missouri, Kansas and Texas Railroad, the "Katy," through eastern Indian Territory, brought a host of undesirables to prey on workers, Indians, or anyone else who crossed their path. Gamblers, bootleggers, thieves, desperadoes, "ladies of leisure," speculators, and drifters thronged the line of the road to ply their various and nefarious trades.

General Sherman, fully apprised of the state of affairs, ordered Grierson to take sufficient troops and, operating out of Fort Gibson, expel "intruders from the Territory." He also instructed General C. C. Augur, commanding the Department of Texas, which since the previous November had included Indian Territory, to spare neither officers nor men in the pursuit and punishment of raiding Indians.[91]

On April 23, Major George W. Schofield assumed command at Fort Sill, and Grierson marched for Fort Gibson with four companies of the Tenth. When he arrived, he found conditions "very unsettled" and hastened to assign each company to a section of the railroad. Scores of unsavory characters were rounded up and escorted to the Kansas line, while those guilty of crimes were arrested and taken to Fort Smith, Arkansas, for trial. Grierson's swift action brought a potentially explosive state of affairs under control, but maintaining order seemed a continuing task, and in May, Augur ordered Grierson to move his headquarters to Gibson. Reluctantly, Ben wrote Alice to "start packing." She would have to vacate the new, comparatively large, and comfortable quarters that had just been carpeted. With Louisa's assistance, though their relationship was again a cool one, Alice quickly made the necessary arrangements and reached Gibson in mid-June.[92]

At the time of her departure, an anti-Grierson "clique" had surfaced at Fort Sill, led by Major Schofield. The discontent stemmed from alleged discrimination in assignment of quarters and unorthodox methods in dealing with the officers and men. Only a handful of officers were involved, but Captain Carpenter, a Grierson friend with a distinguished combat record, was concerned enough to warn Ben that derogatory information was being forwarded to General Augur, who was known to dislike "non-West Pointers" and might believe "the stuff." Others wrote in similar vein, for Grierson was a respected and popular commander.[93]

Ben appreciated the warnings, but he made no effort to defend himself, nor did he take any action to punish his detractors. He had always done his duty to the best of his ability and would continue to do so. Augur would have great difficulty finding any real cause for complaint. It was a typical Grierson reaction to quarrels, complaints, and petty jealousies—he did not choose to be involved.[94]

The unhappiness of a few officers at Fort Sill was far surpassed by the gloom that settled over the Indian agency in the summer of 1872. Tatum's lingering hopes that kindness and fair dealing would bring lasting peace were dashed by Kiowa activity. On June 4, less than two miles from Fort Sill a band of warriors killed and scalped unarmed Frank Lee, an employee of a wood contractor. Five days later, White Horse led a small party across the Red to avenge the death of his brother, killed a few weeks earlier in a raid into Texas. On a clear Sunday afternoon the Indians approached the home of Abel Lee on the Clear Fork of the Brazos, only sixteen miles from Fort Griffin. They spied Lee sitting on the porch reading a newspaper, opened fire, and killed him instantly.

Mrs. Lee and her four children, who were inside the house, ran to his side and then tried to flee as the warriors swooped down on them. Mrs. Lee was overtaken inside the house, shot and killed, and her body mutilated. Rebecca Lee, aged fourteen was caught and slain in the backyard, while Susannah, sixteen, Millie, nine, and John, six, were taken captive. When Tatum learned of the tragedy, all he could do was withhold rations and demand return of the children.[95]

In July, the Five Civilized Tribes, who had suffered severe losses from Kiowa and Comanche incursions into their horse herds, made an effort to promote peace by inviting their unruly neighbors to a council at Old Fort Cobb. Little was accomplished except to provide a forum for belligerent speeches on the part of White Horse and Lone Wolf, though Kicking Bird did promise to do all in his power to return the Lee children.[96]

The Indian Bureau also attempted to impress the Plains tribes with the virtues of peace by arranging for a delegation of chiefs to visit Washington. En route, the Kiowas, among them Lone Wolf, were permitted a brief visit with Satanta and Big Tree, who were brought under guard to St. Louis. It proved the first step in their release, for Bureau officials in Washington promised, in return for Kiowa good behavior, to prevail on Governor Davis to free the chiefs.[97]

Temporarily, the prospect of freedom for Satanta and Big Tree kept the Kiowas in their camps, but Lawrie Tatum, who had lost all faith in their promises, was unalterably opposed to release of the chiefs. He was certain that Satanta, both "daring and treacherous" would resume raiding at the first opportunity. Feeling that his position as agent had been seriously compromised, he resigned effective March 31, 1873.[98]

The Kiowas had been persuaded by Indian Bureau promises to take the peace road, but the Comanches encountered persuasion of another kind. Heeding Augur's instructions, Colonel Mackenzie set out to strike the Kwahadis. On September 29, with a six-company command, he surprised a large camp on the North Fork of the Red, killed twenty-three warriors, captured 120 women and children, and totally destroyed the camp. Mackenzie then marched to Fort Concho, Texas, where his captives were interned in the post corral.

For the first time, the Kwahadies came to the agency and begged Tatum to restore their women and children. They assured him they were prepared to accept the white man's road. As a precondition to any intervention on his part, Tatum insisted that all white captives must be surrendered, and when this was done, he wrote Mackenzie requesting that the Comanche prisoners be returned to their people.[99]

While Satanta and Big Tree remained in prison, and the Comanche women and children stoically bore their confinement at Fort Concho, the Texas frontier enjoyed an unprecedented peace. The question remained, would the peace continue when these prisoners were released? Most observers outside the Indian Bureau were skeptical.[100]

Among the doubters was Grierson. He had no stomach for making war on an entire tribe and remained an advocate of the peace policy. But like Tatum he had come to the conclusion that release of Satanta and Big Tree would prove to be a mistake. Imprisonment of chronic raiders would have a salutary effect if combined with fair and decent treatment for the others.

At Fort Gibson, Grierson again had the opportunity to demonstrate his genuine interest in the welfare of the Indian people, as well as his sincere desire for peace. In August, contending factions in the Creek Nation were at the point of armed conflict. Though divided in their loyalties during the Civil War and suffering severely as a result, the Creeks had resolved these differences. Now a crisis had arisen over implementing a new constitution adopted in 1867. An explosive schism developed, exacerbated by the machinations of railroad promoters who sought to use tribal quarrels as a means of acquiring Creek landholdings.

Grierson hastened to arrange meetings with leaders of both sides, urged them to settle their disputes without resort to arms, and, to his great relief, reached agreement on a truce. This accomplished, he sent for Enoch Hoag, head of the central Indian superintendency and supervisor of Indian affairs in the Territory. Grierson's tact and diplomacy prevented a bloodbath and provided avenues for discussion, although factional quarrels continued among the Creeks for another decade.[101]

With the Creek troubles eased and the intruder problem under control, life for the Griersons at Fort Gibson assumed an easy and pleasant tenor. Louisa's return to Jacksonville spared Alice the aggravation of her presence, the children were free of ills and found ample outlet for their energies in play with other youngsters of the garrison. Though housing at the little post was crowded beyond capacity, the officers knew their stay was temporary and accepted conditions in good spirits. Lieutenant L. H. Orleman of B Company, could joke about his "Quarters"—a hospital tent in Captain Carpenter's backyard.[102]

Frequent parties and hops enlivened the evenings, and at the latter Ben always stayed until the last note had sounded. At one of these affairs, given by the Griersons, the beds in the infirmary were rolled away, the floors were polished, and a four-piece band played by the light of fifty candles until 3 A.M. Alice admitted the music was "good." The routine of post life was broken further when Sheridan and Augur paid a visit. To the Grierson's considerable relief, all went well. Augur was most complimentary and reported officially that "Under his [Grierson's] judicious management the removal [of intruders] has been effected without trouble or a single complaint, so far as I have heard." As for Sheridan, Robert thought him the "stillest" man he had ever seen.[103]

Ben and Alice never escaped very long, however, without encountering some strain either within their immediate family or among their relatives. John Kirk provided the next bombshell of sorts when he married a Youngstown widow and lecturer "on the woman question," Ann Bayne. It was only five months after Susan's death, and though Kirk had known this woman for many years, having worked with her in the temperance movement, his precipitous action angered both his daughter Ellen and his son Tom. In their eyes, their father had shown gross disrespect for their beloved mother, barely cold in her grave. To make matters worse, the new Mrs. Kirk occasionally used profanity and often sat with her husband by the fireside with her feet resting on his legs and her skirts up to her knees.[104]

Kirk had never accepted an invitation to visit Indian Territory, but he now made haste to bring his bride to Fort Gibson to seek Alice's approval. His fears regarding her attitude were groundless, for, to his great relief, Alice gave Ann a warm welcome. During the Kirks' stay the two women found that they shared much in common, including a continuing interest in temperance and woman's rights. After what Ben described as a "pleasant visit," the Kirks returned to Chicago, taking Robert along as a guest.[105]

Alice's approval of the new Mrs. Kirk had, initially, little effect on Tom and Ellen, who made no effort to hide their continuing disapproval. Ann Kirk, an outspoken woman always ready and willing to defend herself, stunned Tom by calling him a "shit," and not long afterward she referred to Ellen in the same fashion. Charlie, still boarding at the Kirk home while in school, was caught in the middle of the family feud and asked his mother for advice. Alice informed him unequivocally that he was to "learn civility to all human beings."[106] Many months passed before cordial relations were restored among members of the Kirk family.

For Ben and Alice, the last few weeks of 1872 were among the most enjoyable of their lives. At Fort Gibson no disturbance occurred to mar the approach of Christmas, and reports from Fort Sill were reassuring. The Kiowas and Comanches, eagerly awaiting the return of their people, gave no cause for alarm. Schofield's clique had clearly failed to influence Augur, for the latter had been both cordial and complimentary while at Gibson.

In November, Ben obtained a brief leave and journeyed to Jacksonville to vote for Grant. That his old commander's first term lacked significant achievement and that charges of graft and corruption were rampant, made no impression on Grierson. He agreed with Grant that his opponent, Horace Greeley, and the Liberal Republicans were like "the deceptive noise made in the West by prairie wolves."[107] He was also pleased to learn that his brother John now agreed with his sentiments, after disputing them earlier, and had also cast his vote for Grant. Ben was even more relieved to learn that John's fortunes had improved. He had relocated from Memphis to Chicago and was now employed in Tom Kirk's reopened hardware business.[108]

On his return to Gibson, Grierson launched a campaign of his

own, asking Sherman for assistance in gaining promotion to brigadier. Sherman was not encouraging. Although he held Ben in high
esteem, there were three major and seven brigadier generals in the
service, and "death alone will produce vacancies."[109] Ben remained
undaunted and, in the years ahead, conducted his quest for promotion with ever increasing and unrelenting vigor.

The holidays were celebrated at Gibson with the usual round of
parties, dances and gift-giving, but they also brought a change in
duties and station for Grierson. Influenced largely by Alice's desire
to enjoy the amenities of city life, he had responded favorably to a
Sherman inquiry concerning his interest in a temporary assignment
as Superintendent of the Mounted Recruiting Service, headquartered
in St. Louis. On December 31, orders arrived confirming the appointment. Lieutenant Colonel Davidson would assume command
of the Tenth in Grierson's absence.[110]

Ben and Alice welcomed the change. It meant two years in an
interesting and lively city, with easy access to family and friends
in Jacksonville and Chicago as well as good schools for Robert and
Edie. Ben felt the new post might enhance his chances for promotion. He could not have known that in his absence his regiment
would engage in a far-flung and major Indian war, and an opportunity once again to prove his effectiveness as a combat officer would
be lost.

CHAPTER 8

Banished to West Texas

T HE FIRST WEEK in January, 1873, after more than six years as commanding officer, Ben Grierson issued a circular bidding farewell to the officers and men of the Tenth Cavalry. After a round of parties given by friends at Fort Gibson, the Griersons left for St. Louis. On arrival they took large and comfortable quarters in the old Arsenal building, and Alice sent for Charlie. The family was united for the first time since the summer of 1871.[1]

Ben's official duties were not demanding, and he and his family took full advantage of the many and varied activities available in the bustling "Gateway to the West." They regularly attended the theatre, concerts, and lectures, dined out on occasion, and frequently entertained visitors. Ben's pocketbook underwent mounting strain, but John Kirk's considerable resources provided loans to maintain a near-continuous vacation.[2]

President Grant also contributed to the Grierson's sense of well-being. Charlie had done well in his studies and was now ready to begin preparing for a military career. At Ben's request, the President appointed Charlie to West Point, contingent on his passing the qualifying examinations. To celebrate, Ben took his son to Grant's second inaugural, where the youngster was introduced to the president, his wife, Julia, and other notables.[3]

While all went well for the St. Louis Griersons, this was not true for some of their Kirk and Grierson relatives. Months had passed before Tom Kirk determined the full extent of his losses from the Chicago fire, but the final figures disclosed that his insurance coverage fell short by twenty thousand dollars. He managed to keep his store reopened throughout 1872, but when the Panic of 1873 ushered in a depression, hard times not only diminished his sales, but curtailed his supply of credit. Finding himself more than fifty thousand dollars in debt, much of it to his father, Tom could borrow no more.

His only hope for averting bankruptcy appeared to lie in an upswing in the business cycle, an unlikely prospect for the present. His book-keeper, John Grierson, watched all of this with growing anxiety, fearing that very shortly he would be forced to look again for another position during a period of business distress and mounting unemployment.[4]

In addition, Louisa Semple plunged into a deep depression. Since returning from Fort Gibson in April, 1872, she had waged perpetual war with John and Elizabeth and quarreled with other family members "from the oldest to the youngest." Now, having "worn out her welcome" at John's home and her sister Susan's, she began brooding constantly over the irrevocable past. Her despondency became so great that John wrote his brother: "Something must be done, if she will allow it—if not I shall expect to see her an inmate of the Insane Asylum."[5]

Ben alone had managed to maintain a close and loving relationship with his temperamental sister, and he provided a partial solution to her difficulties. He had intended selling the Jacksonville homestead, but now he turned it over to Louisa, though both John and Alice doubted the wisdom of this arrangement. Time would prove the move a fortunate one.[6]

Though sensitive as always to family matters, Ben and Alice did not allow the misfortunes of Tom Kirk, John, and Louisa to mar their pleasant days in St. Louis. In August they enjoyed a week at Niagara Falls, and on their return, Alice left for a long visit with friends and relatives in Ohio and then to Sandy Lake, Pennsylvania, where her father and her stepmother had recently settled.

The first year of marriage for John and Ann Bayne Kirk had not been entirely serene. The new Mrs. Kirk expressed her opinions openly, and eight months after the wedding, Alice had received a letter from Ann, bearing the postmark of Geneva, Ashtabula County, Ohio, and containing this message: "Your father and I had a few words and parted one week ago today." Upsetting as this was, Alice was certain that the separation was temporary, for Ann had noted "the time we can enjoy each other's society is short enough at the longest. . . ."[7] Very soon, they were reconciled. When Alice returned to St. Louis, she reported that the couple appeared to be enjoying their new life together, renovating an old house and restoring the grounds and orchard.[8] In her absence, Ben had spent his time catching up on administrative duties, making plans for gaining promotion, and assessing a growing flow of letters on development at Fort Sill.

A long delay in the release of Satanta and Big Tree and the Comanche women and children created concern for the behavior of their tribes. As a result, in March, headquarters of the Tenth was transferred from Gibson to Sill, and eight companies of the regiment were concentrated there. The Indians caused no immediate problems, however, and Davidson seized the chance to reorganize the regimental staff and initiate a program of rigid discipline in contrast to Grierson's more tolerant approach.[9]

Davidson's efforts achieved minimal success. Staff reorganization brought a rebuke from Adjutant General E. D. Townsend, who informed him that, "The Lieutenant Colonel commanding is not authorized to make changes in arrangement of the regimental staff," adding that this applied to "non-commissioned officers" as well. The first to run afoul of the new disciplinary rules was Davidson's son, who was arrested for walking on the grass while crossing the parade ground.[10]

Rivalry and quarrels over quarters also gave Davidson problems. An unseemly feud developed between Captain William Foulk of D Company and several other officers. One of these, Captain T. A. Baldwin, went to Foulk's quarters to smooth over the matter and was set upon by Mrs. Foulk with a horsewhip, while the two Foulk children threw books at him. As a result the Foulks were ostracized by the rest of the garrison, and Davidson arranged the transfer of Foulk and D Company to Fort Griffin, Texas.[11]

An able but erratic commander, Davidson failed to gain support among the officer corps and found himself caught between two groups. The old anti-Grierson Schofield clique sought to discredit him, while Grierson loyalists sent a steady stream of complaints to St. Louis. Sam Woodward thought Davidson issued strange orders, and was subject to "fits," but deserving of sympathy in dealing with Schofield and associates; others simply urged Grierson to return as soon as possible.[12]

Petty strife among the officers and Davidson's unpopularity were minor annoyances when compared with the difficulties of dealing with the Kiowas and Comanches. No serious trouble occurred in the spring and early summer, but in June, when their women and children were returned, the Comanche camps spewed forth numerous raiders. Efforts by Davidson's troopers to turn them back were unsuccessful. Harried post commanders in Texas, with every available man in the saddle, rarely managed an interception.[13]

The Kiowas took no part in these raids, but as the months passed with no sign of Satanta and Big Tree, anger, frustration, and restlessness mounted. Speculation grew among the military and other observers, that the Kiowas might join the Comanches in an all-out war. Pressure mounted on Governor Davis to calm the Kiowas by freeing the chiefs.

Davis had reason to hesitate. Freedom for the Comanche prisoners had resulted in a renewal of assaults on the frontier of his state. He had no guarantee that the Kiowas would not return to their old ways once Satanta and Big Tree were released. At length, however, President Grant persuaded the reluctant governor to yield, though Davis still insisted on a number of conditions.

Early in October, Davis and some members of his staff brought the chiefs to Fort Sill under military escort. After several days of intense bargaining with Commissioner of Indian Affairs E. P. Smith and Superintendent Hoag, Davis gave up all but one of his demands and freed the chiefs. Had he delayed longer, the Kiowas were planning to take them by force.[14]

Davis's lone remaining condition, that five Comanche warriors guilty of recent raids be arrested and imprisoned, was never met. Initially, Commissioner Smith withheld rations while a combined force of troopers and warriors searched for the guilty parties. The search produced no results, but Smith soon ordered Agent Haworth to resume issuing rations. The end result was a rash of Kiowa raids on the Texas frontier.[15]

In the long and frequent letters between Woodward and Grierson, both agreed that the outlook was not promising. To make matters worse, in the face of a number of severe problems, including a probable Kiowa-Comanche outbreak, serious trouble with the Apaches of Arizona and New Mexico, growing difficulties with the Sioux in the Dakotas, and unstable conditions along the Mexican border, Congress intended reducing the army further. After the reorganization of 1866 and cuts in both 1869 and 1870, additional trimming was on the horizon.

Grierson kept a wary eye on the progress of the army bill through the Congress. Debates on consolidation and elimination of units, reductions in manpower, and lower pay scales sent a wave of uneasiness through the military. Many officers feared their days in the service were numbered, and Ben received many letters from friends in the Tenth requesting his assistance if they were marked for dismissal. Some of them believed the Tenth would be either disbanded or consolidated with another regiment.

As finally enacted in March, 1874, the army appropriations bill reduced the overall strength to twenty-seven thousand, half the size of the 1866 establishment, and placed stringent restrictions on recruitment. Pay scales were allowed to remain at the 1870 level. Congress thus ensured even greater rivalry and jealousy among officers, along with erosion of morale. Grierson's chance for promotion remained far distant, and his hopes for a pay increase were blasted, but he still had a command and a regiment. His duties in mounted recruitment, never heavy, were now negligible.[16]

Pessimism at Fort Sill regarding Indian behavior was reinforced in the winter of 1873–74. The usual winter let-up in raiding did not occur, though the Indians paid a high price. In December and January, hard-riding troopers operating out of Forts Griffin and Clark finally scored heavily on their red antagonists. In two fierce encounters they killed twenty warriors, and among the slain were Lone Wolf's son and nephew. The chief was inconsolable, "slashed himself all up," and could think of nothing but revenge. The Comanche camps buzzed with talk of war, and they sought support from the restless Southern Cheyennes.[17]

Revenge was not the only motive. The restraints of reservation life, along with often inadequate rations, created resentment that was stimulated by whiskey, easily obtained from bootleggers. The vast herds of buffalo, central to the Indian way of life, were fast disappearing under the guns of white hide hunters, while white horse thieves constantly raided the Indian pony herds. Little wonder that by late spring most of the Comanches and Cheyennes, and Lone Wolf's faction of the Kiowas, were ready to take the warpath.

In May, a son of the Cheyenne chief Little Robe, while trying to recover some stolen horses, was wounded in a skirmish with Sixth Cavalry troopers, and the lid was off. A large party of Cheyenne warriors came to their agency, assured the agent and his employees that no harm would come to them, "and rode off and began killing people."[18] Red raiders ravaged the Texas frontier, and in June some seven hundred Kiowa, Comanche, and Cheyenne warriors attempted to wipe out a party of buffalo hunters at Adobe Walls in the Texas Panhandle. They were repulsed with severe losses, but two weeks later a band of Kiowas under Lone Wolf badly mauled a company of Texas Rangers.[19]

There was no longer any doubt as to the scale and intensity of Indian hostilities and, under urging from General Sherman, the Secretaries of War and Interior soon reached agreement on measures to quell the outbreak. On July 21, Sherman notified Sheridan to order sufficient forces into the field to inflict overwhelming defeat. Reservation boundaries were to be ignored and Indian hostiles punished wherever found. Care was to be taken to separate the innocent from the guilty by enrolling the former at their agencies. Commissioner Smith informed his subordinates in the Indian service of the change in policy.[20]

Grant's peace program, designed and launched with high hopes in 1869 lay in ruins, a blow to many ardent supporters, including Ben Grierson. He still had no desire to "kill Indians," and ignored inquiries regarding his return to lead his regiment against the hostile bands. Still, he was fiercely loyal to the Tenth, that must now pursue and fight Indian warriors well known to them. He had no doubt that his officers and men would do their duty, a faith that was soon fully justified.[21]

Enrollment at Fort Sill and the Cheyenne agency proceeded without serious difficulty, and when completed on August 8, found most of the Comanches and Cheyennes "out," but a majority of the Kiowas followed Kicking Bird into camps near their agency. Even some of Lone Wolf's followers had enrolled, but their loyalty was subject to question.[22]

Sheridan, meanwhile, had instructed his department commanders, Pope and Augur, to push multiple commands into the field to strike the hostiles from all sides and maintain unrelenting pressure. Accordingly, Pope ordered a column under Colonel Nelson A. Miles to march south from Fort Dodge and another, commanded by Major William R. Price, to move east from Fort Bascom, New Mexico. Augur sent out three columns under Colonel Mackenzie, Lieutenant Colonel Buell, and Davidson. Mackenzie would operate north and west of Fort Concho, while Buell and Davidson moved west from Forts Griffin and Sill.[23]

Miles, Mackenzie, and Price were in the field before the end of August. But Buell encountered delay in securing supplies, while Davidson's preparations were stalled temporarily by sudden and unexpected trouble at Anadarko, site of the agency for the Wichita and Affiliated Tribes.

In the late afternoon of August 21, Davidson received an urgent message from Captain Gaines Lawson, commanding a lone company of infantry at Anadarko. Kiowa hostiles were lurking in the vicinity and a band of non-enrolled Comanches under Big Red Food had actually encamped near the agency commissary. Lawson's force was too small too drive these Indians away or even to protect the agency.

Davidson acted promptly. By noon the following day he reached Anadarko with four companies of buffalo soldiers. He sent for Big Red Food and told him bluntly that the Comanches must give up their arms and return to Fort Sill as prisoners of war. Woodward, with a detachment of troopers, escorted the chief to his camp and began the collecting of weapons. Taunts by Kiowa warriors observing the proceedings led the chief to refuse to surrender bows and arrows, break from his captors, and dash into nearby timber and brush. The troopers fired at him, the Kiowas returned the fire, and the battle was on.

For a few minutes wild confusion reigned as hundreds of friendly Indians, who had arrived for rations issue, scrambled in every direction seeking safety. Once these people were out of the way, Davidson drove the hostiles from the agency grounds and positioned the companies to defend buildings and property. Long-range rifle fire continued until nightfall and was resumed at daybreak. By midday, the Indians broke off the action and retired westward along the Washita River. Davidson had four men and six horses wounded and believed more than a dozen warriors had been "shot off their horses."[24]

The fight at Anadarko served to define clearly the ranks of hostile and friendly bands. The warriors discovered that an agency was no longer a sanctuary for those who chose the warpath, and they gathered in old haunts in the western reaches of Indian Territory and the Texas Panhandle. The military now had well defined targets for their gathering campaign.

Anadarko also provided an answer, for those willing to listen, to the question of the fighting qualities of Grierson's Tenth. Scorn and abuse had dogged their footsteps for five long years at Fort Sill, but they had fought with valor and skill at the Wichita Agency, while ensuring that they did no harm to the innocent. Their old commander, at his desk in St. Louis, could not have wished for more.

While Davidson restored order at Anadarko, the columns of Miles, Price, and Mackenzie, marching in searing summer heat, were converging rapidly on probable points of Indian concentration in the Texas Panhandle. On August 30, as Miles approached a low line of hills bordering the Staked Plains, some six hundred Cheyenne, Kiowa, and Comanche warriors contested his advance. After a five-hour fight among the hills and ravines, the Indians were driven to the plains, where they scattered.

Miles's command was too worn out for effective pursuit, and his supplies were at a perilously low level. He moved back to the Canadian, where he established a supply camp and arranged for two others on the Washita and Sweetwater. From these points he sent out small columns to prevent hostile movement northward and to probe for any of their camps in the area.[25]

Price, after an uneventful march east, joined Miles on September 7. Five days later he set out to link up with his train, which he had sent to the Washita depot for supplies. Along the way he encountered a host of Kiowas and Comanches—the same who had fought Davidson at Anadarko—and was hard put to do more than hold his own. Shortly thereafter, on orders from General Pope, he merged his force with that of Miles.[26]

The movements of Miles and Price served to drive many of the warrior bands southwest to the rough and broken country along the Staked Plains escarpment and straight into the path of Mackenzie. His scouts reported a huge camp in the rugged depths of Palo Duro Canyon and found a steep, narrow trail leading to the bottom. At dawn on September 28, the command made the descent, took the Indians by surprise, and easily routed them. After destroying hundreds of lodges, tons of supplies and equipment, and capturing the entire pony herd, Mackenzie withdrew. After a few of the better animals were eliminated from the herd, the remainder, numbering more than a thousand, were shot.[27]

The rout in Palo Duro Canyon cost the Indians few casualties but was, nonetheless, a devastating blow. Deprived of food, lodging, and animals, many of them gave up the struggle and headed eastward toward their agencies. Mackenzie remained in the field until December, scouring the headwaters of the Red and Brazos rivers, determined that no Indian in his area of operations could be assured of a peaceful night's sleep.[28]

Buell did not solve his problems of transport and supplies until the end of September. Then, with two battalions of buffalo soldiers from the Ninth and Tenth Cavalry, he marched west along the Salt Fork of Red River. On October 9, a deserted camp of fifteen lodges was found and destroyed and a warm trail discovered. Buell pursued with all possible speed as his quarry fled northwest and then northeast in an effort to shake him off. In rapid succession he burned villages of 75 and 475 lodges. Finding the trail littered with discarded camp equipment and worn-out ponies, Buell felt he would soon force the Indians to make a stand. Instead, on reaching the Canadian, the trail broke in all directions.

With Miles now in position to take up the chase, Buell replenished his supplies and headed back south. For the next five weeks he ranged the breaks of the Salt Fork and flushed a few small parties. Not until snow, sleet, and rain made progress impossible did he return to Fort Griffin.[29]

Davidson's Fort Sill column moved out on September 12 to operate between Miles and Buell. A month-long sweep on a broad front, during which they skirted the edge of the Staked Plains, "through some of the most broken country" brought no results. With many of his animals worn out, Davidson came in to rest and refit.[30]

He was on the move again by late October, pushing west from Old Fort Cobb, and almost immediate success rewarded this effort. In less than a week the command surprised and forced the surrender of a small party of Kiowas and a large camp of Comanches. In the latter were five prominent chiefs, including Big Red Food of Anadarko fame. These Indians were among those fleeing from the tenacious Buell. Continuing west, Davidson, on November 8, struck and burned a Cheyenne camp of seventy-five lodges on the North Fork of Red River. He pursued the Indians to the Canadian River, where many of his horses gave out and more than a hundred others froze to death. Davidson had no choice other than to return to Fort Sill, but he kept small patrols in the field until January.[31]

Four months of near-constant fighting, pursuit, and harassment, combined with enormous losses in animals, food supplies, and equipment, wore down the Indian will to resist. In increasing numbers they gave up the struggle, moved into their agencies, and surrendered. At Fort Sill the women and children were quartered in detention camps while the warriors were confined in the guardhouse and corral. When these spaces were filled, others were imprisoned in the icehouse. Many of the horses and mules were shot, and the rest auctioned for a fraction of their value.[32]

Ringleaders of the outbreak and those guilty of crimes were singled out, shackled, and sent to prison at Fort Marion, Florida. Among the more prominent of these were Lone Wolf and White Horse of the Kiowas, and Black Horse of the Comanches. Satanta, who had turned himself in at the Cheyenne agency in October, was returned to the Huntsville penitentiary, where he took his own life in 1878. The last to come in, the Kwahadis, did not reach Fort Sill until June, where they surrendered to Mackenzie, who had replaced Davidson as commander at that post.[33]

The main body of Cheyennes laid down their arms at their agency in March. During the process of separating the guilty from the innocent an event occurred that brought tragedy to the Cheyennes and unwarranted accusations of cowardice to two companies of the Tenth Cavalry. On the afternoon of April 6, while the blacksmith was fitting irons on a number of warriors, one of them bolted. He failed to halt when hailed by the guards, was fired on, and killed. Some of the shots penetrated the Cheyenne camp and brought a volley of arrows accompanied by a stampede.

About 150 men, women, and children fled to a nearby sand hill, dug up weapons buried there before their surrender, and entrenched. Lieutenant Thomas H. Neill, Sixth Cavalry, commanding at the agency, sent his available cavalry, M Company of the Sixth and D and M of the Tenth, to corral the runaways. Deep sand and hot Indian fire held the troopers off until nightfall, when the Cheyennes managed to slip away and escape.

Neill had high praise for his company of the Sixth, but charged that the buffalo soldiers had refused to fight, a charge hotly denied by Captains S. T. Norvell and A. S. B. Keyes, commanding these troopers. Neill never retracted his statements and his official report remained an uncorrected matter of record. This was so even though Norvell and Keyes's men had incurred two-thirds of the casualties. Prejudice continued to haunt the footsteps of Grierson's Tenth Cavalry. Grierson, well informed on the course of the war and outraged by Neill's report, asked for a general court-martial, but the judge advocate general ruled otherwise.[34]

Grierson shrugged off this rebuff from the "powers that be," but he was still smarting from orders received in November transferring his regiment to scattered posts in west Texas and his headquarters from Fort Sill to Fort Concho. Once more he was being exiled to an isolated location that offered little, if any, opportunity for advancement.[35] John Grierson had searched his map in vain to find Concho until Ben pointed it out to him. In John's view, his brother had been sentenced to "the most God-forsaken part of Uncle Sam's Dominions." While it may have been true, John noted, that Horace Greeley had advised men to "go west," he had assumed they would have enough sense at least to "orient themselves."[36]

Aside from Fort Concho's remoteness and lack of promise, there were other reasons for Grierson's reluctance to make the move. He had expected to return to Fort Sill, which he regarded as "his post," and reports indicated that Fort Concho was in deplorable condition. This meant that it would be some time before his family joined him,

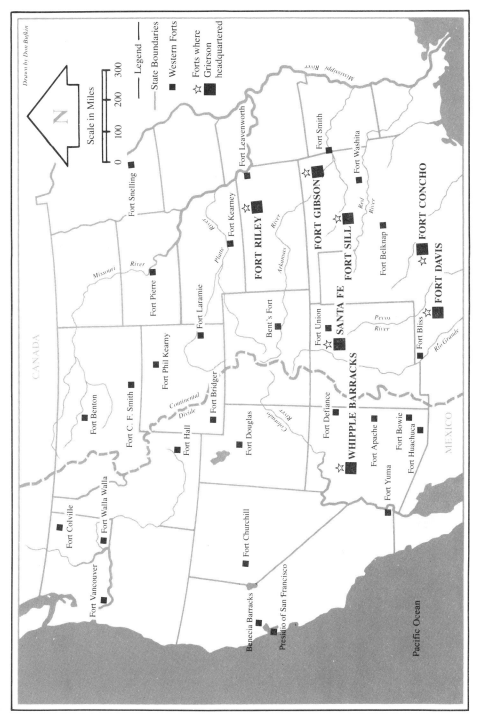

Area of operations for Grierson and the Buffalo Soldiers.

for Alice had informed him flatly that in the future she would remain in Jacksonville until decent quarters were available for herself and the children. There would be no more "tenting on the plains." If the reports about Concho proved true, Ben faced long months of separation from his family.

He was also deeply concerned for his sister Louisa. In the spring of 1874 she appeared to have found an outlet for her vast energies by joining the "terrific woman's movement in this City" and attending its weekly temperance meetings. Organizations of women, determined to close all saloons permanently, had arisen spontaneously during the previous winter, first in Ohio and then spreading to New York, Pennsylvania, Massachusetts, Indiana, and Illinois.[37] By April, 1874, the movement had caught fire in Jacksonville, and Louisa wrote Ben that the local women were "training the Saloon Keepers in the way they should go, pouring over their heads semi-daily vials of wrathful love, cutting their jugulars with a feather until they bleed, singing at them, praying at them, crying at them, and making speeches at them." In the face of all this, the Jacksonville saloon keepers were displaying "manly self control, and an angelic patience," leading Louisa to conclude that "such men are capable of taking more than one step in the right direction."[38]

She reminded Ben that she had personal reasons for becoming involved in the movement. Recently she had witnessed the deterioration, culminating in death, of their mutual friend Richard Yates, who had lost his battle against alcoholism. Nor did she consider Ben entirely immune to overindulgence, and she warned him to remember, when the temptation struck him to drink at his lonely frontier posts, "there are sons to follow in your footsteps." Her concerns increased when she recalled that "our ancestry some generations back were not noted for sobriety; our grandfathers on both sides being drunkards."[39]

By May, however, her new cause had proved inadequate. An immense amount of frustration had been building within her for many years. After the death of her husband in 1865 it had intensified, for she found herself not only widowed but emotionally and financially dependent upon her relatives, first her father and then her brothers. One day she quietly disappeared. When she was next heard from, she was in Chicago, having taken up residence in the Woman's Home. During the day she walked the city streets, looking for employment to enable her to begin making her own way in the world at last.

Her brother John was both astounded and irritated. As he saw it, at least three-fifths of the residents of the Home were either former prostitutes or "addicted to drink," and thus Louisa was attempting to create a sensation or, barring that, had finally gone insane. If the latter were true, then it was time to have her arrested and locked up for her own safety. Ben, however, counseled patience.[40]

During the current widespread depression and considering the customs of the times, there was no work for a woman of Louisa's age, background, or temperament. Shortly thereafter, with an empty purse, she was forced to move in with Alice's brother Tom and his family. All parties understood that this was no permanent solution, although Tom and Mary Kirk did their best to make Louisa feel at home and escorted her to concerts and lectures as a means of reviving her sagging spirits.[41]

On a minor note, young Robert informed his father that he, too, had little interest in going to Texas, having formulated other plans. Enamored by a lecture he had heard on the Arctic by the explorer, I. I. Hager, he had applied for a post on the next expedition. "I am thirteen years old, pretty slim, with dark complexion, blue eyes and very healthy."[42] Ben's sole comfort at this point came from Charlie, who, having passed his examinations, had entered West Point. Charlie had only two complaints—the food was "made of spoiled meat," and during his freshmen hazing he had been forced to stand on a mantle and sing "Mary had a little lamb."[43]

In the face of these considerations, plus the need to attend to some business in Jacksonville, Ben applied for and was granted a leave of five months. His first concern was to persuade Louisa to return to Jacksonville. He succeeded, and once back in the "Old Homestead," as the family called it, Louisa gave up all hope of joining the laboring classes. She continued to be interested in the anti-saloon movement, which by this time had become nationally organized into the Women's Christian Temperance Union. Her involvement reinvigorated a latent interest she had harbored for some time in the whole matter of women's rights.

While she had read widely on the topic, the question of woman's suffrage had never seemed germane to her situation. Now she was beginning to feel different. While still in Chicago she had attended a "Woman's Congress," where a number of "celebrities" had spoken. The event had been so well attended that municipal authorities had brought in extra police to maintain order. A month later Louisa confided to Ben that something "must result from the ferment, for an awful Spirit of unrest is abroad in the world, especially among the women. There is a ghost that will not down at the bidding of any man."[44]

Ben's concerns were not limited to Louisa. He was distressed to learn that his brother John, beset by financial worries, had not only joined the Greenback Party, but having returned to Jacksonville was one of its energetic organizers in Morgan County, Illinois. To Ben this was pure and simple heresy.

What Ben did not understand, indeed was incapable of comprehending, given his strong emotional attachment to Grant, was that in John Grierson's view it was not he who had left the party but the party that had deserted him and millions like him—the farmers, laborers, and small and struggling businessmen—in short, all the would-be and aspiring entrepreneurs who had not yet achieved material success. Since these same groups—labor and small businessmen—had represented the backbone of Republican Party support during its formative years in the late 1850s, John felt a keen sense of betrayal and growing rage.[45]

Yet, despite the political rift between himself and his brother, Ben still agreed to assist John in setting up a grocery and hardware store in Jacksonville. Aside from the old clan loyalty,[46] part of Ben's decision may have arisen from a recognition that had he not established a military career, he, too, would have made his living as a small businessman. Thus he was naturally inclined to be both sympathetic and supportive toward his fifty-four-year-old brother, who once more was starting over.

Before he left for his new post, Ben moved Alice and the children to Jacksonville, where they settled comfortably while awaiting word that suitable quarters were available at their new home. With family matters settled temporarily, Ben started for Concho. He stopped off in San Antonio to call on General E. O. C. Ord, Augur's replacement as commanding general of the Department of Texas. It gave him the chance to tour the old city, and what he discovered impressed him favorably. Here was an "old Mexican City" that was "in almost every particular strange and different," from any he had seen, with broad plazas and "rather beautiful" missions, particularly the Alamo and San Jose.[47] Perhaps Texas had its charms after all.

When he arrived at Fort Concho and saw the post and the neighboring village of Saint Angela (not called San Angelo until about 1880), his spirits fell. The post, "if such it may be called," was in a sad state of disrepair. "In all my Army experience I have never been at a Post where Everything has been conducted in such a haphazzard [*sic*], loose & disjointed manner." There was not "a nail or a board with which to have a coffin made for a soldier in case of death."[48]

It was worse than that. The post surgeon inspected Concho in 1875 and found living conditions that could only be described as "primitive." Sweaty horse blankets and saddles were routinely kept inside the poorly ventilated barracks. The porches were full of holes into which dirty rags had been stuck, and everywhere there were broken windows. The outhouses were so filthy that soldiers were reluctant to use them, which, in turn, caused medical problems. Quarters were in such short supply that Ben took a single room with Lieutenant Kislingbury's wife and her "three noisy children." He could have forced the lady to move, but her husband was in the field, and Ben was too kind a man to cause her that inconvenience. Captain Nolan of A company provided sheets and a pillow, and Woodward moved in, bringing a wash basin, candleholder, and candle.[49]

Few words were required to describe Saint Angela. It consisted of about two dozen "hovels," each one a whiskey shop "or something worse." The sheriff was a saloonkeeper and gambler and "as great a rascal as any." The countryside teemed with "the greatest set of scoundrels that ever lived on the face of the earth." Robbery and murder were frequent, and the only jail was the crumbling guardhouse at the post. These miserable surroundings did have two redeeming features—abundant wild game and the Concho River, "a beautiful stream sporting numerous cascades and abounding in fish of good quality."[50]

Grierson was never one to bemoan his fate for long. Within a few days he had located stone near the post and suitable for building purposes. Quarrying details were set to work and repairs were soon underway. The parade ground, overgrown with weeds, some three feet high, provided work for the occupants of the guardhouse. When it had been cleaned, Ben ordered the officers to keep their dogs—he had counted fifty-one of them—from littering it. While not a "spit and polish" commander, Grierson never tolerated an untidy post.[51]

While Ben thoroughly enjoyed superintending construction and the renovation of Fort Concho, he was deeply concerned over the maintenance of peace and order. The wild tribes of the Southern Plains had been decisively defeated and were no longer a serious threat, but west Texas was far from "civilized." The region, much of it uncharted, overflowed with Anglo and Mexican bandits and

Fort Concho, Texas, about 1876. *Courtesy Fort Concho National Historical Landmark, San Angelo, Texas.*

cattle and horse thieves. Kickapoos, Lipans, Mescalero Apaches, and a few renegade Comanches preyed on unwary travelers, trains, stages, and herds. To make life and property secure from so many antagonists was a very large order for a single regiment.

Grierson outlined these problems in a long letter to Ord and pointed out that his companies were badly scattered, undermanned and poorly mounted. Two hundred additional troopers were needed, along with decent mounts and essential equipment. He also proposed linking the frontier posts by telegraph and the construction of roads to facilitate troop movements and the response to calls for assistance.[52]

Ord's answer was unexpected and to Grierson both inadequate and embarrassing. Lieutenant Colonel William R. Shafter, Twenty-Fourth Infantry, stationed at Fort Duncan, Texas, was ordered to Concho to lead an expedition designed to sweep the Staked Plains of hostile

Indians. In addition, Shafter was charged with mapping and estimating the resources of the country he traversed.[53]

Grierson blamed neither Ord nor Shafter for the order. In one of his rare moments of righteous indignation he laid responsibility at Sheridan's door. It was not the first time that "Sherry Dan," as Ben referred to the general in private, had done him a disservice. Sheridan had deprived him of a Texas command in 1865 in favor of those "toadies," Custer and Merritt. In 1868, after Grierson had organized and prepared the Tenth for service in the Cheyenne War, Sheridan had shunted him off to Fort Gibson, to give Custer, whom Grierson outranked, the major field command. Now an infantry officer would lead half of Grierson's regiment on a march into an area supposedly under Grierson's control. It was both "unjust" and "unfair" to the field officers of the Tenth Cavalry. Even Davidson,

Officers' Row, Fort Concho, Texas. Grierson's quarters are the first on the right. Photographed about 1876. *Courtesy Fort Concho National Historical Landmark, San Angelo, Texas.*

commanding two companies of the Tenth at Fort Griffin, was "outraged." Grierson found some small consolation in the belief that the expedition would accomplish little other than to wear out animals and equipment. Time would prove him at least partially correct.[54]

Grierson's pique at Sheridan was not appeased by the arrival of a letter of invitation to the latter's wedding in Chicago. He wrote Alice that, "The lady married the *Lieutenant General* more than she did Sherry Dan—anyone who would marry the latter for love I think would be rather hard up for a lover."[55] John Grierson shared his brother's view of the fate of Sheridan's bride, "God help the poor woman who gets him for her Lord and Master."[56]

Ben's feelings did not relieve him of the responsibility for assisting Shafter in making preparations for the expedition. Much of his time was spent in arranging for transportation and supplies, and he was greatly relieved, when, on July 14, the long column left Fort Concho for the Staked Plains.[57]

With virtually his entire garrison in the field with Shafter, Grierson could do little other than keep small patrols on the lookout for cattle and horse thieves and continue the work of reconstruction at Concho. It was not enough to offset his anger and frustration, and once again he gave thought to leaving the service. In a long letter to Alice he admitted that he was "rather disgusted with the army and army life."

It was his birthday, and he was almost fifty. "Next year," he noted, he would be "half as old as my Country," a disturbing thought, because it signalled that time was running out. Would he ever achieve the military glory that had seemed so likely after the two brilliant raids through Mississippi? If not, how would he reconcile himself?

There were no clear answers to these questions, and he confided to his wife that at this stage of life he felt the desire to begin setting down his earliest memories, wishing he had done so earlier. True, a friend of the family, Ella Wolcott, had organized his military records chronologically after visiting the Griersons in St. Louis. With these at his disposal, he could begin compiling his Record of Service. But something more was needed. He stood at a crossroads in his journey through life. There were two ways that he could go: forward with the army in spite of his intense dissatisfaction; or he could leave the military and start a new career as a small businessman, as his brother John had done so often, and perhaps with no greater success.

His indecision was intolerable, and he concluded that he should make up his mind in the manner of the old Goths and Vandals who decided matters of importance twice, "once drunk so that the Council would not lack vigor or vim and spirit and once sober— that—due regard should be given to discretion."[58]

Alice fired back an immediate response. It wasn't necessary for her to get drunk to know what they must do. He was to stay in the army, if for no other reason than that his salary was necessary. Since they were "not rich," they could not "indulge in luxuries," including that of ending a career, no matter how frustrating.[59] Aware that loneliness was a heavy contributor to his occasional depressions, she began making arrangements for the move to Concho, although she still had one problem she had not solved to her satisfaction. She had decided to leave Robert behind in Louisa's care so that he could attend secondary school. No one, save Louisa, was happy with this arrangement, and Robert, who was miserable, begged his mother not to leave.[60] But the time had come for her to join her lonesome husband. And since even the most prosaic news from his family was comforting, she encouraged the children to write "Papa." A note from George, now six years old, must have given Ben at least a chuckle.

Dear Papa

Jacksonville june 4th, 1875
I thought I would write to you today. I have had
prfect [*sic*] lessons for four days in reading and
speiling [*sic*] and hoop [*sic*] to have moor [*sic*]
Your son
GEORGE.[61]

Ben welcomed chuckles wherever he found them. Discovering humor in everyday events was one of the ways he coped with less than perfect circumstances. While he waited for Alice and the younger children to arrive, Ben sought occasions for laughter. When swallow droppings hit him while he was sitting on his porch, he wrote Alice that he would "endeavor to talk to these birds . . . and instruct them to be more careful as to their decorations or deposits." And when a skunk sprayed his front yard and porch, leaving a lingering odor, he commemorated the occasion with a long poem entitled "Dissertation of the Skunk," acknowledging that his recent guest had made a lasting contribution. He also warned Alice that the officers and ladies of Concho had succumbed to "fishing on the brain," a disease which was highly "contagious." And finally, as the time for her arrival drew nearer, he asked her to purchase some nightshirts and sew "waits" [*sic*] on the bottom "to keep the wind from blowing the thing up under my arms or perhaps over my head," adding, "You need not put anything of this kind on yours."[62]

Ben met Alice, Edie, Harry, and George at Denison, Texas, on September 5, a ten-day journey from Fort Concho. He had neglected no detail for their comfort and security. A carriage, ambulance, and two wagons carried the family, their clothing, furniture, and food, while a detachment of buffalo soldiers served as escorts. On arrival at Concho, Ben proudly toured his family through renovated quarters smelling of fresh paint and plaster. He gave no further thought to leaving the army.[63]

In the ensuing weeks, long rides, picnics, and fishing parties to the Concho River caused Alice to admit she was beginning to like Texas. Ben's view of the Lone Star State was also changing, but brother John remained unconvinced. "I suppose you have to feel the top of your head every morning before you are certain you still retain your scalp."[64]

After four exhausting months in the field, Shafter returned to Fort Concho on December 9. He rested for a few days as a guest of the Griersons. Alice found him a "jolly man," an opinion shared by few, if any, of the Tenth's officers and men.[65]

A stern, dogged, and driving commander, Shafter had combed the length and breadth of the Staked Plains. His columns had traversed literally thousands of hot, dusty, and often thirsty miles at a heavy cost in horses and mules. A few deserted Indian camps were found and destroyed, and their former occupants pursued. Only one warrior had been killed and four women and a young boy captured — not surprising, for the Comanches, former overlords of this vast region, were confined to the limits of their reservation. Only an occasional hunting party, with a permit from an agent, and a handful of runaways roamed their former kingdom.

From a military standpoint, Shafter accomplished little, but his maps and reports were another matter. While he was cautious about water resources, Shafter regarded much of the old Indian haunt as ideal ranching country. The reports, once published, provided a stimulus for the rapid movement of white settlers into an area formerly regarded as a wasteland.[66]

Far greater problems than a few roving Indians on the Staked Plains faced Shafter and Grierson. Conditions along the Río Grande bordered on anarchy. Civil war in Mexico had produced nearly countless revolutionaries, as Porfirio Díaz sought to overthrow the government of Sebastián Lerdo de Tejada. Díaz was winning the struggle in 1876, but his control of the northern border states was loose at best. Revolutionary chieftains, some no more than bandits, plagued both sides of the river frontier, with slight regard for lives, or property. Added to these activities were raids by the Kickapoos, Lipan Apaches, and Mescaleros. Neither Shafter nor Grierson had enough troops to guard the many river crossings, which meant that the pursuit of Indians, bandits, and revolutionaries was usually futile. They simply recrossed the river and thumbed their noses at their pursuers.[67]

Such conditions were intolerable, and pressure mounted from Texans and their elected officials for more vigorous action to quell the border troubles. The Grant administration, sensitive to diplomatic relations with their troubled neighbor, adopted a vague policy that Ord understood to mean that he could order troops into Mexico if in "hot" pursuit of marauders. And Ord was not the man to interpret "hot" too literally.[68]

Ord's position permitted Shafter and Grierson to plan complementary campaigns to rid the region of intruders. While Shafter made thrusts across the river, Grierson would throw most of his regiment south and west of Concho in a continuing operation. Early in the summer, Kickapoo and Lipan raiders penetrated far into Texas, killed a number of citizens unfortunate enough to cross their path, rounded up a large number of horses and cattle, and returned swiftly to their camps in Mexico.

Shafter received orders from Ord to organize a strong column, cross the river, and strike these Indians. With a body of Seminole-Negro scouts, a battalion of buffalo soldiers under Captain T. C. Lebo, and detachments of supporting infantry, Shafter crossed the Río Grande above the mouth of the Pecos. After a five-day march, a Lipan camp was located near Zaragosa and, at dawn on July 30, a picked detachment of forty scouts and buffalo soldiers attacked the surprised Lipans, killed fourteen warriors, and routed the rest. After burning twenty-three lodges and rounding up ninety horses, Shafter's force retired across the Río Grande.[69]

Captain Lebo, with his battalion of the Tenth, followed up Shafter's strike by destroying a Kickapoo village in the Santa Rosa Mountains and recovering sixty head of stock. He then turned his attention to the rough and broken Devil's and Pecos rivers country, scattering small bands in all directions. Grierson's four additional companies searched along trails and water holes in the Davis and Guadalupe mountains. Only the onset of bitter winter weather brought the troopers in from the field.[70]

In the midst of these operations, Grierson had felt compelled to take the stage to San Antonio and confer with Ord. The latter was reluctant to use black troops in the Río Grande crossings, because Mexican citizens would feel their use "more offensive" than that of white troops. Ord had also been quoted as having doubts regarding the soldierly qualities of blacks. This alone was enough to upset Grierson, but Ord was displeased with receiving "too many complaints" from some officers of the Tenth, and was disturbed by rumors that Woodward was having "a scandalous intimacy" with the wife of another officer.[71]

The Grierson-Ord meeting was a private one and thus not a matter of record, but Ben was satisfied with the outcome. Black troops continued to be used extensively in border crossings and fully justified Grierson's confidence in them. Apparently he convinced Ord that Woodward was the victim of vicious gossip, for no official action was ever taken in the matter. The complaints by some of his officers, Grierson believed, stemmed primarily from Concho's isolation, their low pay, and chronic indebtedness.[72]

While Grierson's troops sought to clear far west Texas of marauders, Alice, with Edie, Harry, and George, made her annual trek east. On this occasion she had more in mind than a visit with relatives. After establishing "headquarters" in Jacksonville, she, Louisa, and Robert moved on to Chicago, where she arranged for her sister Ellen to care for Edie and George. Then, with Louisa, Harry, and Robert, she took the train for Philadelphia, where Charlie joined the party, and they spent several days attending the Centennial Exposition, a celebration of the nation's one hundredth anniversary.

Huge crowds thronged the grounds of Fairmont Park, touring some one hundred buildings that made up the great fair. Machinery Hall, housing the latest in industrial technology, the Main Building, with products from more than thirty countries, and Memorial Hall, crammed with works of art, were the outstanding attractions, but Alice was more impressed with the zoological gardens. Most enjoyable of all was the time spent in the Monkey House, followed by a steamboat ride on the Wissahickon River, which wound through the 450-acre park. When Alice discovered that she had only twenty dollars left of an original three hundred, it was time to "break up the expedition." After putting Charlie on the train for West Point, she wrote Ben that he seemed unhappy, knowing that, in all probability, he would not see his family for another two years.[73]

Charlie resumed his studies at the military academy "in good health but bad spirits," while Alice returned to Jacksonville after stopping off in Chicago to pick up Edie and George. On her arrival she found the house had been burglarized, an increasingly common crime that was attributed to the "tramp problem." Great numbers of drifters wandered the countryside, unable to find employment in the depressed economy. At night they often slept in barns, and recently, before Alice's arrival, Louisa had found evidence that they were using one in the back yard. Since they often set small fires to keep warm, or left their smoldering cigar butts in the hay, Louisa was terrified that someone would set the property on fire while she was sleeping. Now that the house had been pillaged, neither she nor Alice felt secure, especially at night.[74]

If a ransacked house deflated Alice's spirits, her brother-in-law did little to restore them. With the money borrowed from Ben, John had purchased a partnership in a wholesale grocery firm. Business was slow, and John's income was barely enough "to make a living and not much more." And, despite his association with the Greenbackers, John was now fretting over a possible Democratic victory in the upcoming presidential election. If Samuel Tilden defeated Rutherford B. Hayes, it would eradicate all the progress of Reconstruction and "set the country back sixteen years."[75] Disenchanted as he was with Republicans, the Democrats, representing the party of treason, were worse.

As the time drew near for Alice to return to Concho, she was again troubled about leaving Robert behind. Increasingly he became moody at home and unruly and inattentive at school, and she asked "Papa" to give him a stern lecture. Her leavetaking was further delayed when Harry became ill with what at first appeared to be diptheria. Fortunately it turned out that he had simple flu, but as a result she did not reach Concho until almost the end of November, in the midst of the Hayes-Tilden election crisis.[76]

Initially, Tilden appeared the winner. He had a majority of both the popular and electoral votes, and Democrats were jubilant. In Jacksonville Robert lowered the flag to half-mast.[77] Returns from three Southern states still occupied by federal troops—Florida, South Carolina, and Louisiana—were in dispute, as well as one electoral vote in Oregon. If Hayes could capture all the disputed votes he

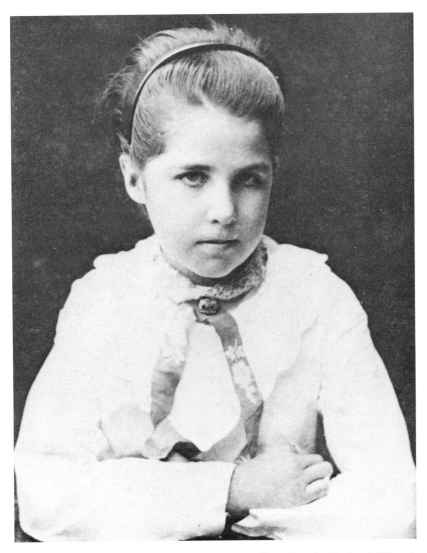

Edith Clare Grierson, age twelve. *Courtesy Fort Davis National Historic Site, Fort Davis, Texas.*

Theodore McGregor Grierson ("George"), age thirteen. *Courtesy Fort Davis National Historical Site, Fort Davis, Texas.*

could win the presidency in the electoral college by one vote. Republican managers quickly claimed them all. If this move went unchallenged, some Democratic partisans talked of taking up arms to put their man in the White House. To both Ben and John Grierson, such talk sounded like the opening guns of the "second rebellion" they had been predicting for over a decade. It seemed that their worst fears might yet be realized.

A tense nation awaited the outcome. Ben, convinced that "Grant and Sherman were in the right place" at such a critical time, remained confident of an ultimate Republican victory. In any event, there was nothing wrong in firing a salute to Hayes. When Ordinance Sergeant Joyce, an avid Tilden supporter, refused to discharge the volley, Grierson found a substitute. In part as celebration and also as a reward to officers and men after a hard year of campaigning, Grierson gave a Christmas party for the entire garrison. Whether doughty Sergeant Joyce attended is not a matter of record.[78]

Fortunately, a peaceful solution was found for the disputed election. Congress created an Electoral Commission to review and certify the correct returns, and all were awarded to Hayes. When no significant disruptions occurred, Hayes was inaugurated peacefully. John Grierson summed up the matter for both himself and Ben when he wrote "The country is safe for the next four years."[79]

Affairs along the Río Grande and in West Texas allowed no lengthy respite to celebrate either the presidential election or the holidays. By mid-January, Grierson's buffalo soldiers, working out of forts Concho, Davis, and Griffin, sought to curb the raids of small Indian war parties. One battalion of the Tenth, however, remained under Shafter's orders and was used repeatedly, in combination with other units, for swift forays into Mexico.

The Lerdo government, fighting for its existence, had voiced little opposition to the river crossings, but Díaz, now in control, protested vigorously. He also began efforts to remedy the chaotic border conditions. When the Ord-ordered and Shafter-led incursions continued and were supported by the Hayes administration, relations between the two countries became severely strained. There was loose talk of war.[80]

Grierson had supported and cooperated in the 1876 crossings, but as they continued into the spring and summer he felt Ord was abusing his authority and exaggerating the need for violating the borders of another country. "Old Ord has gotten the Mexican border troubles on the brain," he confided to Alice. Still, he did not believe there would be a war; the difficulties would "blow over."[81]

Grierson's evaluation proved correct. Although United States–Mexican relations did not improve for more than a year and the crossings continued into 1878, armed conflict was avoided. Grierson's opinion of Ord was shared by both Sherman and Sheridan, though Ord remained in command of the Department of Texas until 1880.[82]

While Grierson remained alert to conditions on the Río Grande, most of his attention was focused on Indian raids west of the Pecos. The Mescaleros were a growing source of trouble, particularly along the San Antonio–El Paso road. When they were pursued, their trails led almost invariably to the Mescalero Reservation at Fort Stanton, New Mexico. Realizing Grierson's problem in overtaking and punishing these marauders, Ord complained to Adjutant General Townsend and recommended that steps be taken to move the reservation farther west—a recommendation that was ignored.[83]

In addition to the Mescalero threat, reports reached Fort Concho in March that a strong band of Comanches under Black Horse had fled their reservation and gone to the Staked Plains. Captain P. L. Lee, stationed at Fort Griffin with C Company of the Tenth, went in search of these Indians, and on May 4 he found and attacked a small camp, killed four warriors, and captured six women and over sixty horses. Continued search failed to locate the main body of Comanche runaways.[84]

Determined to find and punish this band, Grierson planned a two-company sweep of the Staked Plains and selected a close friend and veteran officer, Captain Nicholas Nolan of A Company, to lead the column. Nolan had been with Shafter on the latter's 1875 campaign on the Plains and was more familiar with the country than any other officer of the Tenth. Preparations had not been completed when news of the most distressing kind reached Ben and Alice Grierson.

For more than a year they had been concerned over Robert's behavior and attitude and Charlie's frequent bouts with depression. Robert had been the greater source of worry. Recently there had been complaints that he frequently misbehaved in school, and, on at least two occasions, when told to report to the principal, he had gone home instead. His mother warned him against becoming a "rowdy." Her peace of mind did not improve when her father, who had moved to Jacksonville in the past year, cautioned her that

Robert and his friends were keeping "Bachelor Hall," although "if they had any Irish Revels, amongst them, they were careful to keep it from me." As for Robert's schoolwork, John Kirk thought that "he has been out so much at night that I can hardly see how he could make very much progress at school. What Robert needs most," he added ominously, ". . . is to be placed under restraint, to be taught to submit to authority." Only John Grierson gave her any comfort. While it was true that Robert was "acting up," certainly he was no worse than either John or Ben had been at this same age.[85]

As if all this news was not disturbing enough, Robert complained constantly of sickness, and in one letter confided "I feel so bad some times that I think I'm never going to feel well again." In desperation, Dr. Jones, the family physician in Jacksonville, physicked Robert three times in quick succession, leaving the youth to speculate, "if he does it once more there won't be much left of me. I feel as if I'd been turned inside out." He was left so weak that his condition delayed his arrival at Fort Concho for a summer vacation, thereby increasing his parents' anxiety.[86] But it was Charlie, rather than Robert, who was in severest trouble.

Throughout his third year at West Point, Charlie suffered from "the blues." When he wrote his mother, seeking comfort, he received instead advice. "I don't like to hear you talk of having a blue time until June—you ought to be enough interested in your studies and military drills, so as not to be blue." When he complained of boredom, she reminded him that "it is extremely dull at a frontier army post, for those who cannot interest themselves in quiet, or simple pleasure." She constantly exhorted him to devote all his energies to school, otherwise a low class ranking would consign him to the infantry rather than his father's Tenth Cavalry.[87]

To his great relief, Charlie passed his third-year exams. A few days later, he heard a rousing sermon in chapel that concluded with the words: "There is a point we know not where, there is a time we know not when that shapes the destinies of man for glory or despair." Suddenly Charlie was inspired as never before, and he wrote his uncle John a long letter beginning with the statement "I'm a little enthusiastic Perhaps owing to the great overflow of animal spirits in which I find myself at present." What followed was the most incoherent and grandiose letter John Grierson ever received.

Before long, Charlie asserted, he would be the best-known man in

America, would write the greatest poetry, surpassing that of Homer's *Iliad* and presently, he was "in love with everybody" and "happier than I was ever in my life heretofore." Beneath the bombast was one plaintive statement. "Friends and relatives I have had so little of home life." A few days later, he dispatched a similar letter to his parents.[88]

The next word on Charlie came from officials at West Point. While serving as officer of the day, he had become mentally deranged and so violent that it required four men to subdue him. He was now under restraint. Ben obtained a leave from Ord and left at once for West Point. Robert spared his family additional trauma by appearing at Concho just before his father's departure.[89]

Ben reached West Point on July 12 to find his son's condition worse than imagined. Charlie had torn off all his clothes and was shackled to a bed in the post hospital. He looked and acted in a "wild" manner but seemed genuinely glad to see his father. Ben believed that months of hard study and the excitement of passing his third-year examinations had proved too much for Charlie, bringing on a nervous breakdown. John Kirk assessed the disorder as "brain fever."[90]

Ben never considered committing his son to an asylum. As soon as possible, he arranged to take Charlie to their home in Jacksonville, where rest and treatment would restore his health. He also secured a promise from General John Schofield, commanding at West Point, that Charlie could have a year's leave if necessary. Within a week Charlie had improved enough that Ben could manage him, and they took the train for Jacksonville. It was a difficult ride. Not only did Ben have to pacify his son, but along the way there were reports of rioting and labor strikes among railroad workers in Martinsburg, West Virginia, Baltimore, Maryland, and Buffalo, New York. They passed through Pittsburgh just before that city erupted in violence that claimed lives among the strikers and the state militia and left a number of buildings in flames, including the Union Depot. The trip from Concho to West Point and then to Jacksonville, Ben wrote Alice, "was the most trying experience of my whole life."[91]

Once home, Charlie was confined to the attic room of the house, with only a double mattress as furniture. For a time he continued to talk and act wildly and was able to fend off all efforts by Dr. Jones to force feed him chloral hydrate, a sedative, as a means of quieting him. After conferring with other members of the family,

Ben decided to stay and nurse him personally. He hoped Charlie's condition would improve sufficiently so that when his own leave expired in early September, he could bring his son back to Fort Concho. Alice approved of the plan, but cautioned Ben not to let Louisa see too much of Charlie, because "she will smother him," adding, "If I were sick it would set me nearly frantic to have her take care of me."[92] Grierson's decision to remain in Jacksonville during this period prevented his participation in one of the starkest dramas ever enacted on the Southern Plains—one etched forever in the history of the Tenth Cavalry.

In obedience to Grierson's orders, issued in June, Captain Nolan completed preparations for the "Comanche search," though, instead of two companies, the command was limited to Company A. On July 10, Nolan, Lieutenant Charles Cooper, and sixty troopers with a four-wagon train left Fort Concho and marched up the North Concho River. The weather was dry and very hot, and on the second day out, one of the troopers suffered sunstroke, though he soon recovered. Nolan moved on to the headwaters and then northwest to Big Spring, where he turned due north to the Colorado and across that stream to Bull Creek in present Borden County, Texas. Here Nolan found a suitable site and established a supply camp. He also found reinforcements in the form of twenty-eight buffalo hunters out looking for Indians who had stolen stock from them.

With the hunters was a veteran guide, José Tafoya, who had assisted Colonel Mackenzie in his campaigns, and Nolan welcomed the opportunity to secure his services. Tafoya believed the Indians were at or near Lagunas Sabinas, due west of the supply camp, and Nolan and the hunters prepared to march for that point. Having no pack mules, Nolan took eight mules from his six-mule teams to carry rations and forage and sent his wagons back to Fort Concho for additional supplies.

On the evening of July 19, Nolan set out westward with Lieutenant Cooper, forty troopers, and twenty-two buffalo hunters. Sergeant Allsup and nineteen men were left behind to care for the supply camp. On July 21, the first Indians were seen. They proved to be a party of Comanches under Chief Quanah Parker, but they had a pass from the Indian agent at Fort Sill that had been countersigned by Colonel Mackenzie, commanding at that post, indicating that the chief was on a mission to induce runaway Indians back to the reservation. Nolan was unhappy, but since "he and party were liberally supplied with Government Horses, Equipments, Arms, Ammunition and Rations, I did not feel authorized in detaining him."[93] After the Indians left, Nolan marched on to Laguna Sabinas, reaching it on the evening of July 22. But it had been a dry year, and where Shafter had found plenty of water in 1875, Nolan was forced to dig holes and dip out water by the cupful.

The command rested for a day while Tafoya and a few of the hunters scouted south to the Five Wells for signs of Indians and also for water. They returned next day, after a waterless trip of thirty hours, to report that an Indian trail had been found running northeast toward Double Lakes. Nolan set out in the late afternoon on July 24, preferring to march at night to avoid the deadly heat, and reached Double Lakes about noon the following day. No sign of Indians was found, and once again the men were forced to dig for precious water.

For the next three days the guide led Nolan and the hunters steadily westward along the trail, but the Indians were not overtaken and no water was found. Thirst was becoming acute, the animals were breaking down, and the men beginning to struggle. Nolan, now genuinely concerned, asked Tafoya how much farther it was to water, and when told it was another six or seven miles, he gave the guide one of his private horses and urged him to lead on as rapidly as possible. The command would follow with as much speed as the condition of men and animals permitted.

Tafoya rode off in a westerly direction and then turned northeast. Nolan was doing his utmost to keep up, but it proved impossible, for two troopers suffered sunstroke. Others were so dehydrated and exhausted that they kept falling from their saddles. Nolan halted briefly, detailed Sergeant William Umbles to stay with the two sick men, picked eight of his strongest men, gave them all the canteens they could carry, and sent them on to follow the guide. It was the last he would see of those eight men for many days.

Nolan limped on for a few more miles and then was forced to bivouac. Shortly thereafter Sergeant Umbles and the two sick men passed within easy hailing distance but failed to respond to repeated shouts and disappeared in the darkness. Eleven men were now missing, the guide had not returned, and Nolan's plight was becoming desperate.

At daylight on July 28 there was still no sign of Tafoya or the eight troopers, and the buffalo hunters were "scattered over the plains, their ponies gone." Nolan and Cooper conferred with the hunters, and the decision was made to follow in the direction taken by the guide the day before, but after some fifteen miles with no sign of water or Tafoya, Nolan decided to turn back and make for the Double Lakes some fifty-five miles to the southeast. The buffalo hunters disagreed, believing that water must be nearby somewhere to the northeast, and they bade Nolan farewell.[94]

Every mile was agony now for Nolan and his troopers. The heat was oppressive, exhausted horses were staggering, and the men were constantly falling from the saddle. Discipline became the victim of thirst and fear. Corporal Charles Gilmore deserted after being detailed to care for a trooper who had fainted, and the little column straggled so painfully that Nolan called a halt. One of Lieutenant Cooper's horses, completely broken down, was killed, and the men drank warm blood to partially slake an all-consuming thirst.

The next morning brought out the broiling sun again, to beat down upon half-crazed men. Corporal George Fremont and two other troopers struck off on their own, and forty men had shrunk to twenty-four. Thirst was so overpowering that the urine of both horses and men was sweetened and drunk with relish, which brought momentary relief, then greater suffering. More horses died and their blood was drunk, as tortured officers and men fell, lurched, and staggered another twenty-five miles before sheer exhaustion forced a halt near mid-afternoon beside some scrub mesquite that gave partial shelter from the blistering rays of the sun. All were now despairing of their lives.

Near sundown, Nolan ordered the men to abandon all their rations and surplus property and gird themselves for a last effort. Then the column set out, although this was no longer a disciplined march but an individual struggle to reach life-giving water. Fifteen more agonizing miles brought them at last in little groups to Double Lakes during the early morning of July 30. They had been on the Staked Plains for eighty-six hours without water.[95]

As soon as thirst was quenched, Nolan counted faces. One trooper, Private J. T. Gordon was missing, and a brief search failed to locate him. The men were in no condition for a thorough scout, and Nolan rested his command until the morning of July 31, when he sent out a detail with two pack mules to return to the last camp, gather up the abandoned supplies, and look for stragglers. While awaiting their return, Nolan spied a long column on the horizon to the north and soon welcomed Captain Lee and C Company, scouting out of Fort Griffin. Lee rendered immediate assistance and sent out a strong detachment along Nolan's back trail, with plenty of food and water, to find any men still lost and to retrieve discarded property. Meanwhile, the detail that Nolan had sent out earlier in the day returned with the abandoned rations, but they had found no stragglers.

On August 1, while the command recuperated at Double Lakes, Corporal Fremont and another trooper came in. They reported that they had straggled and become lost, all their animals had died, and Private Isaac Derwin, who had also been with them, had perished. Nolan placed both men under arrest as deserters and sent a detail to bring in Derwin's body, but the men failed to locate the remains. Three days later Sergeant Allsup and fifteen men arrived from the supply camp, overjoyed to find their commander alive and safe.

Sergeant Umbles and the two men with him, as well as Corporal Gilmore, had reached the supply camp and told Allsup that Nolan and the rest of the command had become lost and died of thirst. Umbles, Gilmore, and another trooper had then ridden on to Fort Concho to bear the grim news to the garrison, while Allsup had marched at once to find Nolan. The latter immediately sent a courier to Concho to give the lie to Umbles's story and to request that both he and Gilmore be placed under arrest.

On August 5, Nolan broke camp and, escorted by Captain Lee, marched for his supply camp, which was reached the following day. Here he found the eight troopers whom he sent for water on July 27. Shortly thereafter a relief force from Concho, headed by Lieutenant R. G. Smither and Assistant Surgeon J. H. King, arrived, having marched in response to the news Umbles had brought to the post. After rest and treatment, Nolan set out for Fort Concho, where he arrived on August 14.[96]

Nolan's ill-fated expedition cost the lives of four troopers from thirst and exhaustion. Twenty-five horses and four mules were also lost. Sergeant Umbles, Corporals Gilmore and Fremont, the latter the post librarian, and Private Alexander Nolan, were confined in the guardhouse pending court-martial.[97]

Grierson's first knowledge of the misadventure came from newspaper reports that the entire command had been lost. Hard on the heels of this alarming report, however, was a letter from Alice with assurances that most of the men were safe. A few days later she informed him that Nolan and Cooper "make light of their sufferings but the truth is they were simply horrible." Ben was "very happy" that the outcome had not been worse, and it was typical of him that he wished consideration shown for the men under arrest. He wanted Nolan to be careful in dealing with their case, feeling that "It is probably best not to be too hard on them."[98]

By mid-August, Charlie's condition had improved. While he was still "cross and irritable," he had not attempted to break anything for several days, and recently relatives had moved the furniture back into his room. Ben, finding it "painful" to discuss the disease, urged Alice not to allow the subject to prey on her mind. He advised her to set aside time for healthful recreation and suggested that she take frequent drives in the buggy, though he also cautioned her that while riding beyond the post, she should take an armed guard to protect her scalp, horses, and money.[99] Likewise, Alice was concerned for her husband and urged him to play "a reasonable amount of checkers" at every opportunity with both his brother and her father as a means of relaxation. She knew from her correspondence with John Grierson that Ben, involved in "constant watching," and suffering from "loss of sleep & anxiety of mind," was under greater stress than he had ever experienced before.[100]

When September arrived, Charlie was well enough to travel, and as soon as General Schofield approved a year's leave for him, the "whole family" saw him and Ben off at the Jacksonville depot. They arrived at Concho in midmonth without incident.

For the next year, Charlie enjoyed the family life he had missed for so long. In addition, Ben, subscribing to the common belief that physical exertion and contact with nature were antidotes to the stresses and strains brought on by too strenuous mental exertion, arranged as much out-of-doors activity for him as possible. Some of it was labor, but much of it was recreation, including riding, hunting, fishing, and picnics at the Painted Rock. Ben occasionally brought along his fiddle and regaled family and friends with songs, while Dr. Buell, one of the post surgeons, danced the Irish jig and performed Indian war whoops. Before long, Charlie's mental state changed for the better, and soon plans were being made for his return to West Point.[101]

Grierson's return to duty permitted him little of the healthful recreation he prescribed for others. He was faced at once with the distasteful court-martial of four men of his regiment. And, after reviewing all the circumstances with Nolan, Cooper, and others, he formally recommended leniency. The court was not swayed, and on December 10 sentenced the four to be dishonorably discharged and to serve one year in prison.[102]

Alice Kirk Grierson, about age fifty-five. *Courtesy Fort Davis National Historic Site, Fort Davis, Texas.*

General Benjamin Grierson in civilian dress. *Courtesy Fort Davis National Historic Site, Fort Davis, Texas.*

Grierson also found himself at odds with the Texas Rangers. His troopers often visited sordid little Saint Angela to enjoy the "night-life." Little trouble had occurred until the fall of 1877, when a party of rangers took exception to a number of troopers dancing and drinking in Nasworthy's saloon and administered a pistol-whipping. Grierson demanded an apology from ranger Captain John S. Sparks and received the boastful reply that the rangers could whip the entire garrison at Fort Concho. The response of the offended troopers was to arm themselves and shoot up the saloon, killing a citizen in the process. Sparks, whose responsibility for the unhappy affair was clear, resigned from the ranger service.[103]

A more serious clash occurred a few months later in Morris's saloon, when a group of buffalo hunters and cowboys surrounded, abused, and humiliated a sergeant of Company D. Once free of his tormenters, the trooper gathered some friends at the post and, armed with carbines, they returned to the saloon. The gunfight that followed resulted in the death of one hunter and the wounding of two others. One soldier also was killed and another wounded.

Sparks's replacement, Captain G. W. Arrington, came to the post intent on arresting First Sergeant Goldsby of Company D for allowing the troopers to secure weapons. Grierson refused to give up Goldsby on the grounds that Arrington had no authority on a federal military reservation, but the sergeant did not remain to embarrass his colonel—he fled to an unknown destination. Nine troopers of Company D were indicted and tried for murder and one was given the death penalty, though he later successfully appealed the verdict. Unfortunately it was not the last clash between garrison and town. Tension remained high and the potential for an explosion great.[104]

The year had scarcely been a vintage one at the isolated little post on the Concho even before the onset of racial troubles. In February alone, Captain Nolan's wife had died of "quick tuberculosis," and Lieutenant Hans Gasman's infant was born, died, and was buried while he was away in the field. Loneliness overcame one of the telegraph operators, who went insane, and Harriet Griffin, Assistant Surgeon King's maid, "began eating dirt." Days of anxiety followed the report of Nolan's fate. In addition to bearing the shock of Charlie's illness and continued concern over Robert, Ben and Alice had received the depressing, though not unexpected news, that Tom Kirk's business had failed and he was floundering in a sea of debt.[105]

For Ben Grierson the last half of the year had been exhausting, and he felt the full weight of his fifty-one years. His enormous reservoir of energy seemed drained, and he felt ill and "out of sorts." The digestive problems that plagued him whenever he was under stress were once more making themselves felt. He needed rest, but also more constructive things to do than quarrel with rangers and argue with ill-tempered citizens of Saint Angela.

Fortunately the holidays provided a few days of relaxation, and the growing challenge of marauding Apaches offered the opportunity for rewarding service in the field. Ben's great recuperative powers began asserting themselves, and before the new year was a month old he was planning an intensive campaign to bring peace to the territory under his control.

CHAPTER 9

Taming the Trans-Pecos

THE continuing turbulence and tension along the Río Grande, combined with the Apache problems in West Texas, led General Ord to call for reinforcements. He also gained approval for the creation of a new District of the Pecos commanded by Grierson. Colonel Mackenzie and his Fourth Cavalry were transferred to the District of the Nueces, where Mackenzie replaced Shafter as commanding officer. These changes gave Grierson far greater responsibility and equally significant, a long awaited opportunity for more rewarding service. He could now concentrate most of his regiment in the new district and develop plans for broad-scale operations.

Hit-and-run attacks by raiders from the Mescalero Reservation were increasing, as were those of Lipan war parties crossing from Mexico. Reports consistently came to Concho that Presidio del Norte, a Mexican village on the Río Grande southwest of Fort Davis, was "full of Indians" trading stolen stock for late-model Winchester and Sharps carbines. Of less concern but a constant source of danger were roaming bands of Mexican and American cattle and horse thieves, who were not above attacking a stage on occasion. On the San Antonio–El Paso road west of the Pecos, murder and robbery were common events.[1]

From the major posts in his district, Concho, Stockton, Davis, and Griffin, Grierson followed the normal practice of using detachments to pursue marauders. He recognized that most such efforts were futile. It took hours and often days before reports reached the posts, and by then the trails were cold. Even under the best circumstances, the rough, broken, mountainous, and often waterless region made interceptions difficult. To protect his district effectively, a change in strategy was required. Beginning in February, 1878, Grierson began making adjustments. Troop commanders on pur-

suit were instructed to carefully map the country traversed, including every source of water and possible raider hideouts. He also sent
units into the field solely for the purpose of exploring and mapping
assigned areas. In time, he and his officers would acquire a knowledge of the district equal to that of the Indians, thus greatly increasing their chances for successful operations against them.

The problem of safety along the San Antonio–El Paso road led to
a second step. After correspondence with Ord, a decision was reached
to establish infantry camps at waterholes along the route between
Forts Stockton and Davis. Seizing the opportunity, Grierson decided
to establish other camps and sub-posts throughout his entire district
at both water holes and river crossings. He saw clearly that control of
these places was the key to control of the district.[2]

To assure the proper functioning of this system, Grierson began
constructing a network of roads and telegraph lines to improve
communications and expedite the flow of troops and supplies. He
had no intention of leaving the work to subordinates and instead
decided to select roadways and campsites personally, even though
such tasks required weeks and perhaps even months in the saddle.
Grierson had more in mind than a military campaign. By temperament a builder and developer rather than a destroyer, he set out to
make his district not only safe, but attractive to potential settlers
as well. Still having no desire to kill Indians, he hoped to keep
bloodshed at a minimum. At the same time, finding himself free of
the shackles that had bound him at Fort Sill, he was determined
that never again would he suffer the abuse heaped upon him in the
past for inaction against hostiles.

Before the end of April, Grierson was ready to begin an inspection tour to locate sites for camps and new roads, when a devastating storm struck Concho, delaying his departure. Rain, high winds,
and hail "to foot depth," badly damaged roofs and broke almost every
window at the post. Five troopers were seriously injured and more
than a hundred horses stampeded. Within thirty minutes the streams
overflowed and became impassable.[3]

The delay proved a boon for Robert Grierson, who arrived in
time to join Charlie in accompanying the column. In mid-May,
Grierson, his two sons, and Captain Lebo with K Company, set out
for Fort Stockton, some 160 miles southwest, reaching it on May 18.
The post did not impress Ben, except that it did boast the "great
luxury" of a bathhouse.[4] From Stockton, he pushed nearly sixty
miles south to San Francisco Creek, where he found a fine location

for a camp. From a nearby high point he could see more than forty miles into Mexico. On his return to Stockton he ordered a new road constructed to this site, before marching on to Fort Davis.[5]

Although its location left it vulnerable to enemy attack, Fort Davis delighted Grierson, who found the setting and surrounding country beautiful. He also envied the airy and spacious commanding officer's quarters, "a palace compared to our old rat trap," at Concho. After leaving Davis, he turned north to the Guadalupe Mountains, found another campsite at Pine Spring, and ascended Guadalupe Peak, the highest point in Texas, with an altitude of nearly nine thousand feet. Here Robert, an avid hunter and excellent marksman, killed three bighorn sheep in as many shots and was promptly dubbed "Bighorn Bob of the Guadalupes."[6]

After feasting on wild game, including "quail on toast," the command turned south past the rugged Delaware and Diablo mountains and reached the Río Grande opposite Presidio del Norte. Grierson conferred with the Mexican commander and, after obtaining a pledge of cooperation, marched for Concho. East of the Pecos they traveled over a newly constructed road; beside it ran a fine spring, and a sub-post was soon built at "Grierson's Spring."[7]

The tour had proved invaluable, and Grierson determined on another and more extensive one as soon as possible. Meanwhile, construction could proceed and troops could be stationed at the locations already selected. In addition, the long hours in the saddle had been beneficial to both Charlie and Robert. The former, tanned and healthy, was now eager to return to West Point, while the latter, having enjoyed a "splendid" time, was more relaxed and happier than he had been for a long time.

Upon his return, however, Ben was greeted by an impatient Alice. His niece, Helen Fuller, had lived with the Griersons for more than a year following the death of her mother and the loss of the Fuller home to creditors. She had become engaged to Lieutenant William Davis, Jr., of the Tenth some months earlier, but her frail health and his duties in the field had delayed their marriage. Now that Helen was in fairly good health and Davis was once more at the post, Alice, who at times felt burdened with the care of relatives, wanted the wedding to take place quickly. "It will be a great relief to me to feel free of all responsibility for her." Without further delay, Ben acted as father of the bride and gave his niece away at a small wedding that Alice judged "quite the thing in society."[8] Shortly afterward, Charlie left for West Point and Robert returned to Jacksonville.

With these family matters disposed of, Ben turned his attention to making plans for his fall survey. He also divided the regiment into a number of relatively independent commands, assigning them responsibility for seeking out and pursuing raiders, holdup men, and rustlers. Troops remaining in garrison were used to guard mail stations, escort trains, and protect property.

As the summer wore on, the Griersons planned a gala affair for August 27, when Edie would celebrate her thirteenth birthday. A rather husky, but strikingly attractive girl, she carried on a wide correspondence with relatives and officers' ladies throughout her father's district. She was also deeply attached to Ben. When they were apart, she showered her father with many small gifts, which he not only treasured but proudly displayed.

Shortly before her birthday she complained of not feeling well, but did not seem seriously ill. When the day arrived, Tuesday, August 27, she was still ailing, and as a result Alice gave her only a small, brief party and then put her to bed. The next day she appeared to recover somewhat and visited friends and went horseback riding. On Thursday, however, she took to her bed and the following day began vomiting. Sunday, a physician diagnosed her illness as typhoid fever.

For the next eight days and nights, Alice scarcely left her daughter's bedside, trying to bring down the fever and attempting to force fluids to stave off dehydration. Ice was sent for, but did not arrive until Thursday, and, in the meantime, it was difficult to keep liquids or food on Edie's stomach. Early Monday morning, September 9, she took a turn for the worse and, at eight o'clock that evening, died.[9]

The Griersons buried Edie in the civilian cemetery near the post and built a small rock wall around her grave. For as long as they remained at Concho, Alice usually began her day sitting on a box inside the enclosure, reading her mail, planning the day's activities, and nurturing the plants.[10]

With his family in mourning and his own grief scarcely under control, Grierson left Concho on October 11 for the planned scout and inspection. Accompanied by a twenty-trooper escort, he marched first to Grierson's Spring and from there to the Pecos. He ascended that stream to Pope's Crossing and then turned west along Delaware

Creek and Independence Spring to the Guadalupe Mountains. Here he camped for a week, carefully surveying the surrounding country and exploring Blue River Cañon.

The natural beauty of this wild region, "with the view constantly changing like clouds floating in the sky," left a lasting impression on Ben, and he described it lyrically and in detail to Alice:

> On either side as you enter (the cañon) the mountains rise almost per-
> pendicularly to the height of three thousand feet, and, besides the great
> variety of pine, White oak, Post Oak, Mayple [*sic*], Ash, Wild Cherry,
> Elm and Mansenita abounds . . . frost had set in and the great variety
> of tints and hues of foliage, from dark green to pure carmine, add greatly
> to the life and beauty of the magnificent scenery.[11]

Words were not enough; wishing to share with Alice some tangible evidence, he sent her a wagon load of pines, cactus, shrubs, and fossils he had collected. Obviously he enjoyed the grandeur of his surroundings, but he also noted that, "Edie is never far from my mind."[12]

From the Guadalupes, Grierson rode southwest through "rough and desolate country" and struck the Río Grande at old Fort Quitman. After a brief rest, he turned east, inspected Captain Charles Viele's C Company at Eagle Springs, and then moved on to Fort Davis by way of Van Horn's Wells. Satisfied with conditions at Davis, he again turned south and reached the Río Grande between the two Mexican villages of San Vicente and San Carlos. Here he found an excellent crossing and hot and cold springs. After this thrust through the heart of the Texas Big Bend, he returned to Concho and was immensely pleased that Alice rode several miles out from the post to welcome him.[13] Edie's death was a far greater blow than the loss of infants Kirkie and Mary Louisa, but this time their mutual sorrow, rather than dividing them as it had in the past, brought Ben and Alice closer together.

In his report to Ord, Grierson summarized with considerable pride the activities and accomplishments of 1878. Various commands had scouted and patrolled nearly twenty five thousand miles. Grierson himself had covered more than three thousand miles, and he was confident that his district would soon be clear of marauders. As usual, he had high praise for the officers and men serving under him.[14]

As the new year opened, Grierson completed plans for construction of the remaining sub-posts and camps, as well as the connecting network of roads and telegraph lines. He intended supervising much of this work personally, but in March he was summoned for duty in the dual court-martial of General D. S. Stanley and Colonel Hazen. Before his departure he left instructions for carrying out his projects and orders for aggressive pursuit and determined attacks on raiders. Alice took advantage of Ben's absence by making her annual visit to Jacksonville.[15]

While Grierson's protracted court duties did not allow him to return to Concho until July 4, in between court sessions he enjoyed considerable leisure. He attended the theater with General Pope, who laughed so hard during "Mulligan's Guards" that he brought on a headache. Ben also dined with Generals Sheridan, Schofield, and Sherman, who had been called to New York as witnesses, and in a private conversation with the latter, received encouragement regarding a possible promotion. His most satisfactory visit, however, was with Charlie at West Point. Their meeting was an emotional one, at which Ben unabashedly kissed his son. "How different," he reflected, "my visit now to West Point than the last."[16]

As usual when they were apart, Ben wrote Alice long and endearing letters, describing his activities in detail. He disliked their separations more than ever and impatiently looked forward to her return to Concho. "I love thee darling—love thee still. Youre [*sic*] image fills my heart and mind." Several weeks later he added: "I am Mrs. G —decidedly of the opinion that it is more satisfactory for us to keep house together than for you to be doing so in Illinois & I in Texas." To this Alice replied, "There is really no home unless you are in it."[17] Their affection, having survived twenty-four years of marriage, the death of three children, frequent separations, and occasional misunderstandings, had not only endured, but was now stronger than ever.

Nonetheless, Alice was delayed in returning to Concho. After assisting her sister Ellen and Tom's wife, Mary, in caring for newborn infants, she awaited Charlie's arrival in Jacksonville following his graduation. But her real reason for remaining behind was to spend some time with Robert.

Recently, having decided that he wished to attend either West Point or Annapolis, Robert had begun pressuring his father to obtain an appointment for him. When Ben had given him no response, Robert had concluded that his father's hesitancy stemmed from reports on his behavior. He tried hard to assure both parents that he wasn't a "bad boy"; he neither smoked nor drank, and he swore very little. Though he liked girls immensely (several Jacksonville mothers considered him a menace), he wasn't as "spoony" as before, and he had never been to "one of those houses," and more important, never intended going.[18]

Whatever Robert thought, these were not his parents' primary concerns. Throughout the past year, they had been receiving reports from Louisa that Robert tended to overdo all his activities. After an unpromising start in high school, he had thrown himself whole-heartedly into his studies and, except for mathematics which still gave him some problems, he was now at the head of his class. He was especially proficient in languages, having mastered both French and German.[19] But there was also strong evidence that Robert was often a troubled young man, and both Ben and Alice feared that despite his acute intelligence, the pressures of either academy might prove too much for him. It was difficult to tell him this outright, and Alice hoped that by spending some time with Robert, she could gently redirect his ambitions along other lines.

By late August, feeling that she had achieved some success, she prepared to leave, but an outbreak of yellow fever forced her to secure clearances through rigid quarantines at St. Louis, Little Rock, and Texarkana. Thus she did not reach Fort Concho until late September. When she arrived, she was pleased to discover that water pumps had been placed in each officer's quarters. Shortly thereafter fresh vegetables appeared at the post in plentiful supply and at reasonable prices. These small changes made domestic life a great deal easier at Concho.[20]

During her absence Ben spent much time in the field. His March instructions had been carried out to the letter. Eight sub-posts and a number of camps had been established and work was progressing rapidly on his planned communications network. All of this Grierson inspected personally and, in addition, he located routes for still more roads. His energy and endurance amazed those who rode with him. Assistant Surgeon S. L. S. Smith, who accompanied his commander on several occasions, wrote: "The General [Grierson] travels very rapidly at a fast trot and seemed impatient of every delay, although he frequently permitted the escort to halt and shoot antelope."[21]

Grierson's orders for "aggressive" pursuit of raiders were also followed. Typical was a report from Captain D. D. Van Valzah, commanding at Fort Stockton:

Sergt. Briscoe and 9 men, Co "B" 10th Cav. from Santa Rosa Texas struck trail of Indians on 19th who had stolen 8 horses on Pecos. Pushed it some 80 miles, capturing 6 of the horses, blankets, lariats, etc., near Castle Mountains, on 20th, next day, caused Indians to kill a horse for its blood, after which trail scattered. . . .[22]

Many of the trails continued to lead into the Mescalero Reservation, but even here Grierson's hard-riding troopers achieved some success. On August 29, a detachment from Captain Keyes's Company D recovered twenty-nine horses on the reservation, though Mescalero agent F. C. Godfroy, refused to give up the thieves. Ben informed Alice that, "altogether it is quite lively in my district," and he was certain that the raids were not paying off for the Indians.[23]

Grierson's energies were not confined to the needs of military operations. The more he saw of the region, the more convinced he became that it should be settled and developed. Not only was it ideal cattle country, but many areas were suitable for "health and recreation." Thus his official reports were not simply those of a soldier, but reflected his interests in promoting ranching, farming, and urban development. They contained detailed descriptions of the character of the country, including its water resources, types of grasses, shrubs, and soil, kinds of timber, and the variety of animals.[24]

At least a part of Grierson's strenuous activity—he often rode fifty miles a day—could be traced to Edie's death. From the field a year after her passing he wrote Alice, "I do not think that any father who ever lived loved a child more dearly than I did Edith and I love her still." Sometimes he sang to himself "to dry the tears from my eyes and to change the current of my thoughts."[25]

By the close of 1879, Grierson believed he had rid his district of any major source of trouble, and looked forward to a less "lively time." He was highly pleased with a complimentary letter from department headquarters which read in part:

Thirty-four thousand four hundred and twenty miles of marches; three hundred miles of roads opened; two hundred miles of telegraph contructed,—all, except a portion of the telegraph, consummated in one year,—involve efforts which will lead to lasting results, of which, as tending greatly, to advance civilization, yourself and command may well be proud.[26]

Praise at last for construction rather than killing and destruction, and from crusty "Old Ord" at that.

Charlie's presence was also a source of satisfaction. He was assigned to Captain Keyes's Company D and enjoyed his station at Grierson's

Spring, though he was engaged in little other than routine duty. He did spend a few days at Concho during the holidays, filling one void at the Grierson table.[27]

The period of comparative quiet in Grierson's district was not long-lasting. A major Indian outbreak, which had erupted in New Mexico late in August, 1879, now threatened to expand into West Texas. Ord requested and Sheridan approved concentration of the entire Tenth Cavalry — three companies were on detached service at Fort Sill — in the District of the Pecos, and Grierson strengthened his patrols.[28]

The outbreak stemmed from mistaken federal policy that sought to force the Warm Springs Apaches of New Mexico to live on the San Carlos Reservation in Arizona. Led by Victorio, one of the ablest of all Apache chiefs, these people had twice fled the San Carlos reserve and returned to their old homes at Warm Springs. Not permitted to remain there, they had gone voluntarily to the Mescalero Reservation, where Agent Godfroy allowed them to stay. They remained, however, restive and apprehensive of another move to San Carlos, and Victorio, with his people and a few war-hungry Mescaleros, decided to run and fight.[29]

The task of rounding up Victorio fell to Grierson's old friend Colonel Edward Hatch and his Ninth Cavalry. Throughout the fall and early winter of 1879, Hatch pursued his wily antagonist through mountains, canyons, and deserts, along trails littered with the victims of Apache vengeance. Late in November, Victorio vanished into the mountains of northern Mexico, but by January, he was again harassing the New Mexican frontier and drawing supplies, weapons, and recruits from the Mescaleros.[30]

General Pope, commanding the Department of the Missouri, ordered Hatch to the Mescalero Reservation, where he was to disarm and dismount these Indians. Sheridan instructed Ord to send Grierson to assist Hatch, and Ord issued the necessary orders on March 20.[31]

Grierson swiftly took steps to protect his district while organizing a five-company column of buffalo soldiers — about 280 men — and a detachment of Twenty-Fifth Infantry to guard his train. He set out for the Pecos on March 24, with scouts thrown out over a fifty-mile front. On reaching that stream, through country worth no more than "one and a half hill of beans," he turned northwest. Moving rapidly, he arrived at the Peñasco River on April 10, where he concentrated his entire force. En route, far-flung detachments had killed two warriors, captured four Indian women, and recovered one captive Mexican boy and twenty-eight stolen animals.[32]

Two days later, Grierson reached the Mescalero agency, where he and Hatch "gave each other a good hug." After discussing procedures with Agent S. A. Russell, who had replaced Godfroy, Hatch decided to let the agent collect the arms and horses with a small infantry escort. Grierson agreed reluctantly. He would have preferred to surround the Indians, disarm and dismount them, and move them to Fort Stanton, where they would be under military supervision.[33]

The disposition of troops and the location of the Indian camps also disturbed Grierson. The former were stationed at the agency, on the north side of the Tularosa River, while the Indians were encamped on a timbered ridge on the opposite side of the stream, with a boggy bottom between them and the troops. "It left the Indians on the outside and too far away to be sufficiently under control of the military."[34]

Severe weather, rain, and gale force winds delayed disarming the warriors until the afternoon of April 16. Grierson offered one of his companies to Russell and Captain Charles Steelhammer, commanding the infantry, but they felt no trouble would occur. Russell did agree that if additional assistance was needed, three quick shots would be fired.

Shortly after two o'clock, Grierson noted a number of Indians climbing the ridge toward the mountains, but not until 2:30 did the signal shots reverberate through the valley, "a half an hour late," as Grierson remarked wryly. Moments later he led his troopers at a gallop across the river, through the bog, and up the ridge, where "for a time the firing was quite lively." A battalion of Hatch's Ninth joined the fight and 250 men, women, and children were captured and confined in the agency corral. Ten warriors were killed, but between twenty and thirty escaped and joined Victorio.[35]

Grierson did not fault Hatch or Russell. He regarded the latter as "a good and honest man," not responsible for the breakout. He pitied the "poor miserable creatures" in the corral and blamed the Interior Department, "a Hydra-Headed Monster," for the Apache troubles. His views on Indian policy had not changed since his arrival on the frontier more than a dozen years earlier. Understanding, ample and quality annuities and rations, and strict honesty in all dealings was the answer to the Indian problem.[36]

With his part in the operations at the agency completed, Grierson marched south and, in very cold weather, scoured the Sacramento and Guadalupe mountains. Several small parties of Indians were rounded up and returned to the reservation. Then, with his companies scouting on a broad front, Grierson headed for Concho, where he arrived on May 16.[37]

Victorio, meanwhile, gave Hatch and the Ninth another six weeks of nightmarish campaigning before again retiring across the Mexican border. With his regiment badly used up from constant pursuit and skirmishes, Hatch called for reinforcements. Sheridan obliged by ordering the Tenth Cavalry to New Mexico, but Grierson objected vehemently. The transfer would leave the District of the Pecos wide open to attack, and he was convinced that Victorio's next move would be into Texas. Ord agreed, and persuaded Sheridan to rescind the order.[38]

Grierson had more than mere opinion to support his contentions on Victorio's probable movements. On May 12, a party of citizens were ambushed in Bass Canyon west of Fort Davis by eight Mescalero warriors. One man and a woman were killed, two others wounded, and their wagons ransacked. Captain Carpenter with Company H trailed the Indians to the Río Grande and he was certain they were on their way to join Victorio.[39]

Shortly after the affair in Bass Canyon, Lieutenant Frank Mills, Twenty-Fourth Infantry, and a detachment of Pueblo Indian scouts en route to Fort Davis were attacked at sunrise as they neared a waterhole in the Viejo Mountains. One of the scouts was killed and most of their horses lost. Lieutenant Robert Read, with twenty buffalo soldiers from Fort Davis, went in pursuit but failed to overtake the hostiles. Read believed they were scouts for Victorio.[40]

After receiving these reports and being given a free hand by Ord, Grierson made ready for an extensive campaign. He did not intend, as Hatch had done, to wear down his command in long and often fruitless pursuits. Two years of scouting, patrol, and exploration had given him and his officers a knowledge of the district equal to that of the Indians. He proposed to guard the mountain passes and, above all, the water holes while operating from sub-posts and camps. At one or the other, he would confront Victorio and force him to fight.

On July 10, Grierson left Fort Concho with only eight men, including his son Robert, who, having graduated from high school in June, had arrived at Concho thirsting for adventure. Alice was concerned about the size of the escort and in a note to Ben expressed her hope that "you will take every honorable precaution for your safety."[41]

Grierson reached "his spring" the following day, visited with Charlie and Captain Keyes, and picked up a telegraph operator. Four days later he arrived at Fort Davis where Woodward, just returned from two years on recruiting service, welcomed the party. Four companies of the Tenth were concentrated at Davis, waiting for specific assignments, but neither the company commanders nor Grierson had any reliable information on Victorio's whereabouts. However, on July 18, Colonel Adolpho Valle, commanding a force of Mexican regulars, telegraphed that Victorio was on the move and probably headed for Eagle Springs.[42]

Grierson wasted no time. The companies at Davis were dispatched immediately to take positions in the passes and at water holes along Victorio's likely route, while Grierson journeyed to Eagle Springs to establish field headquarters. When he arrived at Eagle on July 23, he learned that Valle's scouts had skirmished with the Apaches near Ojo del Pino, some fifty miles southwest in Mexico, and that the Indians were definitely heading for the Texas border.[43]

In an effort to gain more precise intelligence, Grierson and his party journeyed to Fort Quitman, where Captain Nolan and A Company guarded the river crossing. They were astounded to see Valle's troops encamping on the opposite bank, and soon learned that the Mexicans were sorely in need of supplies. Grierson provided Valle with more than two thousand pounds of flour and grain, and presented the colonel a few choice items for his own consumption—a few bottles of beer, butter, sugar, crackers, and canned peaches. Valle was grateful, but made it clear that he could not move until properly supplied by his government. This was alarming news, for it meant that now Victorio had a clear path into Texas.[44]

Grierson left Quitman on July 29 and headed for Eagle Springs, where he could more effectively direct operations. His headquarters party still consisted of Lieutenant William Beck, Robert, a sergeant, and five privates. In the early evening, as they approached a water hole called Tinaja de las Palmas, an Indian was sighted on a nearby ridge. Long-range rifle shots put the warrior to flight, and it was believed he was one of Victorio's forward scouts.[45]

Meanwhile, one of Nolan's patrols had learned that Victorio had crossed the Río Grande below Quitman. Nolan immediately sent Lieutenant Henry Flipper, the first black graduate of West Point, with couriers, racing to Eagle Springs with this report. Flipper reached his destination, ninety-eight miles away, in just twenty-two hours and alerted Captain J. C. Gilmore, commanding at Eagle. The latter at once dispatched couriers along the Quitman road to inform Grierson and they found him at Tinaja de las Palmas.[46]

Grierson could play the game of cat and mouse as well as any commander, as his Civil War record clearly indicated. He reasoned that Victorio would avoid prominent water holes, aware that they would be heavily guarded. At Tinaja the water supply, which depended on rainfall, was often meager in amount or lacking altogether. No significant body of troops was likely to be there, and "Old Vic" would surely head for the place and then take a direct route to the Mescalero Reservation.

Although his party numbered only nine men including himself, Grierson decided to bar Victorio's way at Tinaja. Near the road was a steep, rocky ridge, rising to a height of some 125 feet. From positions atop the ridge, riflemen could command the approaches to the water holes as well as the surrounding countryside. The men set to work on "Rocky Ridge," using stones and boulders to erect breastworks, and soon completed "forts Grierson and Beck."[47]

When the eastbound stage came by, Grierson stopped it only long enough to tell the driver to have Gilmore at Eagle Springs send all his available cavalry, and on the double. Near midnight, couriers reached Grierson to report that the Apaches were encamped no more than ten miles from his position. The couriers were instructed to hasten on to Fort Quitman and have Nolan and A Company march for Tinaja as soon as possible.[48]

At 4 A.M., Lieutenant Leighton Finley and fifteen troopers arrived from Eagle Springs to escort Grierson to that camp, but, "Papa thought best to 'hold the fort' and the couriers were sent to Eagle" with strict orders to have the remaining cavalry sent out at once. Grierson then had Finley and his men take positions lower down on the ridge. Well supplied with water and ammunition—Robert alone had 250 rounds—Grierson was "confident of my ability" to hold on to the position until reinforcements arrived or "as long as necessary."[49]

With preparations completed, the little group on "Rocky Ridge" awaited sunrise and then enjoyed a quick breakfast. Near nine o'clock the vedettes shouted, "Here come the Indians." Soon thereafter the Apache vanguard came into view, and it was clear to Grierson that they had seen his fortifications and were attempting to flank his

Victorio, Apache warrior. *Courtesy Western History Collections, University of Oklahoma Library.*

position. He ordered Finley to take ten men and charge the Indians in order to hold them up until reinforcements arrived.[50]

Finley mounted and engaged the Apache advance, but soon found himself also fighting warriors who emerged from a brushy swale and attacked his rear. At this critical point, Captain Charles Viele and Lieutenant S. R. Colladay, with C and G Companies approached from the east. In the smoke and dust they mistook Finley's men for Indians and fired into them at long range. Finley, who thought correctly at first that the new arrivals were troops, now took them

"Rocky Ridge," with waterhole of Tinaja de las Palmas in the middle distance. *Courtesy Douglas McChristian, Fort Davis, Texas.*

to be Indians and fired back. Fortunately no casualties were suffered in the exchange.

Sorely beset, Finley feared he would be overwhelmed and, wheeling about, raced for the safety of Rocky Ridge, with "lots of Indians following howling like coyotes."[51]

Finley reached the fortifications without loss, and as his pursuers neared, Grierson and his party opened fire. "You ought to have seen em turn tail and strike for the hills . . . the sons of guns nearly jumped out of their skins getting away," chortled Robert in his *Journal.* Viele and Colladay now closed with the stubbornly resisting Apaches and drove them south of Grierson's position. Victorio regrouped and made another effort to move northward, but Viele held him in check, and when dust clouds to the west signalled Nolan's rapid approach, the Indians drew off and made for the Río Grande. Grierson placed Victorio's loss at seven killed and an undetermined number wounded, while the Tenth had only one trooper, Private Martin Davis, killed and Lieutenant Colladay wounded.[52]

Grierson pushed out scouting parties and learned that Victorio had crossed into Mexico below Fort Quitman. Colonel Valle was notified, but instead of moving on the Indians, he turned in the opposite direction and marched toward El Paso. Certain that the canny and determined chief would again attempt to move north, Grierson concentrated five companies of the Tenth at Eagle Springs, posted others along trails farther north, and sent patrols to the Río Grande.[53]

Any doubt as to Victorio's intentions was removed on August 3, when a patrol led by Corporal Asa Weaver of Carpenter's H Company, found the Indians near Ojo del Alamo, Texas, and skirmished with them for fifteen miles. Weaver reported that Victorio was moving northeast in the general direction of the Van Horn Mountains. Grierson marched from Eagle Springs with every available man to block the passes south of Van Horn's Wells, but Victorio anticipated Grierson's move and, on the evening of August 4, slipped west of Van Horn's. This information soon reached Grierson through his alert scouts, and a glance at the map indicated that the Apaches were heading for Rattlesnake Springs, sixty-five miles to the northwest.[54]

By three o'clock on August 5, Grierson was under way for the spring and kept a range of mountains between his line of march and that of the Indians. Robert, alternately walking and riding in an ambulance, found the going difficult and at times unsettling. At night the fan-like tops of the giant yuccas seemed like Indians in headdress and presented "a terrifying aspect." The terrain was covered with thorny cactus, bunch grass, and "here and there you'd step in a hole and jar yourself."[55]

Despite the conditions, Grierson permitted few halts, and in less than twenty-one hours reached the springs ahead of the Indians and in time to prepare an ambush. To outmarch Victorio was no mean achievement. A bone-tired Robert obtained some relief when "Lt. Beck and I got the Dr. to give us a little whiskey and we needed it." The liquor tasted much better than the water, for "Rattlesnake Springs is so named because it would soon kill a rattlesnake to drink it."[56]

Early on the morning of August 6, Grierson positioned Companies C and G under Captain Viele in Rattlesnake Canyon and held his remaining companies in reserve. Not until two o'clock were the Indians seen approaching, and Grierson issued orders not to fire until they were within easy range. But Victorio, wary and sensing a trap, halted, and the troops volleyed, creating momentary confusion in the Indian ranks.

The sight of so few troops, however, encouraged the thirsty warriors. They regrouped and advanced, determined to fight their way to the springs. Grierson threw his additional companies into the fray and the Apaches were driven back and scattered among the hills and ravines.

As the fighting lulled, Grierson's train, guarded by Company H, Twenty-Fourth Infantry, and a detachment of troopers, lumbered around a point of the mountains to the southeast. A swarm of warriors raced to intercept the train but were repulsed by a curtain of fire from the defenders. Resorting to one more device in a plentiful bag of tricks, Victorio staged a withdrawal and drew off Captain Carpenter with three companies in pursuit. A strong party of warriors then swept out of a canyon between the troops and their camp in an effort to get at the pack train and the springs, but Grierson was prepared and drove them off.

Outfought and in danger of being cornered, Victorio fled south with Carpenter hard on his heels. The battle at Rattlesnake Springs had been a disaster for the Apaches. At least thirty had been killed and wounded, as well as a large number of their animals. Dispirited, Victorio could only hope for safety south of the Río Grande. Grierson's screen of troopers prevented any escape to the Mescalero Reservation and cut off all avenues for supplies and reinforcements.[57]

On August 3, Captain Lebo with K Company had struck Victorio's supply camp in the Sierra Diablo, routed the warrior guards and captured twenty-five head of cattle, a large quantity of jerked beef, bread, and berries. A day later, Captain William Kennedy with F intercepted a party of Mescaleros in the Guadalupes who were on the way to join Victorio, and pursued them into the Sacramento Mountains.[58]

Victorio managed to outrace Carpenter, whose horses gave out, and crossed into Mexico below Fort Quitman. Scouts reported that the Apaches, with many wounded and most of their stock broken down, were making their way slowly towards the Candelaria Mountains. No Mexican troops had appeared to bar their way.[59]

Grierson, who was not permitted to pursue Victorio into Mexico, had to be content with bringing most of his regiment to the line of the Río Grande. The Díaz government had, however, permitted the entry of a powerful United States force under Colonels Buell and

Eugene Carr to cooperate with a Mexican column under Colonel Joaquin Terrazas.[60]

From the Candelarias, Victorio went to a hideout in the Tres Castillos Mountains. Scouts located his camp early in October. Terrazas informed Buell and Carr that their presence on Mexican soil was unwelcome and they were forced to return to the border. On October 14, Terrazas surrounded Victorio's position and attacked. The Apaches were overwhelmed and the chief, sixty warriors, and eighteen women and children were killed. Sixty-eight women and children were captured.[61]

Victorio and most of his warriors died as they would have chosen, in a death battle with their enemies. Terrazas claimed a great victory, but the real victors were Grierson and the Tenth Cavalry. They had frustrated the great chief at every turn, drained him of resources, and driven him, sorely crippled, into Mexico. There he was an easy target for the Mexican troops.

Following Victorio's death, Grierson pulled in most of his companies to Concho, Davis, and Stockton, but he left patrols on the Río Grande and in the Guadalupe Mountains. On October 28, near Ojo Caliente, a party of thirty Apache warriors who had dallied along the Río Grande, thereby escaping the fate of most of their people at Tres Castillos, exacted a measure of revenge. They ambushed a patrol under Sergeant Charles Perry, B Company of the Tenth, and killed five of his troopers. The Indians escaped into Mexico and the Tenth had paid its final price for a masterful campaign against Victorio.[62]

When Grierson returned to Fort Concho he took justifiable pride in the performance of his officers and men during the campaign. He also felt that he had earned promotion to brigadier. Surely the "powers that be" would recognize his achievements as commander of the District of the Pecos. Extensive exploration, construction of hundreds of miles of roads and telegraph lines, and successful conduct of military operations had brought peace and promoted settlement in a huge and hitherto little-known region. Once again he applied to Sherman for support, an appeal that was strongly endorsed by others.[63]

Sherman, Ord, Washburn, and Hurlbut were joined by members of both the Texas and Illinois delegations in Congress in writing letters of recommendation and, though Sheridan's name was conspicuous by its absence, Ben believed his chances were excellent.[64]

There were critics, however, of both Grierson and his black troopers, and some of them were not without influence. Sadly, most of their charges and complaints were based on blind prejudice supported by gross distortion of information. In general, Grierson was accused of cowardice, inefficiency, and dilatory actions, while the soldiers were portrayed as inept misfits and a disgrace to their uniforms.

Typical was an anonymous letter from "prominent" citizens of Saint Angela to the editor of the *San Antonio Express.* They complained in mid-August that Indians were terrifying West Texas and Grierson was doing nothing to stop them—this even though not a single hostile had penetrated the settlements and Victorio had been decisively defeated.[65]

Retired General J. J. Byrne, serving as chief engineer of a Texas and Pacific railroad survey between Fort Worth and El Paso, was even more caustic. In a letter to a Texas Congressman, he pleaded "for God's sake . . . have some other soldiers sent . . . besides Negroes, and another commander, Mackenzie, Merritt, Davidson—anyone but Grierson or Hatch." He also accused Grierson of fleeing "to an almost impregnable mountain fortress when Victorio appeared."[66]

Byrne's remarks were based on obvious racial prejudice and a willful misrepresentation of known facts about the fights at Tinaja de las Palmas and Rattlesnake Springs. Byrne's judgment was poor in any case, for it cost him his life. On August 9, he and his driver, traveling in a buckboard on the Quitman–Van Horn road, ran squarely into Victorio's warriors retreating from Rattlesnake Springs. Byrne was mortally wounded in the first volley, but the driver lashed his mule team and outraced the Apaches into Fort Quitman. Byrne knew of the danger, and a two-day delay would have seen him safely to Van Horn.[67]

Not until April, 1881, did Grierson learn that once more he had been denied promotion. The vacancy went to Colonel Wesley Merritt, a favorite of Sheridan's. It was a disappointment to Ben, but not a great surprise, for his friend Sherman had warned in January of competition and service rivalries. Charlie and Robert, however, were indignant and thought Merritt's promotion over their father's head an "infamous outrage," and an "insult to the distinguished Generals—living and dead who recommended him [Grierson]."[68]

Ben, who could take comfort in the knowledge of a job well done, consoled himself that the opportunity for promotion would come again. He would continue to seek the star on his shoulder straps, but serious family problems in Jacksonville and Chicago diverted both his and Alice's attention.

John Grierson, once again in deep financial trouble, needed assistance. His business had failed, leaving him deep in debt. He owed more than eight thousand dollars including the mortgage on his home. There were no prospects for employment, for even the rumor of a vacancy brought applicants "as numerous as flies on a barrel of New Orleans molasses." As John contemplated the future, he could only regard it as "dark, dark, dark,."[69]

John still blamed the Republican party for most of his troubles. Their hard-money policies stifled small business and their politicians were rotten and corrupt. The "Grand Ratification" meeting of Republicans in Jacksonville to support the nominations of James A. Garfield and Chester A. Arthur amounted to nothing more than a "Big Drunk, and speeches from Drunken Brains." He wondered, as millions before and since, when politics would assume the lofty position assigned it by Charles Sumner, who had written, "Pure Politics is Morals applied to public affairs." Meanwhile, John would continue to work diligently, much to his brother's chagrin, as the Chairman of the Morgan County Central Committee of the Greenback-Labor Party.[70]

Despite his many reverses and his gloomy prophecies, there was still fire and determination in John Grierson. There was none in Tom Kirk. Though he had managed to salvage his homestead and some capital from his bankrupt enterprise, he sank slowly, but inexorably, into a deep depression. John Kirk feared that his son would succumb to "softening of the brain like his mother." By the fall of 1880, Tom's wife, Mary Fuller Kirk, having borne ten children, was pregnant with yet another. Several of the Kirk children had contracted diptheria, and as she struggled to nurse them, she attempted to bolster her husband's spirits. "If he does not get better & do something to make a living we shall certainly come to starvation," she reported to Alice, adding, "He seems incapable of decision."[71]

Ben sent John a small loan, and Alice bought clothing and other gifts for Mary. Beyond this, there was little they could do, other than write letters of encouragement. John Grierson, after months of searching, found employment with a mining company in Rico, Colorado, but Tom Kirk did not improve, and on January 14, 1881, committed suicide. Mary sold some of the family possessions to pay funeral expenses, and, at Louisa Semple's invitation, moved into the Old Homestead in Jacksonville.[72]

In addition to grief and worry over their relatives, Ben and Alice had to deal with petty controversy and serious racial strife between the garrison and citizens of Saint Angela. For more than two years Grierson and his officers were engaged in a "Post Office War" with William S. Veck, Saint Angela's most prominent civic booster. Veck wanted to transfer the post office from the fort to the town, and Grierson objected on the grounds that most of the postal business was transacted by members of the garrison. The result was a continuing and acrimonious skirmish with Grierson, who was blasted, among other things, as an "incompetent meddler," "spiteful," "egotistical," and "cruel." Officers of the Tenth were labeled as "no gentlemen."[73]

Grierson, often in the field for long periods, relied on his headquarters staff to reply to the charges, and they rose to the occasion. Their attackers were local ne'er-do-wells and chronic troublemakers. Saint Angela was primarily "a resort for desperate characters and is mainly made up of gambling and drinking saloons and other disreputable places." Furthermore, Veck and his associates were "enemies of the present administration."[74]

In January, 1880, Veck, by some means never revealed, managed to get himself appointed as postmaster at Fort Concho and promptly moved the office to the front yard of his home. Grierson countered by conducting garrison business at Ben Ficklin, three miles away on the stage line, until December, 1880, when a new postmaster was appointed for Fort Concho. The "war" ended in the spring of 1881, with postoffices at Saint Angela, Fort Concho, and Ben Ficklin, but the ill-feeling remained.[75]

If Grierson and his officers were unpopular in Saint Angela, the buffalo soldiers were even more so, despite notable service on the Texas frontier. Their pay was another matter, for it contributed more than a little to the local economy. Grierson tried to keep the troopers on post, but many sought the pleasures of the town even though a number of them had been killed and others beaten and robbed. Serious trouble had occurred in 1878, and early in 1881 it flared again.

On January 19, a gambler named Watson shot and killed Private Hiram Pinder in Nasworthy's Saloon. With the aid of local citizens, Watson obtained a fast horse and made good his escape. No outburst came from the garrison; there was only an ominous silence. Twelve days later another unprovoked murder broke the bonds of trooper restraint and a few of them attempted to exact their own justice.

The results reverberated throughout Texas, brought a threat of breaking up the Tenth Cavalry, and, strangely, ended on a wave of good feeling.[76]

Private William Watkins of Company E was singing and dancing for drinks in Charlie Wilson's saloon on the evening of January 31, as he had done on many occasions. In the audience was one Tom McCarthy, a rancher from the San Saba River country. Near one o'clock in the morning, Watkins grew tired and proposed to stop, but McCarthy insisted that he continue. When Watkins refused, McCarthy drew a revolver and shot the trooper in the head, killing him instantly.[77]

McCarthy fled the saloon but was apprehended by post guards as he crossed the Concho River. He was held in the guardhouse until morning, when he was turned over to Sheriff James Spears. The Saint Angela jail was a fragile picket structure, and Spears, fearing his prisoner might be lynched, hid him in Mrs. Annie Tankersley's boarding house.[78]

A small party of troopers, thinking McCarthy had been released, went in search of him but were held off by Mrs. Tankersley, whom they knew and respected. A detachment from the post arrived and escorted the group back to the barracks. In reporting the incident, the *Galveston News* showed considerable sympathy for the angry troopers: "If no better results occur from this move on the part of the soldiers, it will have a tendency to check the lawless manner in which soldiers are mercilessly shot down by men who think it an act of bravado."[79]

On February 2, McCarthy's preliminary hearing began and continued the following day. In the afternoon, shock and fear swept Saint Angela when a few soldiers distributed a printed circular that read:

> We, the soldiers of the U.S. Army, do hereby warn the first and last time all citizens and cowboys, etc., of San Angelo and vicinity to recognize our right of way as just and peaceable men. If we do not receive justice and fair play, which we must have, some one will suffer—if not the guilty the innocent.
> "It has gone too far, justice or death."
>   SIGNED U.S. SOLDIERS.[80]

Grierson informed Ord of the circular, immediately arrested those responsible, and strengthened the guard around the post. McCarthy was held without bail pending action by a grand jury. Grierson provided a detachment to assist Spears, for reasons of security, in conducting the prisoner to Ben Ficklin, where he was jailed to await transfer to Austin, Texas.

All was calm on the morning of February 4, but in the afternoon an odd quirk of fate unleashed the hurricane. John McCarthy, Tom's brother, who closely resembled him in appearance, arrived in town. He was urged to leave at once, but the damage had been done; a report reached Fort Concho that Tom McCarthy had been released. At dusk a party of five white men rode to the banks of the Concho River and fired across the stream at Grierson's pickets. The men rode off in the gloom and were never identified.[81]

Shortly after dark, about forty troopers snatched carbines from gun racks, evaded the guards, and rushed into town. They fired two volleys into the Nimitz Hotel and another into Vroman's Store. Despite the heavy gunfire, more than 150 shots, only one person was slightly wounded.[82]

Alarmed citizens sent for a company of Texas Rangers and lodged a protest with Governor O. M. Roberts. Grierson ordered two companies of troops into town to serve as guards and sealed off the post. When the rangers arrived, Grierson conferred with their commander, Captain Bryan Marsh, and promised all needed assistance. No further incidents occurred and "life returned to normal."[83]

Grierson submitted a detailed report to Augur, Ord's replacement, which included a lengthy list of soldiers killed with no action taken against their slayers. Augur accepted the report, but he was not entirely satisfied and warned that any further outbreak would result in disbandment of the regiment. His reaction was not unexpected, though most of the troopers had taken no part in the affair and Grierson had done all in his power to prevent it.[84]

More insight and encouragement came, strangely enough, from the county grand jury meeting in Ben Ficklin. After hearing the evidence, the jury returned no indictments against the soldiers and: "That body [grand jury] made a report wherein you [Grierson] are complimented for zealous aid rendered the civil authorities in investigation of crime. . . ."[85]

McCarthy was indicted for first-degree murder and tried in Austin, but the jury swiftly reached a verdict of "Not Guilty." Seven years later, despondent over chronic ill-health, McCarthy committed suicide in a Detroit, Michigan, livery stable.[86]

The pace and tenor of life at Fort Concho became more leisurely and pleasant as the riot faded into memory and relations with Saint

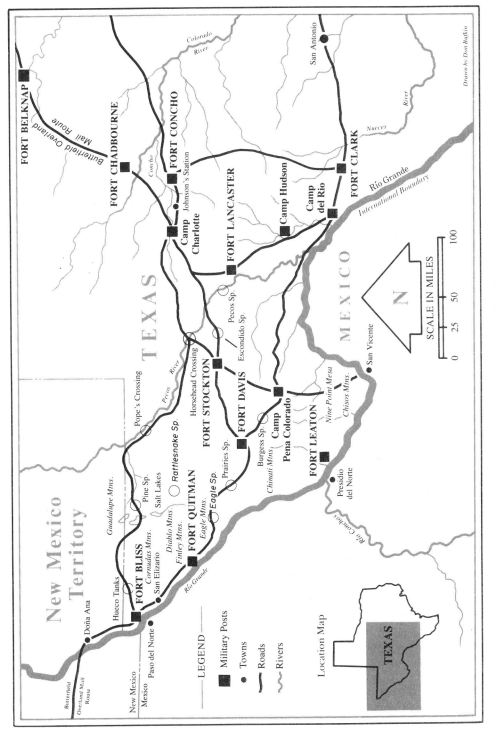

Grierson's area of operations in West Texas.

Angela improved. Grierson and the Tenth could take some time to enjoy the peace they had done so much to bring to West Texas. Detachments were still necessary to provide protection for Texas and Pacific survey crews and assist civil authorities in running down outlaws and cattle thieves. In April, Ord called on Grierson to send a battalion under Major Anson Mills to Indian Territory, where restless Cheyennes and persistent "Boomers" were causing concern, but Mills returned in November after routine patrol duty.[87]

Ben used his spare time to resume his quest for promotion and to compile a family genealogy, the first step in a family biography, which he had assigned to his sister Louisa. On occasion, at the urging of Harry and George, he accompanied them on hunting and fishing trips. Alice began planning an early departure for Jacksonville, because she wanted to settle the problem of Robert's future career by finding a suitable school for him. Meanwhile, Robert passed his time until they left by paying steady court to the belles in Saint Angela and often—certainly without his mother's knowledge—enjoying a drink at Charlie Wilson's saloon.[88]

In June, Alice and Robert journeyed to Jacksonville. After discussions with John Grierson, Louisa, and John Kirk, Robert decided to attend medical school, and arrangements were made for him to enroll at the University of Michigan. With this accomplished, Alice turned her attention to assisting relatives. She not only provided funds for school expenses for Mary Kirk's children, but invited her thirteen-year-old nephew Paul and Ben's niece Grace Fuller to accompany her to Fort Concho. To raise the necessary money, Alice sold 160 acres of Kansas farmland she had acquired through her father.[89]

Alice returned to Concho in September and Grace Fuller, as her sister Helen before her, was soon engaged to an officer of the Tenth. Lieutenant Mason Maxon courted and won her. With this mission accomplished, Ben and Alice could never be accused of failing to pursue the interests of the "clan."

The usual holiday gaiety prevailed at Concho in December, 1881, though party conversation centered on two sobering issues. Lieutenant Flipper was in confinement at Fort Davis on charges preferred by Colonel Shafter, and there were rumors that regimental headquarters would soon be moved to another station.

Flipper, accused of embezzling funds from the post commissary, was awaiting court-martial. Though a few of the Tenth's officers had been cool to him, most of them liked and respected the eager young black. Captain Nolan, in whose A Company Flipper served, was deeply distressed. The two were close friends, and Nolan had once described one of Flipper's critics as "an officer who never smelt powder except on his lady's face."[90]

Grierson, too, was fond of Flipper and regarded him as a brave and talented officer. If the commissary funds were in disorder, not unusual at any post, Grierson was certain it was the result of inexperience or carelessness, and not a question of dishonesty. He wrote a long and laudatory letter of recommendation in Flipper's behalf, asking the court to be lenient.[91]

A new assignment for the Tenth Cavalry was inevitable. Fort Concho was no longer needed, since the Indian troubles had all but ceased, and the adjacent country was filling up with settlers. Grierson had recommended allocating no money for repairs at the post, believing it could best be spent elsewhere. Ord agreed and rumor had it that headquarters would move to Fort Davis. If true, Grierson would not object. He considered Davis a desirable post and had long admired the beauty of its surroundings.[92]

CHAPTER 10

Journey's End

ROBERT GRIERSON completed his first semester at the University of Michigan with a satisfactory performance. He spent the holidays in Jacksonville, enjoying, as he assured his mother, a veritable social whirl, visiting a number of homes and then attending a "grand ball," where he "had the most glorious time I ever had in my life at a dance." After that, he intended paying a brief visit to his aunt Ellen Fuller and her family in Chicago before returning to Ann Arbor, but he failed to appear.

The Fullers were stunned on January 15 to learn that Robert was being held in Chicago's Hamilton Street jail. The day before, he had registered at the Grand Pacific Hotel, bought wine and cigars, and gone to his room. Shortly thereafter, he went berserk, tore up the furniture, barricaded the door, and "prepared for action." The police were called and, with great difficulty, subdued him.[1]

Ellen's husband, Harvey Fuller, Jr., managed to secure Robert's release in order to escort him to Jacksonville, an experience Harvey never forgot. Robert had to be placed in a straitjacket and shackles and guarded closely on the train. Upon his arrival at the Old Homestead he was locked in the attic. Louisa Semple took charge, called Dr. Jones, and employed four attendants to give him twenty-four-hour care. She then notified Ben and Alice, impressing on them that all that could be done was being done. In the meantime she awaited Ben's arrival.[2]

It was another shattering blow to the Griersons. With no leave available and with Robert's expenses mounting daily, Ben arranged through his friend, Jacksonville banker, M. P. Ayres, to provide Louisa with the funds necessary for his son's care. Alice meanwhile sought to learn more details. She had expected Robert to spend the holidays with old family friends, but at the last moment the invitation had been cancelled because of the unexpected arrival of other guests. Robert's only recourse had been to visit relatives in Jacksonville. Despite his frantic efforts to have a good time, in reality he had felt rejected and lonely and sorely missed his family in Fort Concho.[3]

Robert's plight uncovered a deep concern among Alice's relatives that the Kirk family suffered from hereditary insanity. By now the list of those stricken during their youth included a cousin, John Manning, Alice's brother Henry, her deceased sister Maria, and more recently, Charlie and Robert. During the winter of 1881 Charlie had suffered a mild setback but recovered swiftly and now gave no further evidence of disturbance.

Yet, even if heredity was a factor, as it appeared it might be, it seemed possible that it served more as a predisposition to break-down under certain stressful conditions than an inevitable fact. Ellen Fuller, for example, believed that Charlie and Robert would have experienced no trouble "if they had not been sent away to school while still little boys."[4] And while Ben and Alice had no way of determining the accuracy of her statement, the possibility that she might be correct led them to question the value of education for Harry and George. This issue cast a long shadow over the younger boys' future.

For three long and exhausting months Louisa supervised the work of attendants, prepared Robert's meals, and provided as much personal attention as his condition would allow. Other than confinement in the attic, his only treatment consisted of forced doses of chloral hydrate to calm him. His changes of mood could be sudden, ranging from sullen silence to noisy violence, but most of the time he moved and talked incessantly.

On February 13, Louisa, thinking she saw improvement, reduced the number of attendants from four to two and wrote Ben:

All this . . . shows you clearly a marked change in Robert. When the attendant leaves the attic for a short time in the day, I am on guard. The key is turned in the door, on the outside. Robt. is engaged in vehement marching back and forth, with the large red pillow on his head, or he rattles the slats of the window blinds, or he makes furious charges with the pillow on imaginary foes, but never seems to miss the attendant. . . .[5]

Louisa, however, was overly optimistic; Robert's condition remained substantially the same. Mary Kirk, living in the house with her large brood, felt the strain and wrote the Griersons that their son was really no better. Father Kirk, who visited frequently, agreed.[6]

It was too much for Alice. Not content to remain at distant Concho, she reached Jacksonville on April 21, accompanied by George. Immediately she took charge of Robert's care, and Louisa, resentful that her efforts seemed unappreciated, especially since she had recently endured physical abuse from Robert, withdrew from the case entirely.[7]

At first Alice's presence seemed to soothe Robert, and, encouraged by this, she dismissed another one of the attendants. Within ten days Alice was taking her son from the attic and accompanying him on walks and carriage rides, even allowing him to drive. But she underestimated the severity of his condition. Free from all restraint, Robert ran away, tried to catch a freight train, and then wandered from one end of the town to the other, alarming Jacksonville citizens. Friends brought him home, but the police, a "posse," according to Alice, came to the house to take him to jail. Alice, who never flinched during difficult times, appeared at his hearing, spoke in his behalf, and obtained her son's release, but only on condition that she place him in the Oak Lawn Retreat.[8]

When Ben first learned of Robert's confinement "in the vile, filthy, Calaboose," he was angry. On reflection, however, his natural empathy for others asserted itself. Considering Robert's behavior he could well understand why citizens were "alarmed for their own safety," and thus the course taken had probably been justified. Always the comforting optimist, he assured his wife that "Everything will come out all right in the end." And ever the peacemaker, he urged her to reconcile with Louisa, who had cared for their son for ninety-seven days at great cost to her own comfort and leisure. "Taken all together, we are not by any means the worst people in the world."[9]

Ben's concerns now extended beyond Robert's troubles. In a carefully worded letter he shared with Alice the painful thoughts that were difficult for him to acknowledge even to himself.

> We must prepare ourselves to *look* this Family tendency to Insanity squarely in the face. It has been developed in the first two of our children *now living* and under certain circumstances may or might show itself in the two younger boys. It is better that they be *clodhoppers* and go through life with but little education than to be afflicted as Charlie and Robert have been.[10]

He was also distressed that Robert had finally been institutionalized, for unlike his father-in-law, John Kirk, he placed little faith in such treatment. Furthermore, having received Louisa's version of events, he was convinced that Alice had acted precipitously in allowing Robert greater freedom, a point that he made clear to her. And yet there was nothing unkind in his letters; what had happened was irrevocable, and he wished only that his wife would "get all the sleep and rest you can."[11]

Ben's advice was well meant but impossible to take. With the exception of John Kirk, who offered steadfast encouragement and support, Alice encountered criticism from her relatives and embarrassed silence from her friends; Louisa made it clear that she felt vindicated. But the most difficult blow of all was Ben's apparent disapproval, and in a burst of anger Alice fired off her own response to Concho. Noting that she had nursed Charlie back to perfect health, not once but twice, she charged her husband with blaming her for Robert's illness, adding defensively, "I am of the opinion that if you ever look at it squarely, with a willingness to admit that possibly you may be accountable for part of it, you will find it to be the case. . . ." Once again tragedy appeared to have driven a wedge between them, and several days later, Alice wrote in anguish that for the first time in their marriage, she felt there was "little of the affectionate husband left" in Ben.[12]

As he had so many times in the past, Ben responded, not only in a conciliatory fashion, but with great warmth.

> You might as well tell me the *moon is really made of green cheese* my honey—than I *love* thee not—for—if there be one single thing I know and feel absolutely certain about, it is, that, I have loved you devotedly since I was *knee high to a toad* and have been for quite a length of time, whether there be *much or little left of me,* your affectionate husband.

He had other news for her as well. Having succeeded in arranging a four-month leave, he would soon join her in Jacksonville.[13] Robert was still ill, and difficult days lay ahead, but the bonds between Ben and Alice, having survived one more crisis, were as strong as ever.

These welcome words, along with reports from Dr. Andrew McFarland at the asylum that Robert was improving, did much to restore Alice's emotional well-being. She made plans to visit Ellen in Chicago and began assisting Grace Fuller in arranging her September wedding in Jacksonville to Lieutenant Maxon. Alice's mind was relieved on another point as well. She and Ben had decided to purchase enough land somewhere in Texas to give Robert, Harry, and George a start in the ranching business. By September, Robert was well enough to attend the Fuller-Maxon wedding, and in late November, he, along with his parents and George, joined Harry at Fort Davis.[14]

Regimental headquarters had moved to Davis from Concho in July, with Major Anson Mills, Schofield's replacement, in command. The move was accompanied by friction between Mills and Woodward. The former felt the latter was "slow to obey" orders, while Woodward thought Mills "a sorry excuse." Charlie, who was inclined to agree with Sam, wished Papa had not taken a leave. In general, however, morale was good and some funds were available for needed construction and repair.[15]

Harry, in Woodward's care, liked Davis but had two complaints. Woodward's Chinese cook put rice in everything and "Day before yesterday he made peach pie, but it had more rice in it than peaches." Also, he had loaned his rifle to Captain Carpenter, who had broken the stock but promised to replace it.[16]

When he arrived at Davis, Grierson found many of his officers unhappy over Flipper's fate. On December 8, 1881, a court-martial had cleared the lieutenant of embezzlement charges but found him guilty of "conduct unbecoming an officer and gentleman." The court ignored Grierson's recommendation for leniency, and Flipper, after review of the case by the Judge Advocate General, was dismissed from the service. Flipper believed he was the victim of gross prejudice on the part of Shafter and Lieutenant Charles Nordstrom. For the rest of his long and productive life as an engineer, Flipper sought in vain to clear his name. Not until 1976, thirty-six years after his death, was the stain on his record removed.[17]

The Griersons had scarcely settled into their quarters at Davis before Ben began carrying out plans to provide his sons with land for ranching. He disposed of most of his other holdings—acreage in Iowa and in the vicinity of Fort Concho, and with the capital thus acquired and more borrowed on Alice's future inheritance from John Kirk, he bought six sections south of Davis in Presidio County. On a regular basis he continued to acquire choice rangeland, stocking it with cattle and sheep. In the meantime he obtained a position for Robert as forage master in the quartermaster department that paid the "gentlemanly" wage of seventy-five dollars a month.[18]

By the end of 1882 life had returned to normal in the Grierson household. Once more Ben had been passed over for promotion in

Fort Davis, Texas, in the late 1880s. *Courtesy Western History Collections, University of Oklahoma Library.*

favor of Mackenzie, but he was not discouraged, vowing to "give everybody a lively fight for the next vacancy." Alice wasn't sure she liked Davis as well as Concho yet, but in time that would come. She agreed with Ben that the scenery around the post was spectacular. Her only complaint was that her right leg, injured in getting out of a carriage, remained persistently lame. Still, it didn't amount to much, or so she thought. If she had any immediate concern, it was that John Grierson's position in Colorado had given out and, while he again looked for employment, he would need assistance, thus slowing down the Griersons' progress in acquiring land holdings for their sons. And, since neither she nor Ben were young any longer, they needed to begin saving for their retirement to the permanent home they had so long desired.[19]

For more than two years the Griersons enjoyed the comparative peace and quiet at Fort Davis, growing fonder of the place with each passing day. In addition to other holdings, Ben purchased two ranches near the post for Charlie and Robert. He was impressed, not only with the rugged, mountainous beauty of the region, but also with what he sensed was the future of the entire state of Texas. Perhaps at last he had found the place for their long-sought home. His sentiments were accurately expressed by Louisa Semple: "I perceive that Texas is to become one of the most important members of the Union. With its vastness and variety of soil, climate and undeveloped resources, it will yet attract and maintain a vast population."[20] With these thoughts in mind, Ben, ever the developer and promoter, began the organization of a short-line railroad company to link Fort Davis with the Southern Pacific.[21]

As Grierson's property holdings grew, he turned many of the day-to-day operations over to Robert. Feeding cattle, building and repairing fences, raising chickens and turkeys kept Robert busy and out-of-doors, the standard prescription for troubled youths. He appeared healthy and reasonably happy, although his one continuing complaint was the lack of female companionship. He wanted a wife, preferably one "as good and sweet as Mrs. Capt. Keyes."[22]

In the summer of 1883, Alice, for the first time in many years, decided against a vacation in Illinois. She wished to remain near Robert until certain he had fully recovered, and she had also assumed responsibility for tutoring Harry and George. If all went well, she would place Harry in school in Jacksonville in the fall of 1884, and George would follow a year later, well past the time that they were "little boys."

Then, too, since life was very pleasant at Fort Davis, there was not as much need for a change of scenery. It was by then a fairly quiet post, which permitted ample time for hops, parties, and picnics. Evening concerts by Ben's pride and joy, the Tenth Cavalry Band, brought out the entire garrison, and on occasion a traveling troupe presented a play. Typical of these was a six-act drama entitled "A Celebrated Case or the Soldier of Fontonoy," performed by J. G. Stultz and his Mammoth Star Company.[23]

Nor were Ben's military duties demanding. Beyond issuing essential orders and reports and settling quarrels and disputes, he found ample time to pursue his promotion as well as that of others, notably Woodward and Smither, whose advancements were long overdue. Unfortunately the ever-helpful Sherman was no longer in a position to wield much influence. In the summer of 1883 he had relinquished his post to Sheridan, who was now commanding general of the army. Nonetheless, Sherman promised to do what he could, but cautioned Ben not to fret, pointing to Mackenzie, who for fifteen years had "tortured" his friends and correspondents seeking his star. "Now he has it and is in the insane asylum," and Sherman advised Ben to "enjoy your health."[24]

Ben was rarely ill, and though he had suffered many disappointments and had seen his share of tragedy, his sense of humor and the support of his family always sustained him. He also had the capacity for making and keeping friends, another source of strong encouragement. In the summer of 1883 he received a long letter from the old interpreter at Fort Sill, Horace Jones, who spoke of the many friendships formed with the Kiowas and Comanches when Grierson and the Tenth were at Sill. This situation was no longer true, for there wasn't much "in way of relationships now," and Jones couldn't help but wish that the Tenth and their commanding officer were there once more.[25]

The routine at Davis was pleasantly interrupted in September, when Grierson was ordered to San Antonio to assume command of the Department of Texas while Augur took a two-month leave. Ben stayed in the general's quarters and informed Alice—she joined him in October—that he was "nearly all alone in my glory. I trust without being awestruck." Augur had warned that the cook was "old and cranky," and Ben observed that he was "keeping my distance."[26]

The Griersons took full advantage of their few weeks in picturesque San Antonio, touring the Alamo and other missions and dining out in colorful restaurants such as the dining room of the Menger Hotel, a favored oasis for the prominent. An inveterate shopper, Alice drained the family coffers by purchasing gifts for her sons and relatives. Always on the alert for books, she found and purchased the works of Thackeray, Pope, Lamb, and Tennyson for the Fort Davis library.[27]

The following summer, Alice and Harry left for Jacksonville, and Ben spent his spare time writing letters in support of James Blaine's candidacy for the presidency. Whatever defections there had been among family members from the Grand Old Party's ranks, he at least could count on John Kirk to support him in his staunch Republicanism. Both men worried that votes for third-party candidates would give the election to Democrat Grover Cleveland. Kirk wrote his son-in-law that he considered the Greenback and the Prohibition parties "nothing but contemptible tails of the Democratic Kite."[28]

Late in October, Ben joined Alice in order to cast his vote for Blaine, and he later consoled has father-in-law when the "plumed knight" went down to defeat. Perhaps some of the sting was eased by appreciation and amusement over George's labored but faithful efforts to keep his parents informed as promised. He wrote to Alice: "Everything seams upsidedown ever since you have ben gon and it is still worse since Papa has gon. Robtert was not hear to correct the words so I did the best I could." While George never learned to spell very well, he did demonstrate a knack for drawing, and he often made sketches that he presented to his friends among the enlisted men. Recently he had just completed a picture of a herd of antelope, "almost flying" which he gave to D Troop to "remember me By."[29]

In December, Ben visited New York and Washington and then called on Grant, who by this time was struggling to complete his memoirs despite grave illness. His old commander gave Grierson a warm welcome, along with assurances of a strong letter of recommendation for promotion. After visiting several members of the Illinois congressional delegation, Ben took the opportunity to chat with Sheridan and then arranged for a brief audience with President Arthur, all in the hope of enhancing his chances for a star.[30]

The Griersons returned to Fort Davis in time for Christmas, sobered by the news received in Washington that the Tenth would be transferred, probably to Arizona. Grierson had no desire to make this change. Many years earlier, in March, 1862, when he had first embarked on a military career and Alice and Charlie and Robert were living in his parents' home, he had written of his yearning for ". . . some quiet nook on the face of the globe where we could be together permanently and look upon as a home of our own . . . something desirable beyond every other earthly blessing likely to be attained."[31] Now it seemed that they had found that nook. Ben had invested heavily in land and cattle in west Texas, so that his sons would not be "clodhoppers," but prosperous ranchers instead, and he and Alice could live out their lives with them.

Unfortunately, he had plunged deeply into debt and still needed his monthly pay. Moreover, assurance of a decent income in his old age required retirement at the level of brigadier general. In his own mind he had no choice but to continue to do his duty and hope that Robert could manage some of the property efficiently. The rest could be leased.

As a reward for hard work already well performed, Ben gave Robert the funds for a trip to the New Orleans Mardi Gras. He was relieved when his son returned, having had an exciting time and having experienced no problems whatsoever. Among Robert's major purchases was a bicycle, and he was soon "astonishing" the natives at Davis, speeding along the road and racing the train with his "steel steed."[32]

On March 5, Grierson received orders assigning the Tenth to the Department of Arizona. The Headquarters, Band, and Company B were ordered to Whipple Barracks, while the remaining eleven companies were scattered among Forts Apache, Verde, Thomas, and Grant. By the end of the month the entire regiment had assembled at Davis and was ready to march.[33]

Alice, planning to join Ben at Whipple Barracks in the summer, left with George for Jacksonville, to enroll him in school with Harry. She was welcomed with open arms by her father, now eighty and feeling the weight of his years. A few weeks earlier he had written his daughter:

> What a world of trials and afflictions we have to endure . . . your mother, Mary, Maria, John, and last and worst of all Thomas, besides all the little ones, and of my own grandchildren, three of yours, three of Thomas, three of Ellens, and two of Rufus, all gone to their long homes and I expect soon to follow them.[34]

John Kirk was destined to suffer still more "trials and afflictions" before his long life came to an end.

On April 1, the Tenth, united for the first in its history, left Fort Davis. Led by the band, mounted on "dapple greys," the cavalry and train, two miles long, paraded past the post and headed for Eagle Springs. "It almost broke Robert's heart to see Mrs. Keyes leave," Ben informed Alice. Helen Davis, riding in a carriage with satin curtains, was amazed at the efficiency of the soldiers when the column first encamped. Sitting in a willow rocker provided by "Uncle Ben," she watched as the tents went up and the meal was prepared. Next morning, "The whole tent city came down at once like the blowing off of a dandelion puff."[35]

Helen enjoyed the march, as did most of the ladies who "wore suitable clothes." One woman, unidentified, dressed in a gown with long trains "which soon became a fringe of rags at the bottom." At each halt the horses were unsaddled so their backs could cool, for "Woe to the man whose horse had a sore back." In the evenings the band provided music under the stars. The only hitch that developed was "our lady of the trail," who often delayed B Troop's wagons.[36]

When the regiment reached El Paso, the officers were entertained at a formal dance. After that, arrangements were made for crossing the Río Grande "over a corner of Mexico," because of high water on the American side. With "the band playing and colors flying," Grierson's Tenth crossed proudly and set out for Fort Bowie where the companies separated and went to their assigned stations.[37]

Grierson left the march at Bowie to inspect Fort Huachuca and visit Tombstone, "the town too tough to die." After entertaining guests at the Porter Hotel by playing the piano, he toured one of the silver mines. From Tombstone he traveled to Los Angeles, where he reported to Department Headquarters, and then to San Francisco to meet General Pope, an old friend who held similar views on Indian policies and who now commanded the Division of the Pacific.[38]

Grierson journeyed on to Prescott, where he reported to General George Crook, justly famous for his Apache campaigns of the 1870s and early 1880s. Ben found him to be "affable and pleasant" but "considerably annoyed" over a breakout of the Chiricahua and Warm Springs Apaches on the very day of Grierson's arrival. Led by noted raiders Geronimo, Nana, Natchez, Chihuahua, and Mangus, they were capable of inflicting serious damage and would operate from nearly inaccessible mountain strongholds in Mexico.

To Ben, the means of rounding up the runaways was a true "conundrum," but it would end as all Indian raids ended. Eventually they would be driven back to the reservation or killed off, even if it took all summer or longer, "if that's what the army intends doing." He was relieved that he would play no part in this campaign. As to his command at Whipple, feeling it inadequate for his rank, he proposed to seek another appointment.[39]

For the moment, he began repairs on his "old and delapidated" quarters and made acquaintances in Prescott. He liked the little city and found the surrounding scenery "remarkably varied and beautiful." He had not been there long when he accepted an invitation to serve as Grand Marshal of the Decoration Day parade but, by his own admission, he "didn't marshal worth a cent."[40]

The recent travels had clearly been a tonic for him. If he failed to win promotion this year he "wouldn't commit suicide," and he informed Alice that he felt like a boy and "I want you to be a girl again—so brace yourself up—buckle on your armor and fight it out on that line for the balance of your life."[41] On that note, she arrived in Prescott on July 4 with Harry and George and was pleased with the renovated quarters, having already formed a favorable impression of the town. News from Charlie and Helen Davis, however, indicated that all was not going well in the Tenth. The Apache problem was taking its toll on nerves and tempers."[42]

Crook's campaign, launched in June, relied heavily on Apache scouts and comparatively few regular troops. The buffalo soldiers were used primarily to guard water holes and scout the mountain passes. It was monotonous, grinding duty in scorching heat and over incredibly rough and broken country. A steady diet of beans, bacon, bread, and coffee, along with a change in environment, brought a wave of illness. At Fort Thomas the surgeons were unable to check "a very malignant, burning fever," and a number of the troopers died. Cramped quarters, poor food, hordes of insects, and boredom also brought a rash of quarrels among the officers.[43]

Inevitably in a hard-drinking army, liquor exaggerated petty differences, and charges both formal and informal plagued the adjutant's office. Grierson managed to settle most of the disputes short of court-martial but concluded that "Drinking, Gambling and Whoring" were the big problems in the military.[44]

Ben also received a barrage of complaints from another quarter. Robert was now lonely and unhappy at Davis. "My work is perfect drudgery," he wrote, "and is neither beneficial to mind or body." He still felt that he would "like a girl of my own," but acknowledged that there was no way that he could afford a wife, either presently or in the foreseeable future. Moreover, living at the ranch now seemed "like being in jail—a large jail—but a jail nevertheless." But what alternative was there, since Jacksonville held no promise either—he'd "rather be shot with a box full of red hot tacks than go there." A letter from Flipper, who asked to be remembered to the Grierson family, further depressed him.[45]

In August, Alice received a letter from Robert that required an immediate and positive answer: "I would like very much to be with all of you. It would be very nice to "assist" at some of those dinner and birthday parties. It has been so long since I've been to a dinner party or anything of the kind that I'm afraid I've almost forgotten how to act."[46] Robert was invited to spend the Christmas holidays at Whipple, and Ben sent three thousand dollars for the purchase of cattle as a partnership enterprise.[47]

August also brought news of Grant's death from throat cancer, and at Whipple the Griersons attended a memorial service to pay their respects. In addition to providing support and encouragement for Grierson, Grant had always been cordial and friendly. Ben had repaid him with unquestioning loyalty.

All the efforts of Grant, Sherman, and many others had failed to bring promotion, and, in 1885, Grierson once again saw the vacancy go to another. No doubt Sheridan exerted a negative influence, and Ben must have rejoiced to know that Crook shared his opinion of "Sherry-Dan." In his *Autobiography* Crook wrote, "The adulation heaped on him [Sheridan] by a grateful nation for his supposed genius turned his head, which, added to his natural disposition, caused him to bloat his little carcass with debauchery and dissipation, which carried him off prematurely."[48] Crook's criticism may have been too severe, but Sheridan never commanded the respect and affection most officers of the line accorded Sherman.

With his regiment "standing guard" and Crook personally heading operations in the field, Grierson fought off boredom by beginning serious work on his own memoirs and gathering more materials for the family history. In the evenings, he and Alice often entertained their local friends from Prescott as well as Crook and members of his staff.

Robert joined the family in mid-December, had several successful hunting trips with Harry, and satisfied his wish to "assist" at a big party. When Company B sponsored a ball on Christmas night, Robert was the proud escort of Miss Goldwater of Prescott. His good time did not end there. Among his Christmas gifts were funds for him and Harry to visit San Francisco and Los Angeles. While there, they saw the Golden Gate, rode the cable cars, dined in Chinatown, and attended the theater. After two weeks they moved on to Los Angeles before boarding the train for Texas. Robert's depression had ended, and he was able to enjoy Harry's company until school opened in the fall.[49]

Meanwhile, Crook's campaign against the Apaches had struck a snag. After months of seemingly endless pursuit in the mountains, deserts, and canyons of northern Mexico and Arizona, the hostiles agreed to a meeting with Crook in the Cañon de los Embudos, some dozen miles south of the Mexican border. Here, on March 27, 1886, the Apaches agreed to surrender and return to the reservation. Two nights later Geronimo and Nachez, with twenty warriors and sixteen women and children, fled into the mountains. The others, under Chihuahua and Nana, were escorted to Fort Bowie and entrained for Fort Marion, Florida, as prisoners of war.[50]

News of the escape of Geronimo and Nachez, as well as Crook's extensive use of Apache scouts, angered Sheridan. Informed of his displeasure, Crook responded by asking to be relieved of his command. Sheridan did not hesitate. On April 2, Grierson's close friend General Miles was ordered to assume command of the Department of Arizona.

Miles, understanding Sheridan clearly, threw more regulars into the field, but did not discontinue the use of Apache scouts. For the next five months, by giving the renegades no rest, he wore down their will to resist. On September 4, Miles received Geronimo's surrender in Skeleton Canyon, southeast of Fort Bowie. Shortly thereafter the old warrior and his followers were sent to Fort Marion. Two weeks later, Captain Charles Cooper and a detachment of buffalo soldiers scouting in the White Mountains overtook and captured the slippery Mangus and his band. The Apache wars were over.[51]

Though most of the Chiricahuas had taken no part in the recent troubles, Miles was convinced that to insure lasting peace these Indians must be removed from Arizona. Six companies of Grierson's Tenth had the unpleasant duty of arresting nearly four hundred men, women, and children at Fort Apache. They were then taken to Holbrook and shipped to Fort Marion to join the others already there. Few mourned Geronimo's fate, but Louisa Semple expressed her sympathy. "If Geronimo had lived in an early age he would have been crowned with laurels. He has done nothing wrong from his point of view."[52]

Grierson played no part in these events, but Miles had determined on a more active role for him in the Department. In June, friction between white settlers and the Hualapai Indians brought on loose talk of war. Miles ordered Grierson to investigate, and the commanding officer at Fort Mojave was instructed to place his troops at Grierson's disposal. Ben arrived at the scene armed with "a jackknife and a toothpick," and, relying on his powers of persuasion, resolved the difficulties. As he described his achievement to Charlie, "I went, I saw and conquered. All accomplished without bloodshed."[53] It was another demonstration of his concern for Indian welfare, his talent for negotiation, and his remarkable physical courage.

At the end of June, headquarters of the Tenth was transferred to Fort Grant. The move was a temporary one, since in November Grierson was appointed commanding officer of the District of New Mexico, with headquarters in Santa Fe. This post, commensurate with his rank and seniority, demonstrated the confidence Miles placed in him.[54]

The moves from Whipple to Grant and then to Santa Fe, all in the space of six months, were trying ones for Alice. Ben was required to report for duty before completing preparations for packing and transportation, tasks that he had always handled in the past. Fortunately Woodward was on hand to lend his assistance, and Alice was initiated into the art of selling off surplus property — spare horses, a carriage, and even a flock of chickens. But what on earth would she do with George's antelope horns? On Ben's advice, she packed them.[55]

Santa Fe pleased Grierson, who described it in glowing terms to his wife. He attended a number of "blowouts," at which the people were fashionably dressed and the ladies' gowns were described in the local press. Alice wasn't interested in "blowouts," and she owned no dresses worth discussing in newspapers, but she would be happy to leave Fort Grant, an uninspiring post at best.[56]

When Alice arrived she found Ben's enthusiasm for the old city contagious. The climate seemed ideal, and their quarters were neat, clean and boasted the convenience of gas. The market supplied a wide variety of meat, vegetables, and fruit, all rare commodities on most Western army posts. Best of all, she could buy clothing without ordering it from a catalog. Life was gracious in the old territorial capitol, and the Griersons soon had a wide circle of friends.[57]

The rapid changes of station had, however, disrupted George's education and raised again the problem of proper schooling for him and Harry. Alice sought the advice of their old friend in Jacksonville, Dr. Jones, and discovered that he had little use for the "Educational Mills of the country." Louisa Semple volunteered the opinion that the public schools, with their "cramming & crowding and the pressure of examinations, the efforts to fill the mind of the pupil with a vast number of facts without any corresponding mental development or power to use facts," rendered them useless for true learning. Alice agreed, and as a result George was placed in a private school in Tempe, Arizona, and though Alice thought it "risky," Harry was enrolled at Washington University in St. Louis. Some, but not all, of her misgivings eased when Charlie, deciding to accept a year of recruiting service, was assigned to Jefferson Barracks in St. Louis. Harry could stay with his brother, who would see to it that he did not remain out too late or study too hard.[58]

Ben's primary concern was Robert. Severe drought and overstocking of the ranges caused severe cattle losses in the summer of 1886, resulting in little income for his son. In May, he had made a quick trip to Davis and amazed Robert with his endurance. "Papa" wore him out, riding "twelve hours in the saddle without food" while looking over their property. Ben's visit boosted Robert's morale. He convinced his son that the cattle industry would soon recover from the doldrums.[59]

But Harry's departure for St. Louis in August left Robert alone once more. His brother had helped with the chores and, in addition, had enlivened their evenings with music on the guitar. Then, too, Harry had always been ready to go hunting. Robert's quest for a wife "like Mrs. Keyes" had not been realized, though he often wrote of young women, including Maria, "la dulce Mexicana." It was lonely at Davis, and news and excitement were so scarce that an attempted suicide was a sensation. "A man named Cohen, over at Marfa, tried to drown himself in the water tank a few days ago because Jennings danced with his wife," Robert reported to his mother.[60]

He joined Ben, Alice, and George in Santa Fe for Christmas, after a brief visit with the Keyes at Fort Grant. At least some of the time they must have discussed the family's tangled finances. Alice's gift from John Kirk was twenty-five dollars, which Ben was to pay out of interest he owed his father-in-law on a thousand-dollar loan. School expenses for Harry and George were a strain, the cattle business was distressed, and Ben could not collect money due him from other family members, chiefly his brother, who owed him a thousand dollars.[61]

Once more John Grierson was out of work and in such severe straits that he had borrowed $150 from Charlie. His bitterness was increasing daily, as he now railed against the continuing wave of immigration pouring into the United States and destroying, he thought, his chances for employment. "This Country is the receptical for all the downgraded and criminal population of the Globe— this thing must be stopped, or this the *best Government on Earth, will, go to pieces!*" Even local politics had been affected. "A Dutchman and an 'Hinglishman' are running for office in Jacksonville and neither . . . know as much about business as an ordinary hog knows about a holliday [*sic*]."[62]

Louisa Semple eased the strain on her purse by leasing part of the Old Homestead to a man named Steele, "a reformed inebriate." Ellen Fuller complained indignantly that her father's gift was the cancellation of twenty-five dollars in interest on a loan.[63]

A shortage of funds, debt, and a depressed economy did not prevent Grierson from adding to his ranching enterprise. With such cash as he could command, combined with loans, he purchased Confederate land script and used it to buy additional acreage in Presidio County. Through lease and purchase, he accumulated some twenty thousand acres, far more than he could properly stock, equip, and supervise. Grierson was a man of many talents, but none of them were in the field of business enterprise.[64]

The experience gained in the inspection and evaluation of land, water supply, grass, and timber did serve him well in his military duties. On February 11, 1887, he received a telegram from Miles ordering him to investigate troubles between the Navajos and intruders on their reservation. Grierson and Woodward left at once for Fort Wingate, where Ben again displayed his skill for negotiation and peaceful settlement of disputes. He resolved the matter easily and was praised by the Territorial Governor for "prompt and energetic action" in preventing an outbreak and allying fears of the Navajos that the white offenders "would further molest them."[65]

The affair marked the beginning of a keen interest on Grierson's part in Navajo welfare as well as that of the Jicarilla Apaches whose interests he also championed. It was consistent with his long and sincere regard for just and fair treatment of the Indian.

In 1882 the Jicarillas were removed from their reservation near Amargo, New Mexico, at the insistence of ranchers and settlers. Resettled on the Mescalero Reservation, they were soon miserable. About two hundred left and encamped in a starving condition near Santa Fe, to seek assistance from Governor Edmund Ross and General Miles. Miles telegraphed Grierson, then preparing to assume command of the District of New Mexico, to meet him at Willcox. From there they traveled together to Santa Fe.

Here on November 13, 1886, Miles and Grierson met with Jicarilla headmen and promised to do all possible to find them a suitable home. In February, 1887, President Cleveland established a reservation for the Jicarillas in extreme northwestern New Mexico, adjoining the Southern Ute reserve in Colorado.[66]

Efforts were made by ranching and farming interests to block the move, but Special Agent H. S. Welton, with Grierson's cooperation, escorted the Indians to their reservation. According to J. D. C. Atkins, Commissioner of Indian Affairs, "Much of the success attending the removal is due to the valuable assistance rendered by military authorities, particularly by General Grierson, who neglected no opportunity to promote the success of the enterprise."⁶⁷

Throughout the rest of 1887, Grierson kept detachments busy evicting squatters from both the Navajo and Jicarilla reservations. The squatters had the support of Antonio Joseph, territorial delegate to Congress, but Grierson correctly pointed out that, "The real instigators of these projects, however, obscured or disguised, are stock syndicates and other monopolies." And he noted that both tribes had shown remarkable patience and restraint in the face of constant harassment and efforts to occupy reservation lands.⁶⁸

Grierson went beyond merely evicting intruders and affording military protection. He argued persuasively for defining reservation boundaries carefully and enlarging the Navajo reserve. He also emphasized the need for funds to construct reservoirs and tanks to conserve scarce water resources and to build and staff industrial schools to further Indian education.⁶⁹

Both Miles and General O. O. Howard, Pope's replacement as commanding general of the Division of the Pacific, were impressed with Grierson's work and unstinting in their praise. Not Sheridan, however, who abruptly telegraphed Howard in September, asking why Colonel (Eugene) Carr should not be placed in command of the District of New Mexico. Howard's reply was blunt—Grierson was senior. He was also senior in commission in the line of the army, but once more he was passed over for promotion in 1887. Grierson's frustration ran high and doubtless he agreed with brother John that President Grover Cleveland "is the only man in the U.S. who can button his shirt collar and put it on over his head."⁷⁰

At intervals, Ben made hurried trips to Fort Davis to check on ranching operations and to boost Robert's morale. The cattle market remained depressed, and income from the properties low. Robert, working long hours but facing a growing debt, feared "Papa's" disapproval. He also had to wage a constant battle against loneliness. After his father's visits he usually became more cheerful. Ben's determined faith in family investments in Texas was persuasive.⁷¹

George provided a partial solution to Robert's need for company. Bored with school, he informed his parents he "wouldn't stay five minutes" if he could go to the ranch and live with Robert, and he begged them to have "pitty" [*sic*] on him. His wish was granted, and very soon afterward he reported, "I'm as happy as any cowboy you ever saw or heard from." He was "Epluribus Unanimous."⁷²

Harry arrived at Davis after the spring term at Washington University. He planned to return to school in the fall, but funds were not available, perhaps in part because two of his grades were conditional. Neither he nor George had received as strong an academic background as Charlie and Robert. With Ben's reluctant permission, Harry took qualifying examinations for West Point. Failing to pass, he decided to stay at the ranch for a year after which he would try again to enter the military academy.[73]

In the spring of 1887, Ben and Alice were forced to restrict their social activities in Santa Fe. In February she had suffered a fall that injured her "lame leg" and brought on what she thought was "sciatica." Her great discomfort forced her to rely on servants to do all shopping and household tasks. Months passed and her condition did not improve. In May, her Santa Fe physician finally discovered that she had a "broken bone in her leg," along with a developing tumor. But when he consulted a specialist in the area, he was advised the surgery was not a safe procedure. Besides, the condition would undoubtedly mend itself.[74]

The pain was often intense, but Alice continued to maintain a large correspondence with her sons, relatives, and friends. As always, she sent a steady flow of gifts to Ellen, Mary Kirk, Helen Davis, and Grace Maxon. Believing that she was suffering from inflammatory rheumatism, she did not heed Ellen's advice to come to Jacksonville for treatment.[75]

Ben, busy with official duties, plans for development of his west Texas properties, and still another campaign for promotion, was frequently away. His long, detailed, and invariably loving letters revealed some concern, but also the conviction that she would soon be well. If the thought occurred to him that she was seriously ill, he shut it from his mind, refusing to believe it. Once he gained his promotion and they retired to their permanent home, they would at last enjoy "the good time coming" he had promised her so many years ago.

Other worries crowded in, too. John Grierson was now desperate, and Ben sold nearly two thousand acres of his Texas holdings to Mary Kirk for fifty cents an acre in order to assist his brother. Ellen's husband, Harvey B. Fuller, Jr., had recently sustained a damage suit for eight thousand dollars, resulting in the loss of his Chicago home. Since then the family had moved to St. Paul, Minnesota, in search of a fresh start. Ellen had taken the state examination to enable her to teach and contribute to family income. After

Benjamin Henry ("Harry") Grierson. *Courtesy Fort Davis National Historic Site, Fort Davis, Texas.*

Grierson ranch, near Fort Davis, Texas. *Courtesy Illinois State Historical Library, Springfield, Illinois.*

passing with flying colors, she discovered that the school board would not allow married women in the classroom. At present she was looking for boarders and taking in sewing. Lieutenant Maxon developed severe respiratory problems and faced a disability discharge, while Lieutenant Davis, having incurred the wrath of Major Mills, had narrowly escaped court-martial.[76]

Not all was dark, however, in the Grierson circle of family and friends. Tough-minded Louisa Semple threw the Steeles out of the Old Homestead when she caught Mr. Steele drinking, and then plunged more deeply into study and letter-writing. John Kirk's spirits, low for some time, had revived, to Ann Bayne Kirk's great relief, and he seemed more like his old vigorous self. Mary Kirk had carved out a career for herself painting family portraits. She had sold her Chicago property at a substantial profit and now, at forty-seven, she was planning to enroll in college to continue studying art. The only assignment she refused was Louisa's portrait, ". . . it would certainly be a trial to paint such a face."[77]

Sam Woodward, after twenty years as a first lieutenant, received promotion to captain and was ordered to join Company I at Camp Verde, Arizona. Ben praised his ever-loyal friend as "a brave and gallant officer and gentleman," and immediately undertook to have Woodward promoted to major. Charlie returned from recruiting duty and took over as Adjutant of the Tenth Cavalry.[78]

By the spring of 1888, Alice's condition had not improved, and she decided to seek treatment in Jacksonville. Ben put his affairs in order and accompanied her. Dr. Jones, along with two other physicians, King and Prince, examined her. Jones was certain Alice was recovering, and in his judgment the tumor was not malignant, but "borderline." King also took a "favorable view of the case," but Prince thought otherwise. If Alice was his patient, her leg would be amputated the following day. A wooden leg was preferable to the one she had.[79]

Nonetheless, five physicians had been consulted, and four had expressed cautious optimism, leading Alice to believe that Ben's presence was no longer necessary. He returned to Santa Fe, still convinced that her problem was inflammatory rheumatism. One of his first acts was to buy her a comfortable chair as her present when she rejoined him. Early in July he was ordered to Fort Huachuca for court-martial duty and he wrote Alice that he was awaiting word of her "continual improvement." He outlined plans for their future, noting that in two years he would retire and devote himself entirely to her happiness and his business interests.[80]

But there was no news of "continual improvement." Instead she was failing rapidly. When her cousin, Sadie Morley, arrived in Jacksonville late in June to care for her, she discovered that Alice spent her days either in bed or, occasionally, on the couch. By now she was too weak to sit up even for meals. So excruciating was the pain from the oozing tumor and so constant her fever that much of the time she was delirious. John Kirk sent for Ellen, who came at once and began assisting with Alice's care.[81]

Ellen had scarcely reached Jacksonville when a severe thunderstorm struck the city, raged throughout the night, and disturbed Alice's rest. As her sister moaned in agony, hallucinating that she was being evicted from her home, Ellen held her hand and wept. Louisa, barging in on them, pronounced such conduct unbecoming in a nurse. In the storm's aftermath, Alice's strength ebbed swiftly, and Ellen wrote Charlie that his mother would not last another month.[82]

But Ben, unaware that Alice was waging a losing battle, continued to do what he always did—hope for the best. At the end of July he wrote her (by this time she was entirely oblivious to mail) that he had requested a leave and would soon be joining her. "It will be a great pleasure for both of us to be together again." He also urged her to "make the very best fight you possibly can to get well in spite of all unpleasant circumstances or contrary indications." No one had told him the plain truth—Alice was dying.[83]

When Ben received a cryptic telegraph from Dr. Jones, instructing him to "finish your business," he understood for the first time the seriousness of the situation. A letter from Louisa further clarified the matter. "Alice does not appear to be impressed with the idea of a fatal termination of her case. She spoke some weeks ago, when her mind was clear of 'being a cripple for life.' She has wandered in her mind much less in the last two weeks than formerly, and yet, dear Ben, She is really no better."[84]

The day Ben arrived at the Old Homestead, Alice was lucid enough to recognize his footsteps on the walk. Despite her suffering she asked him about their sons, especially Robert, and then insisted that he rest. On August 13, Ben wrote Charlie that there was no hope. Sadie Morley followed with another letter informing Charlie that his mother "would like so much to see and speak to you each day," but given her present condition "she prefers you do not come to see her."[85] Three days later Alice died. On the following day she was buried in the Jacksonville East Cemetery, a stone's throw away from the old family home. For Ben Grierson, thirty-four years of dreaming about "a quiet nook" with "My dear Alice" had ended.

After the funeral, Ben remained in Jacksonville for several weeks, numbed by the shock of his wife's death. When he recovered sufficiently to return to his post, John and Ann Bayne Kirk accompanied him to the station, where he boarded the train to return to Santa Fe. Later Ann related to Charlie, "It seemed so sad to me to see him start to go on such a lonely business." But she had consoling words as well, noting that Ben's presence had been "a comfort" to Alice; "the few days he was here he was so tender and thoughtful of her wishes even before they were expressed." At Davis, Robert received his father's telegraph announcing his mother's death and, after informing Harry and George, wrote Charlie, "May God help us to bear our grief."[86]

Back in Santa Fe, Ben struggled to provide for his children as he thought Alice would have wanted. He arranged for George to board with Mary Kirk while attending school in Jacksonville, and enrolled Harry once more in Washington University. In October, Ben visited Robert at their "Spring Valley Ranch" to give encouragement and praise. Their prize cattle, exhibited at the Dallas Fair, had won four first places, and hard work by Robert was responsible. In addition, he had been elected county commissioner. He was pleased with his father's compliments and encouraged by his assurances of better times ahead, but Robert missed his brothers and, even more, the frequent letters from his mother. As for Ben, he dealt with his sorrow in the only way he knew, by throwing himself into his work.[87]

Shortly after returning from Davis, Grierson's military career took a sudden and welcome turn. He was ordered to Los Angeles to assume command of the Department of Arizona, replacing Miles, who was elevated to division head. Before his departure he paid a warm tribute to the Tenth Cavalry, a regiment he had led for almost twenty-two years:

> The officers and enlisted men have cheerfully endured many hardships and privations, and in the midst of great dangers steadfastly maintained a most gallant and zealous devotion to duty, and they may well be proud of the record made . . . and that it cannot fail, sooner or later, to meet with due recognition and reward.
>
> That the high standard of excellence gained by the regiment for discipline and efficiency in the past will be fully sustained in the future;

The "Old Homestead." *Courtesy Fort Davis National Historic Site, Fort Davis, Texas.*

that the most signal success will ever attend the officers and soldiers of the Tenth Cavalry in all their noble efforts and undertakings, official and otherwise, is the heartfelt wish of their old commander.[88]

Grierson took over his new command on November 24. He appointed Charlie as assistant aide-de-camp and sought unsuccessfully to have Woodward assigned as assistant adjutant general. The principal problem in the Department was the persistent efforts of special-interest groups to enter and exploit the resources of the Indian reservations.[89]

In March 1889, Grierson received reports that a large number of miners had organized and gathered near the Navajo Reservation for the purpose of prospecting on Indian lands. He alerted the commanding officer at Fort Wingate and ordered him to use all necessary force to repel the miners. Grierson then informed leaders of the organization, in cold, blunt terms, that under no circumstances would they be permitted to enter the reservation. As a result the miners disbanded.[90]

Isolated murders and robberies were also a problem, and on May 11, one of the latter made national news. Major Joseph W. Wham, an army paymaster, en route to Fort Thomas with an escort of eleven soldiers from the Tenth Cavalry and Twenty-Fourth Infantry, was ambushed in the hills fifteen miles from the post. A gang, estimated at eight to twenty men, fired into the guards from behind boulders near the road. In the blazing gunfight that followed, nine of the eleven soldiers were wounded, allowing the robbers to make off with nearly thirty thousand dollars in payroll funds.

Troops from nearby posts, with Apache scouts, took up the pursuit and captured seven members of the gang. Grierson believed the remaining robbers would soon be caught and the money recovered, but he was overly optimistic. No further arrests were made, and the payroll was never found. Trial of the seven apprehended resulted in a Tucson jury returning a verdict of "Not Guilty." According to the presiding judge it was the greatest miscarriage of justice in his experience.[91]

Minor affrays involving Indians also gave Grierson concern. Reports of these affairs were usually exaggerated and circulated, he believed, to provide a screen for efforts to encroach on Indian rights and property. In one such instance, two San Carlos Indians killed a teamster and wild rumors had fifty hostiles entrenched in the mountains near the agency. Grierson's investigation revealed that only five Indians were involved, and three of these had assisted authorities in capturing the killers.[92]

These diversions did not distract Grierson from pursuing his two primary interests: the welfare of the Indians in his department, particularly the Navajos and Jicarillas, and promotion of measures to increase productivity in the arid West as an aid to settlement.

He urged enlargement of the Navajo reservation to meet more adequately the needs of nearly twenty thousand people. "It is neither practicable nor just, under the circumstances to try to force them within the limits of their present reservation. . . ."[93] The skills of the Navajos in crafting rugs, blankets, gold and silver ornaments should be encouraged and supported. Finally, a more summary method was needed to deal with whiskey peddlers who plied their iniquitous trade along the borders of the reservation.

Grierson pointed out that the same forces that had earlier caused removal of the Jicarillas were still at work, but should never again be permitted to drive these people from their reservation. If their rate of progress was unsatisfactory to some critics, the fault lay with government mismanagement and dishonest agents. Given assistance in their farming operations and decent schools, Grierson believed these Indians would soon be self-sustaining and capable of assuming citizenship that was rightfully theirs.[94]

Grierson had a vision of the future of New Mexico, Arizona, and southern California, given liberal government assistance in developing water resources and systems of irrigation. Millions of dollars, properly spent, would with "absolute certainty" turn this vast region into "a verdant, blooming oasis where the fatal mirage will no longer delude the way worn traveller, and to which the people of the continent will eagerly flock in search of health, wealth and happiness. . . ."[95] Grierson's prophecies were realized, and at a rate he could not have imagined.

While he efficiently and constructively administered his department, personal and family affairs still troubled Ben. Both Harry and George grew tired of school, quit, and joined Robert at Davis only to discover that "the bottom had fallen out of the ranching business." Ben agreed, but advised them to remember that it was a time of general depression and "the bottom has fallen out of *all* of our business." Under the circumstances they had done as well as could be expected, and he predicted that "everything will come out alright [*sic*]."[96]

John Grierson at sixty-nine was ill and impoverished. His wife, Elizabeth, suffered from crippling rheumatism. By now he had given up all hope of finding gainful employment. Even bookkeeping was closed to him, for women had recently entered the field and were working for salaries a half or even a fourth of those men had earned. Ben offered to try to find a position in the Quartermaster Department, but John thought the physical demands would be too great. Besides, he was convinced that most army officers were "damned fools" for whom he would not care to work. Whatever remnants of faith he had once had were gone. "If there be any God so loving, and all powerful as represented by Orthodox believers—he is guilty of a great misdemeanor—or Malfeasance in office, for allowing so much pain and suffering in this world. I think 'Creator' is a fraud."[97]

Louisa Semple's troubles with tenants continued. The McCoys followed the Steeles, but when one of their children, "a little incendiary" set fire to the barn, she forced the family to move. In her spare time, according to John, Louisa was busy getting Ben remarried and "what she will get up next God only knows."[98] Louisa's efforts at matchmaking were embarrassing, but Ben did not remonstrate with her and instead, as so often in the past, urged John to be more tolerant of their sister's eccentricities.

Inured as he was to family quarrels, erratic behavior, misfortune, and tragedy, Ben was hardly prepared for the news that reached him early in February, 1890. Robert had suffered another breakdown and was being placed once more in the Jacksonville Oak Lawn Retreat. When the Davis County Treasurer had absconded with some two thousand dollars, Robert, along with the other commissioners, had been sureties on the treasurer's bond. Following a court order to make good the deficit, Robert had collapsed under the strain. In truth, he had never recovered from the depression that had set in following Alice's death. There was nothing Ben could do but pray for his son's recovery.[99]

Amidst the welter of discouraging reports came one of a different kind that relieved Grierson of one long-standing frustration. In March, General Crook's death from a heart attack created a vacancy at the rank of major general. When a brigadier was promoted to Crook's former post the way opened for Grierson, and he applied at once. Sheridan, Grierson's nemesis, had died in 1888 and had been succeeded by Ben's friend and supporter Major General John Schofield. Schofield readily endorsed Grierson's application, and President Benjamin Harrison agreed. On April 5, 1890, Ben received his long-sought star.[100]

A flood of telegrams and letters attested to Grierson's many friends in and out of the army. Perhaps he was most pleased with congratulations from his old captains in the Tenth, Woodward, Carpenter, Keyes, Lebo, and Smither, among a large number of others. From Santa Fe, too, where he and Alice had spent their last months together, came such messages as "We feel jubilant," and "Merit is at last rewarded."[101]

The promotion came just three months short of Grierson's intended retirement and the long delay was partly because of Sheridan's petty discrimination, but there were other reasons. Grierson did not fit the popular image of the dashing cavalry leader who routed hordes of red savages, smashed their villages, and counted his victims by the score. He preferred negotiation, conciliation, fair play, and justice, rather than bullets, as solutions to the Indian problem. Kind, humane, and tolerant, he looked forward to the day when adequate support, education, and encouragement would bring the Indian people full-fledged citizenship. Such views were decidedly unpopular in many quarters.

The fact that he commanded black troops, treated them with respect and consideration, and never failed to support and defend them against racial slurs, prejudice, and discrimination, earned him few friends in high places either. His care and concern for his own men extended to enlisted men generally. His list of recommendations for reform in the enlisted service—among them better pay, quality rations, decent libraries, gymnasiums, amusement centers, and shorter terms of service—went unheeded at the time, though all were adopted in the distant future. In his day, his regard for the enlisted ranks left him open to charges of coddling, slack training methods, and condoning poor discipline.[102]

Grierson practiced what he preached in dealing with Indians, blacks, and enlisted men, and he waited twenty-four years for promotion.

Ben retired on July 8, 1890, his sixty-fourth birthday. After visiting with his sons Harry and George at the Spring Valley Ranch at Davis, he returned to Jacksonville, where his sister Louisa and his brother John welcomed him. Ben Grierson's search, spanning nearly four decades, for distinction, fortune, and a permanent home brought him back, on August 15, 1890, to the place where it had started, at the house his father, Robert, had built, the Old Homestead in Jacksonville, Illinois.

Epilogue

B EN GRIERSON's retirement years were not the happy, carefree, and prosperous ones he had anticipated. Misfortune, illness, and death continued to dog his footsteps. Through all, until near the end of his long life, he remained remarkably consistent. He seldom complained and continued to be generous, compassionate, and a very poor business man.

His properties in Texas never yielded significant profits, and the cost of maintenance was a growing burden. He borrowed money at ruinous rates of interest—as much as 25 percent—and some of his investments in stocks and bonds brought serious losses. While never in want, Grierson was always hard-pressed for funds.[1]

For nearly a decade he divided his time between Fort Davis and Jacksonville, maintained a wide correspondence, a keen interest in politics and in the military, and frequently visited old friends. But he was lonely. John Kirk, old and broken by family tragedies, died in 1891. John Grierson, after a long illness, followed in 1894. Louisa Semple's health had failed and, though she lived to the age of eighty-nine, she no longer provided the intellectual stimulus and family continuity that Ben had appreciated.[2]

Difficulties arose with Harry and George over management of the ranch properties because they came to feel that their father was not doing enough for them. The relationship became strained and uncomfortable. Robert never recovered, and in May, 1891, was transferred from Oak Lawn to the state mental hospital. The admitting diagnosis was dementia praecox of the hebrephonic type, probable cause, heredity. He remained there until his death in 1922.[3]

By contrast, Charlie was a source of pleasure and satisfaction. In October, 1890, he married Sarah Joy Merrill of Los Angeles, whom he had met while serving on his father's staff. Two years later the couple presented Grierson with his first grandchild, Alice Kirk Grierson. Two other children followed, Sarah Joy and John Charles.[4]

Charlie's career also progressed steadily, if not spectacularly. By the close of the Spanish-American War—Ben strongly supported a free Cuba—Charlie was a lieutenant colonel in the Tenth Cavalry and looked forward to becoming, as his father had been before him, colonel of the regiment.[5]

In 1897, at the age of seventy-one, Grierson married a Jacksonville widow, Lillian King, with the enthusiastic approval of his sister Louisa. Charlie, however, objected to the union, while Harry and George became totally alienated, regarding this as an insult to their mother's memory.[6]

Thereafter Grierson's visits to Fort Davis became irregular and in a few years ceased altogether. His interest in ranching waned, he allowed leases to expire, and he sold many of his holdings. The remaining property was sublet to Harry and George for a small annual payment of less than three hundred dollars a year.[7]

In the summer of 1907, Ben and his wife traveled to Pennsylvania and Ohio to visit friends. On their return he fell seriously ill with flu, suffered a stroke, and never fully recovered. His memory was impaired and he was subject to "little bursts of temper soon over." Lillian believed that the stroke was brought on by strain and worry over the failure of a Jacksonville banking enterprise in which he and several friends had incurred large losses.[8]

For the next four years his condition slowly deteriorated, and he was confined to his bed. Lillian informed Charlie that "The old fire and grit is gone." In June, 1911, she took Ben to their summer cottage at Omena, Michigan. Here Charlie paid a brief visit and found his father incoherent in speech and very weak. A month later, on August 31, Ben Grierson breathed his last.[9]

Ben was buried beside Alice in Jacksonville's East Cemetery. Reverend F. S. Hayden praised him as an affectionate and friendly man, honest and fearless, and one who had always tried to do what he saw as right. The eulogy was no exaggeration. Fittingly, a black man led the procession to the cemetery, and Sam Woodward, now a retired lieutenant colonel, performed the ceremonial of the Legion of Honor. Of his sons, only Charlie attended the funeral.[10]

Grierson left his affairs in chaos. Charlie, Harry, and George all struggled to unscramble a mixture of land deals and a small mountain of mostly worthless stocks and bonds. An unseemly quarrel, one that Grierson would have deplored, developed between his

General Grierson about 1897. *Courtesy Fort Davis National Historic Site, Fort Davis, Texas.*

sons and Lillian over various parts of his estate. The disputes were never settled satisfactorily, ending only when Lillian died from a stroke in 1914.[11]

The dynasty that Grierson predicted after Harry's birth in 1867 was never realized. Harry and George lived out their lives in modest comfort at Fort Davis. George remained a bachelor, while Harry married, then divorced, and had no children. Harry died in 1934, and his brother in 1950. Both were interred with their parents in Jacksonville.[12]

Charlie's military career ended abruptly in 1915. While commanding Fort Huachuca, Arizona, he suffered a mental breakdown. After a brief stay at Letterman General Hospital in San Francisco he was transferred to St. Elizabeth's Hospital in Washington, D.C., where he spent the rest of his life. The end came in 1928, and he was buried in Arlington National Cemetery.[13]

Of Charlie's children, only his son Jack married, and he left no offspring. Sarah Joy and Alice lived long, quiet, and useful lives in Los Angeles, and with their deaths in 1978 and 1979, respectively, all the direct descendants were gone. Benjamin Grierson's family odyssey had come to an end.[14]

The last survivors. Mrs. Charles Grierson with son John C. and daughters Alice Kirk and Sarah Joy. Photographed about 1900. *Courtesy Fort Davis National Historic Site, Fort Davis, Texas.*

List of Abbreviations Used in Notes

AG: Adjutant General
AGO: Adjutant General's Office
AAA: Assistant Adjutant General
AAAG: Acting Assistant Adjutant General
GM: The Papers of Benjamin H. Grierson, Illinois State Historical Library, Springfield, Illinois
GP: Benjamin H. Grierson Papers, 1827–1941, Southwest Collection, Texas Technological University, Lubbock, Texas
LR: Letters Received
LS: Letters Sent
NA: National Archives
OR: Official Records of the Union and Confederate Armies
PA: Post Adjutant
RG: Record Group
RS: Benjamin Henry Grierson, Record of Services Rendered the Government
SDLR: Selected Documents, Letters Received
SLR: Selected Letters Received

Notes

1. Benjamin H. Grierson, "A Genealogical History of the Griersons and Mac-Gregors or Clan-Alpine with a brief summary from Scotch and Irish History. Etc. Etc. Compiled and Arranged from Family Records and Other Sources." (1886) and "The Genealogy of the Grierson Family, from the Thirteenth Century, or Twelve Generations of the MacGregors. Abridged from Family Records, Standard Register and Other Authentic Sources." (1889) The Benjamin H. Grierson Papers, Fort Davis National Historic Site, Fort Davis, Texas. Hereafter cited as GH, either 1886 or 1889.

2. Grierson, GH, 1886. Pittsburgh remained the Scotch-Irish capital of America well into the twentieth century. See William L. Fisk, Jr., "The Scotch-Irish in Central Ohio," *Ohio State Archaeological and Historical Quarterly* 57 (April 1948): 111.

3. S. Jones, *Pittsburgh in the Year Eighteen Hundred and Twenty-Six, Containing Sketches Topographical, Historical and Statistic. Together with a Directory of the City, and a View of Its Various Manufactures, Population, Improvements & etc.*, pp. 12, 39–40. In 1820, 11,629 persons resided in the Pittsburgh area and 7,249 in the city.

4. Ibid., p. 119.

5. Grierson, GH, 1886; Benjamin H. Grierson, "The Lights and Shadows of Life, Including Experiences and Remembrances of the War of the Rebellion, 1892." Typescript autobiography, The Papers of Benjamin H. Grierson, Illinois State Historical Library, Springfield, Illinois, p. 57. Hereafter cited as Grierson, Auto.

6. Grierson, GH, 1886. Eliza Wright, Jr., agent for the American Tract Society, wrote his fiancée from Pittsburgh: "Every man here seems to be striving every nerve to get rich with the hope of spending his money someday or other in a place that is cleaner." Vincent A. Carrafiello and Richard O. Curry, "The Black City: Eliza Wright, Jr's View of Early Industrial Pittsburgh," *Western Pennsylvania Historical Magazine* 55 (July 1972): 254.

7. *History of Trumbull and Mahoning Counties with Illustrations and Biographical Sketches* 1:359–65.

8. Louisa Semple to Ben Grierson, 4 January 1879, Benjamin H. Grierson Papers, 1827–1941, Southwest Collection, Texas Technological University, Lubbock, Texas. Hereafter referred to as GP for Grierson Papers.

9. Grierson, Auto., p. 56.

10. Ibid., pp. 62–63; Grierson, GH, 1886.

11. Grierson, Auto., pp. 63–67.

12. Ibid., pp. 54–56. John Grierson often commented on the difficulties Griersons had controlling their tempers. John Grierson to Ben, 28 May 1860, 28 July 1873, GP.

13. At log rollings, "Hearty, merry hurry and laughter excluded fatigue, and well-filled jugs of New England rum or homemade corn whiskey added to the hilarity." *History of Trumbull and Mahoning Counties* 1:59–60.

14. Grierson, Auto., pp. 50–54.

15. Ibid., pp. 58–59. An obituary in the *Daily Illinois Courier*, 5 September 1911, stated that when Ben graduated from Youngstown Academy, he passed the West Point examinations. But when his mother objected to her son becoming a soldier, he remained in Youngstown. Bruce Dinges examined West Point applications between 1842 and 1847 and found no evidence Ben ever applied. See Dinges's "The Making of a Cavalryman: Benjamin H. Grierson and the Civil War Along the Mississippi, 1861–1865." Ph.D. dissertation, Rice University, 1978, pp. 54–55.

16. James Leyburn reveals that a quarter of a million Scotch-Irish emigrated to the American colonies between 1717 and the Revolutionary War, driven from Ulster by economic disaster, years of drought, and "rack-renting." See *The Scotch-Irish: A Social History*, pp. 181–82; *History of Trumbull and Mahoning Counties* 1:373; Grierson, GH, 1889.

17. Grierson, GH, 1889; Howard C. Aley, *A Heritage to Share: The Bicentennial History of Youngstown and Mahoning County, Ohio*, pp. 41–42.

18. Grierson, GH, 1889.

19. John Kirk to Ben and Alice Grierson, 31 December 1855, the Papers of Benjamin H. Grierson, Illinois State Historical Library, Springfield, Illinois. Hereafter referred to as GM for Grierson Manuscript.

20. John Kirk to Alice Grierson, 12 January 1857, GP; John Kirk to Alice Grierson, 3 May 1869, 24 May 1869, GM. While husbands, by law and tradition, were dominant members of American households, there is a growing body of evidence that by 1830 most Americans had consigned to mothers the primary responsibility for physical nurturing of children and moral upbringing as well. See Carl Degler, *At Odds: Women Against the Family in America from the Revolution to the Present*, pp. 73–79; Ruth H. Block, "Untangling the Roots of Modern Sex Roles: A Survey of Four Centuries of Change," *Signs: Journal of Women in Culture and Society* 4 (Winter 1978): 237–52; Bernard Wishy, *The Child and the Republic: The Dawn of Modern American Child Nurture*, pp. 26–33.

21. John Kirk to Alice Grierson, 19 September 1867, GM.

22. John Kirk, *Mahoning Free Democrat*, 29 September 1853, 27 February 1854, 24 May 1854; Relatives and in-laws described John Kirk as "jolly." John Grierson to Ben, 16 July 1877, GP.

23. Alice to Ben, 10 August 1862, GM.

24. Grierson, Auto., pp. 69–70.

25. Ibid., pp. 69–72, 100.

26. Ibid., pp. 72–73. In his autobiography Ben did not acknowledge calling John Kirk a "pope," stating instead that his reply was firm, but reasonable. Alice indicated otherwise in a letter to Ben's sister, Mary Grierson, 3 March 1852, GM.

27. Alice complained to Mary that "Ben always had an indifferent manner of treating me that always angered me. . . ." Alice to Mary Grierson, 10 September 1852, GM.

28. Alice to Mary Grierson, 30 January 1850, GP.

29. For information on the early years of the Disciples of Christ, see Sydney Ahlstrom, *A Religious History of the American People*, pp. 447–49. An offshoot of Scotch Presbyterianism, the "Campbellites," as they were often known, stressed a simplified creed based on the Bible and natural law. Their services were distinguished by simplicity and the banning of musical instruments.

30. Paul Angle, ed. and comp., *Prairie State: Impression of Illinois, 1673–1967, By Travelers and Other Observers,* pp. 251, 267. One observer wrote, "a man can live like a prince in Jacksonville [Illinois] for what would barely suffice to pay his house-rent in New York."

31. Ibid., pp. 264–65.

32. Don Harrison Doyle, *The Social Order of a Frontier Community: Jacksonville, Illinois, 1825–70,* pp. 18–31, 68–79. "Yale Band" refers to young theologians from Yale who organized the Illinois Association, a group that played a critical role in bringing education to the frontier state. Two members, Theron Baldwin and Julian M. Sturtevant, founded Illinois College and became prominent citizens in Jacksonville.

Many Southerners moved to Illinois from Missouri, Tennessee, and Kentucky because they were unhappy with their status in a slavery dominated society. At the same time, settlers in the state, whether from north or south, often displayed virulently racist attitudes, and this led to the passage of legislation intended to prevent, or at least discourage, free blacks from settling in the state. See Eugene H. Berwanger, *The Frontier Against Slavery: Western Anti-Negro Prejudice and the Slavery Extension Controversy.* Ohio, Indiana, and Oregon had similar laws.

33. Grierson, Auto., p. 65.

34. Ibid. William Still, writing on the Underground Railroad, maintains that those who knew William Lloyd Garrison intimately always called him Lloyd. Ben's passing reference would suggest that his father knew Garrison well. See William Still, *The Underground Railroad*, pp. 666–67.

35. Ibid., pp. 73–74. The entire Grierson family was united in Jacksonville by October, 1850, a year earlier than Grierson's autobiography indicated. Alice to Mary Grierson, 21 October 1850, GM.

36. Nancy Cott notes that by mid-nineteenth century, schoolteaching had become a common occupation for women. "Between 1825 and 1860 . . . a quarter of all native-born New England women were schoolteachers for some years of their lives." See *The Bonds of Womanhood: "Woman's Sphere" in New England, 1780–1835,* pp. 34–35. Alice received $140 a year. *History of Trumbull and Mahoning Counties* 1:397–99.

37. Alice to Mary Grierson, 3 March 1852, GM.

38. The letters were extremely affectionate, as was common among women in the nineteenth century. Given the rigid distinction in sex roles, based on the "doctrine of separate spheres," women turned to one another for comfort and emotional intimacy. For an illuminating discussion of this peculiarly nineteenth-century phenomenon, see Carroll Smith-Rosenberg, "The Female World of Love and Ritual: Relations Between Women in Nineteenth-Century America," *Signs: Journal of Women in Culture and Society* 1 (Autumn 1975): 1–29.

39. Alice to Mary Grierson, 21 October 1850, 10 September 1852, GM.

40. Mary Grierson to Alice, 20 July 1851, GP; Mary Grierson to Alice, 12 January 1852, GM.

41. Mary Grierson to Alice, 20 July 1850, GM; Susan Bingham Kirk to Alice, 20 November 1853, GP.
42. Mary Grierson to Alice, 12 September 1850, 22 November 1850, GP; Mary Grierson to Alice, 28 August 1853, GM.
43. Alice to Mary Grierson, undated letter [Summer 1853], GM; Alice to Mary Grierson, undated letter [Summer 1853], GP.
44. Alice to Mary Grierson, 3 March 1852, GM; Mary Grierson to Alice, 12 January 1852, GP.
45. Alice to Mary Grierson, 3 March 1852, GM.
46. Alice to Mary Grierson, 21 October 1850, GM.
47. Alice to Mary Grierson, 17 May 1852, GP; Alice to Mary Grierson, 1 July 1852, 10 September 1852, GM.
48. Grierson, GH, 1889.
49. Grierson, Auto., pp. 74–76; Alice to Mary Grierson, 24 September 1853, GM.
50. Undated letter from Alice Kirk to unnamed person or persons in 1854, GM.
51. Ben to Alice, 10 August 1854, GM.
52. Ben to Alice, 12 August 1854, GM.
53. Alice to Mary Grierson, 26 August 1854, GP; Grierson, Auto., pp. 74–75.

CHAPTER 2

1. For a discussion of the nineteenth-century view that women were morally superior to men, and that it was the role of wives to uplift their husbands, see Carl Degler, *At Odds*, pp. 30–32.
2. Alice to Ben, 5 January 1855, GM.
3. Ben to Alice, 11 January 1855, GM.
4. Alice to Ben, 12 January 1855, GM.
5. Grierson, Auto., p. 78.
6. Alice to Louisa Semple, 28 January 1874, GM; Susan Ellen Kirk to Alice, 1 January 1867, Grierson Miscellaneous Collection, Fort Davis National Historic Site.
7. Alice to Mary Grierson, 18 December 1851; Alice to Ben, [20] December 1871, GP.
8. Ben to John Kirk, 29 October 1855, GM.
9. Ben to Alice, 23 October 1855, GM.
10. Alice to John Kirk, 29 October 1855, GM.
11. Ben to John Kirk, 29 October 1855, GM.
12. John Kirk to Ben and Alice, 31 December 1855; Alice to John Kirk, 13 January 1856, GM.
13. John Kirk to Ben and Alice, 31 December 1855, GM.
14. Alice to John Kirk, 15 January 1856, GM.
15. John Grierson to Ben, 9 September 1856, GP; Alice, undated poem describing Meredosia home [1856], GM; Ben to Alice, 17 July 1857, GM.
16. Alice to Mary Grierson, 16 February 1857; Ben to Alice, 8 May 1856, 17 July 1857, GM.

17. Alice to Ben, 9 October 1876, GP.
18. Ibid.
19. Grierson, Auto., pp. 88–92.
20. John Grierson to Ben, 17 October 1856, GM.
21. Grierson, Auto., p. 92.
22. Alice to Mary Grierson, 16 February 1856, GM.
23. Maria Kirk died of typhoid in 1854 and Mary Fitch died in April, 1856, GH, 1889; John Kirk to Alice, 12 January 1857, 19 October 1857, GP.
24. Ben to Alice, 16 August 1857, GM.
25. Alice discussed this aspect of their relationship in a letter to Ben dated 9 October 1861, GM. "You know I'm 'kind of good' sometimes, when I have nothing in particular to do, and nothing to fret me. But when there are many things for me to do, or which I feel I ought to be doing; I am apt to think you might exert yourself more to entertain the young fry & relieve me."
26. Ben to Alice, 23 August 1857, GM.
27. Alice to Mary Grierson, 1 March 1858, GM; Mary Grierson to Alice, 24 November 1856, GP. Despite her good works, Mary Grierson exhibited the racial prejudice so common in the Old Northwest, referring to her students as "niggers."
28. John Kirk to Alice, 29 April 1858, 28 June 1858, 4 October 1858, GP.
29. Grierson, Auto., p. 92.
30. Ben to Alice, 12 November 1858, 2 June 1859; Robert Grierson to Ben, 8 August 1864, GM.
31. John Grierson to Ben, 19 February 1859, GP.
32. John Kirk to Alice, 1 March 1859, GM.
33. John Grierson to Ben, 7 February 1858, 28 February 1858, GM.
34. Ben to John Grierson, 16 June 1859; Ben to Alice, 29 June 1859, GP. See also Douglass North, *The Economic Growth of the United States, 1790–1860,* pp. 214–15 for the declining prices of wheat.
35. Ben to Alice, 5 June 1859; Alice to Ben, 13 June 1859; Ben to Alice, 27 June 1859, GM.
36. John Grierson to Ben, 14 April 1860, 28 May 1860, 5 July 1860, GM.
37. Ben to Alice, 1 June 1860, GM; William E. Baringer, "Campaign Techniques in Illinois — 1860," *Transactions of the Illinois State Historical Society* 39 (1932): 249–50.
38. Ben to Alice, 1 June 1860, GM.
39. John Grierson to Ben, 28 May 1860, GP.
40. John Grierson to Ben, 22 August 1860, GP.
41. John Grierson to Ben, 15 October 1860, 11 November 1860, GM.
42. John Kirk to Ben, 25 July 1860, GP.
43. Alice to Ben, [20] December 1871; Ben to John Kirk, 2 December 1860, GP.
44. John Grierson to Ben, 15 October 1860, GM.
45. John Grierson to Ben, 24 December 1860, GM. Robert Anderson, the commander of federal fortifications in Charleston, withdrew his troops from Fort Moultrie on December 26 and transferred them to Fort Sumter, thus abandoning Fort Moultrie. On the next day, South Carolina seized all federal property in the state with the exception of Fort Sumter, located on a small island at the center of Charleston Harbor.
46. Robert Grierson to Ben, 17 January 1861, GM.
47. Louisa Semple to Ben, 12 August 1864; Robert Grierson to Ben, 17 January

1861, GM.

48. John Grierson to Ben, 26 May 1861, GM.

49. Robert Grierson to Ben, 3 February 1861, GM.

50. Grierson, Auto., p. 92.

CHAPTER 3

1. Allan Nevins, *The War for the Union*, 4 vols., 1:70.

2. Shelby Foote, *The Civil War: A Narrative* 1:51.

3. John Grierson to Ben, 13 April 1861, GM.

4. Ben to John Grierson, 28 April 1861, GM; Grierson, Auto., p. 98.

5. Alice to John Kirk, 2 May 1861, GM.

6. Ben to Alice, 7 May 1861, GM; Grierson, Auto., p. 99.

7. Ben to Alice, 11 May 1861, 14 May 1861, 15 May 1861, GM. A. B. Safford, a Cairo banker, loaned Ben the money to keep him going during this difficult period. Grierson, Auto., p. 103.

8. Alice to Ben, 16 May 1861, GM.

9. Alice to Ben, 17 June 1861, GM.

10. Ben to Alice, 15 May 1861, 18 May 1861, GM.

11. Ben to Alice, 16 June 1861; Alice to Ben, 17 June 1861.

12. Grierson, Auto., p. 116; *The War of the Rebellion: A Compilation of the Official Records of the Union and Confederate Armies* 3:406. Hereafter cited as *OR*.

13. Nevins, *War for the Union* 1:121–22; Thomas W. Knox, *Campfire and Cottonfield: Southern Adventure in Time of War*, p. 29.

14. Nevins, *War for the Union* 1:124–25; Nathaniel Lyon to the AG, US, 12 May 1861, *OR* 3:9.

15. Bruce Catton, *Grant Moves South*, p. 32; General Orders No. 40, War Dept., AGO, 3 July 1861, *OR* 3:390. Frémont's command was the Western Department, which included Illinois plus the states and territories west of the Mississippi and east of the Rocky Mountains.

16. Grierson, Auto., pp. 104–105.

17. Ibid., pp. 106–107; Ben to Alice, 14 June 1861, GM.

18. Alice to Ben, 9 June 1861, GM. Mary Fuller Kirk was the daughter of Susan Grierson Fuller, Ben's sister.

19. Alice to Ben, 16 June 1861, GM.

20. Alice to Ben, 12 June 1861, GM.

21. Ben to Alice, 28 June 1861, GM.

22. Alice to Ben, 30 June 1861, GM.

23. Alice to Ben, 7 July 1861, GM.

24. Ben to Alice, 26 July 1861, GM.

25. Ben to Alice, 25 June 1861, 30 July 1861, GM.

26. Alice to Ben, 25 July 1861; Ben to Alice, 24 July 1861, GM.

27. Frémont had never commanded more than a few hundred men, and while many of his numerous staff were competent, few were familiar either with American political or military tradition and practice. See Nevins, *The War for the Union* 1:317–18.

28. Ibid., p. 316; Foote, *The Civil War*, 1:92–94; Frémont to Prentiss, 15 August

1861, *OR* 3:443-44.

29. John C. Frémont to Benjamin Prentiss, 15 August 1861, *OR* 3:443-44.

30. Grierson, Auto., p. 117; Ben to Alice, 14 August 1861, GM.

31. Grierson, Auto., p. 116; Catton, *Grant Moves South*, p. 27.

32. Grierson, Auto., pp. 129-30.

33. Ibid., p. 133.

34. Grierson, Auto., pp. 134-35; John C. Frémont to B. Prentiss, 28 August 1861, *OR* 3:142-43.

35. Ben to Alice, 27 September 1861, GM.

36. Alice to Ben, 1 September 1861, GM.

37. Ben to Alice, 4 October 1861, GM.

38. Grierson, Auto., p. 147.

39. Catton, *Grant Moves South*, pp. 48-49; *OR* 4:198.

40. *OR* 3:466-67. (These pages contain the complete text of Frémont's Proclamation.); *OR* 4:181-89.

41. *OR* 3:693.

42. Nevins, *War for the Union* 1:337-39.

43. Ibid., p. 382; G. McClellan to H. Halleck, 9 November 1861, *OR* 3:567-69.

44. Ben to Alice, 7 November 1861, GM.

45. Ben to Alice, 4 November 1861, GM. Ben was an avid reader of books on drill, tactics, and strategy. His letters to Alice and his brother John contained numerous requests for the most current works on these subjects.

46. Alice to Ben, 7 November 1861; Ben to Alice, 6 September 1861, GM.

47. Grierson, Auto., pp. 120-21.

48. Ibid., p. 157; Ben to Alice, 24 November 1861, GM.

49. Grierson, Auto., pp. 158-61.

50. Ben to Alice, 18 December 1861, 19 December 1861, GM.

51. Ben to Alice, 21 December 1861, GM.

52. Ibid.

53. Alice to Ben, 27 December 1861, GM.

54. Grierson, Auto., p. 164; Alice to Ben, 30 December 1861, GM.

55. Grierson, Auto., p. 176; Ben to Alice, 9 January 1862, GM.

56. Grierson, Auto., p. 186.

57. Grierson, Auto., p. 186.

58. Nevins, *War for the Union* 1:150-54; *OR* 7:531; D. C. Buell to G. C. McClellan, 20 December 1861, *OR* 7:520-23; Foote, *The Civil War* 1:573.

59. Foote, *The Civil War* 1:172-73; Buell to McClellan, 29 December 1861, *OR* 7:521; Buell to Halleck, 3 January 1862, *OR* 7:528-29.

60. *OR* 7:122-23; Catton, *Grant Moves South*, pp. 143-44.

61. *OR* 7:383-87; Robert D. Henry, *"First with the Most" Forrest*, pp. 50-61; U. S. Grant to Halleck, 16 February 1862, *OR* 7:625.

62. Halleck to McClellan, 3 March 1862, *OR* 7:680; Halleck to Grant, 4 March 1862, *OR* 10, pt. 2,3.

63. *OR* 7:683-84.

64. Halleck to Grant, 13 March 1862, *OR,* pt. 1,32; Grant to Sherman, 4 April 1862, *OR* 10, pt. 2,90-91.

65. Johnston to Soldiers of the Army of Mississippi, 3 April 1862, *OR* 10:396-97.

66. Beauregard to General S. Cooper, 11 April 1864, *OR* 10:385-92; Grant to War Dept. of Miss., 19 April 1862, *OR* 10:109-11. General Prentiss, Grierson's

early sponsor, commanded a division at Shiloh that sustained heavy losses in the fighting of the first day, forcing him to surrender. This marked the end of his military career.

67. Beauregard to General S. Cooper, 11 April 1864, *OR* 10:385-92; Grant to the AAG, Department of Mississippi, 9 April 1862, *OR* 10:109-11.

68. Report of Major General William T. Sherman, 30 May 1862, *OR* 10:740-44.

69. Colonel T. H. Cavanaugh to Major Benj. H. Grierson, 19 February 1862; Ben to Alice, 20 February 1862, GM.

70. Ben to Alice, 24 February 1862, GM.

71. Yates to Stanton, 13 March 1862; B. H. Grierson to A. C. Campbell, 13 March 1862; Ben to Alice, 6 April 1862, GM.

72. Alice to Ben, 13 April 1862; John Grierson to Ben, 29 April 1862, GM.

73. Ben to Alice, 9 April 1862; Petition to Governor Richard Yates, 10 April 1862; Grierson, Auto., p. 209; Ben to Alice, 13 April 1862, GM.

74. Ben to Alice, 1 May 1862, 9 May 1862, GM.

75. Grierson, Auto., p. 219.

76. Ibid., pp. 235-36; Ben to Robert Grierson, 20 May 1862, GM.

77. Ben to John Grierson, 17 May 1862, GP; Ben to John Grierson, 20 May 1862, GM.

78. Alice to Ben, 2 June 1862, 8 June 1862, GM.

79. Ben to Alice, 8 June 1862; Ben to John Grierson, 17 June 1862, GM; *OR* 7:9-10.

80. Grierson, Auto., pp. 231-32; Ben to Alice, 23 June 1862, GM.

81. Wallace had taken a wrong road, an honest mistake, but his division, six miles from the battlefield, did not reach the scene until evening of the first day. It was many years before Grant forgave him for his tardiness.

82. Ben to Alice, 24 June 1862, 11 July 1862, GM; Grierson, Auto., p. 237.

83. Ben to Alice, 24 June 1862, GM.

84. Ben to Alice, 24 June 1862, GM; Grierson, Auto., pp. 246-48.

85. William T. Sherman, *Memoirs of General William T. Sherman* 1:265; Henry, *Forrest*, pp. 335-36.

86. Ben to Alice, 19 June 1862, GP.

87. Grierson, Auto., pp. 256-60.

88. Ibid., pp. 259-60.

89. John Grierson to Elizabeth Grierson, 10 September 1862, GM.

90. Ben to Alice, 13 September 1862, GM; B. H. Grierson to Brig. Genl. Morgan L. Smith, *OR* 17:58-60; Sherman to Grant, 8 December 1862, Letters and Documents, Grierson Papers, Manuscript 343A, Edward Ayer Collection, Newberry Library. Hereafter cited as MS343A.

91. Alice to Ben, 2 August 1862, Ben to Robert Grierson, 20 September 1862; Robert Grierson to Ben, 11 November 1862, GM.

92. Robert Grierson to Ben, 8 October 1862, GM; Grierson, Auto., p. 278.

93. *OR* 7:471; Grierson, Auto., p. 292.

94. Grierson to Sherman, 25 October 1862, *OR* 17:461; Grierson, Auto., pp. 280-85. Woodward enlisted as a private in Company G, Sixth Illinois in February, 1862, and was promoted to second lieutenant in November of that year.

95. Grierson, Auto., p. 292.

96. Grierson to Sherman, 8 December 1862, *OR* 17:517-18.

97. Ben to Alice, 13 December 1862, GM; Samuel Woodward, "Fifty Days

Travel of the Sixth Illinois Cavalry," GM.

98. For details of McClernand's plans, see Catton, *Grant Moves South*, pp. 329-36.

99. Ben to Alice, 9 December 1862, GM.

100. See Henry, *Forrest*, pp. 108-20 for details of Forrest's raid.

101. *OR* 17, pt. 1,518; Edwin C. Bearss, *Decision in Mississippi*, pp. 110-11.

102. Grierson to Colonel J. A. Rawlins, 29 December 1862, GM; *OR* 17, pt. 1,418-19.

103. *OR* 17, pt. 1,519-20; Grierson, Auto., pp. 308-14.

104. Grierson, Auto., pp. 308-14.

105. Alice to Ben, 10 December 1862, GM.

106. Alice to Ben, 27 December 1862, GM.

107. Ben to Alice, 14 January 1863; Grierson, Auto., p. 322.

CHAPTER 4

1. For details of Grant's efforts to assault Vicksburg from the north, see Catton, *Grant Moves South*, pp. 371-406.

2. Ben to Alice, 15 February 1863, GM.

3. Ben to Alice, 10 February 1863, GM.

4. Ben to Alice, 22 February 1863, GM.

5. Alice to Ben, 26 February 1863, GM.

6. Alice to Ben, 8 February 1863, GM.

7. John Kirk to Alice, 14 August 1862, GM; John Kirk to Alice, 9 May 1859, GP; Alice to Ben, 10 November 1861, GM.

8. Alice to Ben, 22 June 1862, 18 March 1863, GM.

9. Alice to Ben, 25 July 1862, 10 August 1862, GM.

10. Alice to Ben, 4 March 1863, GM; Mary Abigail Dodge [Gail Hamilton], "A Call to My Country-Women," *Atlantic*, March 1863, p. 347. For information on Dodge see George M. Fredrickson, *The Inner Civil War: Northern Intellectuals and the Crisis of the Union*, pp. 83-84, 248.

11. Dodge, "A Call to My Country-Women," p. 346.

12. Alice to Ben, 28 March 1863, GM.

13. Ibid.

14. C. S. Hamilton to B. H. Grierson, 14 February 1863; Ben to Alice, 15 February 1863, GM.

15. *OR* 24:481-85; Grierson, Auto., pp. 337-42. Grierson's losses during these actions totaled approximately fifty persons killed and wounded.

16. Grierson, Auto., p. 360.

17. S. Hurlbut to B. H. Grierson, 13 April 1863, GM.

18. Alice to Ben, 16 April 1863, GM.

19. Ben to Alice, 16 April 1863, GM.

20. Grierson, Auto., p. 373.

21. Ibid.; Samuel Woodward, "Grierson's Raid," Manuscript in the GM; D. Alexander Brown, *Grierson's Raid*, p. 18.

22. Larry Underwood, *The Butternut Guerillas: A Story of Grierson's Raid*, p. 9.

23. Brown, *Grierson's Raid*, p. 20.

24. S. Hurlbut to W. S. Smith, 15 April 1863, *OR* 24, pt. 3, 196-97. S. Hurlbut

to Col. J. C. Kelton, AAG, Headquarters of the Army, Washington, D.C., 5 May 1863, *OR* 24:520–21.

25. Grierson, Auto., p. 374.

26. Ibid., p. 376–77.

27. Ibid., p. 380; B. H. Grierson to the AAG, Sixteenth Army Corps, 5 May 1863, *OR* 24:523.

28. Ibid., pp. 523–24.

29. Ben to Alice, 20 April 1863, GM.

30. B. H. Grierson to the AAG, Sixteenth Army Corps, 5 May 1863, *OR* 24:524.

31. Edward Hatch to the AAG, First Division, Sixteenth Army Corps, 24 April 1863, *OR* 24:529–31.

32. Underwood, *The Butternut Guerillas*, p. 23.

33. Grierson, Auto., p. 386; Grierson to the AAG, Sixteenth Army Corps, 5 May 1863, *OR* 24:523.

34. Grierson to the AAG, Sixteenth Army Corps, 5 May 1863, *OR* 24:524.

35. Grierson, Auto., p. 392; Brown, *Grierson's Raid*, p. 79.

36. B. H. Grierson to the AAG, Sixteenth Army Corps, 5 May 1863, *OR* 24:524.

37. Grierson, Auto., p. 397.

38. Brown, *Grierson's Raid*, pp. 101–10.

39. B. H. Grierson to the AAG, Sixteenth Army Corps, 5 May 1863, *OR* 24:525.

40. Ibid., p. 525; Grierson, Auto., p. 402.

41. B. H. Grierson to the AAG, Sixteenth Army Corps, 5 May 1863, *OR* 24:525.

42. Benjamin Henry Grierson, *Record of Services Rendered the Government, 1863*, p. 98, GM. Hereafter cited as Grierson, *RS*.

43. Grierson, *RS*, pp. 98–99; Brown, *Grierson's Raid*, pp. 142–43.

44. Grierson, *RS*, p. 99; Brown, *Grierson's Raid*, p. 117.

45. B. H. Grierson to the AAG, Sixteenth Army Corps, 5 May 1863, *OR* 24:526.

46. Grierson, Auto., p. 415; B. H. Grierson to the AAG, Sixteenth Army Corps, 5 May 1863, *OR* 24:526; Brown, *Grierson's Raid*, p. 158.

47. J. C. Pemberton to John Bowen, 27 April 1863, *OR* 24, pt. 3, 792.

48. J. C. Pemberton to Gen. S. Cooper, 29 April 1863, *OR* 24, pt. 3, 801.

49. Brown, *Grierson's Raid*, p. 158.

50. Grierson, *RS*, p. 106.

51. R. B. Maury to J. C. Pemberton, 29 April 1863, *OR* 5:942.

52. B. H. Grierson to the AAG, Sixteenth Army Corps, 5 May 1863, *OR* 24:527.

53. Brown, *Grierson's Raid*, p. 182.

54. Grierson, Auto., p. 422.

55. Ibid., pp. 425–26.

56. Ibid., p. 429; Brown, *Grierson's Raid*, pp. 200–201.

57. Grierson, Auto., pp. 428–29; Grierson, *RS*, p. 107.

58. Brown, *Grierson's Raid*, p. 204.

59. Ibid., p. 205; Grierson, Auto., p. 432.

60. B. H. Grierson to the AAG, Sixteenth Army Corps, 5 May 1863, *OR* 24: 528.

61. Grierson, Auto., p. 443.

62. W. Adams to J. C. Pemberton, 4 May 1863, *OR* 24:550.

63. R. V. Richardson to J. C. Pemberton, 4 May 1863, *OR* 24:550.

64. Brown, *Grierson's Raid*, pp. 217-19.

65. B. H. Grierson to the AAG, Sixteenth Army Corps, 5 May 1863, *OR* 24: 528-29.

66. Grierson, Auto., p. 483.

67. Foote, *The Civil War* 2:341.

68. Hurlbut to the AAG, Headquarters of the Army, Washington, D.C., 5 May 1863, *OR* 24:520-21.

69. Ben to Alice, 6 May 1863, GM.

70. John Grierson to Robert Grierson, 24 May 1863, GP; See also John S. Abbott, "Heroic Deeds of Heroic Men—Grierson's Raid," *Harper's New Monthly Magazine,* February 1865, pp. 273-81.

71. Ben to Alice, 9 May 1863, GM.

72. Ibid.; Grant to Banks, 10 May 1863, *OR* 24, pt. 3, 289.

73. Brown, *Grierson's Raid*, p. 233.

74. Ben to Alice, 21 May 1863, GM.

75. Ibid.

76. Ben to Alice, 28 May 1863, GM.

77. Grierson, Auto., p. 492.

78. Ben to Alice, 16 June 1863, GM.

79. Secretary of War Stanton to Grierson, 3 June 1863, GM; Grierson, Auto., p. 500.

80. Alice to Ben, 22 May 1863, GM.

81. Alice to Ben, 28 May 1863, 9 June 1863, 16 April 1863, GM.

82. *OR* 26:625.

83. Quoted in Brown, *Grierson's Raid*, p. 236.

84. Grant to Banks, 10 July 1863, *OR* 24, pt. 3, 493.

85. Sherman to Grant, 13 July 1863, *OR* 24, pt. 2, 524.

86. Special Orders No. 174, Headquarters, Department of the Gulf, Nineteenth Army Corps, 18 July 1863, *OR* 26:645.

87. Grierson, Auto., pp. 510-11.

88. *OR* 26, pt. 3, 550.

CHAPTER 5

1. Grierson, Auto., p. 516.

2. Ben to Alice, 8 August 1863, GM.

3. Louisa Semple to Ben, 18 August 1863, GM.

4. Grierson, Auto., pp. 517-19.

5. Ibid., pp. 525-34. The comment was made by George McConnell, brother of Murray McConnell, a leading Democrat in Morgan County, Illinois.

6. Alice to Ben, 9 October 1861, 2 February 1865, GM; Grierson, Auto., p. 555.

7. Henry, *Forrest*, p. 203.

8. Ibid., pp. 204–206.

9. B. H. Grierson to Major Coon, 27 December 1863, *OR* 21, pt. 3, 535.

10. B. H. Grierson to the AAG, Sixteenth Army Corps, 24 January 1863, *OR* 31, pt. 1, 578.

11. N. B. Forrest to Major General Stephen D. Lee, 29 December 1863, *OR* 31, pt. 1, 620–21.

12. Grierson, Auto., p. 560. William Sooy Smith graduated from West Point in 1853, and was appointed colonel of the Thirteenth Ohio Volunteers Infantry in June 1861 and brigadier of Volunteers on April 15, 1862. He resigned July 15, 1864. See Francis B. Heitman, *Historical Register and Dictionary of the United States Army* 1:905.

13. Grierson, Auto., p. 558; Grierson, *RS*, p. 136.

14. Henry, *Forrest*, p. 217.

15. Quoted in Foote, *The Civil War* 2:926.

16. B. H. Grierson to the AAAG, Dept. of Tenn., *OR* 32, pt. 1, 260–61.

17. Ibid.

18. Grierson, Auto., p. 574.

19. Ibid., p. 579.

20. George E. Waring, Jr., "The Sooy Smith Expedition," *Battles and Leaders of the Civil War* 4:417.

21. Ibid., p. 418.

22. Sherman, *Memoirs* 1:422; Ben to Alice, 27 February 1864, GM.

23. Alice to Ben, 26 February 1864, GM.

24. Alice to Ben, 6 March 1864, GM.

25. Ben to Alice, 15 March 1864, GM.

26. Ben to Alice, 31 March 1864, GM.

27. Foote, *The Civil War* 3:108–11; Henry, *Forrest*, pp. 248–68. The latter includes details on the federal investigation of the fight at Fort Pillow.

28. Grierson, Auto., p. 604; Alice to Ben, 1 April 1864, GM.

29. Sherman to Commanding Officer at Memphis, 18 April 1864, *OR* 32, pt. 3, 402. Sturgis, a native of Pennsylvania, graduated from West Point in 1846. He served in the Mexican War and at the outbreak of the Civil War was appointed as major, First Cavalry. He was promoted to brigadier general of Volunteers on August 10, 1861.

30. B. H. Grierson to AAAG, Sixteenth Army Corps, 26 April 1864, *OR* 32, pt. 3, 502; Ben to Alice, 26 April 1864, GM.

31. Sturgis to the AAG, District of West Tennessee, 24 June 1864, *OR* 39, pt. 1, 89–90.

32. B. H. Grierson to the AAAG, Sixteenth Army Corps, 24 June 1864, *OR* 29, pt. 1, 95–96.

33. Ben to Alice, 9 June 1864, GM.

34. Grierson, Auto., p. 567.

35. Grierson to the AAG, Sixteenth Army Corps, 24 June 1864, *OR* 39:90–91.

36. Sturgis to the AAG, District of Tennessee, 24 June 1864, *OR* 39, pt. 1, 93–94.

37. Forrest to the AAG, Department of Alabama, Mississippi, and Eastern Louisiana, 1 July 1864, *OR* 29, pt. 1, 222–24; Grierson to the AAG, District of West Tennessee, 21 June 1864, *OR* 29, pt. 1, 128–30. Grierson's family, reading

accounts of the disaster, feared at first that Ben was among the prisoners. Louisa Semple to Ben, 19 June 1864, GM.

38. Testimony of General B. H. Grierson in Proceedings of Board of Investigation, Memphis, Tennessee, June 1864, *OR* 29, pt. 2, 203.

39. Grierson to Sturgis, 23 June 1864, GM.

40. Louisa Semple to Ben, 12 August 1864, GM.

41. Major General A. J. Smith to the AAG, District of West Tennessee, 5 August 1864, *OR* 29, pt. 1, 250–51.

42. Ibid., p. 252; *Battles and Leaders* 4:421.

43. Henry, *Forrest*, pp. 316–17.

44. *Battles and Leaders* 4:422; Smith to the AAG, District of West Tennessee, 5 August 1864, *OR* 29, pt. 1, 253–54.

45. Smith to the AAG, District of West Tennessee, 5 August 1864, *OR* 29, pt. 1, 253–54.

46. Another source placed Forrest's loss at 1,308 killed, wounded, and missing. See Henry, *Forrest*, p. 322.

47. Alice to Ben, 2 July 1864, GM.

48. Henry, *Forrest*, p. 333.

49. John Grierson to Elizabeth Grierson, 21 August 1864, GM.

50. Maque to "Dear Folks," 14 August 1864, GM.

51. Grierson to Washburn, 26 August 1864; General Orders, No. 1, Headquarters, Cavalry Corps, 25 July 1864, GM.

52. Howard to Grierson, 24 October 1864, *OR* 39, pt. 3, 428.

53. Grierson to Howard, 30 October 1864, *OR* 39, pt. 3, 528–29.

54. Wilson to Grierson, 20 November 1864, *OR* 45, pt. 1, 955; Grierson to Wilson, 1 December 1864, *OR* 45, pt. 2, 9–10.

55. Grierson to the AAG, Department of Mississippi, 14 January 1865, *OR* 45, pt. 1, 845.

56. Grierson to General Dana, 8 January 1865, *OR* 45, pt. 2, 552.

57. Grierson to the AAG, Headquarters, District of West Tennessee, 14 January 1865, GM.

58. Lieutenant General Richard Taylor to Wirt Adams, 27 December 1864, *OR* 45, pt. 2, 741–42; Dana to the AAG, Military Division of West Mississippi, 8 January 1865, *OR* 45, pt. 1, 1000.

59. Grierson to the AG, 9 January 1865, *OR* 46, pt. 1, 1000.

60. Alice to Ben, 2 February 1865, GM.

61. Ibid.; Louisa Semple to Ben, 3 April 1865, GM.

62. Alice to Ben, 21 March 1864, 19 March 1865, GM.

63. Alice to Ben, [20] December 1871, GP. This letter, written years later, contained a lengthy description of how Alice greeted each of her pregnancies.

64. Alice to Ben, 28 January 1865, GM.

65. Alice to Ben, 2 February 1865, GM.

66. Ibid.

67. Ben to Alice, 12 February 1865, GM.

68. Grant to Canby, 9 February 1865, *OR* 48, pt. 1, 786.

69. John Grierson to Ben, 20 February 1865, GM.

70. Ben to Alice, 15 March 1865; Alice to Ben, 24 February 1865, GM.

71. Alice to Ben, 5 March 1865, GM.

72. Alice to Ben, 3 March 1865, GM.

73. Alice to Ben, 8 March 1865, GM.

74. Ben to Alice, 18 March 1865, GM.

75. Ben to Alice, 5 March 1865, GM.

76. Doyle, *Jacksonville, Illinois,* pp. 239–40; Alice to Ben, 4 April 1865, GM.

77. Ben to Alice, 8 April 1865, GM.

78. Ben to Alice, 15 April 1865, GM.

79. Alice to Ben, 16 April 1865, 4 May 1865, GM.

80. General Orders No. 3, Headquarters, Cavalry Forces, Military Division of West Mississippi, 17 April 1865, *OR* 49, pt. 2, 387.

81. Johnston reached an understanding with Sherman after conferences April 13–18. The terms were so liberal that the Johnson administration repudiated the agreement, requiring new terms for surrender. These were accepted by Johnston on April 26. Sherman received widespread criticism for his original terms, and Alice wrote Ben: "Is it not very strange Gen'l. Sherman should have assented to such terms for the surrender of Johnston's army? Father thinks he will be dismissed the service and Mrs. Ramsay thinks he must be insane." Alice to Ben, 27 April 1865, GM.

82. Ben to Alice, 1 May 1865, GM.

83. For details of Davis's capture see Foote, *Civil War* 3:1009–1010.

84. Ben to Alice, 8 May 1865, GM.

85. Ben to Alice, 23 May 1865, GM.

86. Ben to Alice, 25 May 1865, GM.

87. Grierson to the AAG, Military Division of West Mississippi, 4 June 1865, *OR* 49, pt. 1, 301.

88. Ben to Alice, 10 July 1865, GM.

89. Alice to Ben, 5 July 1865, GM.

90. Alice to Ben, 23 July 1865, GM.

91. Special Orders No. 21, Headquarters, Military Division of the Gulf, 9 August 1865, GM.

92. Ben to Alice, 17 September 1865, GM.

93. B. H. Grierson, "Testimony," U.S. Congress, *Report of the Joint Committee on Reconstruction,* H. Report 30, 39 Cong., 1st sess., 1866, pt. 1, pp. 121–24.

94. John Grierson to Ben, 12 August 1865, GM.

95. Louisa Semple to Ben, 31 October 1865, GM.

96. Louisa Semple to Ben, 22 November 1865, GM.

97. Ibid., 23 December 1865, GM.

98. Ben to Alice, 24 September 1865, GM.

99. Alice to Ben, 1 October 1865, GM.

100. Ben to Alice, 5 October 1865, GM.

101. John Kirk to Ben and Alice, 4 December 1865, GM.

102. Grierson, "Testimony," *Report of the Joint Committee on Reconstruction,* p. 122.

103. Grierson to Brevet Major General M. C. Meigs, Quartermaster General, U.S.A., 1 November 1865, GM.

104. Grierson to S. S. Giers, 9 February 1866, GM.

105. Grierson, "Testimony," *Report of the Joint Committee on Reconstruction,* pp. 121–24; Ben to Alice, 2 March 1866, GM.

106. Ben to Alice, 7 March 1866, GM.

107. Alice to Ben, 12 March 1866, GM.

108. Ibid.

109. Special Orders No. 140, War Department, Adjutant General's Office, Washington, D.C., 28 March 1866, GM.

110. Ben to Alice, 16 April 1865, GM.

CHAPTER 6

1. John Grierson to Ben, 23 November 1866, GM.

2. Doyle, *Jacksonville, Illinois*, pp. 248–49.

3. See Doyle, *Jacksonville, Illinois*, pp. 249–54.

4. Grant to Sheridan and Sherman, 4 August 1866, Selected Letters Received Relating to the Tenth Regiment, United States Cavalry, Records of the War Department, AGO, Record Group 94, NA. Hereafter referred to as SLR, Tenth Cavalry; William H. Leckie, *The Buffalo Soldiers: A Narrative of the Negro Cavalry in the West*, p. 7. Grierson's friend, Colonel Edward Hatch, was appointed the commander of the other regiment of cavalry, the Ninth.

5. John Grierson to Ben, 28 August 1866, GM.

6. Special Orders No. 20, Headquarters, Military Division of the Missouri, 10 September 1866, GM: Special Orders No. 18, Headquarters, Department of the Missouri, 17 September 1866, GM.

7. Woodward to Grierson, 21 September 1866, GM.

8. Special Orders No. 484, War Department, 29 September 1866, GM; Ben to Alice, 19 October 1866, GM.

9. Ben to Alice, 22 October 1866, MS343A.

10. Alice to Ben, 4 October 1866, GM.

11. Ben to Alice, 3 October 1866, GM.

12. Alice to Dr. Garlick, 18 November 1866, GM.

13. Grierson to Captain L. H. Carpenter, 5 March 1867, Letters Sent, Tenth United States Cavalry, Records of United States Army Commands, Record Group 98, NA. Hereafter referred to as LS, Tenth Cavalry.

14. Grierson to H. T. Davis, 6 March 1867, LS, Tenth Cavalry.

15. Organizational Returns, Tenth Cavalry, January 1867. Records of the War Department, AGO, Record Group 94, NA. Hereafter referred to as Organizational Returns, Tenth Cavalry.

16. Ben to Alice, 26 April 1867, GM.

17. Sherman to Hancock, 25 January 1867, MS343A.

18. Ben to Alice, 14 January 1867, GM.

19. Lieutenant Henry Alvord to Post Adjutant, Fort Leavenworth, 2 April 1867, LS, Tenth Cavalry; Grierson to Post Adjutant, Fort Leavenworth, 21 June 1867, LS, Tenth Cavalry.

20. Charges and Specifications preferred against Colonel B. H. Grierson, Tenth Cavalry, Brevet Major General U.S.A., 23 June 1867, GM.

21. Leckie, *Buffalo Soldiers*, p. 15; Alice to Ben, 21 May 1867, GM.

22. Grierson to Walsh, 4 May 1867, LS, Tenth Cavalry; Grierson to the Adjutant General, Washington, D.C., 9 May 1867, LS, Tenth Cavalry; Grierson to Lieutenant W. D. Badger, 31 May 1867, LS, Tenth Cavalry.

23. Ben to Alice, 5 May 1867; Ben to John Grierson, 16 May 1867, GM.

24. Alice to Ben, 21 May 1867, GM. Alvord, a Massachusetts native, enlisted

in a Rhode Island cavalry regiment in June, 1862. Five months later he was commissioned as a second lieutenant in the Second Massachusetts Cavalry, where he served for the rest of the war. He was promoted to captain in December 1864 and appointed first lieutenant in the Tenth Cavalry in July 1866. He served as the regiment's first adjutant and later was captain of Company M, resigning in December 1871. See Heitman, *Historical Register* 1:161.

25. Alvord to Badger, 18 June 1867, LS, Tenth Cavalry.

26. Grierson to the Adjutant General, Washington, D.C., 7 August 1867, LS, Tenth Cavalry.

27. Louisa Semple to Ben, 8 august 1867, GM.

28. Leckie, *Buffalo Soldiers*, p. 19; Donald J. Berthrong, *The Southern Cheyennes*, pp. 277–87.

29. Woodward to Grierson, 21 July 1867, GM; Organizational Returns, Tenth Cavalry, August 1867.

30. Organizational Returns, Tenth Cavalry, August 1867; Leckie, *Buffalo Soldiers*, p. 22.

31. Lawrence A. Frost, *The Court-Martial of General George Armstrong Custer*, p. 86.

32. Grierson to H. T. Davis, 16 July 1867, LS, Tenth Cavalry.

33. Alvord to Grierson, 19 September 1867, LS, Tenth Cavalry; Alvord to Grierson, 22 December 1867, MS343A; Alice to Ben, 16 September 1867, GM.

34. Woodward to Grierson, 6 October 1867, GM. Davidson, a graduate of West Point, had served in the Mexican War and in the West before the Civil War. He was appointed a captain in the First Cavalry and by February, 1862, was brigadier general of Volunteers. He became chief of cavalry, Missouri Division of the West, in 1864. At the end of the war, he was a brevet major general with many citations for gallant and meritorious service. Appointed lieutenant colonel, Tenth Cavalry in December, 1866, he remained in that rank until he left the regiment in 1874. He died of injuries sustained when a horse fell on him in 1881. See Heitman, *Historical Register* 1:355–56.

35. Frost, *The Court-Martial of General George Armstrong Custer*, p. 246.

36. Woodward to Grierson, 3 October 1867; Alice to Ben, 3 October 1867; Ben to John Grierson, 4 October 1867, GM.

37. Louisa Semple to Ben, 7 October 1867, GM.

38. For details of the agreements at Medicine Lodge, see Charles J. Kappler, *Indian Affairs: Laws and Treaties* 2:980–89; Alfred A. Taylor, "Medicine Lodge Peace Council," *Chronicles of Oklahoma* 2 (June 1924):100–101.

39. Mrs. C. J. Myrick to Alice, 7 January 1868; E. F. Reynolds to General and Mrs. Grierson, 15 January 1868; An Army Wife at Fort Riley to Mrs. Grierson, 15 November 1867, GM.

40. Louisa Semple to Ben, 26 November 1867, GM.

41. General Orders No. 42, Headquarters of the Army, AGO, 9 July 1868, GM.

42. John Grierson to Ben, 3 December 1867, 16 December 1867; Ben to John Grierson, 11 March 1868, GM.

43. John Grierson to Ben, 29 January 1878, GM.

44. Indian raids and depredations in Texas were devastating during the winter of 1867–68. Colonel Jesse Leavenworth, Agent to the Kiowas and Comanches, was unable to control them and, in May, 1868, fled the Territory in fear of his life. See Leckie, *Buffalo Soldiers*, pp. 29–30; J. W. Wilbarger, *Indian Depredations in Texas*,

pp. 633–36. Organizational Returns, Tenth Cavalry, October–December 1867.

45. Ben to John Grierson, 23 March 1868, MS343A.

46. Louisa Semple to Ben, 6 April 1868, GM.

47. Ben to John Grierson, 6 May 1868, GM; Fort Gibson was on the Grand River in northeastern Indian Territory. Established in 1824, it was for many years one of the most important posts in the Southwest. After the Civil War it served primarily as a quartermaster depot. See W. Morrison, *Military Posts and Camps in Oklahoma*, pp. 28–47.

48. "Journal of an Expedition to the Wichita Mountains, from June 1 to July 13, 1868," MS343A. Fort Arbuckle, some 180 miles southwest of Fort Gibson, was established in 1851 to protect the Chickasaws from the wild plains tribes. United States troops withdrew at the outbreak of the Civil War, and it was occupied by Texas troops and later by Confederate Chickasaws. Reoccupied by federal troops after the war's end, it was abandoned in 1869. See W. B. Morrison, "Fort Arbuckle," *Chronicles of Oklahoma* 6 (1928):26–34.

49. Morrison, "Fort Arbuckle,"; Grierson to the AAG, Department of the Missouri, 14 July 1868; Ben to Alice, 5 July 1868, MS343A.

50. Alice to Ben, 19 June 1868, GM.

51. Alice to Ben, 5 July 1868, GM.

52. The memoirs of frontier army wives testify to the painful dilemma, "the question which, sooner or later, presents itself to the minds of all parents of army children," as Martha Summerhayes wrote in *Vanished Arizona: Recollections of My Army Life*, p. 236. In the latter case, Martha Summerhayes left her husband at Fort Niobrara in Nebraska and took the children back east, where she lived while they completed their secondary schooling during the 1880s, thus experiencing a long separation from her husband. See also Ellen McGowan Biddle, *Reminiscences of a Soldier's Wife*, p. 252, for further discussion of the personal conflict experienced by army wives facing this decision.

53. Ben to John Grierson, 31 July 1868.

54. *Annual Report of the Commissioner of Indian Affairs for 1868*, pp. 68–70; *Annual Report of the Secretary of War for 1868*, pp. 4–5; Leckie, *Buffalo Soldiers*, p. 32; Stan Hoig, *The Battle of the Washita*, pp. 46–51.

55. U.S. Congress, *Senate Executive Document*, No. 13, 40 Cong., 3rd sess., 186[9], pp. 8–11. It is doubtful that the Kiowas and Comanches were truly innocent. Woodward wrote Grierson in September that "Old Horseback" (a Comanche chief) had returned from a raid into Texas with eight scalps, two captive women, and a lot of stock. Horseback had escaped to the Staked Plains before troops could strike him. Woodward to Grierson, 19 September 1868, MS343A.

56. Marvin C. Kroeker, *Great Plains Command: William B. Hazen in the Frontier West*, pp. 74–75; *Annual Report of the Commissioner of Indian Affairs for 1868*, pp. 82–83. Hazen was a graduate of West Point, class of 1855. He served extensively on the western frontier before the Civil War. At the war's onset, he was a captain, Eighth U.S. Infantry, and in October, 1861, was promoted to colonel, Forty-First Ohio Infantry. In November, 1862, he was commissioned brigadier general of volunteers and promoted to major general of volunteers in December, 1864. Appointed colonel of the Thirty-Eighth Infantry in the army reorganization of July, 1866, he transferred to the Sixth Infantry in March, 1869. See Heitman, *Historical Register* 1:517.

57. Kroeker, *Great Plains Command*, pp. 75–76.

58. Alvord to Grierson, 4 November 1868, MS343A; Leckie, *Buffalo Soldiers,* p. 39.

59. Leckie, *Buffalo Soldiers,* pp. 39–40; *Annual Report of the Commissioner of Indian Affairs for 1868,* pp. 388–96.

60. *Annual Report of the Secretary of War for 1868,* pp. 44–45; Philip H. Sheridan, *Personal Memoirs* 2:309. Custer's command, moving south from Fort Dodge, Kansas, consisted of eleven companies of the Seventh Cavalry, a battalion of infantry and the Nineteenth Kansas Cavalry under Governor S. J. Crawford. Marching east from Fort Bascom, New Mexico, was a column under Brevet Lieutenant Colonel A. W. Evans, while two commands under Brevet Brigadier General W. H. Penrose and Brevet Major General Eugene A. Carr pushed southeast from Fort Lyon, Colorado. Four troops of Grierson's Tenth were in Penrose's command, while another four guarded the Kansas frontier. See Leckie, *Buffalo Soldiers,* p. 40, and Hoig, *The Battle of the Washita,* pp. 74–75.

61. For a detailed discussion of Custer's attack on the Cheyenne village, see Hoig, *The Battle of the Washita,* pp. 126–43. Camp Supply was established on November 18, 1868, near the junction of the North Canadian River and Wolf Creek. It served as a base for the "main column" in the winter campaign and later as a major post for controlling the Cheyennes and Arapahoes. See Robert W. Frazer, *Forts of the West,* pp. 124–25.

62. Wilbur S. Nye, *Carbine and Lance: The Story of Old Fort Sill,* pp. 72–74.

63. Ben to Alice, 23 November 1868, MS343A; Charlie to Alice, 6 December 1868; John Grierson to Ben, 16 August 1868, GM.

64. Ben to Alice, 24 December 1868, GM.

65. Ibid.

66. Alvord to Grierson, 2 February 1869; Ben to John Kirk, 4 March 1869, MS343A. Recent scholarship tends to support Grierson's contention. See Berthrong, *Southern Cheyennes,* pp. 327–28.

67. Ben to Alice, 19 December 1868, 1 January, GM: Nye, *Carbine and Lance,* p. 75.

68. Nye, *Carbine and Lance,* p. 77.

69. Ben to Alice, 18 December 1868, GM. Just a few months earlier, Ben had written his brother John that he was considering taking out bankruptcy, for his old debts were burdensome. Ben to John Grierson, 21 February 1868, GM. Matters had not improved a great deal by Christmas of that year.

70. Alice to Ben, 10 December 1868, 16 December 1868, 17 December 1868, GM.

71. Ben to Alice, 20 January 1869, 30 January 1869, GM.

72. Leckie, *Buffalo Soldiers,* p. 46.

73. Gillett Griswold, "Old Fort Sill: The First Seven Years," *Chronicles of Oklahoma,* 35 (1958):3; Nye, *Carbine and Lance,* pp. 89–93. When Grant assumed the presidency, Sherman replaced him as commanding general of the army, and Sheridan succeeded Sherman.

74. For details of Custer's efforts to round up the Cheyennes and Arapahoes, see Berthrong, *The Southern Cheyennes,* pp. 335–38.

75. Alice to Ben, 11 February 1869, GM.

76. Alice to Ben, 26 February 1869, GM. Homicide between troopers of the Tenth Cavalry was rare. A fist fight usually settled their differences, though these could be bloody affairs if the antagonists wore their "drinking jewelry," horseshoe nails bent in the form of a ring.

77. Alice to Ben, 12 March 1869, GM.
78. Alice to Ben, 14 March 1869, GM.
79. Chaplain Grimes to Grierson, 18 March 1869, GP.
80. Alice to Colonel Jones, 12 April 1869, GM. Grierson had arranged with Sheridan for Alice and the children to remain in the quarters at Fort Gibson until he could prepare suitable quarters at Camp Wichita. Grierson to Sheridan, 22 February 1869, GM.
81. Ben to Alice, 5 March 1869, GM.
82. Ben to Charlie, 28 April 1869, GP.
83. Ben to John Kirk, 8 March 1869, MS343A.
84. Ben to Alice, 20 March 1869, MS343A. "Wano" was probably *"bueno,"* the Spanish word for "good."
85. Ben to Alice, 7 April 1869, MS343A.
86. Nye, *Carbine and Lance,* p. 111; Laurie Tatum, *Our Red Brothers and the Peace Policy of President Ulysses S. Grant,* p. 31.
87. Note in file MS343A.
88. Grierson to Lawrie Tatum, 30 September 1869, MS343A.
89. Ben to Alice, 7 April 1869, MS343A.
90. William H. Leckie, *Military Conquest of the Southern Plains,* pp. 133–34.
91. *Annual Report of the Commissioner of Indian Affairs for 1869,* pp. 3–5; Loring B. Priest, *Uncle Sam's Stepchildren: The Reformation of United States Indian Policy, 1865–1887,* pp. 44–47; Leckie, *Military Conquest,* pp. 134–35. The initial appointees were W. E. Dodge and Nathan Bishop of New York, William Welch and George H. Stuart of Philadelphia, John Farwell of Chicago, Robert Campbell of St. Louis, E. S. Tobey of Boston, Felix R. Brunot of Pittsburgh, and Henry Lane of Indiana.
92. Tatum, *Our Red Brothers,* pp. 27–31.
93. Ben to John Grierson, 23 July 1869, MS343A.
94. John Kirk to Alice, 23 August 1869; John Grierson to Ben, 25 June 1869, GM.
95. Ben to John Grierson, 9 August 1869, MS343A.
96. Alice to Louisa Semple, 23 November 1869, GM. Grierson's efforts to "dry" up his post were successful. The post trader, John S. Evans, did a thriving business in "tonics," notably Peruna (26 percent alcohol), which he sold by the case. See Nye, *Carbine and Lance,* p. 101.
97. Leckie, *Military Conquest,* p. 138.
98. Oakes to Grierson, 7 October 1869, MS343A.
99. Post Returns, Fort Sill, October 1869; Leckie, *Buffalo Soldiers,* pp. 49–50; Leckie, *Military Conquest,* p. 138.
100. Louisa Semple to Ben, 7 October 1869, 16 October 1869; Louisa Semple to Edie, 23 October 1869, GM.
101. John Grierson to Ben, 4 October 1869, 1 November 1869, GM.
102. Alice to Ben, 18 October 1869, 25 October 1869, GM. Dr. Storer's book, originally a prize-winning essay in a contest sponsored by the American Medical Association in 1865 for the best anti-abortion tract, made a great impression on Alice. For information on Storer, see Linda Gordon, *Woman's Body, Woman's Right: A Social History of Birth Control in America,* p. 429.
103. Alice to Ben, 22 October 1869, GM; See also Mary Williams, ed. and comp., *An Army Wife's Cookbook, with Household Hints and Home Remedies: Alice Kirk Grierson, passim.* Cookbooks of this era also contained recipes for soap, cleaning fluids, medicines, dyes and ointments.

104. Alice to Ben, [20] December 1871, GP.

105. Alice to Charlie, 16 November 1869, GM.

106. Mrs. M. L. Dodge to Alice, 2 December 1869, GM; Alvord to Grierson, 6 March 1870, MS343A. In a letter to Tatum, Grierson wrote: "It seems from recent events that in certain quarters I am considered rather too much of a Quaker myself for a soldier. . . . had I only launched out and killed a few Indians . . . would no doubt have been considered by certain parties, successful. . . . I will not for the sake of material interests or for personal advancement seek to gain an opportunity to kill some Indians and bring on a war." Grierson to Tatum, 30 September 1869, GM.

107. Alice Grierson's Christmas List, [1869] Manuscript in GP.

CHAPTER 7

1. Jacob Hershfield to Lieutenant John Sullivan, 11 January 1870, SLR, Tenth Cavalry.

2. Leckie, *Buffalo Soldiers*, p. 52.

3. *Army and Navy Journal* 8 (21 May 1870):622.

4. Alice to Ben [20] December 1871, GP.

5. [Susan] Ellen Kirk to Alice, 2 March 1870, GP.

6. John Kirk to Alice, 27 July 1870, GM.

7. Louisa Semple to Ben, 20 June 1870, 6 August 1870, GM.

8. John Grierson to Ben, 9 March 1870, 13 April 1870, GM. The wages paid laborers varied sectionally. In Chicago in 1871 skilled laborers earned between a thousand and twelve hundred dollars a year. See Frederick Law Olmsted, "Chicago in Distress," *Nation*, 9 November 1871, p. 303.

9. H. B. Fuller to Ben, 2 February 1870; Louisa Semple to Ben, 30 May 1870, GM.

10. John Kirk to Alice, 3 May 1869; John Kirk to Ben, 15 September 1869; John Kirk to Ben and Alice, 24 January 1870, GM.

11. Grierson to the AAG, Department of the Missouri, 21 June 1870, 27 June 1870, MS343A.

12. Colonel W. A. Wilson to the AAG, Department of the Missouri, 12 June 1870, GP; Leckie, *Buffalo Soldiers*, p. 53.

13. Tatum, *Our Red Brothers*, p. 35.

14. Grierson to the AAG, Department of the Missouri, 21 June 1870, MS343A; Nye, *Carbine and Lance*, pp. 112–14; Tatum, *Our Red Brothers*, p. 42.

15. Nye, *Carbine and Lance*, pp. 114–15.

16. Leckie, *Buffalo Soldiers*, p. 55; *Annual Report of the Secretary of War for 1870*, p. 9.

17. John Grierson to Ben, 25 July 1869; Woodward to Grierson, 29 September 1870, GM.

18. Louisa Semple to Ben, 10 July 1870, GM.

19. Tatum, *Our Red Brothers*, pp. 40–41; Nye, *Carbine and Lance*, p. 116.

20. Grierson to the AAG, Department of the Missouri, 7 August 1870, Selected Letters Received, Records of the War Department, AGO, Record Group 94, NA. Hereafter referred to as SLR, AGO; Tatum, *Our Red Brothers*, pp. 41–44; Nye,

Carbine and Lance, p. 117.

21. Tatum, *Our Red Brothers,* p. 44.

22. Leckie, *Buffalo Soldiers,* p. 55.

23. Kiowa Files, Depredations, Indian Archives, Oklahoma State Historical Society, Oklahoma City, Oklahoma.

24. Captain A. F. Rockwell, Assistant Quartermaster, USA, to the Quartermaster General, USA, 6 May 1871, MS343A; Nye, *Carbine and Lance,* p. 121; Organizational Returns, Tenth Cavalry, December 1870.

25. Captain Henry Alvord to Grierson, 21 December 1870, MS343A; *Annual Report of the Secretary of War for 1870,* p. 3; Note in Grierson Manuscript for 1870, GM.

26. SLR, AGO, August 1870; Organizational Returns, Tenth Cavalry, August 1870; Ben to Alice, 30 July 1870, GM.

27. Captain William H. Beck to Captain J. W. Meyers, PA, 25 March 1871; Major D. B. McKibben to Meyers, 29 March 1871, GM; Woodward to Grierson, 30 April 1871, MS343A; Louisa Semple to Alice, 10 September 1871, GP.

28. Nye, *Carbine and Lance,* p. 120; Alice to Charlie, 21 June 1870, GM.

29. John Grierson to Ben, 26 August 1870, 21 September 1870, 3 December 1870, GM.

30. I. P. Vollintine, Weatherford, Texas, to E. S. Parker, Commissioner of Indian Affairs, 19 January 1871, Kiowa Files, Depredations; Kenneth W. Porter, "Negroes and Indians on the Texas Frontier," *Southwestern Historical Quarterly,* 53 (October 1949):155–56.

31. Tatum to Grierson, 25 March 1871, Kiowa Files, Depredations; Leckie, *Buffalo Soldiers,* p. 57.

32. U.S. Congress, *Senate Miscellaneous Document,* no. 37, 42 Cong., 1st sess., pp. 1–2.

33. Extracts from Inspector General R. B. Marcy's *Journal of an Inspection Tour While Accompanying the General-in-Chief during the Months of April, May and June, 1871,* Phillips Collection, University of Oklahoma, Norman, Oklahoma. Hereafter cited as Marcy's *Journal.*

34. Nye, *Carbine and Lance,* p. 128.

35. Marcy's *Journal,* p. 191; Sherman to Mackenzie, 18 May 1871; Report of Assistant Surgeon J. N. Patzke, Letters Received, File No. 1305–1871, Records of War Department, AGO, Record Group 94, NA. Hereafter referred to as File 1305-1871; Post Returns, Fort Richardson, May 1871. Damages, other than loss of life, amounted to $29,732.50, and included 46 mules, 550 bushels of corn, 10 wagons, 5 carbines, and camp equipment.

36. Marcy's *Journal,* p. 193; Tatum, *Our Red Brothers,* p. 116; Sherman to General E. D. Townsend, Adjutant General, 24 May 1871, File 1305-1871.

37. Woodward to Officers and Ladies of Fort Sill, 26 May 1871, MS343A; Robert Grierson to Louisa Semple, 25 May 1871, GM.

38. Tatum, *Our Red Brothers,* p. 117.

39. Tatum to Grierson, 27 May 1871, Kiowa Files, Trial of Satanta and Big Tree. Four of Satanta's warriors were wounded in the attack.

40. Tatum, *Our Red Brothers,* p. 118; Marcy's *Journal,* pp. 196–97; Sherman to Townsend, 27 May 1871; Sherman to Sheridan, 29 May 1871, File 1305-1871.

41. Richard H. Pratt, "Some Indian Experiences," *Cavalry Journal* 16 (December 1906):210.

42. Sherman to Grierson, 12 June 1871; Marcy to Grierson, 6 June 1871, GM. Jacksboro, in Texas, was approximately half a mile from Fort Richardson. See Joseph H. and James R. Toulouse, *Pioneer Posts of Texas*, p. 55.

43. Nye, *Carbine and Lance*, p. 145; Grierson to the AAG, Department of the Missouri, 9 June 1871, File 1305-1871.

44. Tatum, *Our Red Brothers*, p. 121; Grierson to the AAG, Department of the Missouri, 9 June 1871, File 1305-1871; Charlie to Louisa Semple, 9 June 1871, GM.

45. Sherman to Townsend, 28 May 1871; Mackenzie to Grierson, 7 July 1871, MS343A; J. W. Wilbarger, *Indian Depredations in Texas*, p. 563; For numerous letters urging commutation see, Kiowa Files, Trial of Satanta and Big Tree.

46. Grierson to War Department of the Missouri, 21 September 1871, File 1305-1871; Mackenzie to Tatum, 31 July 1871, Kiowa Files, Military Relations.

47. Ben to John Grierson, 24 June 1871, GM.

48. Robert Grierson to Louisa Semple, 4 July 1871, GM.

49. Organizational Returns, Tenth Cavalry, June 1871; Heitman, *Historical Register* 1:807.

50. Alice to Charlie, 9 August 1871, GM.

51. Robert to Charlie, 8 September 1871; Ben to Alice, 14 August 1871, GM.

52. Grierson to the AAG, Department of the Missouri, 4 September 1871; Grierson to Sherman, 5 September 1871, MS343A; Major G. W. Schofield to the AAG, Department of the Missouri, 12 August 1871, File 1305-1871.

53. Alice to Ben, 9 September 1871; Louisa Semple to Alice, 20 September 1871, GM.

54. Alice to Ben, [20] December 1871, GP.

55. Alice to Ben, 2 November 1871, 9 December 1871, 27 December 1871, GM.

56. Olmsted, "Chicago in Distress," pp. 302–305; Stephen A. Forbes, *The Great Chicago Fire, October 8–10, 1871: Described by Eight Men and Women Who Experienced Its Horrors and Testified to the Courage of Its Inhabitants.* Introd. and Notes by Paul M. Angle, pp. 2–3; Stephen Longstreet, *Chicago, 1868–1919*, pp. 122–24.

57. Rufus Kirk to Alice, 12 October 1871, GM.

58. Charlie to Alice, 12 October 1871, GM.

59. Forbes, *The Great Chicago Fire*, p. 3.

60. Rufus Kirk to Alice, 12 October 1871, GM.

61. Ben to Alice, 16 December 1871, GM.

62. Alice to Ben, 27 October 1871, 28 October 1871, 30 October 1871, GM.

63. Alice to Ben, 2 November 1871, 27 December 1871, GM.

64. Alice to Ben, 9 December 1871, 18 December 1871, 20 December 1871, GM.

65. Louisa Semple to Alice, 22 December 1871, GP; Ben to Alice, 16 December 1871, 13 January 1872, GM.

66. Louisa Semple to Alice, 22 December 1871, GP.

67. Ben to Alice, 12 January 1872, GM; Grierson, Auto., p. 78.

68. Grierson to the AAG, Department of the Missouri, 21 September 1871, MS343A.

69. Grierson to the AAG, Department of the Missouri, 25 September 1871, MS343A, Organizational Returns, Tenth Cavalry, September 1871.

70. Quoted in Nye, *Carbine and Lance*, p. 152.

71. Leckie, *Military Conquest*, pp. 158–61.

72. Robert to Alice, 25 November 1871, Gm.

73. Ibid.

74. Alice to Ben, 13 December 1871, GM.

75. Ibid., 28 December 1871; Ben to Alice, 12 January 1872, GM.

76. Alice to Ben, 13 December 1871, 9 December 1871, GM.

77. Ben to Alice, 14 December 1871, 16 December 1871, 30 December 1871, GM.

78. Ben to Alice, 16 December 1871, 18 December 1871, 2 December 1871, GM.

79. Alice to Ben, [20] December 1871, GP. Theodore Tilton, editor of the religious journal, *The Independent*, published *Account of Mrs. Woodhull* as a Golden Age Tract in 1871. It shocked most Americans with its description of her liaison with Colonel Blood while still legally married to Woodhull and her accounts of spiritualist practices, trances, and so forth. Buried in this sensationalism, however, was a message many persons were inclined to take seriously—that love, rather than legal marriage, should form the basis of sexual union.

Following this logic, Woodhull and her sister Tennessee Claflin argued that wives should have the right to say "no" to sexual relations and that, in all cases, motherhood should be "voluntary." Other feminists, such as Elizabeth Cady Stanton, agreed whole-heartedly. See Emanie Sachs, *The Terrible Siren, Victoria Woodhull, 1838-1927*, pp. 100-107, and Gordon, *Woman's Body, Woman's Right: A Social History of Birth Control in America*, p. 104; See also Degler, *At Odds*, pp. 196-201.

80. Alice to Ben, [20] December 1871, GP. Most Americans who practiced birth control relied on coitus interruptus. With the exception of the anovulent pill, the major methods of modern contraception were available to Americans before the Civil War. See James Reed, *From Private Vice to Public Virtue: The Birth Control Movement and American Society Since 1830*, p. 10. The Medical profession disseminated such information widely throughout American society from 1831 on. See Wilson Yates, "Birth Control Literature and the Medical Profession in Nineteenth Century America," *Journal of the History of Medicine and Allied Sciences* 31 (January 1976):42-54.

Nonetheless, in the 1870s, many Americans, including feminists such as Stanton, argued for birth control but were not in favor of contraception, preferring to rely on continence, rather than "artificial" means. There was a deep-seated fear of the social consequences of separating sexuality from procreation among many nineteenth-century Americans.

81. Yates, "Birth Control Literature . . ." *Journal of the History of Medicine and Allied Sciences* 31 (January 1976):42-54. Abortion in the nineteenth century was far more common than is generally assumed. James Mohr, in his pioneering study, estimates that at midcentury, there was approximately one abortion for every five or six live births. See James Mohr, *Abortion in America: The Origins and Evolution of National Policy*, pp. 5, 254.

82. Ben to Alice, 20 December 1871, GM.

83. Ben to Alice, 27 December 1871, 30 December 1871, GM. In lamenting his lack of "peach," Ben was using slang of the time for desirable appeal, like that of the popular fruit.

84. Ben to Alice, 31 December 1871, 29 January 1872, GM. The Griersons always used the term "woman's rights" and often referred to the "woman question."

85. Ben to Alice, 30 December 1871, GM.

86. Ben to Alice, 24 January 1872, GM.

87. Ben to Alice, 3 January 1872, GM.

88. Alice to Charlie, 3 April 1872, GM.

89. Ellen Kirk Fuller to Alice, 29 March 1872, GP; Alice to Charlie, 3 April 1872, GM; Organizational Returns, Tenth Cavalry, January–February 1872; Tatum, *Our Red Brothers*, p. 132.

90. Annual Report of the Secretary of War for 1872, p. 55; Leckie, *Buffalo Soldiers*, pp. 101–102; Nye, *Carbine and Lance*, p. 152; Organizational Returns, Tenth Cavalry, March–April 1872.

91. Alice to Charlie, 18 April 1872, GP; *Annual Report of the Secretary of War for 1872*, p. 55.

92. Post Returns, Fort Sill, April 1872; Ben to Alice, 29 April 1872, GM; Ben to Alice, 5 May 1872, 12 May 1872, 20 May 1872, MS343A.

93. Carpenter to Grierson, 27 June 1872; Lieutenant Nordstrom to Grierson, 31 July 1872, MS343A; Captain T. A. Baldwin to Grierson, 15 August 1872, GM.

94. Ben to John Grierson, 16 July 1872, GM.

95. *Army and Navy Journal*, 10 (7 September 1872):52; Tatum to Jonathan Richards, 5 June 1872, 7 June 1872, Kiowa Files, Depredations; *Annual Report of the Commissioner of Indian Affairs for 1872*, p. 247.

96. *Annual Report of the Commissioner of Indian Affairs for 1872*, p. 248; James Mooney, "Calendar History of the Kiowa Indians," *Seventeenth Annual Report of the Bureau of American Ethnology, 1895–1896*, pp. 190–93. Kicking Bird succeeded in recovering the Lees. See Tatum, *Our Red Brothers*, pp. 126–27.

97. *Annual Report of the Commissioner of Indian Affairs for 1872*, p. 250; *Army and Navy Journal* 10 (26 October 1872):165.

98. Tatum, *Our Red Brothers*, pp. 132–33.

99. Ibid., p. 142.

100. Mackenzie to Tatum, 9 November 1872, Kiowa Files, Depredations; Grierson to Augur, 10 November 1872, GM; *Annual Report of the Secretary of War for 1872*, p. 35; *Annual Report of the Commissioner of Indian Affairs for 1872*, p. 248.

101. *Annual Report of the Commissioner of Indian Affairs for 1872*, p. 36; Angie Debo, *A History of the Indians of the United States*, pp. 172–73; Carolyn T. Foreman, "General Benjamin Grierson," *Chronicles of Oklahoma* 24 (Summer 1946):213–14; Alice to Charlie, 8 August 1872, GM.

102. Alice to Charlie, 12 September 1872, 16 October 1872, GM.

103. Augur is quoted in Frank Temple, "Colonel Grierson in the Southwest," *Panhandle-Plains Historical Review* 30 (1957):37; Alice to Charlie, 16 October 1872, 26 November 1872, GM.

104. John Kirk to Alice, 13 August 1872; Louisa Semple to Ben, 9 September 1872, GM; Ellen Kirk to Alice, 14 August 1872. Louisa revealed that she had heard Mrs. Bayne lecture "on the woman question" twenty years earlier. Even John Grierson thought Kirk had remarried "sorta quick." John Grierson to Ben, 18 September 1872, GM.

105. Ben to John Grierson, 30 September 1872; Alice to Charlie, 24 September 1872, GM.

106. Ellen Kirk Fuller to Alice, 27 November 1872; Tom Kirk to Alice, 27 November 1872; Charlie to Alice, 5 September 1872; Alice to Charlie, 24 September 1872, GM.

107. Quoted in William McFeeley, *Grant: A Biography*, p. 384.

108. Charlie to Alice, 7 November 1872, GM.

109. Grierson to Sherman, 22 November 1872; Sherman to Grierson, 29 November 1872, MS343A.

110. Colonel J. B. Fray, AAG, Military Division of the Missouri to General Augur, 31 December 1872, SLR, Relating to Texas, 1873, Records of the War Department, AGO, Record Group 94, NA. Hereafter referred to as SLR, Relating to Texas.

CHAPTER 8

1. Circular Headquarters, Tenth Cavalry, Fort Gibson, Indian Territory, 5 January 1873, GP; Alice to Charlie, 17 January 1873, GP.

2. John Grierson to Ben, 15 June 1873; John Kirk to Alice, 22 December 1873, GP.

3. Grierson to Grant, 27 January 1873, GM; Ben to Alice, 4 March 1873, GP.

4. John Grierson to Ben, 21 January 1873, 4 January 1874, GP.

5. Louisa Semple to Ben, 6 July 1873, 7 September 1873, GM; John Grierson to Ben, 19 August 1873, GP.

6. John Grierson to Ben, 20 September 1873, 27 October 1873, GP. Ben had actually sold the property earlier, but the new owner defaulted on it after a brief period.

7. John Grierson to Ben, 28 July 1873; Ann B. Kirk to Alice, 18 April 1873, GP.

8. John Kirk to Alice, 28 July 1873, 13 October 1873, GP.

9. Organizational Returns, Tenth Cavalry, March 1873.

10. General E. D. Townsend to Davidson, 1 April 1873, MS343A; Leckie, *Buffalo Soldiers*, p. 69.

11. Captain William Beck to Grierson, 19 January 1873, GM; Alice to Ben, 12 March 1873; Organizational Returns, Tenth Cavalry, April 1873.

12. Woodward to Grierson, 26 June 1873, 10 October 1873, GM; Beck to Grierson, 23 June 1873, MS343A.

13. Davidson to the AAG, Department of Texas, 25 July 1873; Lieutenant Colonel George Buell to the AAG, Department of Texas, 15 June 1873, SLR, Relating to Texas.

14. Woodward to Grierson, 10 October 1873, GP; *Annual Report of the Commissioner of Indian Affairs for 1873*, p. 219.

15. Woodward to Grierson, 30 November 1873, 5 December 1873, GM; Colonel W. H. Wood to the AAG, Department of Texas, 1 November 1873, SLR, Relating to Texas. Davis's conditions were: the Comanches were to surrender five recent raiders; the Kiowas and Comanches were to return all stolen stock, camp near Fort Sill, draw rations every three days, and allow agents to live among them. Woodward to Grierson, 10 October 1873, GP.

16. Lieutenant Robert Smither to Grierson, 9 March 1874, MS343A; John Grierson to Ben, 18 March 1874, GP; Robert Utley, *Frontier Regulars: The United States Army and the Indian, 1866–1890*, p. 19. A colonel's pay was $3,500 and a lieutenant's $1,400 annually.

17. Woodward to Grierson, 24 February 1874, GM; *Army and Navy Journal*, 11 (3 January 1874): 324.

18. Mooney, *Calendar History of the Kiowas*, p. 199; *Annual Report of the Commissioner of Indian Affairs for 1874*, p. 233.

19. Walter Prescott Webb, *The Texas Rangers: A Century of Frontier Defense*,

pp. 312–13; Nye, *Carbine and Lance,* pp. 195–200.

20. Sherman to Sheridan, 21 July 1874, LR, File No. 2815-1874, Records of the War Department, AGO, Record Group 94, NA. Hereafter referred to as File 2815-1874; Woodward to Grierson, 8 August 1874, GP; *Annual Report of the Commissioner of Indian Affairs for 1874,* p. 41.

21. Lieutenant Nordstrom to Grierson, 15 July 1874; Woodward to Grierson, 8 September 1874; Captain P. L. Lee to Grierson, 8 October 1874, MS343A.

22. Davidson to the AAG, Department of Texas, 10 August 1874, LR, File No. 3300-1874, Records of the War Department, AGO, Record Group 94, NA. Hereafter referred to as File 3300-1874; *Annual Report of the Commissioner of Indian Affairs for 1874,* p. 238.

23. Woodward to Grierson, 12 August 1874, GM; Pope to Sheridan, 27 July 1874, SLR, Relating to Texas.

24. Davidson to the AAG, Department of Texas, 27 August 1874, LR, File No. 3490-1874, Records of the War Department, AGO, Record Group 94, NA. Hereafter referred to as File 3490-1874; Woodward to Grierson, 3 September 1874; Lieutenant Robert Smither to Grierson, 31 August 1874, MS343A.

25. For details of Miles's movements see, Miles to the AAG, Department of the Missouri, 4 April 1875, File 3490-1874.

26. Price to the AAG, Department of the Missouri, 25 September 1874, File 2815-1874.

27. Sherman to Townsend, 13 October 1874, File 2815-1874; Leckie, *Buffalo Soldiers,* pp. 221–22.

28. Mackenzie to Augur, 8 November 1874, File 2815-1874.

29. Buell to AAG, Department of Texas, 8 November 1874, File 2815-1874; Buell to the AAG, Department of Texas, 24 February 1875, SLR, Relating to Texas.

30. Davidson to the AAG, Department of Texas, 10 October 1874, SLR, Relating to Texas.

31. Ibid.; Davidson to the AAG, Department of Texas, 23 March 1875, File 2815-1874.

32. Nye, *Carbine and Lance,* pp. 229–30; *Annual Report of the Commissioner of Indian Affairs for 1874,* pp. 268–72; Woodward to Grierson, 15 October 1874, MS343A.

33. Mackenzie to Pope, 19 April 1875, File 3490-1874; Post Returns, Fort Sill, June 1875; *Annual Report of the Commissioner of Indian Affairs for 1875,* p. 272.

34. Neill to the AAG, Department of the Missouri, 7 April 1875, SLR, AGO. Of sixteen troopers wounded, eleven were among the buffalo soldiers. See Leckie, *Buffalo Soldiers,* p. 139; Thirty-four Cheyennes were sent to Fort Marion. Of those who escaped from the sand hill, twenty-seven were killed in a fight with Sixth Cavalry troopers on Sappa Creek in Kansas. See Lieutenant Austin Henely to Major Hambright, Commanding at Fort Wallace, Kansas, 25 April 1875, File 3490-1874.

35. William D. Whipple, AAG, Military Division of the Missouri, to Grierson, 16 November 1874, MS343A; Ben to Alice, 20 December 1874, GP.

36. John Grierson to Ben, 23 November 1874, GP.

37. Degler, *At Odds,* pp. 316–17. See also Barbara Leslie Epstein, *The Politics of Domesticity: Women, Evangelism and Temperance in Nineteenth-Century America.* This author sees temperance women as "proto-feminists," and the letters of Louisa Semple suggest that in Louisa's case at least, her involvement in temperance, al-

though short-lived, heightened her latent interest in women's rights.

38. Louisa Semple to Ben, 17 April 1874, GM.

39. Louisa Semple to Ben, 8 December 1873, GM.

40. John Grierson to Ben, 22 May 1874, 7 September 1874, GP.

41. Louisa Semple to Ben, 5 October 1874, GM.

42. Robert Grierson to I. I. Hager, 21 June 1874, GP.

43. Charlie to Alice, 24 January 1874, GP.

44. Louisa Semple to Ben, 27 November 1874, GM.

45. John Grierson to Ben, 13 April 1874, 19 April 1874, GP. John maintained when it came to monetary policies the administration was "filled with imbeciles."

46. Ben to Alice, 20 December 1874; Alice to Ben, 11 January 1875, GP.

47. Ben to Alice, 22 April 1875, GM.

48. Ben to Alice, 1 May 1875, 2 May 1875, 4 May 1875, GM.

49. Medical History of Fort Concho, Records of the War Department, AGO, Record Group 94, NA; Ben to Alice, 6 May 1875, GM.

50. Ben to Alice, 4 May 1875, 8 May 1875, GM.

51. Ben to Alice, 10 June 1875, GM.

52. Grierson to the AAG, Department of Texas, 5 May 1875, SLR, Relating to Texas.

53. The AAG, Department of Texas, to Shafter, 30 June 1875, SLR, Relating to Texas.

54. Ben to Alice, 21 June 1875, GP.

55. Ben to Alice, 12 June 1875, GM.

56. John Grierson to Ben, 3 June 1875, GP.

57. Ben to Alice, 9 July 1875, MS343A. Grierson was not the only army officer who disliked and distrusted Sheridan. See Utley, *Frontier Regulars*, pp. 33–34.

58. Ben to Alice, 8 July 1875, 25 June 1875, GM.

59. Alice to Ben, 6 July 1875, GM.

60. Alice to Ben, 24 July 1875, GP.

61. George to Ben, 4 June 1875, GP.

62. Ben to Alice, 14 July 1875, 5 September 1876, 8 May 1875, 16 July 1875, GM.

63. Ben to Alice, 1 August 1875, GM; Alice to Robert, 5 September 1875, GP.

64. John Grierson to Ben, 19 October 1875, GP.

65. Alice to Charlie, 10 December 1875, GP.

66. Shafter to the AAG, Department of Texas, 4 January 1876, SLR, Relating to Texas.

67. *Annual Report of the Secretary of War for 1876*, p. 26; Ben to Alice, 22 June 1875, MS343A.

68. The AG to Commanding General, Department of Texas, 10 March 1876, Letters Received, Affairs on the Río Grande and Texas Frontier, 1875–81, File No. 1653, Records of the War Department, AGO, Record Group 94, NA. Hereafter referred to as File 1653; *Annual Report of the Secretary of War for 1876*, p. 493.

69. Colonel George L. Andrews, Twenty-Fifth Infantry to the AAG, Department of Texas, 21 December 1876; Shafter to the AAG, Department of Texas, 3 August 1876, File 1653. For an account of the services of the Seminole-Negro scouts see, Kenneth W. Porter, "The Seminole Negro Indian Scouts, 1870–1881," *Southwestern Historical Quarterly* 45 (January 1952): 370.

70. Organizational Returns, Tenth Cavalry, July–November 1876.

71. Leckie, *Buffalo Soldiers*, p. 150; *Army and Navy Journal* 13 (11 March 1876): 502; Ord to Grierson, no date, GP.

72. Ben to Alice, 20 August 1876; Woodward to Grierson, 23 September 1876, GM; Correspondence, AG, Document File, 1876, Records of the War Department, AGO, Record Group 94, NA. Hereafter referred to as Correspondence, AG, Document File, 1876.

73. Alice to Ben, 27 August 1876, 5 September 1876, GP; For information on the Centennial, see Oliver W. Larkin, *Art and Life in America*, pp. 241–42.

74. Charlie to Alice, 5 September 1876, GP; Alice to Ben, 7 September 1876, GM.

75. John Grierson to Ben, 6 November 1876, GP.

76. Alice to Ben, 7 September 1876, 7 October 1876, 15 October 1876, GP.

77. Alice to Ben, 9 November 1876, GP.

78. Alice to Charlie, 6 December 1876, GM; Alice to Robert, 28 December 1876, GP.

79. John Grierson to Ben, 8 March 1877, GP.

80. Organizational Returns, Tenth Cavalry, January–June 1877; U.S. Congress, *House Executive Document*, No. 13, 45th Cong., 1st sess., 1877, pp. 14–15; J. W. Foster to William Evarts, Secretary of State, 28 May 1877; Sheridan to Townsend, 12 June 1877, File 1653.

81. Ben to Alice, 31 July 1877, GP.

82. Utley's *Frontier Regulars*, pp. 351–55, gives an excellent summary of the Río Grande troubles between 1877 and 1880.

83. Organizational Returns, Tenth Cavalry, May–June 1877; Ord to Townsend, 12 July 1877, File 1653.

84. Organizational Returns, Tenth Cavalry, May 1877.

85. Robert to Alice, 11 April 1877, 18 April 1877, 19 April 1877; John Kirk to Alice, 27 April 1877; John Grierson to Ben, 7 February 1877, GP.

86. Robert to Alice, 29 April 1877, GP. Louisa did not ease the Griersons' concerns when she wrote that Robert was afraid of losing his mind. Louisa Semple to Ben, 6 June 1877, GP.

87. Alice to Charlie, 24 December 1876, 18 January 1877, GP. Two years earlier, when Charlie had placed twenty-ninth in a class of fifty-five, Alice had warned him, "You would not like I suppose to be an infantry officer. . . ." Alice to Charlie, 14 January 1875, GP.

88. Charlie to John Grierson, 22 June 1877, GM; Charlie to Alice, 1 July 1877, GP.

89. Alice to Ben, 10 July 1877, Ben to Alice, 12 July 1877, GM.

90. Ben to Alice, 14 July 1877, 17 July 1877, GM; John Kirk to Alice, 17 October 1877, GP. John Kirk was stating a very common view of mental illness. Barbara Sickerman, writing in *The Quest for Mental Health in America, 1880–1917*, p. 155, notes that in the nineteenth century, "psychiatrists and neurologists agreed that insanity was a disease of the brain, or a symptom of such disorder. Mental derangement was the sign of a nervous system which had been subjected to too much strain."

91. Ben to Alice, 20 July 1877, GM; Alice to Ben, 24 July 1877, GP.

92. Alice to Ben, 10 July 1877, GP.

93. Nolan to the AAG, Department of Texas, 20 August 1877, SLR, Relating to Texas.

94. Nolan to the AAG, Department of Texas, 20 August 1877, SLR, Relating to Texas. Late in the day the hunters found water to the northeast.

95. Ibid.

96. Ibid.

97. Ibid.

98. Ben to Alice, 10 August 1877; Alice to Ben, 11 August 1877; Ben to Alice, 13 August 1877; Alice to Ben, 16 August 1877, GP.

99. Ben to Alice, 15 August 1877, 17 August 1877, 31 August 1877, GP.

100. Alice to Ben, 16 August 1877, GP; John Grierson to Alice, 11 September 1877, GP.

101. Helen Fuller to Robert, 1 April 1877; Harry to Robert, 1 April 1877, GM. Joseph F. Kett points out that hard physical labor in the out-of-doors, was the prescription for mental disorders due to precocity or studying too hard. See Joseph F. Kett, "Curing the Disease of Precocity," in *Turning Points: Historical and Sociological Essays on the Family*, pp. S183–S211. Edited by John Demos and Savane Boocock.

102. Susan Miles, "Fort Concho in 1877," *West Texas Historical Yearbook* 35 (October 1969):49.

103. J. Evetts Haley, *Fort Concho and the Texas Frontier*, p. 274.

104. Leckie, *Buffalo Soldiers*, p. 164.

105. Alice to Charlie, 4 February 1877; Alice to Robert, 11 February 1877, GM; Miles, "Fort Concho in 1877," p. 29; Ben to Alice, 20 July 1877, GP.

CHAPTER 9

1. Organizational Returns, Tenth Cavalry, January–June 1878; Sheriff, Brady County, Texas to General Grierson, 18 January 1878, GP; *Army and Navy Journal* 15 (4 May 1878): 4; Captain L. H. Carpenter to PA, Fort Davis, Texas, 24 July 1878; Ord to the AG, Military Division of the Missouri, 21 April 1878, LR, AGO, 1878.

2. Grierson to the AAG, Department of Texas, 8 March 1878, MS343A; Ord to the AG, Military Division of the Missouri, 30 April 1878, LR, AGO, 1878.

3. Grierson to the AAG, Department of Texas, 20 April 1878, LR, AGO, 1878.

4. Ben to Alice, 19 May 1878, GM.

5. Grierson to the AAG, Department of Texas, 25 May 1878, LR, AGO, 1878; Ben to Alice, 25 May 1878, MS343A.

6. Ben to Alice, 29 May 1878, MS343A; Robert Grierson, "A Climb Up Guadalupe Peak," June 1878, GM.

7. Organizational Returns, Tenth Cavalry, June 1878.

8. Alice to Ben, 24 May 1878, 30 May 1878; Louisa Semple to Alice, 14 June 1878, GM. Louisa suggested that the Griersons hook up a microphone to a telephone so that she could listen to the wedding ceremony in Jacksonville. They were unable to oblige. William Davis, Jr., a native of Indiana, was appointed as first lieutenant in the First Missouri Cavalry on June 7, 1862. He joined the Tenth Cavalry as a second lieutenant in August, 1867, and was promoted to first lieutenant and then captain in March, 1873, and May, 1888, respectively. He retired November 6, 1897. See Heitman, *Historical Register* 1:360.

9. File, Ancestry and Children, GM; Susan Miles, "Edith Clare Grierson, 1865–1878," *Fort Concho Report* 10 (Winter 1978): 4–8; Robert to Ben and Alice, 18 September 1878, GM.

10. Miles, "Edith Clare Grierson," pp. 6–7. Miles noted that many years later an old friend of Grierson's, Assistant Surgeon S.L.S. Smith, fearful that the grave would be lost, wrote Ben, then residing in Michigan, asking for permission to move Edie's remains to a site in the doctor's own cemetery plot. Ben agreed, and today (1984) Edie's grave is in the Fairmont Cemetery in San Angelo, Texas.

11. Ben to Alice, 21 October 1878, MS343A; Grierson to the AAG, Department of Texas, 28 December 1878, File 1653.

12. Alice to Ben, 12 November 1878, GP; Ben to Alice, 26 October 1878, GM.

13. Grierson to the AAG, Department of Texas, 28 December 1878, File 1653; Alice to Charlie, 19 November 1878, GP.

14. Grierson to the AAG, Department of Texas, 28 December 1878, File 1653.

15. Thomas M. Vincent, AAG, Department of Texas, to Grierson, 20 March 1879, MS343A.

16. Ben to Alice, 15 April 1879, 19 April 1879, GP; Ben to Alice, 17 April 1879, GM.

17. Ben to Alice, 13 April 1879, 3 May 1879, GM; Alice to Ben, 18 July 1879, GP.

18. Robert to Alice, 24 November 1878, 19 January 1879, 26 February 1879, GP.

19. Louisa Semple to Ben and Alice, 20 October 1878, 11 November 1878, GP. Robert gave every evidence of being what nineteenth-century physicians and educators referred to as a "precocious" child. The common view was that such children were often unstable, indeed, the brighter the child, the theory went, the greater the tendency towards insanity. Thus Robert, who was more gifted than Charlie, would have aroused greater anxiety in his parents. See Kett, "Curing the Disease of Precocity," p. S185.

20. Alice to Charlie, 17 May 1879, GP; Alice to Ben, 29 August 1879, 22 October 1879; Ben to Alice, 18 September 1879, GM.

21. Dr. S.L.S. Smith to his father, 19 September 1879, GP. Grierson's rank was colonel, but it was not unusual for officers to be addressed at the rank held at the end of the Civil War. Thus Woodward, a first lieutenant, was commonly referred to as "Major" Woodward. Custer, a lieutenant colonel, was normally called "General."

22. Captain D. D. Van Valzah to the AAG, Department of Texas, 27 August 1879, LR, AGO, 1879.

23. Grierson to the AAG, Department of Texas, 29 August 1879, File 1653; Ben to Alice, 31 August 1879, MS343A.

24. For one such report, see Grierson to the AAG, Department of Texas, 22 September 1879, MS343A.

25. Ben to Alice, 7 September 1879, GM.

26. Thomas M. Vincent, AAG, Department of Texas to Commanding Officer, District of the Pecos, 11 February 1880, Appointment, Commission and Personal Branch, Records of the War Department, AGO, Record Group 94, NA. Hereafter cited as Appointment, Commission and Personal Branch, AGO.

27. Organizational Returns, Tenth Cavalry, October–December 1979; Alice to Robert, 27 December 1879.

28. Sheridan to Ord, 12 December 1879, File 1653.

29. *Annual Report of the Commissioner of Indian Affairs for 1877*, pp. 34–35; Orga-

nizational Returns, Ninth Cavalry, September 1877. For details of Victorio's final breakout see Dan L. Thrapp, *Victorio and the Mimbres Apaches,* pp. 218–45.

30. *Annual Report of the Secretary of War for 1880* 1, pt. 2, 88; Pope to the AAG, Military Division of the Missouri, 24 September 1879, LR, Selected Documents Relating to the Activities of the Ninth and Tenth Cavalry in the Campaign Against Victorio, 1879–80, File no. 6058-1879-80, Records of the War Department, AGO, Record Group 94, NA. Hereafter referred to as File 6058-1879-80.

31. Sherman to Townsend, 26 May 1880, File 6058-1879-80.

32. Grierson to the AAG, Department of Texas, 21 May 1880, File 6058-1879-80; Ben to Alice, 14 April 1880, MS343A.

33. Grierson to the AAG, Department of Texas, 21 May 1880, File 6058-1879-80.

34. Ibid.

35. Ibid.

36. Ibid.; Ben to Alice, 17 April 1880, MS343A.

37. Grierson to the AAG, Department of Texas, 21 May 1880, File 6058-1879-80.

38. Grierson to Hatch, 29 May 1880; Grierson to the AAG, Department of Texas, 2 June 1880; William D. Whipple, AAG, Military Division of the Missouri, to Ord, 11 June 1880, all Military Division of the Missouri, Special File, Victorio Papers, 1880, Records of the United States Army Commands, RG 98, NA. Hereafter cited as Victorio Papers.

39. Grierson to the AAG, Department of Texas, 18 May 1880, SLR, Relating to Texas, 1880.

40. Lieutenant Robert Read to the PA, Fort Davis, Texas, 25 June 1880, LR, AGO, 1880.

41. Alice to Ben, 6 August 1880, GM.

42. Robert K. Grierson, *Journal Kept on the Victorio Campaign in 1880,* Fort Davis National Historic Site, Fort Davis, Texas, pp. 4–5. Hereafter cited as *Journal, Victorio Campaign.*

43. Grierson to Ord, 24 July 1880, File 6058-1879-80; Grierson to Pope, 24 July 1880, Victorio Papers.

44. R. K. Grierson, *Journal, Victorio Campaign,* p. 11; *Annual Report of the Secretary of War for 1880* 1, pt. 2, 159.

45. R. K. Grierson, *Journal, Victorio Campaign,* p. 13.

46. Henry O. Flipper, *Negro Frontiersman,* p. 16. Flipper was well acquainted with Charlie, whom he had met at West Point. After graduation in 1878, Flipper was assigned to Company A, Tenth Cavalry.

47. R. K. Grierson, *Journal, Victorio Campaign,* p. 14.

48. Grierson to Ord, 30 July 1880, File 6058-1879-80.

49. *Annual Report of the Secretary of War for 1880* 1, pt. 2, 160; R. K. Grierson, *Journal, Victorio Campaign,* p. 14.

50. R. K. Grierson, *Journal, Victorio Campaign,* p. 14.

51. Ibid., p. 15.

52. Ibid.; Grierson to Ord, 30 July 1880, File 6058-1879-80.

53. Grierson to Ord, 3 August 1880, File 6058-1879-80.

54. Grierson to Ord, 4 August 1880,Victorio Papers.

55. R. K. Grierson, *Journal, Victorio Campaign,* p. 22.

56. Ibid.; Robert to Bessie ———, 18 October 1880, MS343A.

57. *Annual Report of the Secretary of War for 1880* 1, pt. 2, 161–62.

58. Organizational Returns, Tenth Cavalry, August 1880.

59. Grierson to the AAG, Department of Texas, 14 August 1880; Commanding Officer, Fort Bliss, Texas to Hatch, 18 August 1880, Victorio Papers.

60. Grierson to the AAG, Department of Texas, 2 September 1880, Victorio Papers.

61. Colonel Terrazas to Colonel Buell, 22 October 1880, File 6058-1879-80.

62. Organizational Returns, Tenth Cavalry, October–November 1880.

63. Grierson to Sherman, 20 December 1880, GM.

64. *Brief Record of General Grierson's Services*, Appointment, Commission and Personal Branch, AGO.

65. *San Antonio Express*, 18 August 1880.

66. Alex E. Sweet and J. Armoy Knox, *On a Mexican Mustang Through Texas*, p. 525.

67. James B. Gillett, *Six Years with the Texas Rangers, 1875–1881*, pp. 252–53; Grierson to the AAG, Department of Texas, 19 August 1880, Victorio Papers.

68. Sherman to Grierson, 4 January 1881, MS343A; Robert to Alice, 25 April 1881, GP.

69. John Grierson to Ben, 6 February 1881, 9 February 1881, GP.

70. John Grierson to Ben, 22 November 1880, GP.

71. John Kirk to Alice, 25 March 1880, 14 October 1880; Mary Kirk to Alice, 28 November 1880, GP.

72. John Grierson to Ben, 6 October 1880; Mary Kirk to Ben and Alice, 1 February 1881; Louisa Semple to Alice, 14 February 1881, GP.

73. *San Antonio Enterprise*, 8 May 1880; Henry Clay Burke to the Secretary of War, 23 February 1880, LR, AGO, 1880.

74. Grierson to the AAG, Washington, D.C., 12 January 1880, LR, AGO, 1880; Grierson to the Honorable James N. Tyner, Acting Postmaster General, 18 September 1879, MS343A.

75. For details on the resolution of the "war," see Susan Miles, "The Post Office War," *Fort Concho Report* 12 (Spring 1980): 5–13.

76. Susan Miles, "The Soldiers' Riot," *Fort Concho Report* 13 (Spring 1981): 1.

77. Miles, "Riot," pp. 5–6; Organizational Returns, Tenth Cavalry, January 1881.

78. Miles, "Riot," pp. 9–10.

79. *Galveston News*, 2 February 1881.

80. *San Saba News*, 12 February 1881.

81. Miles, "Riot," p. 13; Grierson to the AAG, Department of Texas, 8 February 1881, LR, AGO.

82. *San Saba News*, 12 February 1881.

83. Miles, "Riot," p. 16.

84. Grierson to the AAG, Department of Texas, 8 February 1881, LR, AGO; Miles, "Riot," p. 16.

85. Ibid., p. 17.

86. Ibid., p. 19.

87. Organizational Returns, Tenth Cavalry, April–November 1881; *Fort Griffin Echo*, 21 May 1881, 12 November 1881. Mills, a native of Indiana, attended West Point but did not graduate. When the Civil War came, he enlisted as a first lieutenant and rose to the rank of captain in the Eighteenth Indiana Infantry. He

remained in the service and joined the Tenth Cavalry with the rank of major in April, 1878. He transferred to the Fourth Cavalry as the lieutenant colonel in March 1890. See Heitman, *Historical Register* 1:713.

88. Major General W. S. Hancock to Grierson, 24 May 1881, GP; Brigadier General Nelson A. Miles to Grierson, 20 April 1881, GP; Miles, "Riot," p. 3.

89. Alice to Ben, 3 July 1881; Robert to Alice, 30 September 1881; Louisa Semple to Ben, 31 July 1881; Mary Kirk to Alice, 16 October 1881, GP.

90. Organizational Returns, Tenth Cavalry, November 1881; Nolan to Mr. R. N. Price, 4 September 1879, GP.

91. Grierson to Whom It May Concern, 1 November 1881, MS343A.

92. Grierson to the AAG, Department of Texas, 5 April 1882, MS343A.

CHAPTER 10

1. Robert to Alice, 3 January 1882; Statement to Robert Grierson, Grand Pacific Hotel, Chicago, Illinois, 14 January 1882; Ellen Kirk Fuller to Alice, 27 January 1882, GP; *El Paso Herald,* 1 February 1882.

2. Ellen Kirk Fuller to Alice, 27 January 1882; Louisa Semple to Alice, 1 February 1882, GP.

3. Robert to Alice, 21 December 1881, GP.

4. Louisa Fuller to Alice, 20 January 1882; John Kirk to Alice, 4 February 1882; Ellen Kirk Fuller to Alice, 19 February 1882, 2 April 1882, GP.

5. Louisa Semple to Ben, 13 February 1882, GP.

6. Mary Kirk to Alice, 19 February 1882; John Kirk to Alice, 27 March 1882, GP.

7. Alice to Charlie, 27 April 1882, GM; Louisa Semple to Ben, 30 April 1882, GP.

8. Alice to Ben, 9 May 1882, 10 May 1882, 17 May 1882; Louisa Semple to Ben, 11 June 1882, GP.

9. Ben to Alice, 16 May 1882, 20 May 1882, GM.

10. Ben to Alice, 17 May 1882, GM.

11. Ben to Alice, 18 May 1882, GM.

12. Alice to Ben, 24 May 1882, GP.

13. Ben to Alice, 13 June 1882, GM.

14. Ellen Kirk Fuller to Alice, 7 June 1882, GP; Ben to Alice, 8 June 1882, 18 June 1882, GM; Alice to Harry Grierson, 21 September 1882, GP.

15. Mills to Grierson, 1 October 1882; Woodward to Grierson, 10 October 1882; Charlie to Alice, 6 August 1882, GP.

16. Harry to Ben, 15 October 1882, GP.

17. Flipper, *Negro Frontiersman,* p. 20; Organizational Returns, Tenth Cavalry, June 1882. For details of Flipper's case, see Army Board for Correction of Military Records, NNM 372-2, Records of the War Department, AGO, Record Group 94, NA.

18. Warranty Deed, State of Iowa, Crawford County, 29 July 1882; Ben to Charlie, 26 December 1882, GP.

19. Ben to Charlie, 31 October 1882; Louisa Fuller to Alice, 11 December 1882; John Grierson to Ben, 10 October 1882, 4 November 1882, GP.

20. Louisa Semple to Ben, 5 November 1883, GP.

21. Ben to M. P. Ayres, 3 December 1885, GP.

22. Robert to Alice, 30 November 1884, GP.

23. Miscellaneous File, 5 March 1883, GP.

24. Grierson to the AG, U.S. Army, 30 July 1883, LS, Tenth Cavalry; Sherman to Grierson, 28 December 1883, GM.

25. Horace P. Jones to Grierson, 15 August 1883, MS343A.

26. Special Orders No. 210, AG, U.S. Army, AGO, 13 September 1883, MS343A; Augur to Grierson, 22 September 1883, GM; Ben to Alice, 26 September 1883, GM.

27. Alice to Robert, 2 November 1883; Regimental Treasurer, Statement, 15 December 1883, GP.

28. John Kirk to Ben, 24 October 1884, GP.

29. Alice to George, 6 November 1884; Ben to Charlie, 16 November 1884; George to Alice, 27 November 1884, 30 October 1884, GP.

30. Ben to Alice, 3 December 1884, GM; Ben to Charlie, 4 December 1884, GP.

31. Grierson, Auto., pp. 200-201.

32. Ben to John Grierson, 2 February 1885, 1 March 1885; Robert to Alice, 15 February 1885, 23 February 1885, 5 May 1885, GP.

33. General Orders No. 4, Headquarters, Division of the Pacific, 5 March 1885, GM; Organizational Returns, Tenth Cavalry, March 1885.

34. John Kirk to Alice, 23 February 1885, GP.

35. Helen Davis, "An Account of a 10th Cavalry March with General B. H. Grierson from Ft. Davis to Ft. Grant, April 1885," Manuscript in GM.

36. Ibid.

37. Ibid.; Ben to Alice, 10 April 1885, GM.

38. Ben to Charlie, 17 May 1885, GP. For a comprehensive study of Pope's views on Indian policy see Richard N. Ellis, *General Pope and U.S. Indian Policy.*

39. Ben to Alice, 24 May 1885, MS343A; Ben to Alice, 31 May 1885, 5 June 1885, GM; Ben to Charlie, 24 May 1885, 15 June 1885, GP. For an account of Crook's campaign, see John G. Bourke, *On the Border with Crook.*

40. Ben to Alice, 31 May 1885, GM.

41. Ben to Alice, 12 June 1885, GM.

42. Ben to Charlie, 4 July 1885; Charlie to Alice, 22 June 1885, GP; Helen Davis to Alice, 26 May 1885, GM.

43. Anson Mills, *My Story,* p. 189.

44. Ibid.; Organizational Returns, Tenth Cavalry, May-July 1885; Ben to Charlie, 7 September 1885, 10 October 1885, GP.

45. Robert to Ben, 12 June 1885; Robert to Alice, 7 June 1885, 17 June 1885, 22 June 1885, GP.

46. Robert to Alice, 5 August 1885, GP.

47. Ben to Charlie, 10 October 1885, GP.

48. Martin F. Schmitt, ed., *General George Crook: His Autobiography,* p. 134.

49. Alice to Charlie, 15 December 1885, GM; Robert to Alice, 29 March 1886, 4 April 1886, GP.

50. *Annual Report of the Secretary of War for 1886* 1:9-12; Report of General Crook in *Annual Report of the Secretary of War for 1886* 1:147-52.

51. *Annual Report of the Secretary of War for 1886,* 1:169; Organizational Returns, Tenth Cavalry, September 1886.

52. Organizational Returns, Tenth Cavalry, September 1886; Louisa Semple to

Ben, 26 September 1886, GP.

53. M. Barber, AAG, Department of Arizona to Commanding Officer, Fort Mojave, 4 June 1886, MS343A; Ben to Charlie, 20 June 1886, GP.

54. Special Orders, No. 5, Headquarters, Department of Arizona, 30 June 1886; Special Orders No. 35, 6 November 1886, Brief Record of General Grierson's Services, Appointment, Commission and Personal Branch, AGO; Organizational Returns, Tenth Cavalry, July–November 1886.

55. George to Alice, 14 November 1886; Alice to Ben, 16 November 1886, GP.

56. Alice to Ben, 19 November 1886, GP.

57. Alice to Charlie, 5 December 1886, GM.

58. Alice to Charlie, 12 September 1886, GM; Louisa Semple to Ben, 25 September 1886; Charlie to Alice, 15 October 1886, GP.

59. Robert to Alice, 24 May 1886, GP.

60. Robert to Alice, 27 August 1886, 14 October 1886, GP.

61. John Kirk to Ben, 21 December 1886, John Grierson to Ben, 6 February 1885, 30 September 1886, GP; Alice to Charlie, 10 November 1886, GM.

62. John Grierson to Ben, 30 June 1886, GP.

63. Louisa Semple to Ben, 11 April 1886; Ellen Kirk Fuller to Alice, 23 December 1886, GP.

64. W. W. Bissell to Grierson, 2 September 1887; Ben to John Grierson, 4 November 1887, GP.

65. Alice to Charlie, 12 February 1887, GM; C. Meyer Zulick to Grierson, 15 March 1887, MS343A.

66. Miles to Grierson, 2 November 1886; J.D.C. Atkins to Register and Receiver, Santa Fe, New Mexico, 26 February 1887, MS343A; *Annual Report of the Commissioner of Indian Affairs for 1887,* p. lxxii.

67. *Annual Report of the Commissioner of Indian Affairs for 1887,* p. lxxiv.

68. Grierson to the AAG, Department of Arizona, 10 August 1888, GM; William B. Chandler, Clerk in Charge, Jicarilla Agency, 18 October 1887, MS343A.

69. *Annual Report of the District of New Mexico, 1888,* GP.

70. John Grierson to Ben, 8 February 1887, GP; Major General John M. Schofield to the AG, U.S.A., 1 November 1886, GP.

71. Robert to Alice, 8 March 1887, 11 August 1887, GP.

72. George to Alice, 14 January 1887, 24 February 1887, 25 April 1887, 18 June 1887, GP.

73. Alice to Charlie, 26 June 1887, GM; Robert to Alice, 29 August 1887; Harry to Ben, 19 September 1887, GP.

74. Mary Kirk to Alice, 30 January 1887, GM; Ellen Kirk Fuller to Alice, 12 May 1887; Dr. W .S. Harroun to Dr. [Strong], 25 May 1887, GP.

75. Ellen Kirk Fuller to Alice, 29 August 1887, 7 December 1887, 18 February 1888, GP.

76. Alice to Charlie, 2 June 1887, 13 June 1887, GM; Ellen Kirk Fuller to Alice, 10 April 1887, 24 June 1887, 22 October 1887, 16 November 1887, 1 July 1888; Helen Davis to Alice, 29 June 1887, GP.

77. Louisa Semple to Ben, 6 March 1887; Mary Kirk to Alice, 30 January 1887, GP.

78. Orders No. 57, Headquarters, Tenth Cavalry, 26 September 1887, MS343A; Charlie to Robert, 12 October 1887, GP; Miles to Grierson, 10 December 1887, GM.

79. Alice to Charlie, 10 June 1888, 17 June 1888, GP.

80. Ben to Charlie, 13 June 1888; Ben to Alice, 8 July 1888, GM.

81. Sadie Morley to Ben, 2 July 1888, 10 July 1888; John Kirk to Charlie, 23 July 1888, GP.

82. Ellen Kirk Fuller to Charlie, 27 July 1888, GP.

83. Ben to Alice, 27 July 1888, GM.

84. Louisa Semple to Ben, 8 August 1888, GP.

85. Ben to Charlie, 13 August 1888; Sadie Morley to Charlie, 13 August 1888, GP.

86. Ann Bayne Kirk to Charlie, 11 October 1888; Robert to Charlie, 17 August 1888, GP.

87. Harry to Ben, 5 October 1888; Robert to Charlie, 19 October 1888, GP.

88. Quoted in Major E. N. Glass, *The History of the Tenth Cavalry, 1866–1921*, p. 28.

89. Grierson to Woodward, 4 January 1889, GP; "Roster," Department of Arizona in *Annual Report of the Department of Arizona for 1889*, GM.

90. *Annual Report of Colonel B. H. Grierson, Department of Arizona, 1889*, GM.

91. Ibid.; Ray Brandes, *Frontier Military Posts of Arizona*, pp. 68–69.

92. *Annual Report of Colonel B. H. Grierson, Department of Arizona, 1889*, GM.

93. Ibid.

94. Ibid.

95. Ibid.

96. Louisa Semple to Ben, 16 May 1889; Ben to Robert, 20 November 1889, GP.

97. John Grierson to Ben, 17 May 1889, 22 November 1889, GP.

98. Louisa Semple to Ben, 17 November 1889; John Grierson to Ben, 16 October 1889, GP.

99. Louisa Semple to Ben, 5 February 1890, 21 March 1890, GP.

100. Heitman, *Historical Register* 1:478.

101. Second National Bank of Santa Fe to Grierson, 5 April 1890; G. C. Pierson, A. M. Grunsfeld and P. L. Vandever to Grierson, 5 April 1890, GP.

102. *Annual Report of Desertions*, Department of Arizona, 1889, MS343A.

Epilogue

1. John Gano, Dallas, Texas to Grierson, 5 August 1891, GP.

2. Ben to Charlie, 8 February 1891, 4 August 1894, GP.

3. Ben to Charlie, 7 October 1894; George to Charlie, 21 March 1895; Ben to Charlie, 7 June 1896; Harry to Charlie, 3 September 1896; William L. Wilson to B. H. Grierson, Jr. (Harry), 23 July 1923, GP.

4. Louisa Semple to Charlie, 23 October 1890, 8 August 1892; Ben to Charlie, 10 September 1892, GP.

5. Heitman, *Historical Register* 1:478.

6. Louisa Semple to Charlie, 1 August 1897, GP.

7. Ben to Charlie, 20 January 1897, GP.

8. Lillian King Grierson to Charlie, 2 June 1907, GP.

9. Lillian King Grierson to Charlie, 22 August 1908, 8 February 1909, 8 August 1911, GP.

10. *Jacksonville Daily Journal*, 2 September 1911; *Daily Illinois Courier*, 5 Sep-

tember 1911, GP.

11. Harry to Charlie, 25 March 1910; W. C. Veitch, Investment Broker, Jacksonville, Illinois, Memorandum, 2 March 1911, GP.

12. Alice Kirk Grierson to William H. Leckie, 27 April 1977.

13. Mrs. Charles Grierson to CO, Letterman General Hospital, 14 April 1915, GP; Alice Kirk Grierson, Los Angeles, California, interviewed by William H. Leckie, 16 February 1977.

14. "Some Grierson Connections," Benjamin H. Grierson Papers, Fort Davis National Historic Site, Fort Davis, Texas.

Bibliography

I. Manuscript Materials

A. *National Archives, Washington, D.C.*
1. Records of the Office of Indian Affairs
    a. Letters Received by the Office of Indian Affairs, Kiowa Agency, 1864–1880.
2. Records of the War Department, Adjutant General's Office, Record Group 94
    a. Appointment, Commission and Personal Branch, File No. G553 C.B. 1865, B. H. Grierson.
    b. Annual Report of the Department of Texas, 1869–1883.
    c. Medical History of Posts.
    d. Letters Received, 1862–1889.
    e. Selected Documents from Letters Received, 1869–1890.
    f. Selected Letters Received Relating to the Tenth Regiment, United States Cavalry.
    g. Organizational Returns, Tenth Cavalry, 1866–1888.
    h. Post Returns.
        1) Fort Concho   5) Fort Richardson
        2) Fort Davis   6) Fort Sill
        3) Fort Grant   7) Fort Stockton
        4) Fort Griffin
    i. Letters Received, File Nos. 1305-1871, 1653-1875-81, 2815-1874, 3144-1874, 3300-1874, 3490-1874, 4447-1873.
    j. Selected Documents and Letters Received Relating to the Activities of the Ninth and Tenth Cavalry in the Campaign Against Victorio, 1879–80, File 6058-1879-80.
    k. Army Board for Correction of Military Records, NNM 372-2.
3. Records of United States Army Commands, Record Group 98
    a. Letters Sent, Tenth United States Cavalry, 1866–1888.
    b. Letters Sent, Department of Texas, 1875–1885.
    c. Letters Sent, District of New Mexico, 1886–1888.

d. Military Division of the Missouri, Special File, Victorio Papers, 1880.

B. *Illinois State Historical Library, Springfield, Illinois*

1. Grierson, Benjamin H. Record of Service Rendered the Government 1863 [Fort Concho, Texas]. Privately printed.
2. Grierson, Brigadier General Benjamin H. "The Lights and Shadows of Life, Including Experiences and Remembrances of the War of the Rebellion." Typescript autobiography.
3. Grierson, Robert. "A Climb Up Guadalupe Peak." Manuscript in The Benjamin H. Grierson Papers, Illinois State Historical Library.
4. The Papers of Benjamin H. Grierson.

C. *Texas Technological University, Lubbock, Texas, Southwest Collection*

1. Benjamin H. Grierson Papers, 1827–1941.
2. Grierson, Benjamin. Letters and Documents, Edward Ayer Collection. MS343A. Newberry Library, Chicago, Illinois. Two rolls, microcopy deposited at Texas Technological University.

D. *Fort Davis National Historic Site, Fort Davis, Texas*

1. Benjamin H. Grierson Papers.
2. Grierson, Robert K. *Journal Kept on the Victorio Campaign in 1880.* Fort Davis National Historic Site, Fort Davis, Texas.

E. *Oklahoma Historical Society, Oklahoma City, Oklahoma*

1. Indian Archives Division
   a. Kiowa Files.
      1) Agents and Agency.   3) Military Relations.
      2) Depredations.   4) Trial of Satanta and Big Tree.

F. *The University of Oklahoma, Norman, Oklahoma, Manuscripts Division*

1. Extracts from Inspector General R. B. Marcy's *Journal of an Inspection Tour While Accompanying the General in Chief During the Months of April, May, and June, 1871.* University of Oklahoma copy.

2. The Sherman-Sheridan Papers. University of Oklahoma transcript.

II. Government Publications

A. *Federal*

Annual Report of the Board of Indian Commissioners, 1869–75.
Annual Report of the Commissioners of Indian Affairs, 1866–90.
Annual Report of the Secretary of Interior, 1869–90.
Annual Report of the Secretary of War, 1861–90.
Heitman, Francis B. *Historical Register and Dictionary of the United States Army*, 2 vols. Washington, D.C.: Government Printing Office, 1903.
Hodge, Frederick W. *Handbook of American Indians North of Mexico*, 2 vols. Bureau of American Ethnology *Bulletin 30*. Washington, D.C.: Government Printing Office, 1912.
Kappler, Charles J. *Indian Affairs: Laws and Treaties*, 2 vols. Washington, D.C.: Government Printing Office, 1903.
Mooney, James. "Calendar History of the Kiowa Indians," *Seventeenth Annual Report of the Bureau of American Ethnology, 1895–1896.* Washington, D.C.: Government Printing Office, 1898.
United States Army, Military Division of the Missouri, *Record of Engagements With Hostile Indians Within the Military Division of the Missouri from 1868–1882.* Washington, D.C.: Government Printing Office, 1882.
United States Congress, House of Representatives, *H.R. No. 30*, 39 Cong., 1 sess., 1866, Report of the Joint Committee on Reconstruction.
——. *H.R. Misc. Doc. No. 142*, 41 Cong., 2 sess., Vol. 3, 1869, Indian Depredations in Texas.
——. *H.R. Exec. Doc. No. 228*, 41 Cong., 2 sess., Vol. 7, 1870, Sites of military posts in Texas.
United States Congress, House of Representatives, *H.R. Exec. Doc. No. 257*, 43 Cong., 1 sess., 1872, Depredations by Indians.
——. *H.R. Exec. Doc. No. 275*, 43 Cong., 1 sess., Vol. 2, 1874, Depredations on the Texas frontier.
——. *H.R. No. 343*, 44 Cong., 1 sess., 1875, Affairs on the Río Grande.
——. *H.R. No. 354*, 44 Cong., 1 sess., Vol. 2, 1876, Reduction of officer's pay, reorganization of the army, and transfer of the Indian Bureau.
——. *H.R. Exec. Doc. No. 13*, 45 Cong., 1 sess., Vol. 2, 1877, Mexican border troubles.
——. *H.R. Misc. Doc. No. 64*, 45 Cong., 2 sess., Vol. 6, 1878, U.S. relations with Mexico.
United States Congress, Senate. *Sen. Exec. Doc. No. 13*, 40 Cong., 3 sess., 1869, Battle of the Washita.
——. *Sen. Misc. Doc. No. 37*, 42 Cong., 1 sess., 1871, Indian depredations

in Texas.

The War of the Rebellion: A Compilation of the Official Records of the Union and Confederate Armies. 130 vols. Washington, D.C.: Government Printing Office, 1880-1901.

III. Periodicals

A. *Articles*

Abbott, John L. "Heroic Deeds of Heroic Men—Grierson's Raid," *Harper's New Monthly Magazine* (February 1865), pp. 273-81.

Baird, G. W. "General Mile's Indian Campaigns." *Century Magazine* 42 (1891):351-70.

Baringer, William E. "Campaign Technique in Illinois—1860." Reprinted from the Illinois State Historical Society *Transactions*, 1932. Publication No. 39.

Blackburn, Forrest R. "Army Families in Frontier Forts." *Military Review* 49 (October 1969):17-28.

Block, Ruth H. "Untangling the Roots of Modern Sex Roles: A Survey of Four Centuries of Change." *Signs: Journal of Women in Culture and Society* 4 (Winter 1978):237-52.

Carrafiello, Vincent A. and Richard O. Curry. "The Black City: Eliza Wright, Jr.'s View of Early Industrial Pittsburgh." *Western Pennsylvania Historical Magazine* 55 (July 1972):249-54.

Clum, John P. "Victorio." *New Mexico Historical Review* 4 (1929):107-27.

Crimmins, M. L. "General Mackenzie at Fort Concho." *West Texas Historical Association Year Book* 10 (1934):16-31.

Degler, Carl N. "What Ought to Be and What Was: Women's Sexuality in the Nineteenth Century." *American Historical Review* 79 (December 1974):1467-90.

Dodge, Mary Abigail [Gail Hamilton]. "A Call to my Country-Women." *Atlantic* (March 1863), pp. 345-49.

Dorst, J. H. "Ranald Slidell Mackenzie." *Journal of the U.S. Cavalry Association* 10 (1897):367-82.

Ellis, Richard N. "The Humanitarian General." *Western Historical Quarterly* 3 (1972):169-78.

Fisk, William L. Jr. "The Scotch-Irish in Central Ohio." *Ohio State Archaeological and Historical Quarterly* 57 (April 1948):111-25.

Forbes, Stephen A. "Grierson's Cavalry Raid." Illinois State Historical Society, *Transactions*, 1907, pp. 99-130.

Foreman, Carolyn Thomas. "General Benjamin Grierson." *Chronicles of Oklahoma* 24 (Summer 1946):195-217.

———. "General William Babcock Hazen." *Chronicles of Oklahoma* 20

(December 1942):322-42.

Griswold, Gillett. "Old Fort Sill: The First Seven Years." *Chronicles of Oklahoma* 36 (Spring 1958):2-14.

Hazen, General William B. "Some Corrections of Life on the Plains." *Chronicles of Oklahoma* 3 (December 1925):295-318. Writing on American History, Item 998. Reprint of a Pamphlet printed in St. Paul, Minn.: Ramaly and Cunningham, 1874.

Huth, Ronald K. "Louis Kossuth in Ohio." *Norhtwest Ohio Quarterly* 60 (Summer 1968):111-26.

Kett, Joseph F. "Curing the Disease of Precocity." *Turning Points: Historical and Sociological Essays on the Family.* Edited by John Demos and Savanne Boocock. Journal of Sociology 84, Supplement, 1978. Chicago: University of Chicago Press, 1978.

McChristian, Douglas C. "Grierson's Fight at Tinaja de las Palmas: An Episode in the Victorio Campaign." *Red River Valley Historical Review* 71 (Winter 1982):45-63.

Miles, Susan. "Fort Concho in 1877." *West Texas Historical Yearbook* 35 (October 1969):47-57.

———. "Edith Clare Grierson, 1865-1878." *Fort Concho Report* 10 (Winter 1978):4-8.

———. "The Post Office War." *Fort Concho Report* 12 (Spring 1980):5-13.

———. "The Soldiers Riot." *Fort Concho Report* 13 (Spring 1981):1-20.

Morrison, W. B. "Fort Arbuckle," *Chronicles of Oklahoma* 6 (1928):26-34.

Myres, Sandra L. "Romance and Reality on the American Frontier: Views of Army Wives." *Western Historical Quarterly* 13 (October 1982):409-27.

Nunn, W. Curtis. "Eighty-Six Hours Without Water on the Texas Plains." *Southwestern Historical Quarterly* 43 (January 1940):356-64.

Olmsted, Frederic Law. "Chicago in Distress." *Nation* 9 (November 1871): 302-305.

Porter, Kenneth W. "Negroes and Indians on the Texas Frontier." *Southwestern Historical Quarterly* 53 (October 1949):151-63.

———. "The Seminole Negro Scouts, 1870-1881." *Southwestern Historical Quarterly* 45 (January 1952):358-77.

Pratt, Richard H. "Some Indian Experiences." *Journal of the U.S. Cavalry Association* 16 (December 1906):200-17.

Rozett, John M. "Racism and Republican Emergence in Illinois, 1848-1860. A Re-Evaluation of Republican Negrophobia." *Civil War History* 22 (June 1976):101-115.

Smith, Daniel Scott. "Family Limitation, Sexual Control and Domestic Feminism in Victorian America." *Feminist Studies* 1 (1973):40-57.

Smith-Rosenberg, Carroll. "The Female World of Love and Ritual: Relations Between Women in Nineteenth Century America." *Signs: Journal of Women in Culture and Society* 1 (Autumn 1975):1-29.

Taylor, Alfred A. "Medicine Lodge Peace Council." *Chronicles of Oklahoma*

2 (June 1924):98–110.

Temple, Frank M. "Colonel B. H. Grierson's Administration of the District of the Pecos." *West Texas Historical Association Yearbook* 38 (October 1962): 85–96.

——. "Colonel Grierson in the Southwest." *Panhandle-Plains Historical Review* 30 (1957):27–54.

Utley, Robert M. "Pecos Bill on the Texas Frontier." *The American West* 6 (1969):4–13, 61–62.

Welter, Barbara. "The Cult of True Womanhood, 1820–1860." *American Quarterly* 18 (1966):151–74.

Yates, Wilson. "Birth Control Literature and the Medical Profession in Nineteenth-Century America." *Journal of the History of Medicine and Allied Sciences* 31 (January 1976):42–54.

B. *Newspapers and Magazines*

Army and Navy Journal.
Austin Daily Journal.
El Paso Herald.
Fort Griffin Echo.
Flake's Daily Bulletin (Galveston, Texas).
Galveston News.
Harper's Weekly Magazine.
Jacksonville (Illinois) *Daily Illinois Courier.*

Jacksonville (Illinois) *Journal.*
Mahoning Free Democrat.
New York Tribune.
San Antonio Daily Herald.
San Antonio Daily Express.
San Antonio Enterprise.
San Antonio Surprise.
San Saba (Texas) *News.*

IV. BOOKS

Ahlstrom, Sydney. *A Religious History of the American People.* New Haven: Yale University Press, 1972.

Aley, Howard C. *A Heritage to Share: The Bicentennial History of Youngstown and Mahoning County, Ohio.* Youngstown: Bicentennial Commission of Youngstown and Mahoning County, Ohio, 1975.

Angle, Paul, ed. and comp. *Prairie State: Impressions of Illinois, 1673–1967, By Travelers and Other Observers.* Chicago: The University of Chicago Press, 1968.

Athearn, Robert C. *William Tecumseh Sherman and the Settlement of the West.* Norman: University of Oklahoma Press, 1956.

Battles and Leaders of the Civil War. 4 vols. New York: Thomas Yoselof, Inc., 1956.

Bearss, Edwin C. *Decision in Mississippi.* Jackson, Mississippi: Mississippi Commission on the War Between the States, 1962.

Berthrong, Donald J. *The Southern Cheyenne.* Norman: University of Oklahoma Press, 1963.

Berwanger, Eugene H. *The Frontier Against Slavery: Western Anti-Negro Prejudice and the Slavery Extension Controversy.* Urbana: University of Illinois Press, 1967.

Biddle, Ellen McGowan. *Reminiscences of a Soldier's Wife.* Philadelphia: Press of J. B. Lippencott, 1907.

Boatner, Mark Mayo III. *The Civil War Dictionary.* New York: David McKay Company, Inc., 1959.

Bourke, John G. *An Apache Campaign in the Sierra Madre.* New York: Charles Scribner's Sons, 1886.

———. *On the Border with Crook.* New York: Charles Scribner's Sons, 1896.

Boyd, Mrs. Orsemus Bronson. *Cavalry Life in Tent and Field.* New York: J. Selwin Tait & Sons, 1894.

Brown, D. Alexander. *Grierson's Raid.* Urbana: University of Illinois Press, 1962.

Burns, James MacGregor. *The Vineyard of Liberty: The American Experiment.* New York: Knopf, 1982.

Carriker, Robert C. *Fort Supply, Indian Territory: Frontier Outpost on the Plains.* Norman: University of Oklahoma Press, 1970.

Carter, Robert G. *On the Border with Mackenzie.* Washington, D.C.: Eynon Printing Co., 1935.

Catton, Bruce. *The Coming Fury.* Garden City, New York: Doubleday and Company, Inc., 1961.

———. *Grant Moves South.* Boston: Little, Brown and Company, 1960.

———. *This Hallowed Ground.* Grand City, New York: Doubleday and Company, Inc., 1956.

———. *A Stillness at Appomattox.* Garden City, New York: Doubleday and Company, Inc., 1954.

Church, Charles A. *History of the Republican Party in Illinois: 1854–1912, With a Review of the Aggressions of the Slave-Power.* Rockford, Illinois: Press of Wilson Brothers Company, 1912.

Cole, Arthur Charles. *The Era of the Civil War: 1848–1870.* Centennial History of Illinois, edited by Clarence Walworth Alvord. 3 vols. Springfield, Illinois: Illinois Centennial Commission, 1919.

Cott, Nancy. *The Bonds of Womanhood: "Woman's Sphere" in New England, 1780–1835.* New Haven, Connecticut: Yale University Press, 1977.

Custer, Elizabeth Bacon. *Following the Guidon.* New York: Harper and Brothers, 1890.

———. *Tenting on the Plains, or General Custer in Kansas and Texas.* 3 vols. Norman: University of Oklahoma Press, 1971.

Debo, Angie. *A History of the Indians of the United States.* Norman: University of Oklahoma Press, 1970.

Degler, Carl A. *At Odds: Women and the Family in America, From the*

Revolution to the Present. Oxford: Oxford University Press, 1980.

Doyle, Don Harrison. *The Social Order of a Frontier Community: Jacksonville, Illinois, 1825-70.* Urbana: University of Illinois Press, 1978.

Eames, Charles M., comp. *Historic Morgan and Classic Jacksonville.* Jacksonville: Daily Journal Steam Job Printing Office, 1885.

Ellis, Richard. *General Pope and U.S. Indian Policy.* Albuquerque: University of New Mexico Press, 1970.

Epstein, Barbara Leslie. *The Politics of Domesticity: Women, Evangelism and Temperance in Nineteenth Century America.* Middletown, Connecticut: Wesleyan University Press, 1981.

Flipper, Henry O. *Negro Frontiersman.* El Paso: Texas Western College Press, 1963.

Foner, Eric. *Free Soil, Free Labor, Free Men: The Ideology of the Republican Party Before the Civil War.* New York: Oxford University Press, 1970.

Foote, Shelby. *The Civil War: A Narrative.* 3 vols. New York: Random House, 1958-74.

Forbes, Stephen A. *The Great Chicago Fire, October 8-10, 1871. Described by Eight Men and Women Who Experienced Its Horrors and Testified to the Courage of Its Inhabitants.* Introduction and Notes by Paul M. Angle. Chicago: The Chicago Historical Society, 1971.

Foreman, Grant. *Fort Gibson: A Brief History.* Norman: University of Oklahoma Press, 1936.

Forgie, George B. *Patricide in the House Divided: A Psychological Interpretation of Lincoln and His Age.* New York: Norton, 1979.

Frazer, Robert W. *Forts of the West.* Norman: University of Oklahoma Press, 1965.

Frederickson, George M. *The Inner Civil War: Northern Intellectuals and the Crisis of the Union.* New York: Harper & Row, 1963.

Frost, Lawrence A. *The Court-Martial of General George Armstrong Custer.* Norman: University of Oklahoma Press, 1968.

Gibson, A. M. *The Kickapoos: Lords of the Middle Border.* Norman: University of Oklahoma Press, 1963.

Gillett, James B. *Six Years with the Texas Rangers, 1875-1881.* New Haven: Yale University Press, 1925.

Ginger, Ray. *Age of Excess: The United States from 1877 to 1914.* 2nd ed. New York: Macmillan Publishing Co., Inc., 1975.

Glass, Major E. N. *The History of the Tenth Cavalry, 1866-1921.* Tucson: Acme Printing Co., 1921.

Gordon, Linda. *Woman's Body, Woman's Right: A Social History of Birth Control in America.* New York: Grossman Publishers, 1976.

Greene, Duane Merritt. *Ladies and Officers of the United States Army, or, American Aristocracy. A Sketch of the Social Life and Character of the Army.* Chicago: Central Publishing Co., 1880.

Haley, J. Evetts. *Fort Concho and the Texas Frontier.* San Angelo, Texas:

Standard-Times, 1952.

Hayes, Jess G. *Apache Vengeance.* Albuquerque: University of New Mexico Press, 1954.

Heitman, Francis B. *Historical Register and Dictionary of the United States Army.* 2 vols. Washington, D.C.: Government Printing Office, 1899.

Henry, Robert. *"First With the Most" Forrest.* Indianapolis: The Bobbs-Merrill Company, 1944.

Herr, John K. and Edward A. Wallace. *The Story of the United States Cavalry, 1775–1942.* Boston: Little, Brown and Company, 1953.

Hicken, Victor. *Illinois in the Civil War.* Urbana: University of Illinois Press, 1966.

History of Trumbull and Mahoning Counties with Illustrations and Biographical Sketches. 2 vols. Cleveland: H. Z. Williams & Brothers, 1882.

Hoig, Stan. *The Battle of the Washita.* Garden City, New York: Doubleday and Company, Inc., 1976.

Howard, Robert P. *Illinois: A History of the Prairie State.* Grand Rapids, Michigan: W. B. Erdman Publishing Co., 1972.

Johnson, Charles B. *Illinois in the Fifties, or A Decade of Development.* Illinois Centennial Edition. Champaign, Illinois: Flanigan-Pearson Company Publishers, 1918.

Jones, S. *Pittsburgh in the Year Eighteen Hundred and Twenty-Six, Containing Sketches, Topographical, Historical and Statistic. Together with a Directory of the City, and a View of Its Various Manufactures, Population, Improvements, & Etc.* Pittsburgh: Johnston & Stockton, 1826.

Knight, Oliver. *Life and Manners in the Frontier Army.* Norman: University of Oklahoma Press, 1978.

Knox, Thomas W. *Campfire and Cotton-field: Southern Adventure in Time of War.* New York: Da Capo Press, 1969.

Krenkel, John H., ed. *Richard Yates, Civil War Governor.* Danville, Illinois: The Interstate Printers and Publishers, Inc., 1966.

Kroeker, Marvin E. *Great Plains Command: William B. Hazen in the Frontier West.* Norman: University of Oklahoma Press, 1976.

Lane, Lydia Spencer. *I Married a Soldier: Or Old Days in the Old Army.* Foreword by Mrs. Dwight D. Eisenhower. Albuquerque: Horn & Wallace Publishers, Inc., 1964 (first published in 1893).

Larkin, Oliver W. *Art and Life in America.* New York: Rinehart & Company, Inc., 1949.

Leach, William. *True Love and Perfect Union: The Feminist Reform of Sex and Society.* New York: Basic Books, 1980.

Leckie, William H. *The Buffalo Soldiers: A Narrative of the Negro Cavalry in the West.* Norman: University of Oklahoma Press, 1967.

Leckie, William H. *Military Conquest of the Southern Plains.* Norman: University of Oklahoma Press, 1963.

Leyburn, James G. *The Scotch-Irish: A Social History.* Chapel Hill: University of North Carolina Press, 1962.

Longstreet, Stephen. *Chicago, 1868–1919.* New York: McKay, 1973.

Lusk, D. W. *Politics and Politicians: A Succinct History of the Politics of Illinois from 1856 to 1884.* Springfield, Illinois: H. W. Rokker, 1884.

McFeeley, William. *Grant: A Biography.* New York: W. W. Norton & Company, 1981.

McReynolds, Edwin C. *Oklahoma: A History of the Sooner State.* Norman: University of Oklahoma Press, 1954.

Mattes, Merrill J. *Indians, Infants and Infantry: Andrew and Elizabeth Burt on the Frontier.* Denver: Fred A. Rosenstock, The Old West Publishing Company, 1960.

Mayhall, Mildred. *The Kiowas.* Norman: University of Oklahoma Press, 1962.

Miles, General Nelson A. *Personal Recollections of General Nelson A. Miles.* Chicago: Werner Co., 1896.

Mills, Anson. *My Story.* Washington, D.C.: By the Author, 1918.

Mohr, James. *Abortion in America: The Origins and Evolution of National Policy.* New York: Oxford University Press, 1978.

Morrison, W. B. *Military Posts and Camps in Oklahoma.* Oklahoma City: Harlow Publishing Corp., 1936.

Myres, Sandra L. *Westering Women and the Frontier Experience, 1800–1915.* Albuquerque: University of New Mexico Press, 1982.

Nevins, Allan. *Ordeal of the Union.* 2 vols. New York: Charles Scribner's Sons, 1947.

———. *The War for the Union.* 4 vols. New York: Charles Scribner's Sons, 1959–1971.

North, Douglass C. *The Economic Growth of the United States, 1790–1860.* Englewood Cliffs, New Jersey: Prentice-Hall, Inc., 1965.

Nye, Russell. *Society and Culture in America, 1830–1860.* New York: Harper & Row, 1974.

Nye, Wilbur S. *Carbine and Lance: The Story of Old Fort Sill.* Norman: University of Oklahoma Press, 1943.

Potter, David M. *The Impending Crisis: 1848–1861.* Completed and Edited by Don E. Fehrenbacher. New York: Harper & Row, 1976.

Pratt, Richard Henry. *Battlefield and Classroom: Four Decades with the American Indian, 1867–1904.* New Haven: Yale University Press, 1964.

Priest, Loring B. *Uncle Sam's Stepchildren: The Reformation of United States Indian Policy, 1865–1887.* New Brunswick, New Jersey: Rutgers University Press, 1942.

Prucha, Francis Paul. *American Indian Policy in Crisis: Christian Reformers and the Indian, 1865–1900.* Norman: University of Oklahoma Press, 1976.

Randall, J. G. and David Donald. *The Civil War and Reconstruction.* Lexington, Massachusetts: D. C. Heath and Company, 1969.

Reed, James. *From Private Vice to Public Virtue: The Birth Control Move-*

ment and American Society Since 1830. New York: Basic Books, 1978.

Roe, Francis, M. A. *Army Letters From An Officer's Wife.* New York: D. Appleton & Company, 1909; reprint ed., New York: Arno Press, 1979.

Sachs, Emanie. *The Terrible Siren, Victoria Woodhull, 1838-1927.* New York: Harper and Brothers, 1928.

Schmitt, Martin F., ed. *General George Crook: His Autobiography.* Norman: University of Oklahoma Press, 1941.

Scobee, Barry. *Old Fort Davis.* San Antonio: Naylor Company, 1947.

Scott, Donald M. and Wishy, Bernard, eds. *America's Families: A Documentary History.* New York: Harper & Row, 1982.

Seymour, Flora W. *Indian Agents of the Old Frontier.* New York: Octagon Books, 1975.

Sheridan, Philip H. *Personal Memoirs.* 2 vols. New York: Chester L. Webster and Co., 1888.

Sherman, William Tecumseh. *Memoirs of General William T. Sherman.* Bloomington: Indiana University Press, 1957.

Sickerman, Barbara. *The Quest for Mental Health in America, 1880-1917.* New York: Arno Press, 1980.

Smythe, H. *Historical Sketch of Parker County and Weatherford, Texas.* St. Louis: Louis C. Lavat, Printer, 1877.

Stallard, Patricia Y. *Glittering Misery: Dependents of the Indian Fighting Army.* San Rafael, California: Presidio Press, 1978.

Stampp, Kenneth M. *And the War Came: The North and the Secession Crisis, 1860-1861.* Baton Rouge: Louisiana State University Press, 1950.

Still, William. *The Underground Railroad.* Philadelphia: Porter & Coates, 1872; reprint ed., New York: Arno Press, 1968.

Summerhayes, Martha. *Vanished Arizona: Recollections of My Army Life.* The 1908 Edition, Unabridged. Introduction by W. Turrentine Jackson. Philadelphia: J. B. Lippincott Company, 1963.

Sweet, Alex E. and Know, J. Armory. *On A Mexican Mustang, Through Texas, From the Gulf to the Río Grande.* St. Louis: T. N. James & Company, 1884.

Tatum, Lawrie. *Our Red Brothers and The Peace Policy of President Ulysses S. Grant.* Philadelphia: J. C. Winston and Company, 1899; reprint ed., Lincoln: University of Nebraska Press, 1970.

Thomas, Benjamin. *Abraham Lincoln: A Biography.* New York: Knopf, 1952; reprint ed., New York: The Modern Library, 1968.

Thrapp, Dan L. *Victorio and the Mimbres Apaches.* Norman: University of Oklahoma Press, 1974.

Toulouse, Joseph H. and James R. Toulouse. *Pioneer Posts of Texas.* San Antonio: Naylor Company, 1936.

Trachtenberg, Alan. *The Incorporation of American Culture and Society in the Guilded Age.* New York: Hill and Wang, 1982.

Train, Arthur K., Jr. *The Story of Everyday Things.* New York: Harper and Brothers, 1941.

Underwood, Larry. *The Butternut Guerillas: A Story of Grierson's Raid.* Owensboro, Kentucky: McDowell Publications, 1981.

Unger, Irwin. *The Greenback Era: A Social and Political History of the Greenback Era, 1865–1879.* Princeton: Princeton University Press, 1964.

Utley, Robert M. *Frontier Regulars: The United States Army and the Indian, 1866–1890.* The Macmillan Wars of the United States. New York: Macmillan Publishing Company, Inc., 1973.

Villegas, Daniel E. *The United States Versus Porfirio Diaz.* Lincoln: University of Nebraska Press, 1963.

Walters, Lorenzo D. *Tombstone's Yesterday.* Tucson: Acme Printing Co., 1938.

Webb, Walter P. *The Texas Rangers: A Century of Frontier Defense.* Boston: Houghton Mifflin Co., 1935.

Wilbarger, J. W. *Indian Depredations in Texas.* Austin, Texas: Hutchings Printing House, 1889.

Williams, Mary, ed., and comp. *An Army Wife's Cookbook, with Household Hints and Home Remedies: Alice Kirk Grierson.* Globe, Arizona: Southwest Parks and Monuments Association, 1972.

Wishy, Bernard. *Child and the Republic: The Dawn of Modern Child Nurture.* Philadelphia: University of Pennsylvania Press, 1967.

V. Unpublished Materials

Dinges, Bruce. "The Making of a Cavalryman: Benjamin H. Grierson and the Civil War Along the Mississippi, 1861-1865." Ph.D. dissertation, Rice University, 1978.

Temple, Frank M. "Colonel Grierson's Texas Command." M.A. thesis, Texas Technological University, 1959.

Index